MANAGEMENT

in

Higher Education

THAD L. HUNGATE

PROFESSOR OF HIGHER EDUCATION AND FORMERLY
CONTROLLER, TEACHERS COLLEGE, COLUMBIA UNIVERSITY

BUREAU OF PUBLICATIONS

TEACHERS COLLEGE, COLUMBIA UNIVERSITY
NEW YORK, 1964

MANUFACTURED IN THE UNITED STATES OF AMERICA

PREFACE

This work is an analytical study of management in higher education. It is a study of how the enterprise may wisely adapt its important services to the changing needs of modern life. It seeks to present practical ways of effectively involving in management the high abilities of faculty, executives, president, and board. Consideration is given to the four functions of management —the delegating and organizing function, the directive function, the operative function, and the evaluative function. These functions do not stand alone; they continually interact.

Not all the ideas presented are drawn from practice, for the future requirements of higher education must differ in some respects from those of the past.

A brief examination is made of the exercise of state responsibilities. It is included because new designs of institutions and new forms of management are being developed. These new practices should be understood and assessed.

This, then, is a guide to management. It is an effort to assist in fulfilling a strategic need that is widespread and growing and for which neither personnel nor funds are adequately available.

For strengths that may appear in this work I am indebted to many persons; for the weaknesses I alone must answer.

T. L. HUNGATE

CONTENTS

LIST OF TABLES

LIST OF FIGURES

MANAGEMENT IN

HIGHER EDUCATION

CHAPTER *1*

Challenges to Management

In this work, the term management[1] means the management of an institution of higher education. It includes the governing board in which the state has vested responsibility and authority, and all those to whom the board will have delegated responsibility and authority—the president, the executive officers, the faculties, and such agents as the board may employ. The scope of the responsibilities of management is broad. It encompasses the institution's objectives, its educational philosophy and policies, its plans, programs, standards, and finance, as well as personnel, facilities, operations, and the means of evaluation. The many responsibilities of management are thus entrusted to many participants of varying competencies.

In the United States, from the very beginning of higher education, the responsibility and authority for governance have been vested in a lay board, who with the growth of the enterprise in turn delegate major responsibilities

[1] The term *management* has been chosen because of its breadth of meaning. The term *administration* is at times interpreted to exclude policy formation and coordinated planning, and to be restricted to carrying out established policies, and its use is therefore avoided in describing the breadth of responsibilities that must be met. The use of the term management may at first incur some disfavor because there are those who associate it with industrial organizations and who would rightly hasten to point out how different the educational process is from those activities generally associated with business enterprise.

to a career chief executive and to the faculty. Through time the faculty has brought about recognition of its freedom to teach, safeguarded by provisions for tenure. Thus the broad interests of society and professional competence in education are partners in management.

It is the responsibility of management to envision the kind, quantity, and quality of higher education for youth that will afford a preparation for the future that is best for the individual and will best serve the society of which he is a part. It must provide appropriate opportunities and services in order that the talents of youth may be cultivated, and the lives of adults enriched.

To the millions of youth and adults who have utilized or are utilizing the vast array of opportunities offered by institutions of higher education, management may seem to have a minor role, for in the well-ordered institution it is unobtrusive. Instructors exercise full freedom in teaching and in evaluating the student, and supporting services and physical facilities are available as needed. The quality of the environment for learning is based on decisions made before the student arrives. Much of the work of management relates to plans for the future. Much of it is carried on quietly in the various offices, unseen by the public, and students and visitors are scarcely aware of it. Yet it is safe to say that the suitability of higher education to the service of the American people rests on the quality and the adequacy of institutional management. It is therefore important that careful consideration be given to the responsibilities of management for American higher education and how they are exercised.

In the following pages account is taken of the changing role of higher education in American society. Major social policies that give direction to institutional functioning are identified. Technological and social changes are seen as primary causal forces that impose changing requirements on institutions of higher education. The challenges to management posed by growing institutional responsibilities are set forth. How management presently meets these challenges is assessed. The major purpose of this work is to present guides to the appropriate exercise of institutional management commensurate with the present and future responsibilities and challenges. These guides are discussed in the chapters that follow.

The Changing Role of Higher Education in American Society

The role of higher education in American society changes under the influences of the many forces of change within the society of which it is a part. These forces include, but are not limited to, the growth in population, the change from a rural agrarian society to an urban industrialized society, the influence of technological and social changes guided by new knowledge, and the ever-increasing national responsibilities at home and in relation to a changing world. It can confidently be expected that the rate of change will accelerate as the tempo of technological and social change increases.

An enumeration of some of the major changes within the more than three centuries of the history of American higher education will aid in understanding its current and future nature. At the outset the clergy exercised control, but these have been replaced (generally) by laymen. The fixed curriculum that in the earlier period served to train classical scholars, ministers, lawyers, and physicians has been (generally) discarded in favor of diversified curricula. These curricula seek to retain the value of the heritage and to embrace new knowledge of the universe and of man. They offer opportunities for study of many specialized areas of knowledge and seek to relate that knowledge to the needs of modern life. Certain authoritarian dogmas and philosophies have been supplanted by the methods of science; teaching reflects new knowledge of individual differences, of learning, and of social needs. There are now new emphases on research and on field services. As these changes have occurred, the institutions of higher education have grown in size and complexity.

In the period prior to World War II, higher education was looked upon as personal capital whereby the social and economic benefit to the individual and his family was to be assessed in relation to the cost. Higher education was seen as the road to opportunity for gifted youth and for those with the means to attend, and governments were generally benevolent with respect to some public support of such opportunities. Consistent with the social attitude, the institutions were individualistic. Although their programs were changing, the pace was deliberate. Their growth was largely a matter of institutional determination, arising from a sense of responsibility of governing boards, unhurried by social demands. For finance heavy reliance was placed on the student and his family.

Yet before the outbreak of World War II there were a growing number who sought for higher education a new orientation to the industrial age, a far wider availability and greater equality of educational opportunity. Among the more articulate views expressed were those of the Educational Policies Commission of the National Education Association.[2] Observing the panorama of social change, the Commission called for a new emphasis on the social good as well as on individual development. The objects of education identified by the Commission to serve both the individual and society in-

[2] See, for example, Charles A. Beard, *The Unique Function of Education in American Democracy* (Washington, D.C.: Educational Policies Commission, 1937); and William G. Carr, *The Purposes of Education in American Democracy* (Washington, D.C.: The Commission, 1938).

cluded individual self-realization, economic efficiency, human relations, and civic responsibility.

While during the 1930's enrollments in public and private institutions steadily increased, and proponents for a new social policy for higher education grew in number and in influence, no popular consensus emerged prior to World War II. Following the war, however, profound changes were brought about that affected all aspects of higher education. To the earlier proponents of a new orientation of social policy for higher education were added those who from the experiences of the war period saw the demonstrated values of higher education; those who subsequently experienced directly or indirectly the benefits derived from the programs financed for veterans; those who were made aware of the growing demands for leadership and for specialized training in government, business enterprise, and labor. An important impetus to the crystallization of popular consensus was the work of the President's Commission on Higher Education. This Commission, appointed in 1946, reported in 1947.[3] Rightly sensing the quickening tempo of technological and social change, recognizing the vast implications of the newly discovered but as yet unharnessed atomic power, and aware of the new role of the nation in world leadership, the Commission stated its conception of the functions of colleges and universities as follows:

American Colleges and Universities must envision a much larger role for higher education in the national life. They can no longer consider themselves merely the instrument for producing an intellectual elite; they must become the means by which every citizen, youth, and adult is enabled and encouraged to carry his education, formal and informal, as far as his native capacities permit.[4]

This was a call for a widely educated citizenry, and to forestall any complacency on the part of those sharing responsibility for higher education, the Commission added:

Higher education must be alert to anticipate new social and economic needs, and to keep its programs of professional training in step with the requirements of a changing and expanding cultural, social, and economic order.[5]

Identified among major concerns having implications for higher education were accelerating social change, increasing demands for world citizenship, pyramiding technological developments, greater emphasis on ethical ideals.[6]

The Commission further urged acceptance of the concept of higher education as an investment and not a cost:

[3] *Higher Education for American Democracy,* A Report of the President's Commission on Higher Education (Washington, D.C.: U.S. Government Printing Office, 1947).

[4] *Ibid,* Vol. I, p. 101.

[5] *Ibid,* p. 84.

[6] *Ibid,* Vol. IV, p. 61.

It is an investment in free men. It is an investment in social welfare, better living standards, better health, and less crime. It is an investment in higher production, increased income, and greater efficiency in agriculture, industry, and government. It is an investment in a bulwark against garbled information, half truths and untruths; against ignorance and intolerance. It is an investment in human talent, better human relationships, democracy, and peace.[7]

The voice of the Commission joined many others and they were succeeded by many more, so that over the land a consensus grew that higher education should be extended to all who can qualify and benefit, that institutions and programs must serve both the diverse talents of youth and the diverse needs of society, that new world responsibilities call for understanding of other cultures, that equality of educational opportunity for youth is an appropriate goal, and that broad programs of basic research may appropriately be centered in institutions of higher education.

Interdependence and the need for leadership, whether within the country or among nations, and whether political, cultural, or economic, have brought the American people to understand that their security and well-being as a people depend fully as much on their human resources as on their productive capacity and their natural resources. Gardner puts the case well when he states:

Those who receive the most education are going to move into virtually all the key jobs. Thus the question "Who should go to college?" translates itself into the more compelling question "Who is going to manage the society?" . . .

The plain fact is that never in our history have we stood in such desperate need of men and women of intelligence, imagination and courage. The challenge is there—greater than any generation has ever faced.[8]

The American people have come to understand that men and women increase in value both to themselves and to society when they are educated. Thus, in the public mind, higher education has ceased to be solely an individual matter. Henceforth, in a manner suitable for the democratic way of life, the talents of American youth are to be identified and cultivated both for their own good and for the strengthening of the society of which they are a part. Higher education has become social capital as well as personal wealth and capital.

These terms—education as social capital and personal capital—may be defined thus:

Education as personal wealth is the total contribution of education to life, including training for self-realization, human relationships, economic efficiency, and civic responsibility. Education as social wealth or as social capital is the aggre-

[7] *Ibid.*, Vol. V, pp. 26, 28.

[8] John W. Gardner, *Excellence: Can We Be Equal and Excellent Too?* (New York: Harper & Row, 1961), pp. 71 and 153.

gate of the education of the individuals in a society when viewed as personal wealth, account being taken of the fact that the potential possessed by a group is greater than the sum of that possessed by its individual members.[9]

A broadly conceived public policy for higher education based on the concept of both individual and social development is new. It rests on the hypothesis that in a democracy the development of individual interests, aptitudes, talents, and capacities under the free choices of the individual will maximize the over-all social achievement. Society may offer inducements to choice, but short of service to the defense establishment it may not determine the individual's program in higher education. Thus the new social policy, which will take some years to bring to full realization, envisions opportunities in higher education available in extent to all who can profit from them, in breadth to be inclusive of the span of human knowledge, and in depth to reach to and extend the frontiers of that knowledge. It envisions an ultimate equality of educational opportunity, with suitable programs at reasonable cost adapted to changing social needs, and financial support from public funds consistent with the public interest.

In response to this policy major changes have been and are being made by all the states. State governments are planning for enrollments of an increasing proportion of youth. In the development of state systems they are providing various types of programs and institutions and procedures to avoid unnecessary and wasteful duplication of services. Statewide plans are now reaching years into the future, as are those of many private institutions. Philanthropists and corporations are increasing their financial support. The Federal Government has evidenced a growing interest and, although it has not adopted a basic long-range policy of support, it is providing funds in increasing amounts for research, for strengthening aspects of programs deemed vital to defense, for stipends for specialized training, and for loans for institutional residential facilities and for student fees and expenses.

The concept of education as capital received occasional recognition in the past,[10] but the economists took too little account of the fact that human faculties are an important means of economic production.[11] In recent years, however, they have begun to broaden their studies of material capital to include "human capital"[12] and to recognize that higher education as "human

[9] Thad L. Hungate, *Financing the Future of Higher Education* (New York: Bureau of Publications, Teachers College, Columbia University, 1946), pp. 175–176.

[10] Alfred Marshall, *Principles of Economics,* Eighth Edition (London: MacMillan & Co., Ltd., 1936).

[11] *Ibid,* p. 229.

[12] For an excellent treatment of higher education as "human capital" see Mary Jean Bowman, "Higher Education as an Investment in People," in *Economics of Higher Education,* Selma J. Mushkin, ed. (Washington, D.C.: U.S. Department of Health, Education, and Welfare, Office of Education, 1962), Part II, pp. 69 ff.

capital" may be fully as significant to social well-being as material capital. Indeed, such capital development may pace the growth of material capital. Bowman employs the term "human capital" for higher education and analyzes concepts and measures for it. She stresses the distinction to be made in viewing it as a store of capital to be drawn upon in future periods and its productive use in a defined period of time.[13] One of the concerns of the economist, as of the educator, is the relation of this form of capital to the gross national product. The present writer, in 1946, studied the economic implications of the investment in higher education. He recognized that for the individual it meant personal capital and personal wealth; for society it meant social capital and social wealth.[14] For the individual, the cost of higher education could be weighed against the outlook for increased earnings and life enrichment; for society, the cost to be borne could be weighed against the outlook for a better qualified leadership in all aspects of community and national life.

A constant student of economics of higher education for many years has been Professor Seymour Harris of Harvard.[15] Included in his studies have been those dealing with institutional economy and the share of the cost to be borne by the several levels of government, by individuals, and by philanthropists. There has been in recent years a developing interest on the part of many other economists.[16] This interest reached a certain degree of maturity in 1962 with the publication of *Economics of Higher Education*,[17] summarizing the work of a group of able economists in the United States. In England, *The Economics of Education* by Professor John Vaizey of the University of London was published in 1962.[18] The focus of Vaizey's work is on education as an investment in relation to economic growth, with particular relevance to underdeveloped countries. In Germany, the recent work of Professor Edding of the Higher Institute for International Research in Education was also published in 1962.[19] The subject dealt with in this work is the future

---

[13] *Ibid*, p. 70.

[14] Thad L. Hungate, *Financing the Future of Higher Education, op. cit.,* pp. 174 ff.

[15] Among his many writings, see *More Resources for Education* (New York: Harper & Row, 1960); and his chapter on "Broad Issues in Financing" in *Financing Higher Education, 1960–70,* Dexter M. Keezer, ed. (New York: McGraw-Hill Book Company, Inc., 1959). See also his latest book, *Higher Education: Resources and Finance* (New York: McGraw-Hill Book Company, Inc., 1962).

[16] See, for example, Charles Scott Benson, *The Economics of Public Education* (Boston: Houghton Mifflin Company, 1961).

[17] Selma J. Mushkin, ed., *Economics of Higher Education, op. cit.*

[18] John Vaizey, *The Economics of Education* (New York: The Free Press of Glencoe, Inc., 1962).

[19] Friedrich Edding, *Targets for Education in Europe in 1970,* Policy Conference on Economic Growth and Investment in Education. Vol. II with Ingvar Svennilson and Lionel Elvin (Paris: Organization for Economic Cooperation and Development, 1962).

investment in education in Europe in relation to economic growth. We can anticipate from these important beginnings in defining and exploring this new dimension of economics that it will assist in guiding the future investment in the human capital of higher education.

The role of higher education is thus a changing one. The new public policy holds major implications for the future, and these will alter in response to social change. The direction of change is clear: The goal is the extension of higher education to all who can profit, and for so long as they can profit from it. McConnell observes. "This society rests on the service of citizens whose talents are few or modest together with those whose abilities are many or exceptional."[20] The institutions are to serve both youth and adults. The programs for research face major expansion on all levels and in all areas, and the field services of staffs both at home and abroad will grow in volume and diversity. Institutions can be expected to be increasingly responsive to the needs of society as well as to those of the individual.

Identification of Major Areas That Give Direction to Institutional Functioning

The writer, in an earlier publication,[21] set forth six major policy areas in which the continuous conflict of positive and negative wants of society, with respect to higher education, result in what is achieved. These areas are noted below, with comments drawn largely from that source.

1. *The distribution of the benefits of higher education.* Under an ideal expression of democracy, this policy requires equal access to opportunities in the several fields of study for those equally qualified. It is sometimes described as equality of educational opportunity. The criteria of selection are not based on such factors as wealth or social position, or race, or place of residence, but on the personal qualifications of the individual. This does not mean that limits may not be imposed, whether through standards of admission or length of period of study, or share of the cost to be borne by public funds. It means that with equal personal qualifications, the poor may have as ready access to higher education as the rich.

In practice, realization of the ideal of equality of educational opportunity is far removed. Inequality is widespread both within and among the states in accessibility, quality of programs, and cost to be borne by students and their families. Yet substantial progress is being made as institutional public

[20] T. R. McConnell, *A General Pattern for American Public Higher Education* (New York: McGraw-Hill Book Company, Inc., 1962), pp. 46–47.

[21] Thad L. Hungate, *Finance in Educational Management of Colleges and Universities* (New York: Bureau of Publications, Teachers College, Columbia University, 1954), pp. 16 ff.

support mounts, as accessibility is improved through the establishment of new institutions, as programs are adapted to need, and as student aid becomes increasingly available from both public and private funds.

2. *The distribution of the cost burden.* The cost burden must include both institutional cost and student living costs. (Although the total cost includes institutional cost plus cost to the student of his abstinence from earnings, student living costs are assumed here as a substitute for the cost of abstinence from earnings.) For each institution the share to be borne by public funds, by philanthropy, and by the student and his family must be determined. This determination is a responsibility of the management of the institution, importantly conditioned by provisions made by state legislatures and philanthropists. As a principle it may be stated that the share of the cost should be distributed according to the interests of the primary parties —the student and his family on the one hand, and the state and philanthropy on the other. But the major responsibility should not fall on the parents. Since the public interest now demanding realization of the social objectives of higher education is adjudged stronger than the individual's interest, the major share, at least for students of ability, is likely in the long run to be borne by society.

In practice, generally, the major share of the cost continues to be borne by parents; but important progress is being made to assist students, particularly the able ones, to bear the cost. In addition, an impressive extension of publicly financed higher education is under way, in which the fee charges are perhaps a fourth to a third of those found necessary in private institutions.[22]

3. *An appropriate quality of educational opportunity.* That quality of educational opportunity which best serves both individual and social needs is deemed appropriate. This implies that funds must be spent to ascertain the needs and to evaluate both the process and the product. For students, quality will be influenced by the program of educational experiences that are offered to promote their intellectual and personal growth, by the quantity and quality of the staff and the facilities suitable for the undertaking. Abilities, interests, and aptitudes of students, size of classes, competence of professors, suitability of physical facilities, and democratic procedures in policy formation and in operations—all these condition institutional achievement.

In practice, over-all appraisal of the qualities of programs and resources

---

[22] In 1957–1958 student fees were 111.1 per cent of the direct expenditures for instruction in privately controlled institutions and 31.2 per cent in publicly controlled institutions. Source: Calculation based on data, U.S. Department of Health, Education, and Welfare, Office of Education, *Biennial Survey of Education in the United States, 1957–58,* Statistics of Higher Education, Chap. 4, Sec. II, Receipts, Expenditures, and Property, pp. 22, 44.

is limited. But there are many quantitative bits of evidence that afford bases for estimates. The training, experience, and salaries of professors, the adequacy of physical facilities, the quality of teaching, the philosophy and content of the educational program, and the observed performance of graduates are all factors in appraising the quality of programs.

4. *The provision for the availability of educational opportunity.* There should be an optimum distribution of institutional facilities, account being taken of diversity of programs to serve the social need, with optimum freedom for student migration. In general, opportunities should be available within the state of residence. Some states participate in making regional provisions for certain types of programs. The quality of higher education should not be altered to reflect the phases of the economic cycle. This principle is assurance of availability of quality in education through time. Youth cannot for long delay their education; they require it at the proper stage of maturity.

In practice, availability of suitable opportunities at reasonable cost varies markedly among the states. Substantial improvement is being made through the extension of state systems of higher education. These public institutions, state and local, are adding to their number and broadening their programs, and their student fees are generally modest. This development, together with improvement in transportation, is increasing accessibility to higher education academically, economically, and geographically.

5. *The exercise of financial prudence: economy, control of funds, and flow of capital.* There are several principles relating to financial prudence in higher education. The public will wish to derive the maximum benefits from the funds expended, secure honest, careful, and businesslike management and accounting of funds, and be assured that—all things considered—just the right amount is being spent. Institutional economy will require an enterprise of the right size, the right proportions of students, staff, and facilities for the right program. Fund administration must be efficient and honest. The considerations that attend judgment as to the right amount of public funds to be invested relate to the determination of the marginal utility of higher education as social capital. They include not only this weighing of values with respect to costs of the financial and educational plans, but also the relation of such plans to the national economy. Account must be taken of the financial condition of nation and state, of the trends in employment, of national and state incomes, expenditures, tax policies, and tax programs. The percentage of manpower of the nation that should be absorbed in the enterprise of higher education as teacher and learner cannot be ignored. The investment of capital in higher education will require—as do other forms of capital—continuous study, evaluation, demonstration, and experimentation.

It must everywhere be recognized as perhaps the most important of all investments—the investment in the nation's youth.

In practice, interest in and study of the economics of higher education—including the concept of higher education as human capital, the effective use of institutional resources, and financial support—are becoming widespread. Practices in handling funds are usually good. In the states the support of higher education is drawing an increasing share of state revenue, and the Federal Government is searching for its appropriate role. But as yet no method has been agreed on for determining just how much of its income the American people can wisely invest in the social capital of higher education.

6. *The coordination of objectives, functions, and activities of higher education.* Such coordination relates to a vast complex of efforts at all levels, among many agencies, and in numerous ways. Mention of a few major problems will suggest others: institutional design, functions, and size; standards for student admission and for student life; standards for the quality of personnel and facilities; determination of needs, objectives, programs; and the many choices related to operations.

In practice, most states have established procedures for coordinating public higher education, and in some states efforts toward voluntary coordination of public with private higher education are under way. But much more is needed, such as the articulation of the college to the secondary school and to the graduate school or the appropriate role of higher education with respect to providing contractual services to government, industry, and philanthropic agencies.

These six major areas of social policy give direction to the services of institutions of higher education. They reflect the needs of society, which continually change as a result of social and technological changes. Such changes have implications for higher education including the number and characteristics of institutions—their programs, standards, and provision for recognizing the individual differences of students. Consideration of these changes follows.

Certain Social Changes and Their Implications for Higher Education

Changes in American life and culture are taking place at an accelerating rate. For the individual, they have an impact on the conditions of family life, the relationships with others, and the process of earning a living. Mobility of families places new emphasis on the family unit, and tends to decrease involvement in local government. For society, these changes have an impact on the national well-being and the effectiveness of group efforts. They have important implications for higher education and they contribute to the current challenges to its management.

The social changes discussed here are among those which are current and which the reader of his knowledge and experience will recognize. They are neither comprehensive nor equal in significance, but they will serve to illustrate how social change prompts a demand for change in the responsibilities assumed by the higher education establishment.

THE DEMAND FOR LEADERSHIP

The national setting in a changing world imposes responsibilities of extraordinary complexity on both government and citizens. The future well-being of the nation requires of its citizens a broad understanding of the peoples of the world, and a trained leadership for both government and private affairs that will encourage enlightened international cooperation, deter aggression, and promote world peace. The United States, with the other free nations, has assumed leadership responsibility and has strengthened both its economy and its defenses at home; it has enlisted the cooperation of world communities for defense and development such as the North Atlantic Treaty Organization (NATO), the Southeast Asia Treaty Organization (SEATO), and the Organization of American States (OAS), and has sought to work under and in harmony with the United Nations. The policies of the Federal Government in relation to other nations and the implementation of these policies, the influence of the activities of citizens abroad, whether economic, social, or cultural, will importantly affect the welfare of the country. Hence the requirements are for qualified leadership with the support of the citizenry based on understanding. These requirements are no longer for the few leaders but for many in many areas of specialization, to guide the relationships of the people of this country with the peoples throughout the world.

The rise of governmental responsibilities abroad has been paralleled by the growth of domestic governmental functions and activities. The influence of government is pervasive; it affects all aspects of life and economy. The enlargement of governmental activities, federal, state, and local, is seen, for example, in Table 1. This table reveals that the share of government expenditures for goods and services increased from about 10 per cent of the gross national product in 1930 to over 20 per cent in 1961.

The data in this table, however, do not reveal either the increase in functions served or the increase in complexity of operations. Examples of the newer functions assumed by government reflect responsibilities imposed by technological and social changes: social security, unemployment insurance, agricultural price supports and crop controls, labor relations, space exploration and use, a modern defense establishment, oil production and import controls, urban renewal, urban transit, integration, and aid to higher education.

TABLE I.   Growth in governmental purchases of goods and services:
            1930–1961

Year	Population (in millions)	Gross National Product (in billions)	Government Purchases of Goods and Services[a] (in billions)
1930	123.2	91.1	9.2
1940	132.6	100.6	14.1
1950	152.3	284.6	39.0
1960	180.7	504.4	100.1
1961	183.7	521.3	108.7

[a] Includes expenditures of federal, state, and local governments as a component of the gross national product.

SOURCE: U.S. Department of Commerce, Bureau of the Census, *Statistical Abstract of the United States, 1962,* Population, Table 2, p. 5; Gross National Product and Government Purchases, Table 420, p. 312.

The demand for leadership in government is for a large and growing number of workers who possess the knowledge, understanding, and capacity to lead and to meet assigned responsibilities.

There must be leadership, too, in the exercise of the economic power of government. The domains of the public and private economy overlap. In the private economy corporate ownership exceeds private ownership. But the influence of tax policies, monetary policies, and indeed attitudes and opinions of governmental officials is felt throughout the private economy, whether corporate or personal. Interaction between the two areas of the public and private economy based on knowledge of the economic consequences of government economic policies has become important. Economic interdependence is increasing both at home and abroad. The Common Markets of western Europe and of Central America and the accents on lower tariffs are evidences of interdependence among nations. At home the occupational distribution of the work force is changing. Governmental provision is made for relief of involuntary unemployment and for social security. The maintenance of constructive relations between labor and management in the social interest under governmental regulations requires leadership and understanding on the part of union memberships, managements, and the general public.

The population is expected to increase from 180 million in 1960 to an estimated 246 million in 1980.[23] This growth in itself holds major implications for the plans of government, and for the nature and extent of economic, social, and cultural activities of the American society. There will be more

[23] U.S. Department of Commerce, Bureau of the Census, *Current Population Reports,* Series P-25, Nos. 250 and 251, July 1962.

families, more housing, more jobs, more sales, more industrial activity. There will be more need for health services and for education. The age composition of the population of the future will change; there will be relatively more older people and relatively more children. This change too will condition the aggregate demands for goods and services.

In addition, the tastes and habits of the population will alter. There will be more leisure, more opportunity for individual self-development, and at the same time a requirement for greater responsibility and skill in employment. There will be changes in the individual's aspirations regarding ownership and use of things; changes in modes of communication and transportation, in housing, and in social and cultural activities. Increasingly the population will be found in metropolitan areas, surrounded by all the complexities of life in densely populated areas—mass marketing, communication, housing developments themselves changing in response to urban influences. This growth in urbanization will be accompanied by changes in family life, in schooling, in social tensions, in job requirements.

All these changes in growth and characteristics of the population must be taken into account in planning education for leadership of the future.

IMPLICATIONS OF TECHNOLOGICAL CHANGE FOR HIGHER EDUCATION

Underlying and basic to social change is technological change—the change in product design and production methods. Technological change is the result of the application of scientific knowledge and the inventive arts to all aspects of human life and endeavor. In addition to the constant flood of new products, automation and electronic devices speed production, antibiotics aid in the control of diseases, new transportation and communications media affect human relationships. Science aids in the conservation of natural resources in unlocking the vast resources of the seas and in developing a modern defense establishment. The development of nuclear power in itself holds vast implications for the future of mankind. In its peaceful use it may multiply food production and provide access to the universe; in war it may become a threat to the lives of nations. The rapidly increasing diversity of skill requirements for jobs in the work force is well presented in the "Rockefeller Report" published in 1958. It states:

One of the striking features of contemporary life is the growing range and complexity of the tasks on which our social organization depends. This is dramatically apparent in science but is no less a reality in nearly every field of endeavor. It can be seen in the ever increasing range of skills demanded of the doctor, the teacher, the government administrator, the labor leader, and the business executive.

The reasons are not far to seek. They lie in the explosive rate of technological change and the increasing complexity of our social organization. Not only are the tasks that must be performed to keep our society functioning ever more intricate and demanding, they are constantly changing in character.[24]

The report shows that certain selected skills and occupations with high educational requirements accounted in 1910 for 32.9 per cent of the labor force; in 1957, for 47.6 per cent. Wolozin[25] estimates that skilled workers (professional people, proprietors, craftsmen, clerical and sales people) as a percentage of employed persons in the United States will rise from an estimated 54.7 per cent in 1960 to an estimated 61.4 per cent in 1980. To the educational tasks posed by the increasing requirements for skills must be added the requirements for continuing education and retraining resulting from the application of new knowledge derived from research and the extension of automation. The situation is aptly summed up thus: "It is the constant pressure of an ever more complex society against the total creative capacity of its people."[26]

Vaizey, the English economist, makes this observation: "Thus, in general, the requirements of a modern economy, based on the need to provide a vast range of skilled and flexibly-minded people to service it, harmonize with the social situation which the economy creates."[27]

Automation has grown steadily since the turn of the century. It may not materially augment the net number of unemployed persons in the future,[28] but it will increase the number of adults who, having established competence in one job, must re-establish themselves in another. It is estimated that in the coming decade some 200,000 workers each year will be displaced by automation.[29]

DEMANDS FOR RESEARCH

Society relies more and more on research—both basic and applied. This research is conducted in government, in business, industry, and agriculture, and in institutions of higher education. In addition to creating a mounting demand for trained research workers, the programs of research have produced new knowledge at an almost unbelievable pace. As more is learned,

[24] Rockefeller Brothers Fund, Inc., *The Pursuit of Excellence: Education and the Future of America* (New York: Doubleday & Company, Inc., 1958), pp. 6, 7.

[25] Harold Wolozin, *The Outlook for Higher Education* (New York: The Fund for the Advancement of Education, 1963), p. 12.

[26] Rockefeller Report, *op. cit.*, p. 10.

[27] John Vaizey, *The Economics of Education, op. cit.*, p. 123.

[28] For a discussion of the relation of automation to technological unemployment, see John W. Kendrick, *Productivity Trends in the U. S..*, National Bureau of Economic Research, Annual Report, 1962.

[29] Estimate by Commissioner Ewan Clague and Leon Greenberg of the Bureau of Labor Statistics, Reported in the November 1962 Monthly Economic Letter of the First National City Bank, New York, p. 130.

the knowledge gained in earlier years often becomes obsolete. The new knowledge relates both to knowledge of the material universe and to knowledge of man, including how he learns. This knowledge of how man learns guides the establishment and expansion of research enterprises that extend the frontiers of knowledge and in turn form foundations for new knowledge.

These social changes affect the daily lives of the American people—in home and family life, in human relations, in earning a living, and in exercising the responsibilities of citizenship. All in turn affect the requirements for education—the knowledge, skills, habits, and attitudes which each must possess. But in addition there is an educational requirement that grows in importance for all citizens—the readiness and capacity to meet change. The responsibility imposed by this requirement must be borne to an important degree by managements in higher education.

To provide leadership in a world marked by concentration of governmental responsibilities and threats of conflict, to meet wisely the changes owing to population growth and technological change, society has turned increasingly to institutions of higher education. It has entrusted to them the task of providing the kind, quantity, and quality of education needed by individuals and by society itself to meet the challenges of the future. In turn, the institutions must assess the needs for education, both as they now are and as they will be, in order that the programs and services provided may ever be adapted to the requirements of the times.

In the future, as at present, the financial requirements of higher education must be made known to the public, and adequate support must be sought. The public should have a clear understanding of the purposes of each institution, its resources, its students and staff, its facilities, its finance, and its needs for the future. Higher education is essentially a public purpose, and the public must be kept informed and provided opportunities for sharing in its support.

The Outlook for Change in Institutions of Higher Education

The new public policy for higher education, as well as the ongoing technological and social changes, places new responsibilities on American institutions of higher education. Some of the adjustments required to meet these responsibilities are readily apparent; others are less obvious. Certain ones are identified in the discussion that follows, but those cited are neither comprehensive nor equal in significance.

GENERAL INSTITUTIONAL CHARACTERISTICS

The next fifteen years and beyond is a period of major growth for institutions of higher education, both publicly and privately controlled. The growth in the former, however, is expected to be at a much more rapid rate, with the proportion of degree-credit students enrolled in publicly controlled institutions, which was 51.0 per cent in 1938 and 58.7 per cent in 1960, reaching 64.1 per cent by 1975.[30] The trend toward public higher education will doubtless continue beyond 1975. This trend has implications for control, support, and expenditures.

The institutions have been growing both in number and in size, and this trend is expected to continue. In the period 1938 to 1960 the number of institutions increased from 1,694 to 2,026, and their average size from an enrollment of 795 to 1,707. The small colleges account for a smaller proportion of the total enrollment. In 1958 the largest institutional enrollment was in excess of 40,000 students and the smallest, 11.[31] The increase in institutional size adds to the complexity of operations.[32]

The institutions are becoming more diversified. In many instances teachers colleges have become multipurpose institutions, liberal arts colleges have increased in number and in areas of specialization, and universities have extended their programs for professional education. A major development has been the rapid growth of the community college, a locally sponsored public institution providing both degree-credit and terminal occupational programs. These diversities call for specialized programs, faculties, facilities, and managements.

The expansion of public higher education has led a number of states to provide a state lay board charged with responsibility for coordinating existing institutions, including their functions, activities, and support, and for guiding the establishment of new institutions. This agency may promote interinstitutional cooperation in operations. To provide for highly specialized educational services, the states of three regions—the Southern States, the Mountain States, and the New England States—have entered into three interstate compacts whereby a limited number of programs serve the needs of a region. Such arrangements have strengthened the quality of the work and avoided the excessive cost of duplication. Other areas of cooperation are developing as the result of experience in joint efforts. In the future more attention is likely in the planning of public institutional design, and far more cooperation among institutions, public and private, is anticipated.

Perhaps one of the greatest services of a lay board of governance is the

[30] Based on enrollment estimate by Louis H. Conger, Jr., "College and University Enrollment: Projections," in *Economics of Higher Education*, Selma J. Mushkin, ed., assuming that two-thirds of the increase in the period 1960–1971, and three-fourths of the increase in the period 1971–1976, are enrolled in public institutions.

[31] *Biennial Survey of Education in the United States, 1957–58*, Statistics of Higher Education, Chap. 4, Sec. I, Faculty, Students, and Degrees, p. 12.

[32] For institutional numbers see Table 2, Chap. 2. Institutional size is computed from this table.

capacity of its members to bring to the guidance of the institution their understandings and interpretations of the ongoing affairs of the practical world in which they live. The "ivory tower" no longer symbolizes American higher education. Increasingly its institutions are directly related to the functioning of the society—in government, family life, business, and industrial enterprise. And increasingly the institutions' faculties serve abroad. This active partnership in the conduct of human affairs is expected to continue and to expand. To the degree that contact with society is effectively maintained, the quality of the plans to serve society will be enhanced.

THREE MAJOR INSTITUTIONAL FUNCTIONS

The foregoing observations relate to certain general institutional characteristics. Attention will now be given to the functions that the institutions are called on to perform.

The Education of Students. The first of these is the oldest in tradition —the education of students. Traditionally, too, academic achievement has been recognized through the award of degrees. The degree-credit enrollment is expected to rise from 3.6 million in 1960 to 7.1 million in 1975–1976.[33] There is a trend toward more graduate study, and toward a larger number of students who will not continue throughout the period normally required to qualify for a bachelor's degree. There is also a growing number of adults enrolled in degree-credit programs, including housewives who have raised their families. In addition to degree-credit programs, provision for terminal occupational programs for youth can be expected to increase in the community colleges.

It has been pointed out that the rapid increase in knowledge tends to make obsolete that which was the best available only a few years past. Hence there is need for refresher courses or programs to keep the practitioner up to date. Horn states: "The best the college can do is to lay the foundation for a liberal education, to include the habits of mind, breadth of interest, and enlargement of spirit, which, when continued and enriched during the later years, can result in a true liberal education."[34] This requirement for continuing education is especially true in science and mathematics and in business management, law, medicine, teaching, nursing, and other professions or disciplines. Here is an area in which widespread development is foreseen.

[33] Conger, "College and University Enrollment: Projections," in *Economics of Higher Education,* Selma J. Mushkin, ed., *op. cit.,* The median estimate is drawn from Table 8, p. 17.

[34] Francis H. Horn, "A Lifetime of Learning," in *Toward the Liberally Educated Executive,* Robert A. Goldwin, ed. (White Plains, N.Y.: The Fund for Adult Education, 1957), p. 10.

A major segment of education beyond the high school has been largely neglected by institutions of higher education. This is the area of adult education that is not pursued for degree credit. A recent study by Johnstone[35] estimated that from June 1961 to June 1962, in addition to 2.65 million adults[36] enrolled as full-time students, over 17 million enrolled for specified periods (a month or more for 90 per cent of enrollees) in adult education courses, and nearly 9 million more were engaged to some extent in independent self-education.[37] Of the participants about 27 per cent were studying job-related subjects; 16 per cent, hobbies and recreation; 12 per cent, religion, morals, and ethics; and the remainder, a variety of subjects ranging from personal development to public affairs and citizenship.[38] Of all persons enrolled in adult education courses, less than 16 per cent were enrolled under the sponsorship of institutions of higher education.[39] It is safe to say that present programs of adult education, despite their extent, are too limited to provide the adult citizenry of the nation with the knowledge, skills, and understandings needed for effective participation in community and national life. The leadership role in adult education must be assumed by institutions of higher education.

Blakely dealt with the problem aptly when he wrote:

". . . a major responsibility of the university, in cooperation with all sorts of organizations and agencies, governmental and nongovernmental, is to create, to invent and to promote educational opportunities for leaders and emerging leaders in the world beyond the campus, among those who have left the campus and entered the arena of mature affairs.[40]

In the opinion of Liveright,

The state of flux in the field of university and college adult education during the recent past is still its most pervasive characteristic and is likely to remain so for the coming decade. . . . The first and most widespread problem is the fact that

[35] John W. C. Johnstone, *Volunteers for Learning: A Study of the Educational Pursuits of American Adults* (Chicago: National Opinion Research Center, University of Chicago, 1963).

[36] Adults in the sample of over 12,000 American households were defined as twenty-one years of age or over; under twenty-one but married; under twenty-one but head of household; twenty-one or over but living on an armed forces base and having close family ties with some member of an American household; twenty-one or over but living in a school residence or dormitory and closely related to some household member. The number of such adults at June 1, 1962, was estimated at 114 million.

[37] Johnstone, *Volunteers for Learning, op. cit.,* Table 2.4, p. 20.

[38] *Ibid.,* Table 2.8, pp. 33–35.

[39] *Ibid.,* Table 2.13, p. 58.

[40] Robert J. Blakely, in *The Changing University,* A Report on the Seventh Annual Leadership Conference, George H. Daigneault, ed. (Chicago: Center for the Study of Liberal Education for Adults, 1959), p. 60.

adult education is still considered a peripheral and possibly expendable aspect of the university or college program.[41]

Woodburne is in agreement with this view. He states:

Usually it [adult education] does not fit into the pattern of regular departmental arrangements through the teaching colleges and teaching faculties. It is, in most instances, somewhat a side issue from the point of view of regular daytime teaching of students.[42]

It is the writer's opinion that the institutions of higher education must recognize their responsibilities for adult education and give to it the best of their leadership.

Research. In addition to the education of youth and adults, the institutions of higher education have major responsibilities for research that will extend the frontiers of knowledge. The growth of research in institutions of higher education previous to 1940 was slow. It was overshadowed by the development of great research organizations in industry, where qualified men well equipped with facilities demonstrated their capacities for great achievement. At the outbreak of World War II, the extent of organized research in higher educational institutions could be measured in terms of expenditures. In 1940 only $28 million was spent. As a result of expansion during and subsequent to the war, however, the amount increased to $734 million in 1958.[43] This trend is seen as continuing and accelerating, and annual expenditures for this function are expected to reach a range of $5.7 to $7.5 billion by 1975–1976.[44] In this estimate a relationship to the gross national product is assumed.

The institutions of higher education, in thus expanding this function, face a major responsibility in directing the effort, coordinating it with related effort wherever found, and encouraging the work with benefit to and without detriment to the education of students.

Field Service. The third function to be considered here is that of field service, sometimes referred to as public service. Through this function the institution lends its resource personnel to public service at home and abroad for service, consultation, and advisement. Rapid development has been

---

[41] A. A. Liveright, "Adult Education in Colleges and Universities," in *Handbook of Adult Education in the United States,* Malcolm S. Knowles, ed. (Chicago: Adult Education Association of the U.S.A., 1960), p. 214.

[42] Lloyd S. Woodburne, *Principles of College and University Administration* (Stanford, Calif.: Stanford University Press, 1958), p. 186.

[43] *Biennial Survey of Education in the United States, 1957–58,* Statistics of Higher Education, Chap. 4, Sec. II, Receipts, Expenditures, and Property, p. 5.

[44] Herbert H. Rosenberg, "Research and the Financing of Higher Education," in *Economics of Higher Education,* Selma J. Mushkin, ed., p. 319.

seen in these services following World War II. By 1958 expenditures had reached $179 million and by 1975 they are expected to reach $450 to $540 million.[45] The responsibility for this service is being assumed by institutions of higher education. The difficulties they face in freeing their resources to the betterment of social institutions both now and in the future are bound to be great in view of the problem of finding qualified temporary replacements to staff the ongoing programs of instruction and research.

OPERATIONS

In addition to anticipated changes in the functions of institutions of higher education outlined above are foreseeable changes in institutional operations. The extension of opportunities for higher education to all who can profit from it will cause institutions to admit students with diverse interests, aptitudes, and capacities. This will call for more effective programs of advisement and placement. It will also require programs of greater diversity to take into account both the greater range in student characteristics and the growing demand for job knowledge and skills. The new knowledge in many new areas imposes a responsibility both to teach and to learn, and hence programs will require constant revision.

A major problem facing institutions now and in the future is how to instruct students of a markedly wide range of capabilities so that each student will be stimulated and encouraged to exert himself to the best of his ability. This problem has not been as pressing in the past because admissions have been restricted (generally) to those of superior mental ability and academic achievement. In the recent past and in the present, many institutions rely on selective admissions policies to provide a student body within specified ranges of qualifications. Many other institutions have an "open door" policy of admissions, and these have either sought grouping on some basis of homogeneity or attempted to teach in regularly scheduled classes all gradations of ability. In the future it is anticipated that admissions policies will generally become less selective. The search for teaching procedures that will challenge all levels of abilities will thus be intensified, and it will doubtless involve experimentation with basic course content variously supplemented by study in depth for the gifted, and study leading to fuller understanding by the less gifted. Such experimentation may also be expected to include programmed study through the use of teaching machines and communication devices, through group work and independent study, and through class size

[45] See *Economics of Higher Education,* Selma J. Mushkin, ed., Table 6, p. 182. In this table the estimate is made for two activities combined. The rate of increase for the one function discussed is assumed to be the same as that projected by Mushkin for the two.

and teacher aides. The important fact is that the teaching methods in higher education, which for centuries have had to do with the ablest minds, must now be adapted to serve a range of ability.

As public support grows, there will be increased public interest in the quality and cost of education. There is now a growing public expectation of more effective use of institutional resources. This will require management to weigh financial as well as educational implications of all proposals of policies and plans. The mounting interest in the institutional economics of higher education is seen in the growing literature on institutional economy. Among the many publications are those concerned with current planning and management data,[46] operational economy,[47] teaching loads,[48] course proliferation,[49] space utilization,[50] statistical studies,[51] academic calendar,[52] the distribution of expenditures,[53] cost analyses,[54] and uniform accounting definitions and classifications.[55]

Having reviewed the outlook for changes in institutions of higher education, it will be of interest to look briefly at projections of expenditures that are deemed likely in the future. Of the various estimates available, those

[46] *Higher Education, Planning and Management Data, 1957–58 to 1959–60.* U.S. Department of Health, Education, and Welfare, Office of Education (Washington, D.C.: U.S. Government Printing Office, 1961). See also reports on salaries, investments, facilities, etc.

[47] Seymour Harris, *Higher Education: Resources and Finance, op. cit.,* and Beardsley Ruml and Donald H. Morrison, *Memo to a College Trustee* (New York: McGraw-Hill Book Company, Inc., 1959).

[48] *Conference on the Measurement of Faculty Work Load,* Kevin Bunnell, ed. (Washington, D.C.: American Council on Education, 1960).

[49] Earl J. McGrath, *Memo to a College Faculty Member* (New York: Bureau of Publications, Teachers College, Columbia University, 1961).

[50] John Dale Russell and James I. Doi, *Manual for Studies of Space Utilization in Colleges and Universities,* American Association of Collegiate Registrars and Admissions Officers (Athens, Ohio: Ohio University Press, 1957).

[51] *California and Western Conference Cost and Statistical Study,* Financed by a Grant from the Fund for the Advancement of Education (Berkeley: University of California Printing Department, 1955).

[52] Thad L. Hungate and Earl J. McGrath, *A New Trimester Three-Year Degree Program* (New York: Bureau of Publications, Teachers College, Columbia University, 1963.

[53] *The Sixty College Study . . . A Second Look,* Financed by a Grant from the Fund for the Advancement of Education (New York: National Federation of College and University Business Officers Associations, 1960).

[54] Thad L. Hungate, *Finance in Educational Management of Colleges and Universities,* Chap. V; and *Cost Analysis for Collegiate Programs in Nursing* (New York: National League for Nursing, Division of Nursing Education, 1956), Part I; also, *California and Western Conference Cost and Statistical Study.*

[55] *College and University Business Administration* (Washington, D.C.: American Council on Education, 1952), Vol. I.

prepared by Mushkin for current expenditures and by Bokelman[56] for capital outlay are presented here. Mushkin has estimated future educational and general expenditures as follows:[57]

	Expenditures (in billions)	
Function	Actual 1957–1958	Estimated 1975–1976
Student higher education	$2.4	$ 8.6–12.5
Research	.8	5.7– 7.5
Public service and other organized activities	.4	1.0– 1.2
Total	$3.6	$15.3–21.2[a]

[a] In this estimate the projection for student higher education is based on projections of enrollments by Conger, *op. cit.;* the expenditures for research and public services are estimated to vary with the increase in the gross national product.

The annual capital outlay requirement is estimated by Bokelman to rise from $1.1 billion actually expended in 1958 to a range of $1.5 to $2.2 billion in 1975–1976.[58]

Thus the annual requirement for institutional expenditures, exclusive of those for auxiliary activities and student aid, is expected to rise from $4.7 billion in 1957–1958 to a range of $16.8 to $23.4 billion in 1975–1976.

Expenditures of this magnitude will require corresponding increases in support. The debate is mounting over appropriate principles of finance of this institutional enterprise—how much by students and their families, who are further burdened by student living costs, how much by philanthropists, and how much by local, state, and federal governments. The practices among the states are highly diverse. The Federal Government, which has in recent years provided increasing support for research, instruction, facilities, and student aid, appears to be groping for a long-range policy for participating in financing higher education.

The Challenges to Managements of Institutions of Higher Education

In a matrix having to do with social policies, institutional objectives, and the economics of higher education are to be found the mechanisms for

[56] See Selma J. Mushkin and Robert Bokelman, "Student Higher Education and Facilities of Colleges and Universities: Projections," in *Economics of Higher Education,* Chap. 11, pp. 173–194.

[57] *Ibid.,* p. 182.

[58] *Ibid.,* pp. 193–194.

control, both formal and informal; the arrangements for support and expenditures; the roles of governing boards, faculties, and administrators; the development and conduct of institutional plans and programs—all in relation to student growth and development and to the growth of knowledge. The focus of attention is institutional achievement, and the key to such achievement is management.

The managements of institutions must seek to understand how institutional objectives are best determined and modified; how policies consistent with objectives are chosen and implemented; how performance under policy is best achieved; and how evaluation of that performance in turn will permit reassessment of objectives and policies. Always, as a part of the enterprise, must be concern for the quality of the environment for learning, the values of research programs, the growth and development of both academic and nonacademic personnel, and the holding forth of incentives to creativity.

Any appropriate examination of management of higher education must be concerned with the values demanded by society, must take account of the degrees of uniqueness in institutions, and must recognize that the institutional environment must be conducive to both teaching and learning.

Society has called decisively for access to higher education for all youth that can benefit. This change in orientation is without precedent in history. It imposes on state governments responsibilities for the development of state systems consistent with the new concept. It imposes on institutions the task of modifying objectives, resources, programs, and methods developed to serve the earlier concept and of turning to those deemed appropriate for the new.

In summary, the challenges to management are seen in the increasing magnitude of the tasks, in the growth of knowledge, in the changing leadership requirements, in the devising of new programs to match the range of student interests and capacity on the one hand, and the desired outcome on the other. They are evident in the need for adequate and suitable resources and their effective use. They are indicated particularly in the suitable delegation and exercise of responsibilities of management itself—in relation to objectives, philosophies, plans, programs, resources, operations, and evaluation.

The Challenges to Managements Call for Rapid Upgrading of Their Quality and Adequacy

It is believed that in many institutions the new demands on management are presently greater than the organized institutional resources of management to meet them.[59] In such institutions, on occasion or to some extent, may be found:

1. A board of control that is overworked and unclear concerning its role.
2. Lack of clear-cut institutional objectives and absence of long-range planning.
3. Lack of provision by the board of control for suitable supervision of delegated policy responsibilities to faculty and staff.
4. A president too preoccupied with administration to give as much as half his time to educational leadership.
5. Lack of faculty awareness of existing institutional weaknesses and their implications for the institution.
6. Inadequate procedures in relation to faculty and staff for communication and participation.
7. In varying degrees, psychological barriers to effective joint efforts between faculty, president, executives, and board of control.
8. An inadequate and cumbersome records system.
9. Lack of evaluative procedures related to all phases of plans and operations.

If this assessment is valid, there is need to seek ways in which management may be strengthened in order to discharge more effectively its important responsibilities.

It is the purpose of this work to formulate guides for management of institutions of higher education appropriate to present and future needs. Despite the exercise of similar functions, such management calls for standards, procedures, and evaluations markedly different from those in management in government and industry. It is considered likely that a systematic analysis of the responsibilities of management in higher education in its new setting will afford the best basis for evaluating forms and practices, and for forming concepts of ways of meeting such responsibilities within the limitations of institutional resources. The present and future needs of management of institutions of higher education are not to be met solely by adopting practices found in past experience. The outlook is for marked institutional changes that call for new understandings, new ways of cooperation, and new sets of value judgments concerning what constitutes good per-

[59] "Why," asks Gross, "is there so little attention given to problems of coordination, control and appraisal in the universities? . . . Nowhere in the administrative structure of most universities, at the president's level, dean's level, or departmental level, do we find individuals whose energies are primarily devoted to the systematic examination and appraisal of academic affairs." (Neal Gross, "Organizational Lag in American Universities," *Harvard Educational Review*, Vol. 33, No. 1, Winter 1963, p. 70).

formance. It is this fact that justifies the effort to assess what management in the future will be called on to do, and to formulate appropriate guidelines to assist institutions in strengthening their managements to meet the challenges they face.

As a background for the consideration of institutional management, a review of institutional diversity and authority for management within the states is first presented (Chapter 2). This is followed by a chapter dealing with appropriate principles for management (Chapter 3) and by chapters to serve as guides to the exercise of its functions: the delegating and organizing function (Chapter 4), the directive function (Chapter 5), the operative function (Chapter 6), and the evaluative function (Chapter 7). In Chapter 8 the exercise of state controls of higher education is considered. A summary is presented in the final chapter.

CHAPTER 2

The Diversity of Institutions

In a democratic society, the final authority rests with the people. They exercise this authority through their formal organizations of government and through the influence of voluntary agencies, associations, and individuals. Thus the governments of the states and often the governments of localities, through their executives and agencies, exercise direct control of public higher education. Institutions privately controlled operate under charters granted by the states in which they are established. Among these are institutions that operate within the range of authority granted in their charters and are governed by lay self-perpetuating boards of trustees. Also included are chartered institutions that operate under the control of religious denominations.

The Federal Government does not exercise direct legal control over institutions of higher education (a few federal service institutions excepted). Yet through large programs of financial support, its influence throughout American higher education is pervasive. Pursuant to applications of institutions, federal funds are made available for designated purposes through grants or negotiated contracts. Such funds are subject to federal audit. In the public interest the Federal Government, through its Office of Education, its armed services, or any of a number of its branches or agencies, enters into contracts with institutions for low-interest loans for student housing and student aid, for support for aspects of the teaching program, for research or field services. Substantial sums are appropriated for certain programs of research, instruction, and student stipends. Because the funds thus made available are large, the programs of cooperating institutions are modified to provide and coordinate the institutional activities and resources that are financed from this source of support.[1] Such control as is exercised is defined in the contracts and appropriations.

Supplementing the direct controls of governments and religious bodies are the many indirect controls to which institutions must respond in the interest of fulfilling their purposes. These controls are state licensure, job demands, and standards of accrediting agencies.[2] There are numerous professional associations to be heeded, such as, to name but a few, the American Medical Association, the American Chemical Society, the American Psychological Association, the American Association of University Professors, the National Education Association. There are associations of institutional specialists that promote standards in institutional operation, such as those for admissions officers, registrars, plant managers, business officers, personnel officers. There are institutional associations that promote better practices and standards and exchange information. Among the latter are the American Council on Education, the Association of American Colleges, and the Association of Land-Grant Colleges. To all these indirect controls must be added the influence of philanthropists—foundations, corporations, and individual donors. Ever present, too, is the influence of tradition and the attitudes of the general public, and of the public that is of special concern to the institution—the students; the broader community around it, of which the students are a part; and the alumni.

The influence of tradition is shown in the tendency of an institution to

[1] The American Council on Education, in its December 20, 1963 issue of *Higher Education and National Affairs* (Vol. XII, No. 46), reported that the President, on December 16, 1963, signed into law (Public Law 88–204) the Higher Education Facilities Act of 1963. Under this act, expenditures of $1,195 million were authorized for the first three years of a five-year program of grants and loans for the construction of academic facilities.

President Johnson, on the occasion of the signing of the act, stated: "This legislation is dramatic, and it is concrete evidence of a renewed and continuing national commitment to education as the key to our Nation's social and technological and economic and moral progress. It will help meet the demands of our economy for more skilled personnel; it will enable many more of our young people to cope with the explosion of new knowledge and to contribute effectively in a world of intellectual, political, and economic complexity."

[2] For an excellent view of accreditation as a means of control of standards, see William K. Selden, *Accreditation* (New York: Harper & Row, 1960), especially pp. 29–54.

For a description of the work of the National Commission on Accrediting, see John S. Brubacher and Willis Rudy, *Higher Education in Transition* (New York: Harper & Row, 1958), especially pp. 345–346.

continue to carry on in the same manner practices that have persisted for many years, even though they are at variance with current thought or use. The influence of attitudes of institutional publics is reflected in changes that institutions make in their programs or practices in response to ascertained wishes of the various publics, whether for initiation of new services or for modifying practices, where such changes are consistent with institutional objectives and values.

These influences have brought about the great diversity among institutions that is to be described. Hardy speaks of it thus:

Here is an educational system that matches the diversity of American society. It is not, however, anarchic. What relates these many independent, competing educational establishments within an elastic but durable organization is educational tradition, method, and purpose.[3]

Brubacher and Rudy found such diversity consistent with the heterogeneity of the country, and they note its value in these words:

Diversity had furthered equality of educational opportunity, with all that this meant for American social mobility. It had made it easier to maintain freedom in general, and academic freedom in particular. It had afforded the opportunity for original and fruitful experiment, for the serving of the public need with a multiplicity of institutional types and academic programs, for a healthful competition which might never have existed under a more authoritarian and centralized system.[4]

Gardner sees need to foster and extend this diversity. He states:

If we are to do justice to individual differences, if we are to provide suitable education for each of the young men and women who crowd into our colleges and universities, then we must cultivate diversity in our higher educational system to correspond to the diversity of the clientele. There is no other way to handle within one system the enormously disparate human capacities, levels of preparedness and motivations which flow into our colleges and universities.[5]

Thus each institution, whether publicly or privately controlled, is responsive to social demands for higher education expressed through individuals and agencies with authority for direct control or through the indirect controls of those influences relating to institutional support, public relations, academic programs, academic standards, and the demands of and for graduates.

The focus of this chapter is on the authority for management—its nature

[3] Richard Hofstadter and C. DeWitt Hardy, *The Development and Scope of Higher Education in the United States* (New York: Columbia University Press, 1952), p. 143.
[4] John S. Brubacher and Willis Rudy, *Higher Education in Transition, op cit.,* pp. 380–381.
[5] John W. Gardner, *Excellence: Can We Be Equal and Excellent Too?* (New York: Harper & Row, 1964), p. 83.

and its diversity. But this of itself has limited meaning until it is related to the diversity of the institutions managed. Among major responsibilities that are exercised and that afford some measure of institutional diversity is degree-credit student enrollment. If this measure is used to describe institutional diversity, consideration may then be given to other areas of responsibility, including organized research, adult education and other nondegree programs, and public service.

ENROLLMENTS

It has been noted in the preceding chapter that the outlook for growth in higher education is enrollment of over 7 million degree-credit students by 1975. Table 2 shows the increase in degree-credit enrollments in higher education between 1937–1938 and 1959–1960. It also shows the increase in the number of institutions. The data are not strictly comparable because the enrollments for 1937–1938 are those reported for the regular session, whereas the enrollments for 1959–1960 are the census figures for the third week of the fall term. Thus the reported size of institutions in 1937–1938 is larger than it would be had the census figures for that year been used.

From Table 2 it can be seen that in the twenty-two-year period more than 300 institutions were established and the number of students enrolled in the larger institutions (2,500 and over) increased from 659,476 or 48.9 per cent of the 1938 total to 2,329,095 or 67.6 per cent of the 1960 total.

TABLE 2.   Increase in degree-credit enrollments classified according to size of student body: 1937–1938 and 1959–1960

Size of Student Body	1937–1938		1959–1960	
	NUMBER OF INSTITUTIONS	STUDENTS[a]	NUMBER OF INSTITUTIONS[b]	STUDENTS[a]
2,500 and over	95	659,476	316	2,329,095
1,000–2,499	161	251,266	387	597,931
500– 999	276	193,674	426	303,845
250– 499	438	157,979	407	148,864
Under 250	724	85,034	480	62,919
Total	1,694	1,347,429	2,016	3,442,654

[a] Students enrolled in federal service schools omitted. In 1959–1960 ten schools in six states and the District of Columbia enrolled 16,039 students.

[b] Seventy-five separate campuses in nineteen states representing component parts of universities are not separately reported. Of these, 14 are in Indiana, 15 in Pennsylvania, 6 in West Virginia, and 9 in Wisconsin; all other states have fewer than 5 each.

SOURCE: For 1937–1938, Enrollment: *Biennial Survey of Education in the United States,* Statistics of Higher Education, Table 18.   Control: *Education Directory, 1939,* Part 3.   For 1959–60, Enrollments and Control: *Education Directory, 1960–1961,* Part 3.

In the same period, the number of institutions enrolling fewer than 500 students declined, as did the number of enrollees and the proportion of total enrollment. Thus the number of institutions that enrolled fewer than 500 students declined from 1,162 to 887; the aggregate number of students enrolled in them declined from 243,013 to 211,783; and the percentage of total student enrollment found in them declined from 18.0 per cent to 6.2 per cent.

This brief survey of student higher education reveals something of the nature of institutional growth. New institutions have been and are being founded, and those now existing are growing in size. Two out of three degree-credit students are now found in institutions that enroll more than 2,500 students, the average size being about 7,400 students. It must be borne in mind, also, that concurrently with the exercise of responsibility for student higher education the programs of adult education, of research, and of field services have developed in varying degrees.

The new social concept for higher education earlier described has brought and will continue to bring change to these institutions. This is in a sense a transition period in which institutions seek to conserve their established values while adapting and extending their services to fulfill the responsibilities that the new concept and the requirements of technological and social change place upon them.

To meet the rising demand for student higher education, institutions face not only the problems of numerical expansion, but also the problems associated with a widening range of student interests and capacities. As will be shown, the responses of managements within the states to the new demands are highly diverse. We can speculate that such diversity results from a variety of causal forces—the outlook for demand for institutional services, the geographic distribution of the population, varying concepts of what constitutes desirable educational programs, financial considerations, and diverse objectives and policies of privately controlled institutions. Many parents prefer, for financial and other reasons, to have their sons or daughters enroll in local institutions. At times political considerations enter, whether in the design and financial support of a state system, in the provision made for control and support of local community colleges, or in the incorporation of a private institution into the public system.

Aspects of Institutional Control

Since the focus of this work is on the management of institutions, it is essential to set forth at the outset both the manner and the extent to which the states delegate authority for management and to define terms. The word *control* when used here means the final authority of management. Privately controlled higher education includes institutions with independent self-perpetuating boards and those subject to the direct authority of religious denominations or governed by boards subject to the superior authority of religious denominations. Publicly controlled higher education includes institutions established under the authority of the state and subject to direct control of the state through state boards, or subject to control delegated by the state to a regional authority or to local government. The degree of autonomy of publicly controlled institutions varies widely.

INSTITUTIONAL CONTROL IN RELATION TO STUDENT ENROLLMENTS

At the turn of the century, with fewer than a quarter million degree-credit students enrolled, less than 40 per cent were found in publicly controlled institutions. The remaining 60 per cent were enrolled in institutions controlled either by independent self-perpetuating boards or by religious denominations. In the fall of the academic year 1961–1962, with a degree-credit enrollment of 3.9 million, over 60 per cent were in publicly controlled institutions. The reversal in percentages indicates that the trend toward publicly controlled higher education is likely to increase despite the continuous growth of privately controlled institutions. By 1975 it is expected that more than two-thirds of degree-credit students will be enrolled in publicly controlled institutions. The reason is found in the new conception of higher education as human capital—social and personal—and in the readiness and ability of governments to provide the financial support.

Private institutions rely largely on student fees for support. To many students and their families these fees, together with living costs, present a financial barrier. Public institutions charge modest fees, and many tend to be located in centers of population so that students may live at home while in attendance. Thus the cost of attending a public institution is usually much lower than the cost of attending a private one. As enrollments mount, a larger percentage of students from families of lower socioeconomic status enroll. These students require educational opportunity at low cost which only the public institutions can provide. There is another reason for the emphasis on public institutions. The private institutions have traditionally relied on philanthropy to provide the physical plant. The flow of philanthropy for this purpose is no longer adequate to modernize existing plants and provide for expansion as well. In addition, those institutions that rely on endowment income to finance current operations find that with every increase in enrollment the nontuition income per student declines. Finally, many private institutions find educational values in a relatively small institution. This type also has public appeal. For these reasons private institutions are likely to expand but at a much slower rate than public institutions.

Student enrollment classified by types of formal control of institutions is shown in Table 3. The data given are for the years 1937–1938 and 1959–1960. As in Table 2 they are not strictly comparable, inasmuch as the figures for 1959–1960 are from the census taken the third week of the fall term and those for 1937–1938, for the academic year. The latter figures are usually larger than the inventory figure, and hence the data for 1937–1938 are larger perhaps by about 10 per cent than strictly comparable data. The derived percentages, however, are comparable.

It is apparent from Table 3 that marked increases in enrollment have occurred in institutions under all categories of control. Consideration of percentages, however, will afford perspective on the present relative strength of the several types of control as well as the trends that have occurred in the twenty-two-year period. Enrollment in institutions under public control (all governments) increased from 50.9 per cent of the 1937–1938 total to 58.6 per cent of the 1959–1960 total. The proportion of enrollment found in independently controlled institutions, including proprietary, declined from 28.6 to 22.3 per cent. The proportion of enrollment in Protestant and other non-Catholic institutions declined from 13.3 to 10.4 per cent, whereas the proportion enrolled in institutions under Catholic control rose from 7.2 to 8.7 per cent.

In Table 4 student enrollment is classified by both size of institution and type of control for the years 1937–1938 and 1959–1960. It shows that for the nation as a whole, those institutions with enrollments above 1,000 stu-

TABLE 3. Degree-credit enrollment classified by type of institutional control: 1937–1938 and 1959–1960 [a]

Type of Control	1937–1938		1959–1960	
	ENROLLMENT	PERCENTAGE	ENROLLMENT	PERCENTAGE
Public (state and local)	685,434	50.9	2,015,876	58.6
Independent (including proprietary)	384,968	28.6	768,722	22.3
Protestant and other non-Catholic	179,502	13.3	357,803	10.4
Catholic	97,525	7.2	300,253	8.7
Total	1,347,429	100.0	3,442,654	100.0

[a] Enrollments in federally controlled institutions not included. In 1959–1960 there were ten institutions in six states and the District of Columbia that enrolled a total of 16,039 students.

SOURCE: For 1937–1938, Enrollment: *Biennial Survey of Education in the United States,* Statistics of Higher Education, Table 18. Control: *Education Directory 1939,* Part 3. For 1959–1960, Enrollment and Control: *Education Directory, 1960–1961,* Part 3.

TABLE 4.   Degree-credit enrollment classified according to type of control: 1937–1938 and 1959–1960 (federally controlled institutions excluded)

	1937–1938		1959–1960	
Type of Control	NUMBER OF INSTITUTIONS	ENROLLMENT	NUMBER OF INSTITUTIONS	ENROLLMENT
All institutions:	1,694	1,347,429	2,016	3,442,654
Total enrollment in institutions with enrollments of 1,000 or more	256	910,746	703	2,927,026
Per cent	15.1	67.6	34.9	85.0
Institutions under public control:	597	685,435	696	2,015,876
Total enrollment in institutions with enrollments of 1,000 or more	152	536,160	384	1,882,990
Per cent	25.5	78.2	55.2	93.4
Institutions under private control:	1,097	661,195	1,320	1,426,778
Total enrollment in institutions with enrollments of 1,000 or more	104	374,582	319	1,044,036
Per cent	9.5	50.5	24.2	73.2

NOTE: In this table the 75 component parts of public institutions operated as branches or as separate campuses in nineteen states are treated as a part of the parent institution.

SOURCE: For 1937–1938, Enrollment: *Biennial Survey of Education in the United States,* Statistics of Higher Education, Table 18.   Control: *Education Directory, 1939,* Part 3.   For 1959–1960, Enrollment and Control: *Education Directory, 1960–1961,* Part 3.

dents accounted for 67.6 per cent of all enrollments in 1937–1938 and 85.0 per cent in 1959–1960. They also accounted for 93.4 per cent of all enrollments in publicly controlled institutions and 73.2 per cent in privately controlled institutions. In the same period institutions under public control enrolling fewer than 1,000 students declined, and institutions of like size under private control gained slightly, in both number and enrollment.

Student enrollments classified according to type of institution and control are shown in Table 5. For the nation as a whole, in 1959–1960, the degree-credit enrollment in two-year colleges was 13.9 per cent of the na-

TABLE 5. Degree-credit enrollment classified according to type of institution and control: 1959–1960 (excluding ten federally controlled institutions with 16,039 students)

Type of Institution Classified According to Highest Degree Awarded	Public Control			Private Control			Total		
	NUMBER OF INSTITUTIONS	STUDENTS	PERCENTAGE	NUMBER OF INSTITUTIONS	STUDENTS	PERCENTAGE	NUMBER OF INSTITUTIONS	STUDENTS	PERCENTAGE
Two but less than four years beyond twelfth grade	329	397,756[a]	19.7	256	80,561[a]	5.6	585	478,317[a]	13.9
Bachelor's and/or first professional degree	91	109,443	5.4	637	402,351	28.2	728	511,794	14.9
Master's and/or second professional degree	175	594,253	29.5	286	378,147	26.5	461	972,400	28.2
Doctor of philosophy and/or equivalent degrees	96	912,174	45.3	115	554,412	38.9	211	1,466,586	42.6
Other and unclassified	5	2,250	0.1	26	11,307	0.8	31	13,557	0.4
Total	696	2,015,876	100.0	1,320	1,426,778	100.0	2,016	3,442,654	100.0

NOTE: In this table, the 75 component parts of public institutions operated as branches or as separate campuses are treated as a part of the parent institution.

[a] The *Junior College Directory* published by the American Association of Junior Colleges reports junior college enrollments at October 15, 1959, as follows:

Freshmen	346,568
Sophomores	163,674
Total in degree programs	510,242
Special students and adults	130,285
Total (not including summer sessions)	640,527

In the tabulation made by the author from the *Education Directory*, the total enrollment in degree programs as reported was 478,317, or 31,925 below the number reported by the Association. The tabulation, as indicated in Appendix B-2, does not separately account for 75 branches of four-year or more institutions in nineteen states. The special students and adults are not included in the tabulation.

SOURCE: Appendix B-2.

35

tional total, 19.7 per cent of enrollment in institutions under public control, and 5.6 per cent of enrollment in institutions under private control. As stated in the note to Table 5, the proportion would be greater if enrollments in university branches had been included. The enrollment in the four-year colleges accounted for 14.9 per cent of the national total, 5.4 per cent of enrollment in institutions publicly controlled, and 28.2 per cent of enrollment in institutions privately controlled. The enrollment in institutions offering the master's and/or second professional degree was 28.2 per cent of the national total, 29.5 per cent of that in institutions publicly controlled, and 26.5 per cent of that in institutions privately controlled. The largest percentage of total enrollment was in institutions offering the doctorate; it was 42.6 per cent for the nation, 45.3 per cent for institutions publicly controlled, and 38.9 per cent for institutions privately controlled.

This distribution of institutional types for the nation affords a view of what the authorities in control of higher education—public and private—have to date (1959–1960) designed for higher educational opportunities for American youth. Over two-thirds of all students are enrolled in institutions that grant graduate degrees. There is a trend toward the establishment of two-year colleges as a part of a public coordinated system of higher education. These institutions find favor for their availability to the youth of the community, for their adaptability to serve local needs by reason of local control, and for support often provided from state funds. While for the most part enrollments in institutions of all types tend to be drawn from the geographic area in which institutions are located, there is substantial migration of students from their states of residence to the state in which the institution of their choice is located.[6]

In Table 6 the classification shown in Table 5 is expanded to show for each of the four types of institution the kinds of programs being offered. Thus, of the 1960 degree-credit enrollment of 478,317 in 586 two-year institutions, 347,971 students were enrolled in 286 institutions with programs described as liberal arts and general and terminal occupational; 45,456 in

---

[6] In the fall of 1958, the percentage of enrolled students in the United States who had migrated from their home states was 17.1 per cent of undergraduate students, 21.6 per cent of graduate students, and 35 per cent of professional students.

For undergraduates, who account for about 86 per cent of the total enrollment, the percentage migrating from their home states varied markedly. The range was from 5.8 per cent in Utah to 48.2 per cent in Delaware. In six states (Oklahoma, Michigan, Louisiana, California, Texas, Utah) the percentage was less than 10; in six states (Hawaii, Idaho, Connecticut, Nevada, New Jersey, Delaware) it was above 35 per cent.

SOURCE: *A Fact Book on Higher Education* (Washington, D. C.: American Council on Education, 1958—), pp. 115, 116. Data compiled from *Home State and Migration of American College Students, Fall 1958* (Washington, D.C.: American Association of Collegiate Registrars and Admissions Officers).

49 institutions offering solely terminal occupational programs; 61,779 in 114 institutions offering programs described as liberal arts and general, terminal occupational, and teacher preparatory. The remainder were in institutions that are classified under seven different types of program.

In the four-year colleges offering the bachelor's or first professional degree, 511,794 students were enrolled in 1960 in 728 institutions classified according to 11 varieties of program. Chief of these groups were 248,929 students enrolled in 328 institutions with programs described as both liberal arts and general and teacher preparatory and 82,687 in 108 institutions with programs described as liberal arts and general, terminal occupational, and teacher preparatory.

The total enrollment in institutions offering the master's and/or second professional degree was 972,400, distributed among 461 institutions. The three chief classifications were: 279,893 students in 142 institutions classified as both liberal arts and general and teacher preparatory; 242,362 students enrolled in 45 institutions classified as liberal arts and general, with three or more professional schools; 145,093 students enrolled in 41 institutions classified as liberal arts and general, terminal occupational, and teacher preparatory. The remainder were in institutions in six additional classifications.

The enrollment in institutions offering the doctor of philosophy and/or equivalent degree was 1,466,586 in 211 institutions. Most of this enrollment (1,323,225) was in 131 institutions with programs classified as liberal arts and general with three or more professional schools. The remaining institutions were found in eight other classifications.

This summary of enrollments according to institutional types will suffice to show the great variation among the institutions that in the aggregate offer opportunities for higher education to the millions of American youth.

ORGANIZED RESEARCH

One of the major functions now being performed by institutions of higher education is that of research. In general, research may be in support of and incidental to teaching, and hence included as part of the instructional process. Or it may be separately financed and carried on primarily for the purpose of advancing knowledge. Research for the latter category is described as *organized research*. The growth and expansion of organized research since World War II in institutions of higher education have been tremendous. Expenditures for this purpose in all institutions in the United States rose from $28 million in 1940 to $161 million in 1948 to $734 million in 1958.[7] It is being financed to a large extent by the Federal Govern-

[7] *Biennial Survey of Education in the United States, 1957–58,* Statistics of Higher Education, Chap. 4, Sec. II, Receipts, Expenditures, and Property, p. 5.

TABLE 6.   Degree-credit enrollment classified by institutional type[a]

	Type I		Type II	
Character of Program	NUMBER OF INSTITUTIONS	ENROLLMENT	NUMBER OF INSTITUTIONS	ENROLLMENT
Terminal occupational (below bachelor's degree)	49	45,456	1	731
Liberal arts and general	44	6,436	69	36,684
Liberal arts and general and terminal occupational	286	347,971	22	12,654
Primarily teacher preparatory	32	2,134	35	21,566
Both liberal arts and general and teacher preparatory	42	8,065	328	248,929
Liberal arts and general, terminal occupational, and teacher preparatory	114	61,779	108	82,687
Professional and technical only (not including teacher preparatory)	7	1,237	62	18,009
Professional and technical and teacher preparatory	7	1,607	20	7,142
Professional and technical and terminal occupational	4	2,629	17	11,032
Liberal arts and general, with one or two professional schools	1	1,003	61	54,005
Liberal arts and general, with three or more professional schools	—	—	5	18,355
Total	586	478,317	728	511,794
Unclassified				
Grand total				

NOTE: In this table, the 75 component parts of public universities operated institution. Ten federally controlled institutions which enrolled 16,039 students
[a]Institutional Type I: Two but less than four years of work beyond
Institutional Type II: Bachelor's and/or first professional degree.
Institutional Type IV: Doctor of philosophy and/or equivalent degrees.

ment and by private sources—foundations, corporations, and indivduals.

A study of institutional finance will reveal that organized research tends to be concentrated in the great universities, both public and private. Such research (separately financed) in the junior college and the four-year college is very limited. This finding is consistent (generally) with the purposes of these institutions. It is the universities and the technological schools that strive to advance knowledge and that seek to train advanced students in research methods. While the two-year and four-year colleges do provide and character of program: 1959–1960

Type III		Type IV		Total	
NUMBER OF INSTITUTIONS	ENROLLMENT	NUMBER OF INSTITUTIONS	ENROLLMENT	NUMBER OF INSTITUTIONS	ENROLLMENT
—	—	—	—	50	46,187
14	12,003	2	1,913	129	57,036
—	—	—	—	308	360,625
52	101,159	2	7,624	121	132,483
142	279,893	6	11,360	518	548,247
41	145,093	2	2,944	265	292,503
66	33,316	38	34,654	173	87,216
34	19,877	12	41,528	73	70,154
4	1,475	1	6,530	26	21,666
63	137,222	17	36,808	142	229,038
45	242,362	131	1,323,225	181	1,583,942
461	972,400	211	1,466,586	1,986	3,429,097
				30	13,557
				2,016	3,442,654

as branches or as separate campuses are treated as a part of the parent
are not included.
twelfth grade.
Institutional Type III: Master's and/or second professional degree.
   SOURCE: Appendix B-2.

some programs of specialized training (see Table 6), their emphases are on liberal studies and teacher preparation. Because in these institutions the advancement of knowledge is not (generally) a primary purpose, the extent of faculty involvement in research is limited.

In 1958, the aggregate of institutional expenditures for organized research was approximately $734 million. Of this amount, $709 million or 96.5 per cent was expended by universities and technological institutions, and the rest—$25 million or 3.5 per cent—by liberal arts colleges, teachers colleges, theological schools, and junior colleges, including the technical institutes.[8] The universities and technological schools are included in the category of institutions that grant the doctor's degree or equivalent. While these institutions enroll but 42.6 per cent of all students,[9] their enrollments include most of the students who are seeking to qualify for advanced degrees. The research that a teacher carries on in relation to his teaching is not separately accounted for, and its extent is not known. The effect of the presence and extent of organized research on the quality of teaching in an institution remains to be assessed. There is need for evaluation of the desirability of present practice, in which so many institutions have none or little research, whereas in so many others heavy concentrations are found.

FIELD SERVICES

The field services performed by faculty members of colleges and universities are increasing, and the trend is expected to be accelerated in the future. The cooperation between institutions and the Federal Government is placing many specialists in foreign lands for extended periods of service in various fields. In this country, too, the demand for the services of such specialists in government, industry, agriculture, and labor is growing. There is also an increasing demand for both adult and continuing education.

The extent of field services is difficult to measure because not all of it is reflected in institutional reports. Leaves of absence for extended periods of time are often granted to faculty members to perform such service. The reported expenditures for field services in 1958 were about $179 million; and as stated in Chapter 1, they may exceed a half billion dollars by 1975. This estimate may well prove to be a conservative one.

SUMMARY

In summary, the trend in institutional control is toward increase in the domain of public control. By 1975, over two-thirds of all students are expected to be enrolled in institutions under this type of control . Accompanying this trend is growth in institutional size and diversity of offerings. Organized research, largely concentrated in the universities, is growing rapidly, expenditures for this purpose having risen 2,521 per cent since 1940.

Aspects of Public Control

As shown above, public control is becoming dominant in higher education. In 1960 publicly controlled institutions enrolled 2,015,876 or 58.6

[8] *Biennial Survey of Education in the United States, 1957–58*, Statistics of Higher Education, Chap. 4, Sec. II, Receipts, Expenditures, and Property, p. 27.

[9] Enrollment percentage derived from data in Table 5.

TABLE 7.   Nature of public control of higher education in fifty states, Puerto Rico, and District of Columbia: 1959–1960

Type of Control	Number of State Boards	Local Boards	Number of Institutions[a]	Degree-credit Enrollment
For fifty states				
1. State planning- coordinating boards	12			
2. State supervisory or accrediting boards	28			
Local boards under their supervision		254	254	336,789
3. State governing boards each responsible for a single institution	108		108	440,446
4. State governing- coordinating boards	66			
a. Institutions under direct control			286	1,128,803
b. Institutions with local boards under supervision of seven of these boards		40	40	49,058
5. Local boards not under supervision of state boards		6	6	41,615
Total, fifty states	214	300	694	1,996,711
Puerto Rico		1	1	17,891
District of Columbia		1	1	1,274
Total	214	302	696[a]	2,015,876

[a] In this table the 75 component parts of public institutions operated as branches or as separate campuses in nineteen states are not separately counted as institutions.

SOURCE: Appendixes B-1 and B-3.

per cent of all students.[10] The outlook is for further growth both actually and relatively.

An overview of the nature of public control may be gained from Table 7. It will be observed from this table that twelve of the fifty states have statewide planning-coordinating boards. These boards do not exercise direct responsibility for governance. The twenty-eight state supervisory or accrediting boards are often the same state boards that exercise responsibility

[10] See Table 3.

for the supervision of elementary and secondary education. These boards supervise 254 institutions governed by local boards that in 1960 had a total degree-credit enrollment of 336,789. There are 108 boards each responsible for governing a single institution. The 1960 degree-credit enrollment in these institutions aggregated 440,446. There are 66 governing-coordinating boards each responsible for more than one institution. These boards exercise responsibility for planning, coordinating, and governing the institutions for which they are responsible. Together they are responsible for 286 institutions that in 1960 enrolled 1,128,803 students. Under the supervision of seven of these boards are 40 institutions that in 1960 enrolled 49,058 students. Finally, there are six institutions that are not supervised by state boards. These institutions enrolled 41,615 students. The aggregate 1960 degree-credit enrollment in institutions under public control in the fifty states was 1,996,711 students.

In addition to the enrollments shown for the fifty states, the student degree-credit enrollment was 1,274 in one public institution in the District of Columbia and 17,891 in the University of Puerto Rico. Ten federal higher educational institutions located in six states and the District of Columbia enrolled 16,039 students.

Of the four types of state boards shown in Table 7, the oldest in tradition are the governing boards responsible for a single institution. The supervisory and accrediting boards (generally) exercise assignments of responsibilities for higher education that they have customarily performed for elementary and secondary education. While these boards are not new, the growth of local institutions calls for new services of supervision and accreditation, and hence the responsibilities assigned to such boards are increasing.

The governing-coordinating board is not new, but the growing concentration of responsibility in many of these boards has developed since World War II. Three forces operate to increase this concentration of responsibility. One is the increase in size and complexity of institutional student bodies; the second is the introduction of new institutions or branches in new locations; the third is a growing need for statewide planning and coordination. It is this need that has brought into being the newly formed state planning-coordinating boards. The exercise of state responsibility will be further discussed in Chapter 8.

The governance of public higher education in the United States varies from the older stereotype—an undergraduate college concerned almost entirely with the education of youth, governed by a lay board of trustees with wide latitude for independent action, and having the faculty a valued partner in the enterprise—to a new pattern comprising a complex system of many institutions. These include graduate and professional programs and perhaps large programs of organized research, all governed and coordinated by a lay board whose independence of action has been curtailed by the assignment of powers to central state agencies and whose procedures of control necessarily restrict the freedom of individual institutions. The trend is strongly toward the latter pattern. It is claimed that within this pattern the necessary decisions are made by those best qualified and that the process takes full account of both the broad public interests and the interests of the students and the teaching profession. A major consideration is whether under this type of control provision has been made for adequate participation in management by the institutional faculty, for securing its creative contributions to the development of the institutional program, and through consensus with other elements of management for promoting personal understanding and commitment to institutional plans and accomplishments. The net advantages and disadvantages in the exercise of controls by the several state agencies deserve careful evaluation. Further consideration of this development is given in Chapter 8.

Aspects of Private Control

As shown in Table 3 the total resident student enrollment in 1959–1960, excluding 16,039 in federal institutions, was 3,442,654, of whom 2,015,876 or 58.6 per cent were enrolled in publicly controlled institutions and 1,426,778 or 41.4 per cent in institutions privately controlled. It will be of interest to examine further the nature of private control.

Public policy for higher education in the United States, which fosters the establishment and growth of privately controlled institutions, ensures to the citizenry the opportunity for freedom of teaching and inquiry and freedom to transmit the religious heritage. Although the major purposes of institutions under the control of religious denominations and private independent boards differ markedly, their programs tend to have certain common purposes, such as the fostering of self-development, ethical values, human relations, economic efficiency, and civic responsibility. Also, whether denominationally or independently controlled, there exists a great diversity of institutions within the two groups, ranging from small to large, from the two-year college to the complex university.

The types of private control of higher education are shown in Table 8. In 1960 there were 824 institutions, with a total enrollment of 658,056, controlled by religious bodies. The institutions operated under state charters, with boards elected or appointed by the controlling denominations. These religious bodies may in varying degrees formulate objectives, plans, and policies within which individual institutions operate. As many as 67 religious groups exercised institutional controls in 1960. The Roman Catholics controlled 304 institutions, with aggregate enrollments of 300,253. Con-

TABLE 8.   Types of private control of higher education in fifty states, Puerto Rico,[a] and District of Columbia[b]: 1959–1960

Type of Control	Number of Institutions	Degree-credit Enrollments
Control by religious denominations or groups		
Roman Catholic	304	300,253
Methodist	94	91,886
Lutheran	48	35,607
Southern Baptist	33	34,154
Baptist	66	33,608
Presbyterian	57	31,957
Latter-day Saints	3	11,836
Disciples of Christ	13	10,457
Seventh Day Adventists	11	8,154
Christian Church	2	6,638
Church of the Brethren	11	6,286
YMCA	6	5,553
Jewish	6	5,524
Evangelical United Brethren	9	5,306
All others: 53 church organizations, each enrolling fewer than 5,000	161	70,837
Total	824	658,056
Proprietary	38	24,904
Independent (nonprofit)	458	743,818
Total	1,320	1,426,778

[a]Includes 6,178 students enrolled in four institutions in Puerto Rico—3,428 in two independent institutions and 2,750 in two Catholic institutions.

[b]Includes 41,497 students enrolled in 19 institutions in the District of Columbia —19,127 in six independent institutions; 1,849 in three proprietary institutions; 11,657 in seven Catholic institutions; and 8,864 in three institutions controlled by non-Catholic religious denominations.

SOURCE: *Education Directory, 1960–1961,* Part 3, Higher Education.

trols exercised by Protestants were through many different denominations, the five leading ones being Methodists with enrollment of 91,886 in 94 institutions, Lutherans with enrollment of 35,607 in 48 institutions, Southern Baptists with enrollment of 34,154 in 33 institutions, Baptists with enrollment of 33,608 in 66 institutions, and Presbyterians with enrollment of 31,957 in 57 institutions. Each of the other denominations controlled 13 or fewer institutions and had an aggregate enrollment below 12,000.

As would be expected the institutions under the control of religious denominations are located geographically somewhat in accordance with denominational strength in the population.

The institutions under proprietary control in 1960 enrolled 24,904 students in 38 institutions. For the most part these are two-year colleges offering business training.

The institutions under private independent control in 1960 numbered 458 and enrolled 743,818 students. Each institution has a state charter, a self-perpetuating board, and freedom to chart its course. Under this type of control are operated institutions of considerable diversity as to size, policies, and programs. In the group are many of the well-known endowed universities, including Harvard, Princeton, Columbia, Chicago, and Stanford, and many endowed colleges, including Swarthmore, Wesleyan, Oberlin, and Carleton. It is the independent privately endowed institution that has in the past set the standards of excellence in higher education, standards made possible by freedom of control, by availability of funds, and by the quality and objectives of management.

There is much to be learned from a study of the exercise of control of private institutions—whether of the character of the institutions themselves, the mechanisms of control, the selection of students, the conduct of programs, or the evaluation of their operations. It is reasonable to expect that the best examples of effective institutional management are to be found in institutions privately controlled. They have greater freedom than do public institutions in student selection, staff selection, range of faculty salaries, and choice of program. A lay governing board for each institution permits faculty involvement in the development of plans to a degree not feasible in public state systems governed by a single governing-coordinating board.

The Complex of Institutional Controls Within the States

The character of higher education for the nation as a whole is determined by the aggregates for the several states. Because education is a primary state responsibility, attention must be given to the characteristics within each state. Each state differs markedly from the others in enrollments, controls, institutional types, and institutional programs. These differences have roots in the historical development of higher education. Public institutions predominate in the newer states of the West; private institutions still predominate in a number of the older states of the East, although strong public programs are developing that may within a few years alter this generalization. These differences arise in part from the quality of attention that has been given to determining state policies for higher education. Some states have made long-range plans and have adopted forward-looking policies to meet the new social demand for higher education; others have done little beyond expanding existing public institutions.

The responsibilities of state governments for the character and quality of higher educational opportunity for the youth of the state is everywhere recognized, and this responsibility is expressed in the design of institutions in state systems, due recognition being given to resources of private higher education. New York, for example, has traditionally relied to a large extent on private institutions to provide educational opportunities for her youth. In establishing the state university the state's initial policy was to so design public institutions as to supplement but not supplant the private institutions. California, on the other hand, where public higher education predominates, has developed a clear policy of limiting enrollment in the university and state colleges and establishing a network of junior colleges with much broader admissions policies. There are states that are slow to make provision for adequate higher educational facilities for the future. In these states, little change can be seen in institutional numbers, types, or programs. The major change is in the size of the institutions, which has been increasing rapidly.

All states are active in planning for the future of higher education. State systems have been formed and are being formed and re-formed. The institutions and their controls are diverse, and so also are the institutional patterns. The current organizational structures and controls for public institutions have for the most part been adapted from those existing in the past. But a growing number of states have initiated bold new patterns, and as the diversity of students increases, and the study of higher education provides new evidence, further adaptation of the institutional patterns and the structures and mechanisms will be made. It must be borne in mind, too, that existing patterns were developed to a considerable extent in a period in which admissions policies were more selective than they are at the present time.

A review of state provisions for institutions and their controls will add to an understanding of their characteristics.

ENROLLMENTS

The size of degree-credit enrollments in the states will afford some idea of the magnitude of the management task. As shown in Appendix B-2, the range in numbers is from a few thousand in Alaska and Nevada to about 370,000 in New York and 425,000 in California. As summarized in Table 9, at one extreme are sixteen states and Puerto Rico, each with degree-credit enrollments in 1959–1960 of less than 30,000, for an aggregate of 222,349. At the other extreme are four states with aggregate degree-credit enrollments of 1,158,268. These four states include California (421,972), New York (366,733), Illinois (187,619), and Pennsylvania (181,944).

The proportion of student enrollment in 1960 for each state, Puerto Rico, and the District of Columbia in institutions under public and private control is shown in Table 10. It will be observed from Table 10 that the

TABLE 9. State degree-credit enrollment classified by size and institutional control: 1959–1960 (not including ten federally controlled institutions with 16,039 students)

Enrollment	Number of States	Public Control		Private Control		Total	
		NUMBER OF INSTITUTIONS	ENROLLMENT	NUMBER OF INSTITUTIONS	ENROLLMENT	NUMBER OF INSTITUTIONS	ENROLLMENT
Under 30,000	17[a]	87	166,312	91	56,037	178	222,349
30,000 to 59,999	19[b]	221	540,257	381	303,721	602	843,978
60,000 to 119,999	8	127	348,904	241	240,622	368	589,526
120,000 to 180,000	4	100	357,176	214	271,357	314	628,533
Over 180,000	4	161	603,227	393	555,041	554	1,158,268
Total	52	696	2,015,876	1,320	1,426,778	2,016	3,442,654

[a] Includes Puerto Rico.
[b] Includes District of Columbia.
SOURCE: Appendix B-2.

TABLE 10. Proportion of degree-credit enrollment in fifty states, Puerto Rico, and District of Columbia, in institutions under public and private controls: 1959–1960 (not including ten federally controlled institutions with 16,039 students)

Proportion of Enrollment, in Percentage	States	Aggregate Enrollments Classified by Type of Control		
		PUBLIC	PRIVATE	TOTAL
1. Pb* 10.1 to 20.0 Pr 80.0 to 89.9	Massachusetts, District of Columbia	20,753	151,622	172,375
2. Pb 20.1 to 30.0 Pr 70.0 to 79.9	Pennsylvania	37,878	144,066	181,944
3. Pb 30.1 to 40.0 Pr 60.0 to 69.9	Connecticut, New York	150,851	263,366	414,217
4. Pb 40.1 to 50.0 Pr 50.0 to 59.9	Illinois, Iowa, Missouri, New Jersey, Rhode Island, Vermont	198,288	232,832	431,120
Pr 50.0 to 59.9 Pr 40.0 to 49.9	Florida, Indiana, New Hampshire, North Carolina, Ohio, South Carolina, Tennessee	277,180	216,199	493,379
6. Pb 60.1 to 70.0 Pr 30.0 to 39.9	Georgia, Kentucky, Maine, Maryland, Utah, Virginia, Wisconsin	199,087	108,943	308,030
7. Pb 70.1 to 80.0 Pr 20.0 to 29.9	Alabama, Arkansas, Colorado, Idaho, Louisiana, Michigan, Minnesota, Nebraska, Oklahoma, Oregon, Puerto Rico, South Dakota, Texas, Washington, West Virginia	618,940	213,767	832,707
8. Pb 80.1 to 90.0 Pr 10.0 to 19.9	California, Delaware, Kansas, Mississippi, Montana	430,735	92,758	523,493
9. Pb 90.1 to 100.0 Pr 0 to 0.9	Alaska, Arizona, Hawaii, Nevada, New Mexico, North Dakota, Wyoming	82,164	3,225	85,389
Total		2,015,876	1,426,778	3,442,654

proportion of students enrolled in publicly controlled institutions was below 50 per cent in ten states and the District of Columbia. Most of these states are in the East, where traditionally greater reliance has been placed on privately controlled higher education. Together, these states account for 34.8 per cent of the nation's enrollment. At the other end of the scale are twelve states in which more than 80 per cent of the enrollment is found in publicly controlled institutions. These states in the aggregate enroll 17.7 per cent of the total for the nation, and the leadership in higher education—whether in teaching or in research—for the most part is found in the publicly controlled institutions. (The detailed data for Table 10 appear in Appendix B-1.)

American democracy is undergirded by the freedom given to initiative of private citizens to organize and maintain institutions of higher education. Thus the limitations or restrictions which may be imposed in publicly controlled institutions, and which to such citizens may be objectionable—whether in courses of study, standards, or methods—can be counteracted. Special interests, consistent with the public welfare, such as training in systems of ethical values or in religion, can be provided for. These institutions by reason of generous private support and endowments, and by their devotion to standards of excellence and freedom of inquiry, thought, and expression, have attained prestige and broad public good will. The freedom that in them is traditional is consistent with public policy. If ever this freedom should be encroached on in the governance of publicly controlled institutions, voices in protest from these private institutions can be expected to be heard.

A percentage distribution of 1959–1960 degree-credit enrollments among institutional types for the fifty states, Puerto Rico, and the District of Columbia is given in detail in Appendix B-2. To assist understanding of practices, the states have been grouped according to patterns of institutional design. Eight patterns are identified and described in Table 11 and are graphically illustrated in Fig. 1. Here the variations in the percentages of students enrolled in the four types of institutions are shown in relation to the unweighted averages for each type for all the states. It will be seen that the variations from the averages and from other patterns are often marked. Such variations reflect not only the influences of the past, but the changes that are being made to meet the new responsibilities for higher education. In presenting these data the aggregate enrollments for each state have been used, including those of both public and private institutions, because to a considerable degree they supplement each other.

The unweighted averages of state percentages of distribution by institutional type were 9.2 per cent in the two-year colleges; 17.3 per cent in the four-year colleges; 24.4 per cent in institutions granting the master's degree; and 48.7 per cent in institutions granting the doctor's degree. The groupings

TABLE 11.   States classified according to like degree-credit enrollment patterns in institutional types: 1959–1960[a]

State Groups (including District of Columbia and Puerto Rico)	Percentage for Each Institutional Type[b]			
	I	II	III	IV
Group 1: (BBBA)[c] Alaska, District of Columbia, New Mexico, Hawaii, Maryland, Montana	4.1	7.8	9.2	78.8
Group 2: (ABBA) Arizona, Colorado, Delaware, Utah, Wyoming, Oklahoma, Florida	16.2	5.9	6.7	71.1
Group 3: (BBAB) Connecticut, Nevada, New Hampshire, New Jersey	3.0	8.5	62.0	26.0
Group 4: (BAAB) Arkansas, Louisiana, Nebraska, Ohio, Puerto Rico, Tennessee, Kentucky, Virginia	3.7	23.6	41.4	31.1
Group 5: (BABB) Iowa, Maine, Pennsylvania, South Carolina, South Dakota, West Virginia	5.1	38.2	15.8	40.6
Group 6: (BABA) Indiana, North Dakota, Vermont, Wisconsin, Oregon	5.2	26.9	12.5	54.6
Group 7: (ABAB) California, Idaho, New York, Texas, Washington, Illinois, Kansas, Michigan	20.4	8.5	30.0	40.8
Group 8: (Unclassified) North Carolina, Mississippi, Georgia, Missouri, Rhode Island, Massachusetts, Alabama, Minnesota	10.0	19.4	23.5	46.1
All states: Unweighted	9.2	17.3	24.4	48.7
Weighted	13.9	14.9	28.2	42.6

[a] Enrollments of 16,039 students in ten federally controlled institutions not included in calculation of percentages. The aggregate of percentages for the four institutional types may be a fraction of 1 per cent less than 100. This difference is accounted for by a few unclassified institutions (see Appendix B-2).

[b] Institutional Type I: Two but less than four years of work beyond twelfth grade.
Institutional Type II: Bachelor's and/or first professional degree.
Institutional Type III: Master's and/or second professional degree.
Institutional Type IV: Doctor of Philosophy and/or equivalent degree.

Table 11 is to be read as follows: For the six states in Group 1, the average enrollment in 1959–1960 was 4.1 per cent in Type I, 7.8 per cent in Type II, 9.2 per cent in Type III, and 78.8 per cent in Type IV. One-tenth of 1 per cent of enrollment is in unclassified institutions.

[c] The enrollment pattern is described according to the relationship of the percentage of enrollment in each institutional type in each state to the unweighted average for all states of the percentage of enrollment in each institutional type. Thus for Group 1 the percentage of enrollments in Types I, II, and III is below (B) the national average, and in Type IV it is above (A) this average. The pattern is thus described as BBBA.

SOURCE: Appendix B-2.

FIGURE I.   Enrollment patterns in institutional types: 1959–1960

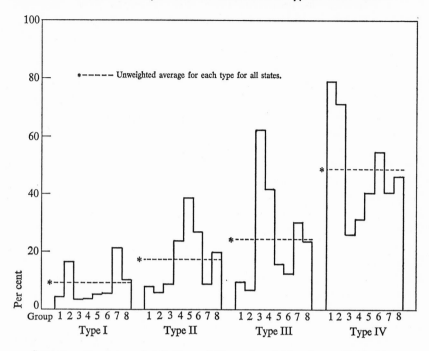

SOURCE: For data and definition of "Group" and "Type"—see Table 11.

in the table were formed according to enrollment distribution patterns related to state averages. Thus in State Group 1 are six states in which the percentages of enrollment are below the unweighted averages in institutional Types I, II, and III and above in Type IV. Eight groups are identified in this way. Thus, in Group 1 the primary reliance is on institutions granting the doctor's degree; Group 2 is similar except that considerable use is made of two-year colleges; Group 3 relies heavily on institutions granting the master's degree; Group 5 strongly supports the four-year colleges. These examples illustrate the diversity of institutional design within the states.

The data in Appendix B-2 show the eight states that in comparison with other states had the highest percentages of enrollment in each of the four types of institution listed in Table 11:

Type I   California, 49.1; Wyoming, 30.1; Idaho, 28.5; Mississippi, 24.5; Texas, 20.1; Florida, 20.1; Arizona, 18.1; Washington, 16.5

Type II   West Virginia, 54.5; Maine, 45.5; South Dakota, 36.7; Arkansas, 35.6; North Dakota, 34.6; Iowa, 34.1; Wisconsin, 31.2; Vermont, 29.8

Type III   Nevada, 100.0; Puerto Rico, 74.3; New Jersey, 55.5; Connecticut, 49.7; Nebraska, 42.9; New Hampshire, 42.8; New York, 41.03; Tennessee, 39.6

Type IV   Alaska, 100.0; Hawaii, 91.2; Utah, 88.6; District of Columbia, 85.4; Delaware, 81.3; New Mexico, 76.3; Colorado, 75.8; Arizona, 74.2

From Table 11 it will also be observed that in the majority of states a large proportion of degree-credit enrollments is found in institutions granting advanced degrees. It is perhaps too early in this transitional and developmental period to judge whether this circumstance will be found consistent with the requirements of the future. Many institutions can be expected to become larger; many new community colleges may be established; and new provisions may be made for adult education, and research and field services. The changes that come will be influenced in part by those who seek to adapt programs and resources to the requirements of the future; in part by those who seek to promote prestige and support for particular institutions; in part by those who seek to conserve the institutional values demonstrated in the past; and in part by those who seek to cling to the old and to resist the new. In the actions taken, the political implications will not pass unnoticed by those affected by them.

ORGANIZED RESEARCH

The place of organized research is unique within each institution. While the data for individual institutions are not readily available, certain differences found among the states will serve to illustrate the quantitative relationships of organized research and teaching. In Table 12 are shown the 1958 expenditures within each state for organized research expressed as a relative of the 1958 direct expenditures for instruction and departmental research.

The wide range in state expenditures for organized research poses a question as to its appropriate role in institutions of higher education. Are there principles or guidelines that will serve to maximize the value of such research within these institutions? As noted earlier, the greater part of organized research is found in institutions granting the doctor's and/or equivalent degree. It is generally recognized that there are values in relating research to teaching, and that higher education has a responsibility to provide research and field services for the benefit of society and its institutions. It is possible, however, that in some instances the college or university may assume responsibilities beyond its resources, and so hinder achievement of its primary purpose—the education of students. At the other extreme, as has been noted, is the college or university that has no ongoing program of organized research and field services. This lack may be undesirable. There

TABLE 12. Expenditures within states (including Puerto Rico and District of Columbia) for organized research expressed as a relative of direct expenditures for instruction and departmental research: 1958

Number of States	Range of Percentage	Average Percentage	States
6	10 – 19.9	14.9	New Hampshire, West Virginia, Vermont, Ohio, Oklahoma, Maine
17	20 – 29.9	25.9	North Dakota, South Dakota, South Carolina, Kentucky, Mississippi, North Carolina, Indiana, Virginia, Missouri, Kansas, Nebraska, Idaho, New York, Texas, Louisiana, Montana, Alaska
12	30 – 39.9	34.0	Nevada, Tennessee, Connecticut, Michigan, Oregon, Pennsylvania, Arkansas, Wyoming, Rhode Island, Arizona, Minnesota, Utah
9	40 – 49.9	43.3	Colorado, Washington, District of Columbia, Wisconsin, Puerto Rico, Hawaii, Iowa, Georgia, Florida
2	50 – 59.9	55.2	Delaware, New Jersey
6	60 and more	120.1	New Mexico, 64.9; Illinois, 82.7; Massachusetts, 112.6; California, 130.5; Alaska, 162.7; Maryland, 166.9
52	Unweighted average: 41.5%		
	Weighted average: 49.7%		

SOURCE of expenditure data from which relatives were derived: *Biennial Survey of Education in the United States, 1957–58,* Statistics of Higher Education, Chap. 4, Sec. II, Receipts, Expenditures, and Property, p. 73.

is an appropriate balance to be sought in the over-all program of teaching, research, and field services. Determination of the relation between these aspects of program is a matter of major importance.

STATE INSTITUTIONAL DESIGN AND CONTROL

The recent surge of enrollments, accompanied by the broadening range of student interests and capacities, has imposed on institutions (and on authorities responsible for higher education in state and local governments) the responsibility of offering suitable programs either through newly created institutions or through adaptations within existing institutions. Institutions that operate under selective admissions policies can choose students who may be expected to profit from an established program. But to the extent that admissions policies have become less selective, the curricula, courses, student assignments, and requirements for scholastic achievement call for adaptation to fit the interests and capacities of the enrollees. Each student must be challenged to achieve according to his capabilities. Consideration also must be given to new requirements for teaching skills. To the extent that such adaptations cannot be successfully achieved, we may expect to find, in varying degrees, a rise in the drop-out rate and an academic experience both frustrating for the less gifted and unchallenging to the gifted. Neither the machinery nor the techniques of evaluation nor any extensive organized experimentation of recognized merit exists to guide institutional design and development. This is a need that in the near future can be expected to be the focus of major study.

McConnell recognizes the need when he writes:

Although the arrangements for post-high-school education should be organized in more orderly fashion, we do not yet know enough about careers, student characteristics, and the character of college environments to establish a tidy array of differentiated institutions and to enable students to distribute themselves among them according to their individual traits. Neither do we know enough at this stage to pair students and specialized curricula with great precision.[11]

An examination of state practices reveals that the states exercise authority for the development of higher education in many different ways. For some, the new demands are met with minimal change; for others, new philosophies have called for new institutional design and new forms and procedures for the exercise of state authority. California and Florida are among the states that have taken the lead in adopting a philosophy of higher education as a guide to institutional development. These states seek to provide local two-year community colleges, for full-time and part-time students, that are geographically accessible so that the students may live at home. They also provide programs that permit qualified students to transfer to senior colleges, and terminal occupational programs that afford training to those who do not wish or may not qualify for degree programs, and they serve community needs through programs for adults.

The plan in California is to develop junior colleges to accommodate a major share of the enrollments in the first two years, thus limiting the demands on the four-year colleges and the universities.[12] That the plan is far advanced is evidenced by data in Appendix B-2, which show that about 60 per cent of the enrollment in California public higher education is found

[11] T. R. McConnell, *A General Pattern For American Public Higher Education* (New York: McGraw-Hill Book Company, Inc., 1962), pp. 179–180.

[12] See discussion in McConnell, *A General Pattern for American Public Higher Education, op. cit.*, pp. 114, 123.

in the junior college. In Florida the master plan provides for the major development of junior and community colleges. Rapid progress is being made. Four community colleges were established in 1960. Also in 1960, over 20 per cent of the total state enrollment in institutions of higher education, public and private, was in the two-year institutions.

The following summaries for three states—Ohio, New Mexico, and New York—for 1959–1960 will further serve to illustrate diversities in types of institutions and provision for control.

1. *Ohio* is a state which in 1960 relied on voluntary coordination of its public institutions, with each of six public institutions provided with a governing board appointed by the governor. In addition there are three chartered municipal institutions.

Type of Control	1959–1960 *Degree–credit* Enrollment
PUBLIC CONTROL	
Six state boards:	
1 university	10,559
1 university and land-grant college combined	23,166
1 four-year college with master's program	6,614
1 four-year college	1,343
1 four-year college with master's program	10,622
1 four-year college with master's program	9,942
Three municipal boards:	
1 university	5,181
1 university	16,650
1 four-year college with master's program	5,492
9	89,569
PRIVATE CONTROL	
19 independent institutions	32,971
11 Catholic institutions	18,477
4 Methodist institutions	7,476
25 institutions (22 denominational groups)	19,153
59	78,077
68 Total	167,646

SOURCE OF STATE DATA: *Education Directory, 1960–1961,* Part 3; and S. V. Martorana and Ernest V. Hollis, *State Boards Responsible for Higher Education,* U.S. Department of Health, Education, and Welfare, Office of Education, 1960.

The enrollments classified according to institutional types follow:

	Public Control		Private Control		Total	
	1959–1960					
Classification	NUMBER OF INSTITUTIONS	ENROLLMENT	NUMBER OF INSTITUTIONS	ENROLLMENT	NUMBER OF INSTITUTIONS	ENROLLMENT
Type I	—	—	4	3,775	4	3,775
Type II	1	1,343	37	38,678	38	40,021
Type III	4	32,670	15	25,124	19	57,794
Type IV	4	55,556	3	10,500	7	66,056
Total	9	89,569	59	78,077	68	167,646

Thus 46.6 per cent of Ohio's enrollment is found in private institutions. The public institutions are relatively few. The six institutions, each governed by a state board, are responsible to the governor. The three municipal institutions are responsible directly to local governments. There exists no over-all state coordinating board. The six state institutions also carry on a program of voluntary coordination in defining their financial requirements and other general matters.[13]

2. *New Mexico* is a state in which 95 per cent of the enrollment is found in publicly controlled institutions. Coordination of public higher education is provided by a board set up for that purpose, and each of the seven publicly controlled institutions has its own governing board. Private higher education is limited to two Catholic-controlled junior colleges.

Type of Control	1959–1960 Degree–credit Enrollment
PUBLIC CONTROL	
Governing-coordinating board:	
7 governing boards for 7 institutions	
1 university	7,367
1 land-grant college	3,845
4 four-year or more colleges	4,243
1 two-year college	278
7	*15,733*

[13] A new state-wide coordinating board for public higher education in Ohio was established in 1963, as reported by the Ohio Educational Association in *Ohio Schools,* Vol. XVI, No. 6, Columbus Ohio: The Association, September 1963.

Type of Control	1959–1960 Degree–credit Enrollment
PRIVATE CONTROL	
2 Catholic two-year colleges	842
2	842
9 Total	16,575

The enrollments classified according to institutional types follow:

| | 1959–1960 | | | | | |
| | Public Control | | Private Control | | Total | |
Classification	NUMBER OF INSTITUTIONS	ENROLLMENT	NUMBER OF INSTITUTIONS	ENROLLMENT	NUMBER OF INSTITUTIONS	ENROLLMENT
Type I	1	278	2	842	3	1,120
Type II	—	—	—	—	—	—
Type III	2	2,811	—	—	2	2,811
Type IV	4	12,644	—	—	4	12,644
Total	7	15,733	2	842	9	16,575

Thus in New Mexico higher education is primarily a public undertaking. Coordination of public institutions is an assigned responsibility. Enrollment is concentrated in institutions offering advanced degrees.

3. *New York* is a state that for many years has relied to a large extent on private institutions to provide higher educational opportunities for its youth. In recent years a major expansion of public effort has been undertaken. The Board of Regents has supervisory authority over the two governing-coordinating boards set up for all of New York State public higher education— one to serve New York City and one to serve the rest of the state. Unlike Ohio and New Mexico, a single board coordinates all public institutions

Type of Control	1959–1960 Degree–credit Enrollment
PUBLIC CONTROL	
Board of Regents Governing-coordinating board (New York City) :	
4 colleges with master's program[a]	72,265

[a] More recently organized as universities and empowered to grant the doctor's degree.

Type of Control	1959–1960 Degree-credit Enrollment

PUBLIC CONTROL *(Continued)*

Governing-coordinating board (State University
of New York):

4 professional schools or colleges with doctor's program	4,905
11 colleges with master's program	24,821
2 colleges with bachelor's program	1,931
22 local boards (22 two-year colleges)	28,784
43	*132,706*

PRIVATE CONTROL

55 independent institutions	174,243
47 Catholic institutions	45,018
20 institutions (20 denominations)	14,766
122	*234,027*
165 Total	366,733

outside New York City, governs 17 institutions directly, and supervises the governance of 22 community colleges, each of which has its local governing board.

The enrollments classified according to institutional types follow:

Classification	Public Control		Private Control		Total	
	NUMBER OF INSTITUTIONS	ENROLLMENT	NUMBER OF INSTITUTIONS	ENROLLMENT	NUMBER OF INSTITUTIONS	ENROLLMENT
Type I	22	28,784	27	7,784	49	36,568
Type II	2	1,931	40	22,702	42	24,633
Type III	15	97,086	32	53,119	47	150,205
Type IV	4	4,905	22	149,830	26	154,735
Total	43	132,706	121	233,435	164	366,141
Unclassified					1	592
Total					165	366,733

1959–1960

Thus in New York is found an above-average use of the two-year college and a heavy concentration of responsibility in two boards for the control of public higher education.

These three examples illustrate the differences in institutional patterns, in the proportion of student higher education controlled by governments, and in the means of coordination utilized. In the fifty states many experiments in the exercise of controls are under way. We may expect to learn from them how best to supply the appropriate types of institutions to serve both the student and society and to govern and coordinate such institutions.

Institutional Management in Relation to Authorities for Control

The quality of institutional objectives and plans depends importantly on the capabilities, the dedication, and the leadership of the governing board and its chief executive, the president. The translation of policies and plans into quality programs of educational opportunities and services is dependent in large measure on the quality, concepts, understandings, and motivations of the faculty and staff. Plans must be interpreted, courses designed, students guided, personnel and facilities acquired, and the whole enterprise conducted to achieve objectives as they are understood. This is to say that the heart of management resides in the institution. Institutional achievement can be maximized if the lay board seeks consensus with faculty and executives. It can be handicapped if the lay board does not. But institutional advancement, however aided, will not rise (generally) above the purposes, competencies, and understandings of those who perform the day-by-day responsibilities of management.

It is with awareness of the importance of affording to each institution effective leadership for its development and support that the provisions for management in the several states will be summarized here.

A summary of institutions in the fifty states classified roughly according to the degree of autonomy exercised by an institutional entity is presented in Table 13. From this table it will be seen that in 1959–1960 as many as 599 institutions (enrolling 1,226,379 degree-credit students) exercised a substantial degree of autonomy. A total of 1,106 other institutions (enrolling 1,020,632 degree-credit students) were governed by lay boards subject to supervision and/or policy decisions of a higher board or agency. In a third category are those public institutions in state systems that are governed by lay governing-coordinating boards. In this category 66 lay governing-coordinating boards exercised direct responsibility for 286 institutions with degree-credit enrollments of 1,128,803, or about one-third of all students.

It will be noted from Table 13 that the 1,705 institutions, each with its own lay board, enrolled 2,247,011 students, an average of 1,317 students under the governance of each board. The 66 governing-coordinating boards governed 286 institutions enrolling 1,128,803 students. This is an average

TABLE 13.   Institutional authority for management in fifty states: 1959–1960
(institutions classified according to provision of authority for
management)

Category	Number of Institutions	Degree-credit Enrollment
I. Institutions with separate lay boards, each with broad powers:		
A. Private independent control with self-perpetuating board	450	721,263
B. Private, proprietary	35	23,055
C. State institutions with separate governing boards not under state boards	108	440,446
D. Local institutions with separate governing boards not under state boards	6	41,615
	599	*1,226,379*
II. Institutions with separate lay boards subject to supervision and/or policy decisions of higher boards or agencies:		
A. Public local boards subject to state supervisory or accrediting boards	254	336,789
B. Public local boards subject to state governing-coordinating boards	40	49,058
C. Private lay boards subject to supervision and direction of Catholic denomination	295	285,846
D. Private lay boards subject to supervision and direction of 66 non-Catholic religious denominations	517	348,939
	1,106	*1,020,632*
III. Institutions subject to direct multi-institutional control of 66 state lay governing-coordinating boards	286	1,128,803
Total, fifty states	1,991	3,375,814

NOTE: Institutions under federal control enrolled 16,039. Puerto Rico enrolled
24,069 in five institutions. Of these, one public university under a governing-coordinating board enrolled 17,891 students; two institutions under Catholic control, 3,428; two
institutions under non-Catholic religious denominations, 2,750. The District of Columbia enrolled 42,771 students in 20 institutions: one institution under a public local board,
1,274 students; six institutions under private independent boards, 19,127 students; three
institutions under private proprietary control, 1,849 students; seven Catholic institutions,
11,657 students; and three institutions under control of non-Catholic religious denominations, 8,864 students.
SOURCE: Tables 7 and 8.

of 17,103 students for each board. While great variations in institutional size are to be found in each grouping, the heavy concentration of authority for governance is vested in the governing-coordinating board. The summary presented in Table 13 reveals that two-thirds of all students are in institutions under a separate lay board, whether independent or subject to supervision. These institutions represent 85.6 per cent of all institutions. In Chapter 8 consideration is given to the exercise of state responsibility for higher education, including the exercise of delegated authority by the multi-institutional governing-coordinating boards.

CHAPTER 3

The Functions and Principles
of Management

Current trends in the management of institutions of higher education are indicative of changes in many directions. These changes include increased delegation of authority by the board of control to the president (and his administrative officers) and the faculty; sharper delineation by the governing board of what responsibilities it will retain to itself, and greater attention to its manner of working; markedly increased emphasis on identifying objectives and planning for the near term and for the longer term; strengthening of the staffs of major executives; greater concern for the economics of institutional operations. They also include new procedures within the institution for communication and participation; a new look at faculty exercise of delegated responsibility; more attention to recruitment and leadership development of professional personnel (faculty and executive officers); a records system to facilitate planning, decision making, and evaluation in all aspects of institutional operations; stronger emphasis on public information and fund raising. Yet these changes come about slowly, as institutions adapt themselves quantitatively and qualitatively to serve the requirements of the new social policy for higher education.

In this chapter, the functions performed by management are considered and appropriate guiding principles are identified.

As shown in the preceding chapter, 86 per cent of American institutions of higher education in 1960, with 67 per cent of the total degree-credit student enrollment, were governed by separate lay boards (whether fully autonomous, or subject to supervisory or coordinating controls) and 14 per cent, with 33 per cent of the total degree-credit enrollment, were governed by lay boards each of which exercised responsibility for more than one institution. In this chapter attention is centered on the management of institutions that have individual governing boards, leaving to a later chapter consideration of the management of institutions governed by boards responsible for governance of two or more institutions.[1] For the most part, even taking into account such restrictions as are imposed by supervisory boards or religious bodies, individual boards of control exercising responsibility for a single institution have large responsibilities for management.

Management exercises responsibility for what the institution will do—how it will organize; how it will select its students, faculty, staff, and physical facilities; how it will conduct its programs and modify them in light of experience; and how it will build and maintain the morale of students and staff. Management thus pervades the entire institution. All institutional personnel are subject to it and all participate in it in varying ways and degrees.

There are degrees of similarity between the enterprise of higher education and other human endeavors. It has defined purposes toward which all efforts are directed. Its claim for public approval and financial support rests on the quality of its services. Its services are carried out through the planned, organized, and coordinated activities of many persons and are subject to evaluation. The services change or are adapted to reflect social changes and advances in knowledge. Such adaptations can be aided by research and experimentation in all aspects of institutional performance. Heneman compares management of the college or university with that of business. He says:

The job of managing a college or university is more difficult and complex than the task of running a business of comparable size. Notwithstanding his responsibility, the university president usually is not as well paid as his business counterpart; he often will not have the staff aides to assist him in discharging his duties; and his attitude toward the significance of sound management often is underdeveloped as compared with the attitude of his business opposite.[2]

The unique characteristics of institutions of higher education as institutions dedicated to freedom of teaching and learning impose on their manage-

---

[1] For selected observations and opinions concerning the role of governing boards, see Appendix A-1.

[2] Harlow J. Heneman, "Opportunities for Improved Management in Higher Education," in *Financing Higher Education, 1960–70,* Dexter M. Keezer, ed. (New York: McGraw-Hill Book Co., 1959), p. 121.

ments certain requirements that are markedly unlike those of other organized forms of human endeavor. The dominant institutional purpose is service, not profit. It deals more with the intangible aspects of the spirit and intellect than with the tangible aspects of places and things. The defined status and privileges of the major institutional productive force—the faculty —limit, on the one hand, the freedom of management in the assignments of work load and require, on the other hand, imaginative programs for professional growth. Institutional personnel, and especially the faculty, are regularly involved in formulating institutional policies and plans. The amount of time the enterprise consumes in close relationship with each unit of output—the graduate—is considerable. The concern of the institution is with human growth and development. In this field the qualitative measures of individual traits and achievements cannot be precise and the methods and procedures used cannot be standardized. Evaluation of services and resources presents varying degrees of difficulty, partly because of individual differences among both students and faculty, partly because defined standards of quality may be lacking, and partly because available evidences— objective and subjective—may afford inadequate bases for forming value judgments. These unique characteristics of institutions of higher education require that the responsibilities of management be shared by all concerned —governing board, faculty, and executives.

The management of an institution of higher education must be developed and exercised with a high degree of sensitivity to all aspects of the environment that will contribute to motivation of faculty and students to teach and learn and serve. The individual, not the conformist, is to be nurtured. The interests, aptitudes, capacities, motivation, health, and strength of students and teachers are constant central concerns. The productive energies of students and faculties are to be stimulated and encouraged. They cannot successfully be driven.

Some of the unique characteristics of college and university management are described by Ruml and Morrison in these words:

The chain of command in a college is at most a tenuous line of influence. The President and deans must rely primarily upon departmental chairmen to direct and influence the departments. But, as already noted, the chairman's ability to meet this expectation is based upon a delicate and unreliable relationship. He does not have the sanction of dismissing recalcitrant colleagues. In carrying out institutional policies, he requires strong backing from the President and dean, and he must depend largely upon his ability to persuade colleagues that the decision is at least pragmatically right and that acceptance is in the long-run interests of the department. When matters of staffing, of curriculum and of teaching methods are involved, a department's capabilities for resistance are almost unlimited—To impose upon him [the teacher] a change in curriculum or teaching method which does not evoke his enthusiasm in self-defeating. His teaching is likely to be less effective than it was before the change.[3]

Consideration of cost accompanies every decision on plans and policies, programs, personnel, and facilities and their uses. The cost of what is desired is usually more than society is willing to pay. This limitation on spending imposes on the institution the need to search for the greatest marginal utility of the dollars spent, and calls for the utmost understanding and cooperation of faculty, executives, and governing board. This understanding has been achieved to only a limited degree in most institutions, partly because traditionally the faculty have been concerned with program and generally uninformed of financial implications of program decisions, and partly because administrative officers and governing boards have not generally sought to involve the faculty in matters of facilities and finance. It is possible that their long but successful fight for status may have developed in faculties a certain coolness toward administration. This attitude, too, may have been fostered in some institutions by administrative officers who did not understand or seek to understand the requirements of academic programs.

Some common blocks to good management, however, are found in varying degrees: the placement of untrained persons in administrative posts; a lack of understanding of the functions to be performed and what is expected of each member—whether governing board, president, major executives, or faculty; a lack of channels of communication and of democratic procedures; poor personnel policies; inadequate or unavailable meaningful records and reports; insufficient staff provision for planning and evaluation. Although institutions are improving their managements, it is doubtful whether the rate of improvement is rapid enough to meet the new demands on management.

The Institution Is the Focus of Management

Despite the great diversity among and within the states with respect to the characteristics of institutions of higher education, the functions of management and the principles that guide its performance are in large measure common to all institutions. The reason is readily apparent. Each institution is an instrument through which the objectives of higher education are to be realized. It is within the institution that organized opportunities and experiences for student learning are provided—faculties, libraries, laboratories, classes, association with other students, and experiences of residential and social life. It is here, too, that research is conducted and public services

[3] Beardsley Ruml and Donald H. Morrison, *Memo to a College Trustee* (New York: McGraw-Hill Book Company, Inc., 1959), p. 56.

are performed. And it is within the institution that institutional policies and plans must be applied.

The quality of the institutional environment for learning must be achieved within the institution itself. It cannot be imposed from the outside. The quality of countless day-by-day decisions required for institutional operations contributes as fully to institutional achievement as does the quality of the plans. Such decisions, for example, have to do with the choice of faculty and staff, the selection of students, the provision of physical facilities and books, the content of programs, the provision of interaction of student with student and student with faculty. Lack of human and material resources will restrict achievement, but a full measure of them will not of itself ensure quality. Motivation of institutional personnel through leadership toward worthy objectives, the continuous development of optimum plans for programs and physical facilities within the limitations imposed by availability of funds, and the translation of plans into appropriate actions demand an informed and responsible relationship between institutional personnel and the governing board. There are aspects of public higher education that are external to the institution. These include state-wide plans for establishing institutions as needed, for assignment of functions, for coordinating their services, and for projecting plans for financial support. In like manner, consistent with their respective purposes, religious denominations have responsibilities to be performed that to a degree are external to the institution. But it remains an unalterable fact that the focus of management of the institution is within it and not external to it.

Participation of Institutional Personnel in Management Is Essential

It is vital that faculty, executives, and board fully understand the financial implications of all proposed policies, plans, and actions. If this understanding is not achieved, rational judgment based on knowledge of the best use of funds cannot be exercised. There is a positive relationship between institutional objectives, plans, and resulting activities and the money spent. When an institution has defined for a given period of time the kind, quantity, and quality of its services, and has further determined its methods and procedures, it will have fixed the requirements for personnel and physical facilities. And these requirements in turn define the need for expenditures. In order to limit expenditures to available income many choices of alternative values and costs must be made—choices of purpose, of program, of techniques, of quality and extent of library service, of class size, of teaching load, and of personnel and physical facilities. It will be seen at once that these choices involve judgments concerning education, human relations, and economics.

The board, in fulfilling its responsibilities for management, requires the aid of the faculty and executives in part because the task is too big to be carried unaided, but more especially because the board does not, unaided, possess the best judgment on all matters involved. Whatever the historical reason for lack of common understanding and cooperation among them, there can be no room in the modern institution for conflict, among those responsible for management, arising from distrust and noncooperation. Nothing less than close teamwork will suffice.[4] This calls for broad understanding by executives of the total program and its needs, by faculty of institutional finance and fiscal policies, by the board of the best ways of eliciting cooperation. It calls for joint involvement of all in a common cause.

In the exercise of its legal responsibility for management, the board must ever retain its power to act. If it delegates authority, it must retain the power to over-ride even though this power may rarely be used. The reservation of this power may be described as "reserved control." Such provision may foster the achievement of consensus in governance.

The Four Functions of Management

There are four major areas of management responsibility. They may be termed the functions of management.[5] They are the delegating and organizing function, the directive function, the operative function, and the evaluative function. The exercise of these functions may be stated in other terms. The delegating and organizing function requires the determination of how responsibilities shall be borne. The directive function includes the formulation of objectives, policies, plans, and standards. The operative function is concerned with the actual day-by-day performance of institutional services. The evaluative function is the continuous application of value measures and judgments to all aspects of institutional life. The first three functions interact, and evaluation is an ever-present force for change in any or all of them.

THE DELEGATING AND ORGANIZING FUNCTION

The delegating and organizing function of management is exercised through the determination of how the responsibilities of management shall be borne. The responsibility of the board is great. It ranges from objectives,

---

[4] For a review of observations and opinions concerning faculty participation in policy formation, see Appendix A-3.

[5] Writers describe the processes or functions of management in different ways. For example, Millett identifies five: (1) decision making, (2) programming, (3) communicating, (4) controlling, (5) reappraising. Masterson identifies four: (1) planning, (2) organizing, (3) executing, and (4) controlling. See John D. Millett, *The Academic Community: An Essay on Organization* (New York: McGraw-Hill Book Company, Inc., 1962), pp. 20–21; Thomas Masterson, "Management Functions," *College and University Business*, Vol. 28, No. 2, February 1960, p. 21.

plans, and policies to programs, often highly diversified, to faculties, facilities, and finance, and to student selection and achievement. These responsibilities are assumed in the public interest and generally are beyond the range of abilities and attention that a board can possibly directly provide. The board therefore must delegate responsibility and authority in order to function under its reserved control. It must enlist the services of professional administrators, outside consultants, faculty, and students in such way as to maximize achievement. What must be sought is a common accord of faculty, executives, and board on institutional objectives, philosophy, plans, and programs. And, to afford a basis for the cooperation of all, this accord must be won through the exercise of participation, debate, and leadership, not through the dictates of superior authority. "Community of power rather than a hierarchy of power," says Millett, "is the organizational basis of American colleges and universities."[6] This is an appropriate guide to practice, with the governing board ever retaining its power to act.

As a basic step, the board must determine how it can best function— what responsibilities it may delegate to others, and what it must reserve to itself—and devise its own organization through officers and committees. Then it must define concurrently the organization of the institution, the responsibilities and authorities of its officers and the faculty, and equally important, the status and privileges of personnel and the processes of working together.

The exercise of this function of delegation and organization is a continuous one. The board may wish to delegate to the president the responsibility and authority for acting with respect to lesser policies—means, methods, and procedures—and to the president and faculty certain matters of educational policy—the content of the educational program, standards of student admissions, conduct, retention, and degrees. All such delegations may be subject to the reserved control of the board.

THE DIRECTIVE FUNCTION

The exercise of the directive function of management is through policy determination. Policies are defined as "settled courses adopted and followed."[7] The policies governing the complex of institutional life are necessarily many and diverse. They include both institutional objectives and the plans to achieve them—their determination, review, and modification. All policies are subject to change to take account of new conditions and new procedures. Subject to state law and the institutional charter, they are the responsibility of the governing board. It will exercise this responsibility directly with respect to the more important and controlling policies, and may

[6] John D. Millett, *The Acadamic Community, op. cit.,* p. 64.
[7] *Webster's New Collegiate Dictionary,* Sixth Edition.

to the extent desired delegate to the president responsibility for lesser policies. The president may in turn distribute this responsibility. The delegation of responsibility for policy by the board implies responsibility for supervision, and how this is to be achieved should be an integral part of the act of delegation.

The controlling policies of an institution are found in the education laws of the state and the institutional charter, bylaws, and statutes. The charter of the institution, granted by the state, defines in broad terms its general purposes, and confers on its board the responsibility and authority for its governance. The bylaws are the procedures established by the board for the conduct of its affairs. They define its organization and procedures, the delegation of responsibility and authority to officers, committees, and agents, including fiscal agents, auditors, and legal counsel. The statutes generally define the internal organization, with the president as the chief executive. Also defined are the delegation of responsibility and authority to officers, faculty, and committees, the status and privileges of academic appointees, and student status and privileges. Other matters dealt with may be the academic calendar, the academic costume, and procedures for amendments. Policies primarily of temporary concern are found in the legislation of the board recorded in the minutes of the proceedings.

The elements of institutional policies include (1) the objectives sought, (2) the delegated responsibility for devising plans and supervising operations necessary to achieve the purposes, (3) the organization required to achieve the purposes, and (4) the methods and procedures appropriate to realization of the objectives sought. Each determination of policy will have been taken after consideration of alternate courses of action. Each policy matter requires an analysis showing the implication (including cost and benefits) of various courses of action. The act of choice is based on value judgments. It is the act of the philosopher, a primary function of the governing board.

Policy changes are prompted by necessary modifications in objectives, new conditions imposed within or without the institution, unsatisfactory results from operations under existing policies, and financial requirements.

Ordinarily policy considerations reach the board through one of its committees, of which the president is usually an ex officio member. As will be seen, the president, through his organization, is prepared to deal with policy matters—identification of matters needing attention, analyses required, and justification for recommendations. The committee of the board weighs the need for action, the relevance and adequacy of the evidence, and the quality of the analysis. It may elect to use outside resources and secure evidence that is more extensive or of a different kind. This action is not usually taken, for the president, in making his recommendations, is in a sense presenting the best evidence and judgment that he and his organization can provide with respect to the outcomes.

Thus, while choice of policy is a primary responsibility of the governing board, the board ordinarily places heavy reliance on the president and through him on his executive officers and the faculty for identifying, canvassing, and proposing action relating to policy formation.

Policies are implemented through plans of action. Such plans supplement and become elements of adopted policies. Usually they define the means, methods, and procedures to be used in achieving policy objectives. Plans involve expressing in quantitative and qualitative terms the projection of operations into future periods—the short-range (or annual) projection of program, resources, and finance, and the long-range projection reaching five, ten, or more years into the future. The plans reflect judgments through time as to programs, personnel, facilities, and finance consistent with the objectives sought.

THE OPERATIVE FUNCTION

The operative role of management is its exercise of responsibility for performance of programs and activities envisioned in approved plans. The exercise of this responsibility requires knowledge of the work to be done, the choice of techniques, the supply of necessary materials, and the assignment of qualified personnel with a desire to perform it. The governing board has primary responsibility for this function, but it delegates it to the president, and through him to administrative officers responsible to him. Although the plans of operations may have been carefully drawn, many decisions not envisioned in the plans will be needed. Operational decisions are ordinarily made by the president or under his delegated authority. They must be consistent with the institutional values sought. At all levels the president will have established procedures for policy interpretation and for staff assistance as needed. But the primary reliance for appropriate exercise of this function must be on shared knowledge and experience of all participants concerning institutional purposes, policies, and plans. This implies a major concern for sharing information and for including staff as participants.

Careful control of operations must be exercised in order that the efforts of all will be coordinated to promote achievement of institutional purposes. This is as necessary for supporting services as it is for teaching, research, and field services. It is only natural for those with an interest in and an enthusiasm for their own particular area of responsibility to seek expansion of the work. There may be those who exercise less rigorous individual commitment, or who are slow to respond to immediate changes. These are challenges to both the planners and the administrators. Increased cost in a particular aspect of program may require corresponding decrease elsewhere. Clear channels for communication to, from, and among faculty and administrators are vital. Participation in and advisement on aspects of operational management are also important, such as selection of staff, assignments of teaching and research, provision for office space. Each individual area, as well as the institution as a whole, must see to it that operating procedures and standards are administered fairly and in a manner acceptable to the participants. This is another way of saying that if trouble spots are developing, the channels should quickly bring them to the attention of the oppropriate executive so that they can be dealt with intelligently.

THE EVALUATIVE FUNCTION

The exercise of the evaluative function of management is a basic responsibility of the board of control which it delegates to the president and through him to his executives and to the faculty. Such evaluation relates to all aspects of delegation and organization policies, operations, and resources. Only through careful evaluation of performance can plans for the future be projected with assurance. Each major executive seeks appropriate evaluative measures for his own area. These measures may be in part objective and in part subjective. They may involve institutional personnel within and without the area, and persons from outside the institution. The faculty participates in evaluation of teaching and research, student growth and development, and perhaps other areas. Meaningful evaluation reports relating both to operation and to resources will be made by all executives to the president and through him to the board of control. These reports permit a review of the year's operations in relation to the plans. They permit identification of strengths and weaknesses in both programs and management that may have important implications for modification of both near-term and long-range plans.

This brief outline of the functions of management—delegating and organizing, directing, operating, and evaluating—will afford a background for an examination of principles of management that are judged suitable for the enterprise of higher education. It is an enterprise that must be held responsive to the public, that requires settings conducive to productivity and creativity of both faculty and students, that must enlist the faculty in management in appropriate ways and degrees, and that must limit expenditures to available income.

Guiding Principles of Management

The analyses of the tasks and requirements of management for the performance of its several functions as presented in subsequent chapters can best be carried on under a few assumed guiding principles. These principles, enumerated below, are considered basic and are believed to have wide acceptance. They are by no means comprehensive.

1. *Institutional government by consensus is essential.* A governing board, in the exercise of its assumed legal responsibility, delegates to administrative officers and faculty a vast amount of responsibility and authority under its reserved control. In practice, the board, through its chief executive, the president, seeks to achieve a consensus of faculty, administrators, and its own members in all primary matters. The relationship is based on shared information and mutual respect. This conception of what is desirable in management will be found a demanding one, yet no other course holds the promise of enlisting as widely spread commitment and application of energy to the fulfillment of the purposes of the institution. The fundamental importance in management of consensus of trustees, administration, and faculty is widely recognized.

Dodds sees it as essential in securing and retaining faculty support. He says:

Successful university presidents from non-academic life soon learn to curb their old compulsions to make rapid-fire decisions. They learn to cultivate patience and the habit of conferring. The academic president who cannot secure faculty consensus through methods of consultation exceeding those obtaining in modern business, even where the consultative process is most highly developed, cannot expect to command faculty support.[8]

Ruml and Morrison emphasize the importance of consensus. They say:

The most pervasive concern is to win the continuing consent of the three major elements—faculty, administration, and Trustees. Here the central problem is to develop within the college a concept of public and institutional interest which is paramount to departmental and other special interests, and in accordance with which the curriculum will be designed and administered.[9]

Corson, too, recognizes the importance of consensus in government. He recognizes that the task of gaining and maintaining it is a challenge to the leadership. He says:

But each faculty member and most administrative officers are engaged in separable, specialized activities that make up the work of the modern college or university. . . . The task of gaining consensus on what an institution shall be and how it should carry on its work is made difficult by this broad range of activities, by the various interests of the specialists, by the relative independence of many of the activities that are carried on, and by the inherent nature of many teachers

[8] Harold W. Dodds, *The Academic President—Educator or Caretaker?* (New York: McGraw-Hill Book Company, Inc., 1962), pp. 16–17.

[9] Beardsley Ruml and Donald Morrison, *Memo to a College Trustee, op. cit.,* p. 75.

(e.g., a professor, it has been said, is a man who thinks otherwise). The problems raised for decisions by this diversity of activities are further complicated by a wide variety of opinion on what a university should be and do. This difference of opinion makes itself apparent in the decision-making councils on many issues.[10]

Millett recognizes some requisites for consensus when he says: "all the constituent elements of the academic community—faculty, students, alumni and administration—must be united in good will if consensus is to be achieved. Shared power can be preserved only in a society of shared respect."[11]

2. *In the delegation of responsibility and authority to institutional personnel, reserved control should be retained by the board, and the organization of the institution should be designed to promote and facilitate government by consensus.* This principle insists that the board retain responsibility for all things done under its delegated authority. The test of organization is whether it facilitates the achievement of general agreement of board, president, executives, and faculty on major policies and plans.

3. *In setting and guiding the course of the institution, the long-term view with respect to objectives and plans is essential.* Traditionally, the reflection of expressed objectives in the institutional program has not been easy to discern; and plans have tended to be short term. However, as brought out in Chapter 1, the rapid technological and social changes, the span of time required to achieve institutional change, the variability of resources in the longer term, and the time made available for debate—all argue for the long-term view to provide perspective and guidance to the annual plans for programs, resources, and finance.

4. *In the conduct of institutional programs, effective use of personnel and facilities should be achieved.* This principle is supported by two primary considerations. The first is that able teachers are in short supply, as are suitable libraries, laboratories, and other physical facilities. More effective use of personnel and facilities will extend to many more youth and adults educational opportunities of quality. The second is that such effective use may save money, and hence may provide ways to increase the quality of program, such as through increases in salaries of teachers—or it may lower the cost. The alternative to effective use may be waste.

5. *The personnel policies and practices should provide to personnel satisfaction in work, motivation to perform the work well and efficiently, and opportunity for growth—personal and professional.* The institution of higher education must achieve its purposes through the efforts of many people. To the degree that they have understanding of purpose, are superior

---

[10] John J. Corson, *Governance of Colleges and Universities* (New York: McGraw-Hill Book Company, Inc., 1960), pp. 19–20.

[11] John D. Millett, *The Academic Community, op. cit.*, p. 257.

in ability to perform assigned duties, and are motivated by a desire to provide superior performance, the institution will achieve that which it provided for in the plans. There are, of course, many elements included in successful personnel policies, and many more in the leadership that translates them.

6. *Assessment of values with respect to all aspects of the institution is an important basis for institutional improvement—whether of objectives, plans, policies, programs, operations, or resources.* Unless there exist bases for judgment of merit of all aspects of an institution, how can it grow in excellence? Some aspects are capable of objective evaluation; others must be judged subjectively. Yet the evidence must be sought, whether opinions or facts indirectly or directly relevant.

If from operations, for example, unworkable aspects of a plan can be identified, the plan must to that extent be amended. If a common fault in educational achievement is discerned among graduates, this fact has implications for program. If student dissatisfaction arises over some phase of the program, the causal forces are to be examined and considered. If cost of a particular service appears far in excess of the values to be derived, a better use of funds is indicated. If the existing plant is not well utilized, the case for a new structure is weakened. As this brief list indicates, the scope of evaluation is as broad as the institutional program itself; and responsibility for evaluation is to be shared by all who participate in institutional operations, and desirably, in addition, by those who employ its graduates.

In the analyses that follow, other principles will doubtless be identified. But of primary interest and concern—and the very reason for the analyses—is how these principles can in practice be realized. The principles identified above, while basic, are stated in general terms.

What kind of organization will promote and facilitate government by consensus? How can the diverse talents of faculty, executives, president, and board be brought to contribute most to institutional achievement? How does the board organize? How can the president free himself of routine tasks to assume the leadership role? What is his appropriate role in the institution? How is faculty leadership expressed?

Again, how does an institution chart its course? How are objectives assessed; and how are the guidelines for program fixed? What planning instruments are necessary? How are they developed? How are they used?

In the academic area, in light of the claims for temporary services of seasoned staff to perform research and field services, and in light of the growth in institutional size and complexity, can the academic department remain as the basic administrative unit? How can the dean free himself to exercise faculty leadership? What is the best way to coordinate teaching, research, and field services?

In the area of student personnel services, to what extent and in what way should students participate in government? How can student freedoms and student opinions be continually impressed on those who exercise responsibility for management? What is the appropriate faculty relationship to the plans for admissions, records, health, and all aspects of student life? How can leadership in this area be fostered?

In the area of business and finance, how can understanding and cooperation of faculty and executives be developed? How can faculty be brought to consider the economic implications of proposals they make? How can officers in the area of business and finance be brought to understand the educational implications of proposals they initiate?

Questions may be asked, too, concerning public relations and fund raising, institutional research, and the coordination of the plans. But the nature of the task of the analyst in all areas is made clear.

In the area of finance, how can all the participants in management be brought to understand the nature of decisions made necessary by the limitation of available funds? How can the search for economy be a shared enterprise rather than a circumstance to promote misunderstanding?

In the area of personnel, how is faculty best recruited? How is merit appropriately recognized and rewarded? What are the best ways to develop professional competence and growth?

In programs, plans, policies, and all other aspects of institutional life, how can value judgments be brought to bear to enable management to discard that which has not worked well and to replace it with that which holds promise? Whose job is evaluation? How is a program initiated? Who uses it? How important is evaluation?

These are questions related not to the intent of the principles, but to the ways in which institutional values are to be realized. The following chapters are addressed to these questions through the analyses of the functions of management.

CHAPTER 4

The Delegating and Organizing Function of Management

The responsibilities for governance of both public and private institutions of higher education are vested by the several states in boards of control. The vestiture of responsibility, with its corresponding grant of authority, is defined in the institutional charter. Boards of control may range in size, in method of member selection, in weight of responsibility assumed, from a small institution to one that is large and complex, to a system with many component institutions. The small institution will (generally) have one, possibly two, related programs, a small student body, and few faculty members. Its programs will (generally) lead to an associate's or a bachelor's degree. A large, complex institution may have an undergraduate college and a number of graduate and professional schools, each with a separate faculty. Attached to the graduate and professional schools may be such resources as extensive laboratories, libraries, museums, experiment stations, research bureaus, hospitals, and laboratory schools. In this institution the span of age between the entering freshman and the doctoral candidate is wide; programs are diverse; faculty are highly specialized.

Yet most boards have broad areas of similarity. Most of them are composed of laymen—often leaders in business or professional life who assume board membership as a public service, usually without compensation. The grant of responsibility and authority to boards (despite checks often imposed by governments and religious bodies) is characteristically broad, requiring independence of judgment and action.

The basic legal responsibilities of the board are well defined by the special Trustees Committee of Columbia University in a report adopted by the Trustees on November 4, 1957, as follows:

a. To select and appoint the president of the university;

b. To be finally responsible for the acquisition, conservation and management of the university's funds and properties;

c. To oversee and approve the *kind* of education offered by the university and make certain that the *quality* meets the highest standards possible.[1]

To carry out these heavy responsibilities must involve the active, constructive cooperation of institutional personnel. It is vital that delegation and organization cultivate, on the one hand, the freedom and initiative of institutional personnel to contribute to institutional achievement, and on the other, to promote the kind and quality of education of which the board approves.

Institutional achievement will depend in large measure on the wisdom and devotion of the board members, the development and maintenance within the institution of the necessary resources, quantitative and qualitative, for management, and the establishment and maintenance of government by consensus achieved through leadership and through the delegation of responsibility and authority to institutional individuals and groups subject to board supervision and reserved control.

It must be recognized that there are many possible conceptions of what constitutes wise management. In institutional affairs, as in other fields of endeavor, there will be differences in opinion and judgment concerning their management. Nevertheless, it is generally believed that institutional achievement through time will be maximized only through the harmonious exercise of responsibilities by faculty, executives, and the governing board.

Citing the need for consensus in institutional management as opposed to domination or compromise, Millett writes:

I know of no way to guarantee that organization based upon a concept of community will necessarily achieve action based upon consensus. I can only observe that consensus has in fact been realized by most colleges and universities. . . . When consensus is not possible, then new leadership is usually needed.[2]

Clearly a government by consensus is desirable, for it will have widespread and purposeful support. To achieve consensus requires a free flow of information concerning policies, programs, and finance. It requires op-

[1] Columbia University Special Trustee Committee Report on *The Role of the Trustees of Columbia University* (New York: Columbia University, 1957).

[2] John D. Millett, *The Academic Community: An Essay on Organization* (New York: McGraw-Hill Book Company, Inc., 1962), pp. 244–245.

portunities for interaction of faculty, executives, and members of the governing board. The more important matters on which to achieve consensus are considered to be the objectives of the institution and the long-range plans for educational programs, resources, and finance. If consensus cannot be achieved on these matters, the institutional short-range operations can be only expedient.

It is the purpose of this chapter to present a general outline of organization, with delegated responsibility and authority appropriate to management. But first, two positions that are taken need justification. One is that a board should delegate responsibility under its reserved control; the other, that all delegation of responsibility should be to a unified organization with a single executive head who will serve both as a medium of communication with the board and as a coordinator of all aspects of institutional management. Such provision places responsibilities on the president, but it also provides to him the setting for the exercise of his leadership. It is the exercise of this leadership that is of primary importance—that distinguishes the successful president from the routine caretaker.

Reserved control means delegation by the board of authority to act, subject to its review, modification, or change.

The retention by the board of reserved control is necessary to permit the board on its own responsibility to take action in the event that in its judgment delegated responsibility and authority have been either misused or misdirected; or actions proposed or taken are without board approval; or lack of action through indecision of institutional personnel is deemed more harmful than action based on board judgment. Thus the reserved control of the board is a reservation of authority that it is hoped will not be needed, but whose very existence will spur all those responsible for management to the achievement of consensus. There may be times when new leadership is needed and the circumstances call for interim action.

A unified organization with a single executive who will serve both as the medium of communication and as the coordinator of policy, program, and finance and other management matters is essential both for efficiency and for safeguarding the leadership role of the president as chief executive. It is argued by some that the faculty should have free access to the board, sometimes with, sometimes without, the president's approval. As will be seen later in this chapter, provision for access of faculty to the board should be made, but *only as arranged by the president*. Any other course will relegate the president to what Dodds[3] refers to as the role of "caretaker" rather than strengthen his role as leader.

[3] Harold W. Dodds, *The Academic President—Educator or Caretaker?* (New York: McGraw-Hill Book Company, Inc., 1962).

Millett writes of the importance of organization. He says:

There can be no social progress which is not founded upon the ever improving output of organized units of group endeavor. There can be no knowledge of social institutions and of social process which is not founded upon a science and art of organization.[4]

Corson observes that

The expanding size of institutions has forced the same delegation of authority to subordinate officers as has characterized the evolution of commercial and industrial organizations. . . . Yet there is little evidence that a carefully thought-out design underlies the delegation pattern that obtains.[5]

Masterson states that the test of organizing is how efficiently it accomplishes its tasks. Organizing, as he sees it, has four phases—the technical aspects, human relations, responsibility relationships, and staffing.[6]

Duryea relates organization to process:

What is important is not only its arrangement, but the consciousness of its operation on the part of participants. . . . Operationally, any process is subject to the effects of human values, self interest, and varying abilities. Yet as Simon points out, organizations are formed with the intention and design of accomplishing goals; and people who work for organizations believe at least part of the time that they are striving toward these same goals.[7]

Delegation of carefully defined responsibility and authority fixes the role of each person or group in the enterprise, and it is this definition of relationship, responsibility, and authority that constitutes organization. The test of institutional organization is how well it facilitates the wise performance of the functions of management. Because the services provided by the institution require the efforts of many persons, both the quality of the personnel and the policies and procedures that affect them will importantly condition performance. Further, appropriate measures for facilitating communication, consultation, and participation in the various aspects of management, and especially in the development of policies and plans, will provide stronger bases for obtaining superior achievement.

[4] John D. Millett, *The Academic Community, op. cit.,* p. 3.
[5] John J. Corson, *Governance of Colleges and Universities* (New York: McGraw-Hill Book Company, Inc., 1960), p. 45.
[6] Thomas Masterson, "Management Functions," *College and University Business,* Vol. 28, No. 2, February, 1960, pp. 22–23.
[7] E. D. Duryea, "The Theory and Practice of Administration," in *Administrators in Higher Education,* Gerald P. Burns, ed. (New York: Harper & Row, 1962), pp. 33–34.

THE ELEMENTS OF MANAGEMENT

The basic pattern of institutional organization is derived from the interdependence of the elements of management—policy, program, and finance. Their relationship is shown diagrammatically in Fig. 2.

Program as used in Fig. 2 includes the organized activities of educational services, student personnel services, and business services, together with the resources of personnel and physical facilities requisite to them. In every policy, there are implications for program and finance; in every aspect of program, the elements of policy and finance are involved; in every financial act is interwoven a relationship to policy and program.

FIGURE 2.   Elements of and organization for management of institutions of higher education

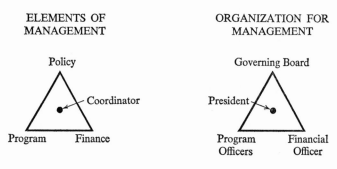

Thus, in its simplest terms, the board exercises major responsibility for policy determination; the president as the chief executive is aided by major executives for the areas of program and finance and sees that in all proposals for action full attention has been given to the interaction of the three major elements of management.

In practice the program officers may be a chief education officer, a chief student personnel officer, and a chief business officer. The chief education officer assumes responsibility for programs of instruction, research, and field services. The chief student personnel officer assumes responsibility for student personnel services and represents in management all aspects of nonacademic student life and values. In some institutions a chief business officer assumes responsibility for the supporting services of a business nature—plant management, purchases, and the management of auxiliary activities. In others this responsibility is associated with finance and is delegated to a chief business and financial officer, inasmuch as the important issues arising in the management of business affairs are often financial at base.

The president as chief executive is the coordinator of the elements of management. He may be assisted by a chief officer of institutional planning and research. He usually exercises direct responsibility for public relations and fund procurement and may be assisted by a chief public relations and fund-raising officer.

It is commonly assumed that each institution has a single organization. This is true only in the sense that each person is assigned to one and only one organizational unit and is responsible to the head of that unit. But in performing the functions of management the responsibilities of persons and their ways of working together alter markedly. Thus in performing the directive function, faculty members are assigned a policy role in which their primary responsibility is the quality of advice or judgment they are asked to provide. When personnel are assigned such a role of advisement, whether in the academic areas or in the areas of the supporting services, their assignment is best described as a staff responsibility.

In developing policies, plans, and standards, in affording advice on operating procedures, in assisting in planning an evaluation program, institutional personnel perform a staff responsibility. When personnel are performing assigned tasks under such supervision or direction as is appropriate, they are performing a line responsibility. When exercising staff responsibility they provide advice and judgment concerning what is to be done; when exercising line responsibility they perform the work to which they are assigned.

Organization must be conceived as multipurpose—its personnel must direct the institutional course, perform the planned services, and evaluate all aspects of the institution. This concept is not generally understood. Thus, the description of a single organization must represent a composite of delegations and relationships necessary to carry out the several functions of management. Moreover, to any formal organization are added *ad hoc* assignments and relationships as needed to achieve particular purposes. This means that organization exists to facilitate the work; whenever a change in it is needed, additional personnel may be involved. For example, the supervision of residence halls requires a management conversant with both student personnel services and business and financial services. Major responsibility is in practice assigned to either the chief student personnel officer or the chief business and financial officer. In either case, close liaison should be provided between these two officers concerning planning, operating, and evaluating. This is the kind of relationship that may or may not be provided for in formal delegation. Through agreed-upon *ad hoc* arrangements between executives, interarea or interdepartmental cooperation can be arranged so that the specialized competencies of one area can be brought to the service of another.

Basic Pattern of Organization

A basic pattern of organization appropriate for institutions of higher education is shown in Fig. 3. The chart indicates the primary areas to which major delegation of responsibility and authority is made. This basic organization must be expanded to reflect provisions for achieving consensus on major policies and plans, and to promote understanding and participation of institutional personnel in the exercise of the responsibilities of management.

FIGURE 3. Suggested basic general organization of institutions of higher education

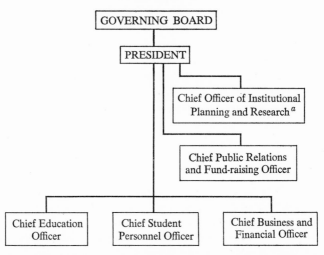

[a] In large institutions, it is likely that the president will need, attached to his office, an officer of institutional planning and research.

The essential idea in Fig. 3 is that there should be only one executive directly responsible to the board. Responsible to him, in turn, are major executives in charge of broad areas of institutional activity. Because the public relations and fund-raising officer and the chief officer of institutional planning and research work in close cooperation and under the direct supervision of the president, they are shown in Fig. 3 as being attached to his office. Figure 3 is descriptive of the primary line relationships and the assignments to major executives.

In the following discussion of the component elements of the basic organization outlined in Fig. 3, attention will be given to the exercise of staff advisory or consultative responsibilities as well as of responsibilities for service under the line organization.

The Governing Board

An examination of the organization may well begin with the governing board.

Observations and opinions of competent observers concerning the governing board are summarized in Appendix A-1. These relate to board size, trustee qualifications, board responsibility, and board organization. Also treated is the exercise of board responsibility for educational policy—an area now receiving renewed attention.

It is the opinion of the writer that in the light of modern educational developments, governing boards should reassess their responsibilities, re-examine their organizations and ways of working to the end that they make their maximum contribution to society in fulfillment of the obligations they have assumed.

The typical state governing board responsible for public higher education has nine or eleven members, including one or two ex officio members. As Martorana and Hollis state: "Ideally, boards should have an uneven number of members, not fewer than 9 nor more than 15."[8] Boards governing private institutions are generally larger. The board must determine how it will conduct its affairs, and if it is small it may elect to have all matters receive the attention of the entire board. In such cases, if the enterprise is complex and many issues, both immediate and long range, press for decision, the board must meet frequently or must restrict the breadth and depth of the consideration it gives to institutional affairs in favor of increased reliance on the guidance of the president and his advisers. As will be seen, heavy reliance on the president and his advisers is required in any circumstance. On balance, there appears to be merit in a board whose size (say about 15 to 18 members) permits committee organization. (This is the form in most private institutions.) The increased resources of a larger board both in manpower and in areas of competence may then be applied to more searching consideration of institutional affairs. Figure 4 suggests an organization appropriate for a board large enough to avail itself of the services of committees.

In this organization, an executive committee is empowered to act for the board between its sessions. A committee on investments exercises responsibility for fund investments, subject to the general supervision of the board. All other committees are advisory. A committee on objectives,

[8] S. V. Martorana and Ernest V. Hollis, *State Boards Responsible for Higher Education* (Washington, D.C.: U.S. Department of Health, Education, and Welfare, Office of Education, 1960), p. 29.

FIGURE 4. Suggested organization of governing board

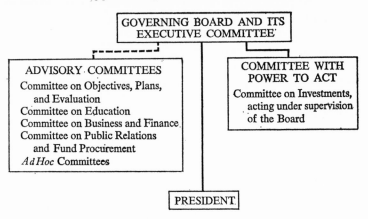

plans, and evaluation is concerned with the institutional purposes; long-range plans for program, resources, and finance; and assessment of current operations in relation to the plans. A committee on education is concerned with developments and proposals concerning the educational program. A committee on business and finance deals with business affairs, current operations, and review of the annual budget. A committee on public relations and fund procurement is concerned with these aspects of institutional life. *Ad hoc* committees may be set up as needed. The president, in the writer's opinion, should be an ex officio member of all committees. Through reports of proceedings to all members of the board and through discussions at board meetings, these committees function in harmony with each other and with the board as a whole.

Board organization is ordinarily defined in the institution's bylaws. Unless otherwise provided by law, the bylaws define the membership, indicating how chosen, term of office, provision for filling vacancies or for removal. The bylaws provide for regular and special meetings and the requirement of notice for such, define the quorum, and the order of business. The bylaws also provide for the designation and appointment of officers, and may provide for the appointment of fiscal agents, public auditors, and legal counsel. The committees of the board, and their method of appointment, officers, quorum, and meeting, are provided for in the bylaws. Basic policies of financial administration, including the preparation of the budget and the authority for expenditures, may also be included. Finally, the procedure for amendment is set forth.

The officers of a board are normally a chairman, who presides at meetings; a vice chairman, who is sometimes designated to preside at meetings of the executive committee and who chairs board meetings in the absence of the chairman; and a secretary, who is the recording officer of proceedings of the board and the executive committee, keeps the seal of the corporation, and attests authorized signatures to documents and actions of the board or its executive committee as may be required.

It may be desirable to have a paid employee of the president's office act as assistant secretary. This removes the clerical burden from the board member who serves as secretary, although he may continue to exercise responsibility for the prepared minutes. Such an arrangement serves to keep the official minutes of the institution readily available and permits their being indexed. It also means that an officer is always available to certify to authorized signatures or to actions taken by the board or its executive committee. While in the past a member of the board has frequently been designated as treasurer, this function is now often delegated through the president to the chief business and financial officer. Corporate funds or securities are in depositories chosen by the board, and are controlled by carefully defined fiscal procedures. Thus, if a treasurer is required, the chief business and financial officer is best designated. If such title is assigned to a board member for reasons of prestige or possible advantage in fund procurement, the assigned duties should in no way interfere with the exercise of full fiscal responsibility under the direction of the president.

The investment of funds is a board responsibility and must be carried on under board supervision. In institutions with large endowments direct responsibility for investment services may be assigned to the chief business and financial officer, who in turn may employ an investment officer, and/or such financial advisory services as are deemed necessary, to function under the direction of the board committee on investments. As an alternate plan, the board may employ an investment officer and financial advisory service directly responsible to it, with the chief business and financial officer serving as secretary to the committee on investments.

Thus a board exercises its powers by delegating much responsibility and authority to and through a chief executive of its choice and subject to its reserved control. It gives consideration to institutional purposes and plans in relation to social needs and resources; it authorizes current operations through approval of programs and budgets; and through evaluation reviews experience for implications for the future. In its exercise of the legal responsibility assigned to it, the board has woven a complex of relationships and responsibilities in its search for maximum institutional achievement.

Some presidents are elected or appointed to serve on the governing board. This appears to be good practice. It gives the president a standing of equality with board members, and fosters the mutual respect and friendly, informal atmosphere conducive to discussion of the wide range of institutional affairs. Some authorities advocate that the president serve as chairman of the board. Because a board must be free to assess the achievements of the executive, this is not a desirable provision.

Considering the nature of the responsibility placed on board members, the importance of their complete understanding of the institution—its strengths and limitations, the range of its activities, its resources, both material and human—can readily be seen. Lack of such understanding means that their background for making appropriate decisions is to that extent limited. This poses a problem of how busy lay members of a governing board can be continuously brought to a growing awareness of all aspects of the institution. Part of the necessary understanding is supplied through the normal activities of a board member. It is importantly supplemented by systematic plans of a chief executive to present to the board and its committees selected aspects of the program, and by systematic joint meetings of board and faculty for discussion of programs and an exchange of views. A program for orientation of new board members may prove exceedingly valuable.

Meetings of faculty and executive officers with the board or its committees should be on invitation of the president. Joint standing committees of board and faculty are not desirable because such an arrangement is likely to promote communication and plans around rather than through the president. In matters of common concern—long-range planning, for example—separate committees of board and faculty are to be preferred. When desired, joint meetings may be arranged by the president.

There doubtless is an advantage in designating the chief business and financial officer as secretary of the board committee on investments and the board committee on business and finance. The president, as a member of these committees, may approve their agenda; but because many of the matters dealt with relate to business and finance, the presence of the chief business and financial officer is desirable both to contribute to the discussion and to keep informed of the background of decisions arrived at. The president may wish to invite the chief education officer to attend meetings of the board committee on education and the chief public relations and fund-raising officer to attend meetings of the board committees concerned with these matters.

At times a committee made up of board members and institutional personnel assigned to perform a specific task may be desirable. An example is an *ad hoc* building committee to guide the erection of a new building. A committee composed of, say, two board members, the president, the chief business and financial officer, the plant manager, the chief education officer, and faculty representatives qualified to define the educational requirements of the building may be authorized to develop and approve specifications of need and approve architectural design.

The President

As the chief executive of the governing board, the president assumes a heavy responsibility. It is vital to the success of his leadership that he have the support of the board and that in the exercise of his responsibility he delegate in such a way that the machinery of management does not interfere with his leadership role.

Dodds observes the qualities possessed by great academic presidents. He writes:

The careers of these eminent past presidents call for study by today's academic chief executives, less because of their administrative methods (although they were not inferior administrators) than because of their educational competence and contributions. They had scholarly tastes; each came to the office possessing an academic background. Each was a man of broad interests; several were leaders in political and diplomatic, as well as the educational, life of the country. Although none was able to ignore the undergirding functions, including fund raising, without exception they gave educational philosophy, policy, and program top priority.[9]

There is great need for this type of leadership today. Dodds recommends that 50 per cent of the president's time (not 10 per cent or 20 per cent) be spent on the college and university main function—education.[10]

The most critical areas for the president-administrant, concludes Dodds, can be reduced to three.

Each is familiar, easy to express in words, but difficult for many to apply in practice. They relate to (1) the practice of consultation, (2) the principles of delegation, and (3) the structure and staffing of the administrative organization.[11]

The president is the medium of communication between (1) the students, faculty, staff, alumni, the public, and (2) the governing board. He is the spokesman for the institution, including the governing board. Subject to the approval of the board, he is responsible for the internal organization, including the delegation of responsibility and authority. Under approved policies and programs he is responsible for decision making with respect to program, personnel, physical facilities, and finance. He often exercises immediate responsibility for public information and fund procurement. He is responsible for the program of evaluation of organization, plans, and performance.

A suggested organization for the office of president is shown in Fig. 5.

[9] Harold W. Dodds, *The Academic President, op. cit.*, p. 41.
[10] *Ibid.*, p. 60.
[11] *Ibid.*, p. 72.

In this organization, the president is provided with a chief public relations and development officer who works closely with him, advising constantly on aspects of public relations and coordinating the fund-raising effort, matters that require first-hand presidential attention. Brandon states: "The officer of public relations should be close to the president strategically, intellectually, and geographically."[12] Johnston takes about the same position for fund raising. He writes:

The President is traditionally the chief fund-raiser of the institution. There are few effective programs in which this is not the case. . . . The officer designated to be in charge of fund-raising by the president is employed primarily to minimize the amount of preparation and detail in which the president is involved.[13]

This chief public relations and development officer is coordinate in rank and stature with the chief education officer, the chief student personnel officer, and the chief business and financial officer. For a large institution, the president may need a coordinator of institutional research and planning to assume duties concerned with research on institutional affairs and the coordination of long-range planning.

It can be seen that all aspects of management are of growing importance. There is some reluctance on the part of faculties to see the office of the president expand, but the work must be done. Adequate staffing of the president's office is of major concern to the president and the board and to the faculty, too, for that matter.

Cowley states that most presidents are "always short of time to do the crucial business which they alone can do—that is to organize, to coordinate, and to carry forward the institution to new intellectual and social fronts."[14] Dodds expresses similar views. He writes:

Presidents have been given more administrative assistance than they used to have, but the expansion in the administrative force has too seldom kept pace with the expansion of institutional activities. The faculty is bound to criticize the added cost of any expansion of administrative staff, and too often the administration defers to them.[15]

If the president is to guide the institution wisely, he needs information on all aspects of institutional affairs, and the work incident to coordination of long-range planning is exacting.

[12] Arthur L. Brandon, "The Vice-President or Director of Public Relations," in *Administrators in Higher Education,* Gerald P. Burns, ed., p. 160.

[13] W. Noel Johnston, "The Vice-President or Director of Development," in *Administrators in Higher Education,* Gerald P. Burns, ed., p. 172.

[14] W. H. Cowley, *What Does a College President Do?* An address presented at Oregon College of Education, Monmouth, February 5, 1956, p. 14.

[15] Harold W. Dodds, *The Academic President, op. cit.,* p. 17.

FIGURE 5.   Suggested organization for office of president

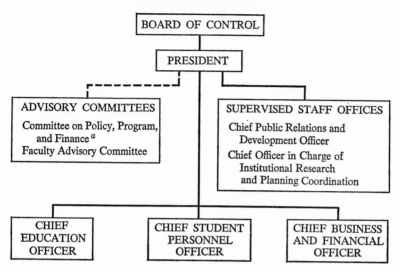

ᵃ Responsible for the quality of advice on (1) objectives, long-range plans, and budgets; (2) annual programs, budgets, and operations; and (3) systematic evaluation audits and reports.

Two committees advisory to the president are suggested. One is a faculty advisory committee. This committee is chosen by the faculty as a whole and its function is to assist the president to resolve personnel difficulties of faculty and staff members that cannot readily be settled within existing channels. In an institution sensitive to the welfare of its staff, such problems should be minimal.

The other committee, the committee on policy, program, and finance, is designed to mobilize the strength of the institution around the president. On it are major executives and strong representatives of the faculty. As shown in the note to Fig. 5, this committee is an over-all planning and advisory committee. Its function as a representative body is to advise the president and participate in planning with respect to (1) objectives, long-range plans, and budgets, (2) annual programs, budgets, and operations, and (3) systematic evaluation audits and reports. The committee has an interest in common both with the committees of major institutional areas discussed later and with the board committee on objectives, plans, and evaluation. Woodburne clearly states the value of such a general committee which is here termed a committee on policy, program, and finance. He says:

The knowledge and understanding that will be represented in any general faculty-administrative committee which is wisely selected is of tremendous importance in developing the basis of judgment necessary to any over-all plan which has meaning for the institution. The reason for this, of course, is that the development of priorities involves a series of comparative judgments based upon knowledge and understanding. This is practically beyond the compass of a single person acting alone."[16]

The president must lead institutional personnel to maximum commitment to the realization of institutional purpose. They must be brought to share in management. They must contribute to the definition of objectives and plans, and they must be kept informed on institutional activities and especially on matters of concern to them. This means that adequate channels to elicit and disseminate information must be provided. The usual channels are through meetings in which information is provided and discussed. Typical of such meetings are those of faculty, faculty and professional staff, administrative officers, research officers, other officers, line organizations, committees of all kinds, and others as arranged. There are meetings of individuals with groups and with individuals; there are student assemblies and student organizations. Supplementary media of communication are newspapers, bulletins, and letters. Letters afford two-way communication vertically and horizontally, within and between departments and areas. There must be adequate recognition by the president of the desire of personnel to participate in matters affecting them. The amount and kind of involvement is of critical importance. Too much involvement wastes valuable time; too little lowers morale. What all personnel want is an opportunity to discuss matters important to them before action is taken.

While it has been suggested that responsibility for guiding academic affairs be delegated by the president to a chief education officer, it is conceivable that for the institution that wishes to develop a strong adult education program, a new educational division for adult education, paralleling that for degree-credit programs, may have advantages. The reason is that the standards, procedures, and methods of the degree-credit program may not be suitable for adult programs. A separate division for adult education would permit freedom to develop new standards and new programs. The criteria for selection, assignment, and evaluation of faculty personnel will be different for adults than for youth. Experimentation, unhampered by the traditions and practices of the education of youth, might then seek to discover what is best for the education of adults. Such programs in established institutions will succeed only if the board is committed to them, and if the faculty appointed to this service receives recognition in status and salary equal to that accorded faculty personnel of equal merit in relation to their assignments in degree-credit programs.

[16] Lloyd S. Woodburne, *Principles of College and University Administration* (Stanford, Calif.: Stanford University Press, 1958), p. 147.

Chief Education Officer

The academic management is under the direction of the chief education officer, who may have a title such as dean, or in some large institutions, that of vice president for academic affairs. In this discussion it may be helpful to consider first an organization for educational services appropriate for an institution with one faculty, and then the adaptations necessary for institutions with more than one.

In the assumed simple structure the dean is responsible to the president for proposing definitive plans consistent with established policies, and for organizing, operating, and evaluating the educational services, for participating in faculty selection, and for the assignment of duties to individual faculty members. He may preside over the faculty or its major committee as it formulates recommendations concerning educational matters pursuant to responsibilities delegated by the board.

As Enarson points out, the academic dean is not "trained" in any sense for the job, and the gap between what he has done and what he is now expected to do is wide.[17] In the larger institutions, the deans bear major responsibility for leadership of faculty, even though, as Dodds[18] notes, they reflect and implement the policies and attitudes of the President:

"The 'conscience of the corporation'," writes Enarson,[19] "is reflected in the values of the teacher; values may be reinforced or weakened—but not created or enforced—by the dean." And because his own competence, "viewed against the wide range of university activities, will be limited," he must constantly seek the judgment of others.

The faculty under the chairmanship of the dean has three major responsibilities for policy formation. The first is to propose to the president and the governing board for approval academic objectives and long-range academic plans and their modification, based on continuous evaluation. The second is to develop, evaluate, and modify academic programs of instruction, research, and field services consistent with approved objectives and plans. These programs include the curricula of instruction and the policies for undertakings of research and field services. The third is to establish criteria and policies for student standards—their selection, retention, and the award of degrees and honors. In assisting the faculty in the exercise of these responsibilities, the dean serves to keep them informed on general institutional matters, such as plans, operations, finances, personnel, facilities, and public relations. On such matters he elicits their suggestions and comments. Through such communication the faculty is more fully informed.

[17] Harold Enarson, "The Academic Vice-President or Dean," *Administrators in Higher Education*, Gerald P. Burns, ed., pp. 122.

[18] Harold W. Dodds, *The Academic President, op. cit.,* p. 112.

[19] Harold Enarson, *op. cit.,* p. 115.

ACADEMIC DEPARTMENTS

The educational program of a student affords opportunity for study in depth in the fields of his major interest. In addition, he is afforded an opportunity to study and become conversant with the broad aspects of a number of subject areas. In these he seeks understanding and knowledge, but not mastery. Thus in most subject areas, courses must be offered to facilitate study in depth for some students, and other courses must be offered as a part of a general education program.

In proposing an organization of educational services appropriate to the optimum achievement of both policy and administrative responsibilities, consideration must be given to the place, in the modern institution, of the traditional basic academic unit—the academic department. The academic department consists of a number of scholars engaged in teaching and research in a specific subject. It has been, and is likely to continue to be, administered by the outstanding professor among them as department head. For planning purposes, the department head serves as chairman of the group. As administrator, he is concerned in varying degrees with staff selection, development, and assignment, and with salaries, supplies, and equipment. As chairman, he is concerned with the organization of knowledge of his subject, what shall be taught, in what sequence and degree of specialization, and under what standards. In this organization, the department historically has been a segment of institutional life, with students majoring in the subject and with the faculty seeking to extend their scholarship in it. Under this organization, departmental course offerings for nonmajors as well as majors have required careful attention. Because traditionally institutions of higher education were neither large nor complex, nor the demands of the society pervasive, nor the requirements for long-range planning imperative, this organization has served well.

The developments of the recent past, however, as outlined in an earlier chapter, have markedly increased the responsibilities to be borne by the faculty. The pressure of enrollments (both in numbers and in range of individual differences) has caused and is causing institutional offerings to become more complex. At the very time that increasing enrollments require more faculty members as teachers, the growth of organized research and field services at home and abroad requires more faculty members for these services, and the demand is for temporary assignments of the ablest teachers. The difficulty of securing and maintaining a qualified faculty is thus increased. There are varying standards among departments of the same institution for student selection, retention, and honors. At the same time, the subject-matter departments, in adjusting to the rapid growth of knowledge in their own and other fields, find that interrelationships of subject matter result in considerable overlapping in what is being taught. Each department has vested interests in its own subjects, and usually is reluctant to evaluate departmental offerings in terms of over-all institutional objectives. Departmental student advisement frequently is related to the subject rather than to the needs of those who for job purposes seek a degree of knowledge in but not mastery of a subject. The values to the student to be derived from institutional resources outside the department may thus to some extent be overlooked.

The rapid increase in organized research requires for each institution clearly defined objectives and polices with respect to: (1) the appropriate relation between instruction and research, (2) organizational arrangements consistent with objectives, and (3) personnel compensation policies designed to support the desired relationship. Gross puts the problem in perspective when he writes:

. . . although the value and reward system of the university now gives highest priority to the advancement of knowledge among its several objectives, the organizational set up as it relates to *the great majority* of the permanent faculty members in most universities is one that is still basically geared to functions as an agency whose primary function is the transmission of knowledge.[20]

Mooney further defines the problem in these words:

Two systems are developing, side by side, in the university, one for the normal lines of budgeting and responsibility centering on teaching, and the other for special agencies and operations centering on research.

The former is embedded in the historical and philosophic tradition of the university as an agency independent of all others, free and responsible for its own evaluations, and the latter is embedded in a newer perspective of the university as dependent on other agencies and responsible for serving their interests.[21]

In light of the nature of the problems associated with the departmental organization, the question may well be asked whether an alternate form of organization would offer a safeguard to scholarship in the individual subjects and also expedite planning, coordination of standards, curriculum development, and relate research and field services to teaching so as to afford the optimum participation of the teaching staff. One must be aware that the answer to this question has implications for the organization of the total institution as well as the department.

[20] Neal Gross, "Organizational Lag in American Universities," *Harvard Educational Review*, Vol. 33, No. 1, Winter 1963, p. 63.

[21] Ross L. Mooney, "The Problem of Leadership in the University," *Harvard Educational Review*, Vol. 33, No. 1, Winter 1963, p. 44.

A review of observations and opinions of competent authorities concerning the academic department is presented in Appendix A-4. The debate on academic organization, it will be noted, is widespread. Yet it seems to the writer that new forces—i.e., the increase in institutional size, the increase in research, and the new imperative for long-range planning—will require a reassessment of traditional departmental organization.

A DIVISIONAL ORGANIZATION

An alternate form of organization that has promise in serving the total institution is one based on divisions rather than departments. This type of organization may be based on one of two concepts or a combination of the two. The first is the interrelationship of subject matter. Thus, in a liberal arts college of some size, there might be established these divisions for both planning and administration: (1) the sciences, both physical and biological; (2) mathematics and statistics; (3) the social sciences; and (4) the humanities. The second idea for organization is grouping by purpose. Here several disciplines are brought together in a program in specific areas of responsibility large enough to justify full-time trained administrators, each of whom may have scholarship in a specific area but whose interest is the over-all quality of the total environment for learning. The professional schools offer examples of grouping according to purpose. A school of engineering may include, in addition to technical subjects, courses in the liberal arts, management, economics, and finance. A school of education may incorporate studies in the social sciences, economics, and public finance. In these schools, the achievement of their primary purpose requires inclusion of a group of specialists in other areas. In a divisional organization, planning with respect to subjects could be developed and coordinated and much overlapping of courses could be eliminated. Standards would generally be division-wide. Staff selection and budget formulation and administration would be centered in the divisional office, provision being made for wide faculty participation in policy matters. Student records for advisement could also be centered there. Subgroups for planning purposes could be organized within the division on the basis of subject matter.

It is likely that a small liberal arts college of, say, 750 full-time students can be administered directly from the office of the dean. Beyond this, when there are more than fifty on the faculty, the dean will first seek to strengthen his office staff, but at some point soon he will find a divisional organization advantageous. Such organization would provide broader bases for policy formation, better coordination of program, greater continuity of experience in academic planning and performance, more efficient administration, and greater freedom to chairmen of subject-matter groups to develop and conduct the academic program.

ORGANIZED RESEARCH AND FIELD SERVICES

For the most part the institutional programs of organized research and field services grow out of and are related to instruction. These programs are administered by the dean. Each area draws its staff from the teaching faculty and also employs some staff directly. The term of service of a faculty member may vary from a few months to some years. But when it is over, the faculty member resumes his teaching. The release of this faculty member for research and field service is usually mutually advantageous: It affords competent and experienced personnel to the research and field service activities; it affords rich experience to the faculty member and, upon his return, may improve the quality of his teaching. Yet the staffing problems posed are difficult ones.

In the opinion of many competent observers, the rapid increase in organized research, in which often the objects are defined by outside agencies, poses important problems—problems of educational policy, of supervision and coordination, and of staffing. And interwoven with these problems is the problem of graduate education. A review of some relevant findings and opinions on these matters is presented in Appendix A-5.

Under a divisional organization, the divisional officer would have a voice in staff assignment. This will facilitate the preparation of staffing plans. Once the programs are approved and a staff is assigned to them, they may be managed under the immediate direction of the dean or administered by the divisional officer.

In the initiation of research, there is an advantage in centralizing the assessment of the merits of research procedures and the conduct of contract negotiations. There is advantage in closely relating teaching to research and field services. It is possible that both advantages can be achieved by placing on divisional officers responsibility, under the supervision of the dean, for managing these services after the projects have been defined and contracts have been drawn with the aid of staff specialists.

Concerning graduate education, the writer holds the view that a separate organization is preferable to submerging both graduate policy and administration in the undergraduate college.

PROPOSED ORGANIZATION FOR EDUCATIONAL SERVICES

In the organization now to be proposed, the basic unit for both policy formation and administration, at least for undergraduate institutions, is the division, not the department. There are important reasons for this departure from a long tradition. As knowledge increases, so do areas of specialization. As specialization increases, the interest, aptitude, and ability of faculty members in dealing with over-all academic responsibilities, particularly as they relate to general education, are likely to be less than was true in the past. Subject-matter departments, when exercising assigned responsibility for plans and programs, tend to measure the success of a department in terms of the breadth of course offerings, and because all faculty members are also members of departments, departmental proposals for course offerings are generally accepted. This has resulted in wide-scale proliferation of courses and small classes, a practice generally not in the best interest of the student and often uneconomical.

A single department is usually too small to afford a qualified trained administrator, and hence the ablest professor of the department often serves in that capacity. This scholar frequently becomes involved in the time-consuming duties of administration, to which he may not be suited and which he may dislike, to the detriment of the work he can do and do well. Departmental proposals are made, and faculty action is taken, generally without assessment of their economic aspects.

These are faults that need to be corrected, and such correction can be more readily effected through an organization based on divisional units rather than on departmental units. For the evaluation of course sequences, of teaching and learning, the divisional organization is superior to the departmental for these reasons: A better balance of general education with specialized education can be obtained; the depth of specialized education can be better related to institutional purpose; a few trained administrators can relieve the many department heads of administrative tasks; more effective coordination of teaching, research, and field services can be anticipated; better procedures for staff selection can be foreseen; and long-range plans can be more readily developed and coordinated.

In short, the needs of the future for effective long-range planning, for coordination of programs and standards, for economy, and for evaluation require both trained administrative personnel and an organization unit wider than the department as it is now found. Departmental subgroups within the division will be useful in proposing subject-matter programs and in relating such programs to the divisional or institutional objectives. The trends toward the increase and specialization of knowledge will accentuate these needs in the future.

Figure 6 presents an appropriate organization for educational services for an institution with a single faculty. In this organization two advisory committees to the dean are proposed: (1) an administrative council consisting of the heads of primary operational units who work with the dean on program schedules, staff assignments, budgets, and the coordination of activities; (2) a faculty committee on personnel, appointed by the dean, to

FIGURE 6.   Suggested organization for the area of educational
services

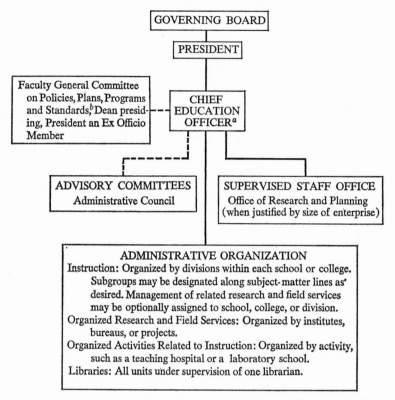

GOVERNING BOARD

PRESIDENT

Faculty General Committee
on Policies, Plans, Programs
and Standards, [b] Dean presiding, President an Ex Officio
Member

CHIEF
EDUCATION
OFFICER [a]

ADVISORY COMMITTEES
Administrative Council

SUPERVISED STAFF OFFICE
Office of Research and Planning
(when justified by size of enterprise)

ADMINISTRATIVE ORGANIZATION
Instruction: Organized by divisions within each school or college.
    Subgroups may be designated along subject-matter lines as
    desired. Management of related research and field services
    may be optionally assigned to school, college, or division.
Organized Research and Field Services: Organized by institutes,
    bureaus, or projects.
Organized Activities Related to Instruction: Organized by activity,
    such as a teaching hospital or a laboratory school.
Libraries: All units under supervision of one librarian.

[a] Also maintains flow of information to and elicits suggestions from faculty
members.
[b] Membership appointed by president from panel chosen by faculty. Subcommittees and divisional committees as needed. Representation on and
close working relations with president's committee on policy, program, and
finance. Areas of responsibility: objectives, long-range plans, and evaluation; student selection, retention, degrees, and honors; curricula, research,
and public service, including criteria, programs, and evaluation.

assist him in setting standards and procedures for staff selection, development, assignments, and evaluation.

The policy responsibilities delegated to the faculty should be subject to
such control or reserved control as the board may deem desirable. Because
the elements of management of policy, program, and finance are so closely
interrelated, the manner of involvement of the faculty in educational policy
formulation is of the utmost importance. What must be sought is a coopera-

tive relationship in which the board, the administration, and the faculty can work together with mutual understanding and respect.

There appears to be fairly wide agreement among writers on the desirability of involving the faculty in policy formation. Practices among institutions in the degrees of participation are highly diverse. And opinions of extent and methods of involvement differ. A review of such observations and opinions of writers in this field is presented in Appendix A-3. It will be seen that there are proponents of extremes, together with the concept of partnership.

The board must place heavy reliance on the faculty and president for guidance with respect to educational activities. Yet it must be recognized that the faculty, like any other group, is composed of individuals with diverse interests and capacities. Not all of them have the interest, willingness, and ability to contribute in a major way to the development of policies and plans. Ruml and Morrison conclude that "the liberal college faculty *as a body* is not competent to make judgments and evaluations required to design a curriculum in liberal education."[22] McGrath shares this view.[23] Each individual must be encouraged, however, to contribute his best thought. It is this recognition of individual differences that leads to the conclusion that the exercise of policy responsibilities by the faculty can best be carried out by a committee representative of faculty interests and carefully chosen for this service from the membership. It is suggested that this committee be called the faculty general committee.

The faculty general committee will exercise the responsibilities delegated by the board with respect to educational objectives, plans, programs, and standards. The committee should be represented on the president's committee on policy, program, and finance (see Fig. 5) and, in turn, if there is a divisional organization, interlocking membership with parallel divisional committees may be desirable. In this way the faculty will have ready access to final authority in the decision-making process. It is likely that both the faculty general committee and the divisional committees may require subcommittees to expedite their work.

It is important that these committees, informed as they must be on institutional over-all plans, policies, and finance, guide the faculty to realistic endeavor on the one hand and assist the president and governing board in choosing optimum institutional goals on the other. They must exercise a responsible leadership role and retain the trust and confidence alike of faculty, president, and governing board.

[22] Beardsley Ruml and Donald H. Morrison, *Memo to a College Trustee* (New York: McGraw-Hill Book Company, Inc., 1959), p. 7.

[23] Earl J. McGrath, *Memo to a College Faculty Member* (New York: Bureau of Publications, Teachers College, Columbia University, 1961), pp. 53–54.

The choice of such committees is of considerable importance. If it is a committee appointed by the president, it is not likely to be claimed by the faculty for its own. If it is elected by the faculty, those commanding the votes may not enjoy the confidence of the administration, and election may in some instances be based on vote-getting ability rather than qualification for the services to be performed. The selection of the members must therefore be a cooperative matter. One possible way to achieve this is for the faculty to elect an *ad hoc* nominating committee, which may present to the president an eligible list or panel from which presidential appointees can be selected. By this procedure the membership of the committee will have the approval or acceptance of both the faculty and the president.

Parallel divisional committees, if provided, may be appointed by the president from panels prepared by divisional nominating committees, and, as indicated above, interlocking of memberships would seem to be desirable. Because the faculty general committee is concerned with the very foundations of the institution, it should call on the best minds of the faculty for membership. There should be provision for rotation or change of committee personnel through term appointments. The quality of the committee and its relationship with the president's committee on policy, program, and finance would assure that the best thought of the faculty was incorporated in over-all institutional plans, plans that before adoption will have been weighed for their desirability and their feasibility by the governing board. The chairman of the faculty general committee should be the dean.

Once the committee is established and operating on a basis of cooperation, understanding, and common purpose, formal definition of working relationships for the exercise of delegated responsibilities may not appear necessary. And it is true that nothing can take the place of leadership and good will. Nonetheless, such definition is of great importance.

DELEGATION OF EDUCATIONAL POLICY RESPONSIBILITIES

The responsibility for policy formation assigned to the faculty must be undergirded with sufficient authority to elicit their full assumption of important assignments. At the same time the leadership position of the president must be respected. The following guides for delegating educational policy responsibility to the president and the faculty are suggested.[24]

1. The faculty general committee should be responsible for formulating proposals defining educational objectives and philosophy and long-range plans. These are to be considered and evaluated by the president and his committee on policy, program, and finance. Such consideration may with

[24] For observations and opinions of authorities concerning faculty role in policy formation, see Appendix A-3.

common consent lead to revision. At such time as the president deems the proposals ready for consideration by the board, they should be presented by him, accompanied by a written evaluation by the president and his committee on policy, program, and finance, through the appropriate committee of the board. Affirmative action by the board is required to validate the proposals.

2. Policy actions taken by the faculty general committee, pursuant to approved objectives and plans, may become effective, subject to the reserved control of the board, when approved by the president.

3. Policy actions taken by the faculty general committee, which are deemed by the president to be inconsistent with established objectives and plans, should be disapproved by him and the action should be referred back to the faculty general committee, together with the written opinion of the president. The committee may at its option propose the necessary modification of objectives and/or plans, and such proposal, if made, should be considered by the president and his committee on policy, program, and finance and should be presented to the board through its appropriate committee, accompanied by the written opinion of the president and his committee on policy, program, and finance. To be effective such proposal must have the approval of the board.

4. Policy actions taken by the faculty general committee that require current or capital expenditures for implementation may be disapproved by the president on financial grounds, whether with respect to present or future requirements; and the president should inform the committee of his action and the reasons therefor. The committee should, in connection with the preparation of the next annual budget, review all proposals so rejected and may present to the president a renewal request for approval and implementation of such of the proposals as they may choose for reconsideration, together with their estimate of the ranking in importance, in order that further consideration may be given to their implementation by the president and his committee on policy, program, and finance. It should be the duty of the president in presenting the annual budget to the board to draw attention to proposals so made and to review with the board his recommendations with respect to each of them, and the board should act with respect to each of them.

5. Actions taken by the faculty general committee which are deemed by the president to be educationally less desirable than alternate action or inaction, but which do not appear to be inconsistent with established objectives and plans nor to have objectionable financial implications, should be disapproved by the president, and the faculty general committee should be informed in writing, together with the reasons for his action. The faculty general committee may reconsider, and an affirmative vote of two-thirds

of the membership of the committee should suffice to validate the action. In a university setting, a committee or council of the faculties will be needed to coordinate and synthesize the policy actions of the faculties. The members of the coordinating committee may be made up of faculty representatives chosen by each faculty general committee from its membership.

In considering a form of organization for the educational program, its suitability will be measured by its net advantages to students and faculty. In large measure this means provision of a setting in which the faculty member can work creatively. The faculty member is an appointee, not an employee in the ordinary sense of the term. He is assured the freedom to teach, to speak, and to write in the area of his competence, and arrangements for his work will be by common agreement. Yet there must be administrative decisions on what responsibilities he will assume, what classes he will teach, what advisement of students he will undertake, and what institutional services he will assume. Ordinarily, involvement of faculty members in administration should be minimized to prevent it from interfering with their professional service.

At times there may arise problems in relation to the faculty member's personal or professional development or the performance of his work. The development of a vigorous, cooperative faculty that is happy in its work is a responsibility not fulfilled by rules of negation but by thoughtful planning and fair-minded leadership of the highest order. The whole range of selection, professional assignment, compensation, incentives to growth and development, morale and motivation, and evaluation must remain a central concern. The faculty is the foremost resource of the institution. It is to be nourished, nurtured, and caused to grow in both stature and service.

In the proposed organization, all staffing, program schedules, assignments, coordination of teaching, research, and field services would be administered by divisional officers directly responsible to the dean.

The library in the organization as proposed remains a responsibility of the dean. A major reason for fixing this responsibility is the library's immediate and continuous service to the educational needs of teachers and students. Other organizations that serve the educational program should also be a responsibility of the dean. Common examples are organized activities related to instruction, including the teaching hospital, laboratory school, and the like.

Chief Student Personnel Officer

A major executive coordinate with the dean and the chief business and financial officer is the chief student personnel officer. To this officer, ordinarily, is delegated by the president the major responsibility of management of student personnel services. The organization for student personnel services as shown in Fig. 7 is presented as an appropriate one.

It must not be overlooked that the characteristics of students enrolled in higher education are changing. They now represent a wider range of ability and aptitudes than heretofore. Of those who enter, perhaps 60 per cent graduate, and 40 per cent drop out for lack of funds, academic difficulties, or lack of motivation to pursue the chosen course. They tend to retain closer ties with their families and home communities than in earlier years. A growing proportion are found in the graduate schools.[25, 26]

The chief student personnel officer exercises responsibility for services related to the academic program and for student services. Services related to the academic program include those concerned with student recruitment, admissions, records, and placement. Services for individuals include health services, chapel, financial aids, and nonacademic counseling. Services related to social and cultural opportunities include those concerned with the conduct of social organizations, student unions, recreational programs, residential programs, and the student newspaper.

The justification for centralized coordinated student personnel administration, according to Bursch,[27] is its contribution to more effective institutional operations. "Here also, in the extracurriculum," he states, "the dean of students may serve the college by increasing the number and variety of relationships possible between members of the faculty and of the student body."

Millett notes that with the establishment of such centralized services,

Faculty members have tended to withdraw from direct contact with students except in the classroom and in the office where an immediate academic problem is involved. . . . Most faculty members now defer to this specialized competence [providing student personnel services] and acknowledge that they have little basis in knowledge or experience for handling the complex social problems of present-day students.[28]

For these many and varied services, plans for both program and finance must be drawn not only for the ensuing year but for the longer terms as well. A staff must be recruited, trained, and developed. Policies for records management must be maintained. Evaluation of both current operations and future plans must be continuous. As with the function of the chief education officer the function of the chief student personnel officer has many facets.

[25] John Summerskill, "Dropouts from College," in *The American College*, Nevitt Sanford, ed. (New York: John Wiley and Sons, Inc., 1962), pp. 631, 643.

[26] W. Max Wise, *They Come for the Best of Reasons—College Students Today* (Washington, D.C.: American Council on Education, 1958), pp. 15–19, 42.

[27] Charles W. Bursch II, "The Vice-President or Dean of Students," in *Administrators in Higher Education*, Gerald P. Burns, ed., pp. 144–145.

[28] John D. Millett, *The Academic Community, op. cit.*, p. 204.

FIGURE 7.   Suggested organization for the area of
student personnel services

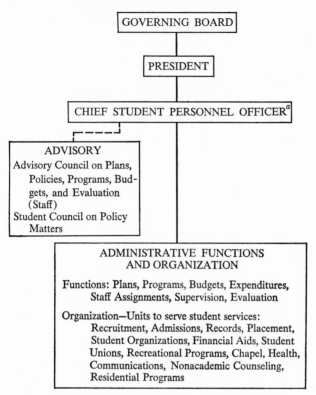

^aAlso maintains flow of information to area staff and stu-
dents and elicits suggestions.

The relationships of the personnel of this area with all other aspects of the
institution must necessarily be numerous and varied.

The chief student personnel officer provides staff advisory service to
the president through membership in the committee on policy, program, and
finance. He may set up his own advisory committee to assist him in over-all
planning and coordinating of area affairs. Such a committee, which may be
designated as a student personnel council, will in turn serve as a channel of
communication and assure that performance will be carried out in the manner
envisioned in the plans. In addition, he will maintain a close relationship
with the student council. It is through this council that student opinion is
readily available on all aspects of student life. Early recognition and adjustment of difficulties that arise from time to time are thus more readily
achieved.

Much attention has been given to the desirability of involving students in various aspects of management. Such participation is advocated as valuable training for citizenship and for developing responsibility, providing experience in policy making and student expression, and contributing to the development of leaders and followers.[29]

While there has been and is wide experimentation in the degrees of responsibility assigned students, the following are the more common provisions: a council for expressing or eliciting student opinion; under staff supervision, varying degrees of responsibility for aspects of extracurricular activities, fraternities, sororities, residence hall living, and the student paper; responsibilities for some aspects of honors systems; and in a few institutions sharing in evaluation of courses and teaching. Participation is not found to any appreciable extent in respect to academic rules and regulations, student marks, academic discipline, curriculum development, and classroom presentation.

Students should be kept informed on institutional affairs—program, finance, facilities, personnel, public relations, and placement. Their opinions should be sought on both academic and student life matters. Student involvement should be based on consideration of net student advantages. It is the author's opinion that students should not participate extensively in institutional budgeting, partly because of their immaturity, partly because at most only a few could participate, and partly because the burden on executive officers could be expected to rise by reason of such involvement.

Chief Business and Financial Officer

A third major executive coordinate with the chief education officer and the chief student personnel officer is the chief business and financial officer. Major responsibility for managing institutional business and financial affairs is ordinarily delegated to this officer by the president. An organization appropriate for this area is presented in Fig. 8.

The relationships of the chief business and financial officer with all aspects of institutional life are exercised through both formal and informal channels. He may perform services relating to the board committee on investments, either as its responsible executive or as its secretary. He may

[29] For an enlightening study in this area see Frances E. Falvey, *Student Participation in College Administration* (New York: Bureau of Publications, Teachers College, Columbia University, 1952). *See also* John S. Brubacher and Willis Rudy, *Higher Education in Transition* (New York: Harper & Row, 1958), especially page 333; Algo D. Henderson, *Policies and Practices in Higher Education* (New York: Harper & Row, 1960), pp. 232–234; and Gordon Klopf, *College Student Government* (New York: Harper & Row, 1960), pp. 10, 43, 47, 58, 71.

desirably serve as secretary of the board advisory committee on business and finance. He serves as a member of the president's committee on policy, program, and finance and shares in the experience of its institution-wide responsibilities. He organizes and chairs the advisory committee for his own area—the committee on business and financial affairs. He is likely to be found on numerous committees with institution-wide representation that deal with such matters as use of academic space, student loans, student housing, student food service, bookstore operation, and intercollegiate athletics.

Because the services for which he is responsible are institution-wide his contacts are widespread—whether in participation in institutional long-range planning, in the formulation and administration of budgets, in contract negotiations, in supervision of policies for nonacademic personnel, or in the management of finance, plant, and auxiliary activities. Beyond this he is often called upon for advisement in the affairs of individuals in the insti-

FIGURE 8.   Suggested organization for the area of business and finance

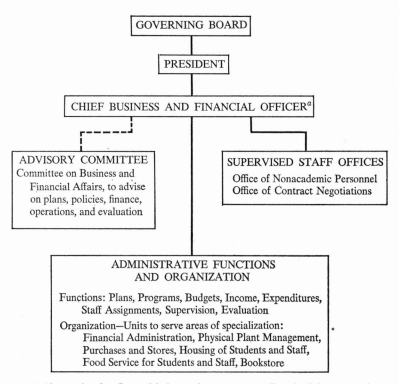

ᵃ Also maintains flow of information to area staff and elicits suggestions.

tutional environment, and frequently he is to be found active in community development.

As indicated in Fig. 8, the chief business and financial officer may organize an advisory committee made up of the executives of his particular organization. This committee can be helpful in the exercise of responsibility for planning, both in the near term and for the long-range period; for advisement on area responsibilities, policies, budgets, operations, and evaluation. Such a committee also affords an opportunity to better relate the services of the area to all aspects of institutional operations. The necessary interaction between this committee and the president's committee on policy, program, and finance is evident.

A substantial share of institutional expenditure is required for the services of nonacademic personnel, including clerical, building service, and food service employees. The institution has much to gain from a first-rate program for employee selection, job placement, job evaluation, employee training, employee rating, and compensation. These responsibilities are often assigned to a personnel officer for nonacademic personnel. It is sometimes advocated that this personnel officer, because of the importance of his duties, be made directly responsible to the president. The major objection there is that the president cannot and perhaps should not devote the time to acquire the background that effective supervision requires. An alternate arrangement is to assign personnel responsibilities for clerical employees to the chief student personnel officer, and for all others to the chief business and financial officer. There is some justification in such division of responsibility because of the dissimilarities generally found between the two groups of employees in personal characteristics, sources of recruitment, hours of work, pay, and fringe benefits.

Another area of staff responsibility that may be delegated by the chief business and financial officer, if volume warrants, is the area of contract negotiations. In the larger institutions numerous contracts are drawn with respect to teaching, research, and field services for which a sponsor agrees to pay. The terms of such contracts require approval of academic administrators concerning the services to be performed, the resources required and to be made available, and the costs, both direct and indirect. Beyond this is required negotiation with the sponsor by both the academic and the financial officers to reach agreement. One way to expedite this rather specialized financial service is to develop wide experience in a single individual to whom the responsibility can be delegated, to be performed under the supervision of the chief business and financial officer. In a small institution, where the demand for such service is infrequent, the chief business and financial officer would perform the service.

DELEGATION TO MANAGERS OF BUSINESS AFFAIRS

The delegated operational responsibilities are exercised by specialized officers, under the supervision of the chief business and financial officer. The officer responsible for financial administration will assist in financial planning, annual and long-range, and will participate in budget administration. He will have charge of cash receipts, including the collection of accounts, and cash disbursements, including the audit of all accounts payable. In addition, he will keep the financial accounts under suitable classifications and render financial reports as requested by the president. He will provide services as desired by the board committee on investments. Finally, he will conduct such studies, including cost analyses and trends in income and expenditures, as may be requested or as he may deem useful.

The physical plant manager assumes responsibility for developing and maintaining physical facilities suitable to the program, including arrangements of furniture and equipment, cleaning services, utility services, repairs, and replacements. He may be assigned the responsibility for new construction, communication, and protection services. If he has a large staff of building service employees, he may exercise or participate in the exercise of responsibility for policy formulation and services related to nonacademic personnel. As elsewhere in the organization, this officer is responsible for plans, policies, operations, and evaluation pertaining to his area. It is likely that in most institutions, the large investment which the academic plant represents will justify employment of a full-time staff member to study space use and to establish policies for such use. An imaginative program in class scheduling and in office assignments may both enhance the program and achieve economy in space use.

The purchasing agent assumes responsibility for centralized purchasing and for the operation of central stores of materials and supplies. To secure the quantity and quality of goods and materials at the lowest available prices under approved business procedures is of continuing advantage to the institution. The purchasing agent may also be assigned responsibility to sell or otherwise dispose of materials found unusable. He must foresee the needs for purchases, and must maintain close liaison with the operating units of his area and, so far as possible, with all other areas of the institution.

The manager of housing for students and staff assumes these responsibilities under the supervision of the chief business and financial officer. Over-all institutional plans will define the extent to which institutionally managed housing will be provided. This officer is responsible for apartment and room assignments and leases, standards for operations and room services, and in addition, for keeping tenants informed of matters of concern to them, for enlisting their cooperation in the development of rules governing the use of shared facilities, and for receiving, considering, and acting upon suggestions and complaints. Maintaining suitable plans and policies, performing operations effectively, and evaluating the quality of housing is a continuing function.

There are those who advocate that the management of housing should be under the supervision of the chief student personnel officer. Assuming the competence of the officer, no objection to such delegation is seen. In any event the chief student personnel officer should have and should exercise substantial responsibility for social, health, and counseling programs provided in the residence halls. Because the greater part of the operational function of this office relates to business and finance, the writer would place over-all responsibility for it on the chief business and financial officer.

The manager of food service assumes responsibility, under the supervision of the chief business and financial officer, for student and staff food services, including meals with service, cafeterias, catering, snack bars, and the like. The designated purpose of this office is to provide the type and standard of service required by the institution, to keep prices low and expenditures within available income. A number of institutions contract with commercial concerns to carry out this function. Such contracts may offer advantages in economical purchasing, a more effective use of the work force which can be assigned to other services during long institutional vacations, and expert supervisory services. Food service is an area of operations to which, understandably, students are quite sensitive. It will be of value to keep the student council informed and to elicit suggestions from that body.

The bookstore manager assumes responsibility, under supervision of the chief business and financial officer, for operation of the college bookstore. A bookstore that offers students and staff the needed institutional and reference materials at a reasonable price, maintains an inventory of appropriate size and composition in relation to sales, and restricts expenditures (including all charges, direct or indirect, properly chargeable to the store) to available income is an institutional resource. As with other student services, there will be value in keeping the student council informed concerning it and in enlisting their suggestions.

One other institutional activity should be mentioned here—intercollegiate athletics. If this activity is maintained primarily as an educational enterprise, it should be classed as an educational activity. If it is maintained for the primary purpose of institutional prestige or profit, it should be classed as an auxiliary activity. Under the former arrangement the major responsibility belongs to the chief education officer, who will wish to involve the chief business and financial officer and others in advisement on its operations. If classed as an auxiliary activity, the primary responsibility belongs to the chief business and financial officer, and he in turn will involve both the chief education officer and the chief student personnel officer in its operations.

General Institutional Organization

The general organization as outlined and discussed above is presented in Fig. 9 (pages 110–112) in considerably more detail than in Fig. 3.

Figure 9 outlines an organization for a sizable institution (say, 3,000 students) with a single faculty. For a small institution, no change in organization of the board is seen. The president may need to assume directly the burdens of coordination of plans, public relations, and fund raising. No change is seen in the organization of the chief education officer, although among the activities for which he is responsible, organized research and field services may not be present. The organization of the area of student services is not altered, but the programs required for the smaller institutions would be less extensive. The organization for business and finance might be altered through reduction or elimination of the supervised staff offices for nonacademic personnel and contract negotiations because these responsibilities may be exercised to the extent required by the chief business and financial officer. Conceivably some of the operational areas might be of little importance or might be nonexistent; for example, some small colleges do not have dormitories, others do not have bookstores.

For a large and complex institution such as a university, no change is seen in the governing board and in the office of president. Larger staffs of needed competencies may be expected to assist the president in institutional research and coordination of plans, in public relations, and in fund raising. In the area of business and finance, no change is needed, but it is recognized that in some universities the functions of business management and financial management are organized separately. In the area of student personnel services, needed changes in the complex institution would appear to relate primarily to adaptations to afford close working relationships with the several faculties.

In the area of educational services of a university comprised of a number of faculties, the policy actions of these faculties require coordination. This can be achieved by an educational coordinating council composed of representatives of the several faculties and the chief education officer (who may exercise responsibility for the president). In such circumstances, actions by a particular faculty require the concurrence of the council. Each faculty should have its chairman or dean, with an organization similar to that proposed on pages 95–99. Each chairman or dean should serve as a medium of

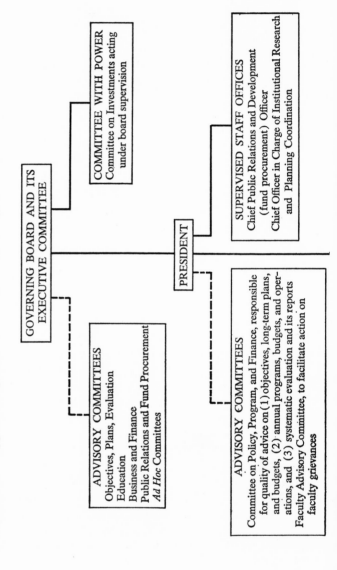

FIGURE 9.   Suggested organization for institutions of higher education

GOVERNING BOARD AND ITS
EXECUTIVE COMMITTEE

COMMITTEE WITH POWER
Committee on Investments acting
under board supervision

PRESIDENT

SUPERVISED STAFF OFFICES
Chief Public Relations and Development
(fund procurement) Officer
Chief Officer in Charge of Institutional Research
and Planning Coordination

ADVISORY COMMITTEES
Objectives, Plans, Evaluation
Education
Business and Finance
Public Relations and Fund Procurement
Ad Hoc Committees

ADVISORY COMMITTEES
Committee on Policy, Program, and Finance, responsible
for quality of advice on (1) objectives, long-term plans,
and budgets, (2) annual programs, budgets, and operations, and (3) systematic evaluation and its reports
Faculty Advisory Committee, to facilitate action on
faculty grievances

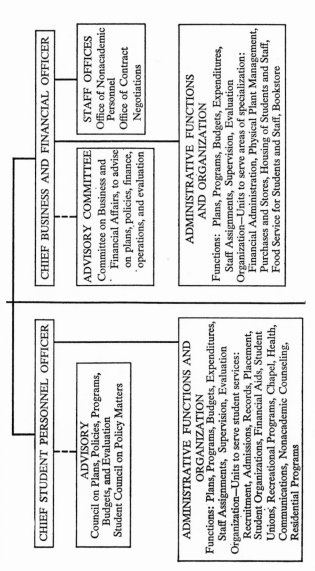

CHIEF BUSINESS AND FINANCIAL OFFICER

STAFF OFFICES
Office of Nonacademic Personnel
Office of Contract Negotiations

ADVISORY COMMITTEE
Committee on Business and Financial Affairs, to advise on plans, policies, finance, operations, and evaluation

ADMINISTRATIVE FUNCTIONS AND ORGANIZATION
Functions: Plans, Programs, Budgets, Expenditures, Staff Assignments, Supervision, Evaluation
Organization—Units to serve areas of specialization: Financial Administration, Physical Plant Management, Purchases and Stores, Housing of Students and Staff, Food Service for Students and Staff, Bookstore

CHIEF STUDENT PERSONNEL OFFICER

ADVISORY
Council on Plans, Policies, Programs, Budgets, and Evaluation
Student Council on Policy Matters

ADMINISTRATIVE FUNCTIONS AND ORGANIZATION
Functions: Plans, Programs, Budgets, Expenditures, Staff Assignments, Supervision, Evaluation
Organization—Units to serve student services: Recruitment, Admissions, Records, Placement, Student Organizations, Financial Aids, Student Unions, Recreational Programs, Chapel, Health, Communications, Nonacademic Counseling, Residential Programs

[Continued on page 112]

FIGURE 9, Continued

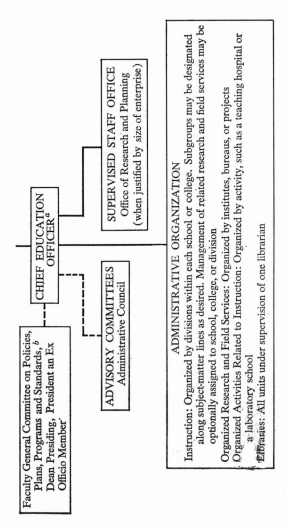

Faculty General Committee on Policies, Plans, Programs and Standards,[b] Dean Presiding, President an Ex Officio Member'

CHIEF EDUCATION OFFICER[a]

ADVISORY COMMITTEES
Administrative Council

SUPERVISED STAFF OFFICE
Office of Research and Planning
(when justified by size of enterprise)

ADMINISTRATIVE ORGANIZATION

Instruction: Organized by divisions within each school or college. Subgroups may be designated along subject-matter lines as desired. Management of related research and field services may be optionally assigned to school, college, or division

Organized Research and Field Services: Organized by institutes, bureaus, or projects

Organized Activities Related to Instruction: Organized by activity, such as a teaching hospital or a laboratory school

Libraries: All units under supervision of one librarian

[a] Also maintains flow of information to and elicits suggestions from faculty members.

[b] Membership appointed by president from panel chosen by faculty. Subcommittees and divisional committees as needed. Representation on and close working relations with president's committee on policy, program, and finance. Areas of responsibility: objectives, long-range plans, and evaluation; student selection, retention, degrees, and honors; curricula, research, and public service, including criteria, programs, and evaluation.

communication between faculty members, other faculties, and the chief education officer, and through him to the president and the governing board. The educational coordinating council may serve also to weigh and coordinate institutional objectives and plans, including financial plans for program. Vital to the plans is the exercise of continuous assessment of the use of resources—human, material, and financial—and the implications of proposals for their use. This means that at each level, the effective use of resources must be sought. Such use calls for awareness of the financial implications of proposals formulated by the faculty or faculties.

In the university the president should have an advisory committee on policy, program, and finance, whose membership must be competent to provide advice of high quality. On this committee must be the executives of the four major areas—education, student personnel, business and finance, public relations and development. To this nucleus may be added four or five faculty members (the limit dictated by need to retain an optimum size for discussion) representative of the educational program. It is likely that these members may be drawn from the educational coordinating council, which has central concern for over-all educational objectives, plans, and policies.

Thus, an appropriate exercise of the delegating function will provide an organization qualified to define the institutional goals, to develop the plans and policies, to operate effectively, and to evaluate both resources and programs. It is an organization which recognizes democratic procedures and the necessity for maintaining channels of communication to attain the maximum values to be derived from appropriate staff participation.

Because each institution is unique, whether in student characteristics, programs, resources, finance, or environment, each can evolve only under an organization which provides a high degree of freedom and self-determination. A governing board for each institution with the maximum of freedom is most desirable. Consideration of the exercise of governance by a board responsible for more than one institution is dealt with in Chapter 8.

In the following chapter attention is focused on how, through the organization described here, management guides the course of institutional development. The exercise of this guidance is the directive function of management.

CHAPTER 5

The Directive Function
of Management

The directive function of management is exercised through policy actions based on policy discussion. It is through policy discussion that institutional goals are set; scope, functions, and standards are fixed; plans and programs are devised; organizations are established; resources and techniques are utilized; and achievements are evaluated. It is imperative that policies, which together direct the functioning of the institution, be continuously studied and adapted to take account of ever-changing social needs, broadening ranges of student interests, aptitudes, and capacities, the changes in institutional resources, and new techniques and procedures.

Policies: The Guide of the Directive Function

The policies that guide operations in institutions of higher education are found in state laws relative to higher education, the institutional charter or legislative grant of authority, the bylaws and statutes or codified legislation of the governing board, the operational legislation of the board incorporated in its minutes, faculty legislation, and administrative rules and regulations.

Authorized by and consistent with the body of institutional policy are the long-range plans concerning program, finance, and resources, both of personnel and material. These plans are the concrete expressions of policy, and represent the best judgment of those concerned as to the services most useful to society that the institution can render.

CHARTER

Each state has laws providing for the establishment of institutions of higher education and the grant of authority to the governing boards. Under such laws charters are granted for the founding of private institutions. The establishment of publicly controlled institutions may be authorized, and the grant of authority to the governing board may be fixed, by special act of the legislature. The charter or special act defines the field of service of the institution, specifies the size and method of selecting the governing board, grants it the power to organize and to act subject to state law, provides that it may hold property, may sue and be sued, and specifies the academic degrees that may be granted. These powers and others that may be conferred may from time to time be amended by act of the appropriate authority.

BYLAWS

The bylaws define the membership of the governing board—number, method of selection, term of office, authority, and powers. Provision is made for regular and special meetings and notice thereof. A quorum for the transaction of business and the order of business are defined. Provision is made for officers, their designation and appointment, their several powers and duties. Agents, including fiscal agents, auditors, legal counsel, and others, may be authorized. Standing committees may be established, and their terms, selection of members and officers, and delegated powers and duties defined. The bylaws may include provision for statutes that define the institutional organization and fix the president as the single executive head. Regulations for fiscal administration may include preparation of the budget, approved procedures for financial transactions, the designation of depositories, and the authorization for withdrawal of funds. And finally the procedure for amending the bylaws may be defined.

Thus the bylaws of the governing board set forth the manner in which it will organize and conduct its affairs under the authority and responsibilty of the charter. Of special importance is the designation of a president as the chief executive, and provision for statutes in which the delegation of responsibility and authority is provided through defined organization and procedures applicable to the entire institutional personnel.

STATUTES

The statutes define institutional internal organization and working relationships. It is here that the philosophy of management must be expressed —whether the board seeks to impose authority, or whether it seeks government by consensus under shared responsibility subject to reserved control. In the statutes are set forth the form of organization, that is, the designation of major areas for which responsibility and authority are delegated to major executives responsible to the president. These areas include (1) instruction, research, and field services, (2) student services, (3) business and finance, (4) public information and fund procurement, and (5) institutional research and planning, if justified by the size and needs of the institution.

Next may be defined the powers and duties of administrative officers, their appointment and tenure. The faculty or faculties will be designated, their powers and duties defined, including meetings and voting procedures, committees, and provision for meeting with trustees. If the president has an institution-wide advisory committee, whether called a council or a committee on policy, program, and finance, its composition, meetings, powers, and duties are defined.

In addition to these provisions, the status and privileges of academic appointees and nonacademic employees are defined, together with student status and privileges. The academic calendar and academic costume are designated. Finally provisions are defined for amending the statutes.

ACTION OF BOARD

The legislative action of the board will relate to all aspects of institutional affairs. Much may appear to be routine; for example, consideration and approval of budgets, appointments of personnel, acceptance of gifts and bequests; but there should be constant concern that proposals be consistent with approved objectives, standards, policies, and plans of the institution. The real contributions of the board are its perception of the social role of the institution; its achievement of identity with the faculty, president, and administrative officers; its focus both on long-range plans of program, finance, and facilities and on current operational plans; its provision of institutional information concerning its services to the public and its enlistment of public support; and its promotion of a continuous program of evaluation of both plans and performance.

POLICIES

The elements of each policy are easy to identify: (1) objectives, (2) responsible agents, (3) organization, and (4) appropriate methods and procedures. To be effective all policies must have these elements. The board may, with respect to some policies, define objectives and fix responsibility, delegating to the president responsibility for choosing the organization and selecting methods and procedures.

All policies present choices. They require, first, an examination of the conditions to which the proposed policies relate and justification for their consideration. Second, they require a scientific analysis of possible courses of action and the implications for the institution of each course. Third, they require an assessment of the analysis and a recommendation of choice and the justification therefor. Fourth, they require consideration and action by the governing board. While on occasion a board member may initiate policy, the first three of these requirements are most likely to be fulfilled under the direction and leadership of the president, within whose organization the necessary resources are usually found. Cowley describes the leadership of the president in the process of policymaking in the following words:

Indeed, in the best governed colleges and universities over the country faculties propose almost all academic policy to boards of trustees, but they largely depend upon the leadership of their presidents. Traditionally and usually legally presidents have the right to propose policy, and they are expected to exercise it. All groups associated with colleges and universities look to them for such leadership, and no one respects those who do not exert it or whose proposals fall short of obvious needs.[1]

The board through its committees may then review the policy proposal showing the need, the analysis, and the justification for choice. It is here that the board brings its combined judgments to bear on the necessity for action, the adequacy and quality of the evidence, and the merits of choices available. Conceivably, further evidence may be requested, or reasons may be identified that lead to a choice of action other than that recommended.

It can be seen that an ongoing institution operates under a complex and comprehensive policy system. Such policies are the established rules of action that will serve until new concepts call for new goals or until specific experiences reveal the need for change to improve operations or to take account of new conditions. Thus policy formation in an ongoing institution is centered on changes in institutional objectives and their implementation and on evaluation and modification of existing policies.

COMMUNICATIONS

In the modern institution, more than ever before, there is an imperative need for communications—to, from, and among institutional personnel and with both the general public and those groups who have special interests in institutional affairs. While this requirement is stressed throughout this work, there is some value in considering more fully the various aspects of this need, and the views of thoughtful writers concerning them.

Communications are basic to the development, conservation, and wise use of resources. This view is held by Dressel and Lorimer, who state:

[1] W. H. Cowley, "What Does a College President Do?" An address given at the inauguration of the President of Oregon College of Education, Monmouth, Oregon, 1956, pp. 18, 19.

The human resources of a college—board of trustees, administrative officers, faculty, non-academic employees, alumni and friends, and students—are its most important assets. Adequate communication which fosters mutual understanding and cooperation among these groups is commonly one of the weakest elements in fully exploiting human resources. The aim in communications should be to apprise all groups fully of the purposes of the institution and of its problems and its successes (and failures) in attaining them. On occasion it has been found that the quality and content of some of the communications to these groups not only misrepresent the institution but insult the intelligence of the recipients. . . . The development, conservation and wise use of resources are obviously applicable to finances and physical plant, but they are equally applicable to human resources.[2]

The weakness in communications noted above by Dressel and Lorimer are observed too by Ruml and Morrison. They state:

The individual faculty member usually does not have basic information about the way the teaching resources of the institution are being used. If information about teaching loads, course offerings and enrollments is available to administrative officers, it is not likely to be distributed routinely to the faculty. Lacking this basic information, it is small wonder that the individual teacher does not see the possibilities of improving his economic status by means of an institutional program utilizing total faculty resources more efficiently.[3]

Woodburne emphasizes the value to the institution of wide discussion. He writes:

As a result of this general process, one further step of importance is almost automatically taken care of. This is the extent to which all of the agencies of an institution are informed, by such a process of discussion, as to where the institution is going, and what it is trying to do. In general, this puts everyone in rapport with the major purposes of the school or college, in such a fashion that all of the subordinate decisions become more intelligent and more integrated with the major policy decisions, which must be made at higher level.[4]

Burns stresses the need for public understanding. He writes as follows:

A final problem worthy of consideration is that of the lack of public understanding, cooperation, and appreciation connected with higher education. Evidence

[2] Paul L. Dressel and Margaret F. Lorimer, "Institutional Self-Evaluation," *Evaluation in Higher Education,* Paul L. Dressel and Associates (Boston: Houghton Mifflin Company, 1961), pp. 406–407.

[3] Beardsley Ruml and Donald H. Morrison, *Memo to a College Trustee* (New York: McGraw-Hill Book Company, Inc., 1959), p. 60.

[4] Lloyd S. Woodburne, *Principles of College and University Administration* (Stanford, Calif.: Stanford University Press, 1958), pp. 148–149.

of the magnitude of this problem abounds in the deterioriation of "town and gown" relationships, the derision that is heaped on intellectuals as "eggheads," and the old hack about "absent-minded professors." Some progress has been made in securing greater understanding between the higher institutions and the general public, but more is needed. College public relations practitioners should stop talking to themselves in solemn conclave and spend more time enlightening the public. One of the reasons why the private colleges are in difficult financial circumstances is that the significant contributions they make are little known by the people who should be supporting them. But here, too, the situation is improving. Trustees, college administrators, and even faculty members are coming to the realization that they have a significant story to tell but that it must be *told*. Support is contingent upon appreciation; appreciation is contingent upon understanding; understanding is contingent upon interpretation. The story needs and deserves telling.[5]

Vital to institutional well-being are the ways of policy determination. Corson describes the distinctive process of decision making in the college or university thus:

The process of deciding is distinctive in the college or university in the degree to which *final* responsibility for making decisions is diffused. Substantial independent authority for making various types of decisions is allocated beyond the trustees and the president to the faculty as a group, to individual teachers, to department heads, to deans, to coaches, and to administrative officers. It follows, hence, that the government of a college or university poses distinct problems in finding ways of enlisting and integrating the energies, initiative, and zeal of the relatively larger number among whom responsibility for decision making is shared.[6]

How responsibility is shared, how those concerned participate, determines whether in fact the institution is a hierarchy of power, or whether it is governed by consensus under the reserved control of the board. The path is difficult, particularly in an institution's early stages of development. This is so because results are achieved through leadership and understanding of many rather than a few. The achievement of consensus is a slow process. It requires patience and leadership and an atmosphere of mutual respect and confidence. But an institution thus run can be expected to give evidence of greater cohesion of all those concerned with institutional goals and programs.

[5] Gerald P. Burns, "Summary and Evaluation," in *Administrators in Higher Education: Their Functions and Coordination,* Gerald P. Burns, ed. (New York: Harper & Row, 1962), p. 222.

[6] John J. Corson, *Governance of Colleges and Universities* (New York: McGraw-Hill Book Company, Inc., 1960), p. 11.

The Scope of the Directive Function: Diversity of Institutional Policies

Policies are pervasive. They pertain to a wide range of institutional matters—from basic objectives to training programs for clerical personnel; from course sequences for French majors to a campus development plan; from levels of compensation for faculty to standards for degrees. Though each institution is unique in emphasis, there are many common elements. At any one time, the policies that guide the institution can be seen through observation of its practices. Most policies are the result of deliberate choice, but many that may have served well when adopted become obsolete as a result of inattention and drift. For an institution that seeks development through deliberate choice, awareness of the scope and nature of its policies and the implications for both program and finance of possible choice is an imperative of management. A comprehensive analysis of an institutional policy system is not practicable here, but an outline of some of the common areas is presented below. It will be evident that the mere mention of a single policy area may require substantial elaboration.

THE SCOPE OF THE DIRECTIVE FUNCTION:
AN OUTLINE OF IMPORTANT INSTITUTIONAL POLICY AREAS

A. General Institutional Guidelines
   1. Objectives and areas of service
   2. Philosophy for student individual growth and development
      a. Academic program: sequences of guided experiences, general and specialized subject areas
      b. Channels and programs for interaction of students and teachers
      c. Student independent study, work experience, and travel
      d. Cocurricular activities
      e. Evaluation and guidance of student experience, growth, and development
   3. Philosophy for research and field services
      a. Values sought
      b. Criteria for programs
      c. Relationships to teaching

B. Delegation of Responsibility and Authority (see Chapter 4)
   1. Board of control
   2. President
   3. Faculty and faculty committees
   4. Chief education officer
   5. Chief student personnel officer
   6. Chief business and finance officer

7. Chief officer for public relations and fund procurement
8. Officer for institutional research and planning

C. The Student Body
   1. Objectives and long-range plans
   2. Criteria for policies of selection and retention
   3. Criteria for student academic advisement (see Instruction)
   4. Criteria for honors and degrees
   5. Records
   6. Reports useful in management, including reports on student qualifications, achievement, program, composition
   7. Evaluation of performance of student selection and retention

D. The Faculty
   1. Criteria for faculty qualifications
   2. Policies and procedures for staff selection and promotion
   3. Policies and procedures on compensation (salary and benefits)
   4. Policies and procedures for faculty development
   5. Criteria for staff assignments (teaching load, etc.)
   6. Faculty tenure and dismissal policy
   7. Individual records of faculty members
   8. Statistics to be derived, and their uses in management
   9. Evaluation of staff performance: quality of teaching, writing, research, and public service
   10. Procedures for policy evaluation and modification

E. Academic Program
   1. Aims and long-term plans for development
   2. Academic calendar
   3. Criteria for program
   4. Exercise of responsibility for program
   5. Course offerings and enrollments, actual and projected for each area, both required and elective
   6. Accreditation
   7. Class scheduling
   8. Procedures for systematic evaluation of program
   9. Procedures for evaluation and modification of objectives and long-range development plans

F. Instruction
   1. Objectives
   2. Student academic advisement
   3. Flexibility in use of techniques (methods of teaching)
   4. Faculty program for improvement of instruction
   5. Faculty standards for student achievement
   6. Records to be kept
   7. Statistics to be derived to aid management in decision making

8. Special consideration of the gifted and those with achievement below standard
9. Evaluation of instruction
10. Implications of evaluation for policy, program, and finance

G. Library Services
   1. Objectives
   2. Relationship of librarians to faculty and students (staff committees)
   3. Program of education in use of library facilities
   4. Records to be kept
   5. Statistics to be derived for use by management
   6. Evaluation in terms of
      a. A learning environment for students, faculty, research workers
      b. Student use

H. Organized Research and Field Services
   1. Policy, scope, and objectives
   2. Criteria for accepted projects
   3. Actual and projected programs
   4. Evaluation of program and identity of limiting factors

I. Cultural, Recreational, and Residential Programs
   1. Policy, scope, and objectives
   2. Programs, actual and projected
   3. Student and staff participation
   4. Evaluation of programs and identity of limiting factors

J. Student Personnel Services
   1. Objectives of program for student life
   2. Scope of services; administration of student affairs (including student aid, admissions, student records, student counseling, placement, student organizations and activities, chapel, health and infirmary services)
   3. Programs, actual and projected
   4. Participation of faculty and students
   5. Evaluation of programs and identity of limiting factors

K. Physical Facilities
   1. Objectives, concepts, and standards—functional and esthetic
   2. Inventory of physical facilities
   3. Evaluation as resource in environment for learning
   4. Criteria and standards of use as guides to space assignment and utilization
   5. Criteria for operation and maintenance
   6. Records to be kept
   7. Statistics to be derived for use by management
   8. Evaluation of operation and maintenance

L. Community Relationships
   1. Policy, scope, and objectives
   2. Programs, actual and projected
   3. Involvement of community in institutional affairs
   4. Involvement of students and staff in community affairs
   5. Evaluation of programs and identity of limiting factors

M. Alumni Relations
   1. Policy, scope, and objectives
   2. Programs, actual and projected
   3. Evaluation of alumni relations

N. Public Information Service
   1. Objectives and policies
   2. Organization and procedures
   3. Evaluation

O. Fund Procurement
   1. Objectives and policies
   2. Organization and procedures
      a. Public appropriations
      b. Private philanthropy
   3. Records to be kept
   4. Statistics to be derived as an aid to management
   5. Evaluation

P. Finance
   1. Policies and objectives
   2. Scope and nature of fiscal policies
   3. Classification of accounts
   4. Budget policies and procedures, long-term and annual
   5. Fiscal services and fiscal procedures
   6. Records to be kept
   7. Reports to be made, regular and special
   8. Cost analyses
   9. Relations to faculty, other administrators, chief executive, and board of control
   10. Evaluation of fiscal policies and fiscal services

It is the business of management in the exercise of its directive function to maintain policies that define appropriate objectives and guide institutional performance to their realization. The objectives must be continuously evaluated in relation to present and foreseeable social needs and institutional resources. The effectiveness of policies as guides to the achievement of objectives must likewise be continuously under review and adaptation.

Two major directive instruments of management embody the concrete interpretation of institutional policies: (1) long-range institutional objectives and plans, for resources, activities, and finance, and (2) annual plans. These will now be discussed.

Long-range Plans as Instruments of the Directive Function

American institutions of higher education have been slow to adopt comprehensive long-range plans. Historically, they have not given heed to the urgent need for such plans. Since World War II the leadership in this direction has been found mainly in state agencies responsible for the development of the state systems. In the institutions themselves, numerous though exceptions are, long-range plans are generally not found.

In recent visits by the writer to more than twenty institutions, no comprehensive long-range plan was found; planning was often uncoordinated and lacked participation of interested staff members. Adequate assistance to the president in the exercise of this function too often was not provided, whether from lack of understanding of the need or from false concepts of economy.

The institutions that do have long-range plans generally limit them to certain aspects of institutional development. Among the more common areas of such planning are (1) plans for campus development, (2) institutional enrollment projections, (3) fund raising, and (4) plans for certain aspects of program development.

There are now two compelling reasons why institutions of higher education must employ long-range planning as a directive instrument. First, the speed of technological and social changes requires a longer span of time in which to assess implications for the institution and to make the necessary institutional adaptations to meet new needs. Second, government by consensus requires time for debate, and sufficient institutional adaptability to permit change in objectives, resources, and programs. Neither of these requirements can be met in short-range plans. And there is an added advantage to a focus on long-range planning: it requires decision on major matters, and the necessary debate on these will promote understanding of the institutional purposes, policies, and resources and hence will promote faculty commitment to program.

The observations and views of authorities in this field concerning the need, the values, the scope, and the procedures of long-range planning are presented in Appendix A-2.

Long-range planning involves assumptions. The conditions of the future cannot be fully foreseen, and to the extent that they affect plans, assumptions must be made. Careful attention must constantly be given to these assumptions so that as needed, changes in them, together with corresponding changes in plans, can be effected.

These assumptions are projections based on the realities of the present. They may include assumptions concerning society and higher education in general, and the institutional environment in particular. The outlook in state and nation concerning population, employment, and economic conditions will be relevant. The general outlook for higher education in terms of enrollments, resources, programs, and finance will also have implications for the particular institution. The outlook for the community in which the institution is located will have implications for the future of the institution, whether in terms of the quality of environment, the nature of community cultural resources, or the need for institutional services. On the basis of the assumptions made, the outlook for the particular institution may be anticipated in terms of its objectives and functions, enrollment, programs, resources, and finance. These institutional projections represent the best judgments available and serve as the basis on which the short-range (annual) plans must be made.

Tickton, in his pamphlet *Needed: A Ten Year College Budget*,[7] stresses the values of long-range planning: (1) It gives direction and quality to annual plans. (2) It permits a check on the feasibility of financing proposed developments. (3) It keeps the focus on essentials and does not permit drift through temporary, expedient actions. (4) It affords a basis for consensus of the leadership—faculty, administration, and the governing board. The shared responsibility of faculty, administration, and board in the development of the plans affords opportunity both to select wisely the undertakings of the institution and to develop cooperation, support, and understanding among all the participants in the program.

There are four major elements of long-range planning: (1) institutional guidelines—objectives, philosophy, and criteria for the plans; (2) plans for programs; (3) plans for resources—personnel and facilities; and (4) plans for finance. These elements are closely interrelated. No one of them can stand alone. An outline of each is presented below. The outlines, although comprehensive, are suggestive only, both because institutional emphases differ and because experience has not yet taught us the point of diminishing return on effort. It is clear, however, that what an institution does must contribute not only to achievement of objectives in a manner consistent with institutional philosophy but, at the same time, to achievement of these objectives with the utilization of suitable resources within its available income.

For example, the establishment of a graduate program in the physical

[7] Sidney G. Tickton, *Needed: A Ten Year College Budget* (New York: The Fund for the Advancement of Education, 1961).

sciences may be an undertaking of some magnitude. Time will be needed for planning the nature of the program, the qualifications for students, the requirements for staff, and the facilities, including the buildings and specialized equipment. Time will be needed also for the acquisition or construction of facilities, the employment of faculty, and the selection of students.

Another example may be a liberal arts college which decides to discontinue its program in the teaching of Latin. The program has been reduced through the years so that now there is but one professor who teaches a light assignment of small classes. He is a distinguished scholar with tenure who has served the institution for over twenty-five years and is fifty-eight years of age. In this case management decides to defer change until this scholar reaches the normal age of retirement.

A third example is a school for nurses that seeks to qualify them for state licensure as registered nurses. Assume that the standards for licensure have just been raised and that the new requirements include experience and training not at present provided. In this case, the school will act quickly to make its offering conform to the new standards.

In all long-range plans there are some matters that will require many years for fulfillment—some that may require, say, four or five years, and others that can be completed in a short period of, say, less than a year.

It is suggested that five years be accepted as a span of time for comprehensive plans, that projections be made for the tenth year, and that longer-range projections or projections in greater detail for the sixth through the ninth years be made as needed. The reasons for this suggested basis are these. First, the ability to foresee detailed requirements beyond five years is open to question. Second, the projection to the tenth year permits recognition of and attention to foreseeable major institutional requirements and changes, without undertaking the work incident to comprehensive planning for the years between the fifth and tenth years. As each current annual plan for programs, finance, and resources shortens the time span of long-range plans to four and nine years respectively, these plans should be revised to maintain the long-range span for comprehensive plans at five and ten years. Third, where detailed plans are needed for periods beyond five years, or where plans require extension beyond ten years, the additional plans can be supplied as supplements.

In long-range planning, care must be exercised that fresh and alert minds evaluate and modify as needed the assumptions, objectives, and philosophies on which the institutional programs are based. The study methods used and the choice of persons to perform the service, and possible advantages of rotation of personnel, should be considered.

The first major element of long-range planning is outlined below. This element provides the guidelines of institutional development. It defines what the institution strives to achieve; the general nature of the activities deemed appropriate to the realization of its objectives; and finally the criteria for the plans.

LONG-RANGE PLANNING ELEMENT NUMBER ONE:
OBJECTIVES, PHILOSOPHY, AND GUIDELINES FOR THE PLANS

1. Objectives for the institution
    a. Kind of education, research, and field services
    b. Quantity of education, research, and field services
    c. Quality of education, research, and field services
2. Philosophy of education
    a. Academic calendar
    b. General qualifications of students
    c. Academic programs
    d. Social, cultural, and recreational programs
    e. Guidance programs
    f. Scope and relation of organized research and field services to instruction
3. Guidelines for plans
    a. Guidelines for student personnel
    b. Guidelines for programs
    c. Guidelines for resources
    d. Guidelines for finance

Institutional objectives have received much attention from scholars. Umbeck sees one concern of the sixties as a "long-overdue program of clarifying and updating institutional objectives." He notes that many institutions have lost sight of earlier objectives and need to establish "new, vital purposes."[8] "If purpose is to permeate the life and work of the institution," writes Henderson, "it must be thought through and accepted as a basis for action by those who compose the institution."[9]

Townsend speaks for "the concept that whatever happens to the student during college is 'educational' in the sense that education is the training and guided development of the whole person."[10] Fischer insists that "moral

[8] Sharvy G. Umbeck, President, Knox College, "The Challenge of the Decade Ahead." An address at the Second National Assembly of the National Federation of College and University Business Officers Associations, French Lick, Indiana, and published in the Proceedings of the Assembly, 1960, p. 15. Printed by News-Record Publishing Co., Inc., Moscow, Idaho.

[9] Algo D. Henderson, *Policies and Practices in Higher Education* (New York: Harper & Row, 1960), p. 41.

[10] Agatha Townsend, *College Freshmen Speak Out* (New York: Harper & Row, 1956), p. 99.

and social values ever accompany intellectual development."[11] Gardner writes, "It is the sacred obligation of the schools and colleges to instill in their students the attitudes toward growth and learning and creativity which will in turn shape society. . . . the schools and colleges must of course give particular attention to the intellectual aspects of growth."[12] Wise urges a closer relation of college experience to real life and community affairs.[13] For the graduate school, the central tasks, as seen by Berelson, are the training of research scholars, and the training of teachers.[14] Weidner observes that "applied knowledge can give a student an opportunity to develop his capacity for independent critical thinking just as well as can knowledge for knowledge's sake."[15] Henderson stresses the importance of programs adapted to individual need. He says:

To gain the objective of individual excellence we must also maintain a degree of individualization within the institution. Acceleration where achievement has been demonstrated, honors reading and research, independent study, individualized opportunities within a particular course—various devices are available if we will but remain conscious of the individual nature of learning.[16]

Hill and Dressel find that objectives should be reflected in course content and the method of teaching it.

The relative emphasis on knowledge and intellectual abilities, the attention to affect, and the extent to which transfer of these factors to practical problems is expected in a particular course must be decided in terms of the students to be instructed, the intrinsic nature of the discipline, and the total educational experience. The instructor's own predilections and competencies must also be considered.[17]

In fixing objectives, the competencies sought for graduates must be defined in terms of knowledge, skills, habits, and attitudes. Then must follow

[11] John H. Fischer, *Administration and the Leadership of Education.* Alfred D. Simpson Lecture on Administration, given at Harvard University, April 26, 1962. Published by the New England School Development Council, Cambridge, Mass., p. 8.

[12] John W. Gardner, *Excellence: Can We Be Equal and Excellent Too?* (New York: Harper & Row, 1961), p. 143.

[13] W. Max Wise, *They Come for the Best of Reasons—College Students Today* (Washington, D.C.: American Council on Education, 1958), p. 45.

[14] Bernard Berelson, *Graduate Education in the United States* (New York: McGraw-Hill Book Company, Inc., 1960), p. 46.

[15] Edward W. Weidner, *The World Role of Universities* (New York: McGraw-Hill Book Company, Inc., 1962), p. 25.

[16] Algo D. Henderson, *Policies and Practices in Higher Education, op. cit.,* p. 304.

[17] Walker H. Hill and Paul L. Dressel, "The Objectives of Instruction," in Paul L. Dressel and Associates, *Evaluation in Higher Education* (Boston, Mass.: Houghton Mifflin Company, 1961), pp. 27–53, 45.

the delineation of institutional services. Will the institution offer a two-year, four-year, master's, or doctoral program? Will it offer programs in liberal arts, occupational, or professional fields; degree-credit or non-degree-credit programs? Will its services be available to youth and adults? Will it serve its immediate community? Can it undertake programs of organized research and field services? What must be the quality of its work, and what guidelines for institutional size can be drawn?

Then the questions relating to the philosophy of education that holds most promise for achieving the results envisioned must be searched. In the four-year liberal arts college, for example, some have sought to emphasize the great books, others to relate work experience to the liberal studies, and some have placed emphasis on current knowledge of world affairs. Will the college offer specialized courses addressed to the professions, such as pre-medical, predental, or pre-engineering, or will it leave such specialization to the professional schools? What combination of study in breadth and in depth will it select? Will it require for graduation a major in one, two, or three subject areas? In how many subject areas will it offer opportunities for advanced scholarship? Finally, will students be given opportunities to learn at first hand of other cultures and the life of the underprivileged, and to do some type of remunerative work? These questions relate to decisions that define the character of the institutional program. Each decision affects the nature of educational opportunities offered, the personnel and facilities required, and the money expenditures that must be made.

These decisions on objectives and philosophy lead to further decisions. For students, decisions must be made concerning number, age, and sex; standards for selection, retention, degrees, and honors; student mix as defined by areas of specialization; full-time or part-time; residential or commuting. For programs, the general scope and design of the curriculum must be defined. For finance, there may be general guides concerning the relation of income to expenditures in budgeting, investment policies, debt for construction of buildings, general principles for financing current expenditures —what part by students, what part by government and philanthropy. These institutional guidelines—objectives, philosophy, and plans—once fixed, are subject to constant change as the conditions and needs of society change. This is the justification for continuous study of them.

The second long-range planning element, outlined below, has to do with program. Here is concrete expression of all institutional activity outlined in detail for five years, and for the tenth year. Each year, the annual plans for program, resources, and finance reduce the span of time of the long-range plans, and hence, the long-range plans must be revised annually. In the program plans, the requirements for finance and resources are indicated.

LONG-RANGE PLANNING ELEMENT NUMBER TWO:
PLANS FOR PROGRAMS

1. Degree-credit instructional programs (including departmental research)
   a. Curricula—requirements, electives, sequences
   b. Teaching methods
   c. Standards for class size and teaching assignments
   d. Academic counseling
   e. Management and supervision
   f. Requirements for personnel—kind, quantity, quality, and standards for compensation
   g. Requirements for housing and equipment—kind, quantity, and quality
2. Non-degree-credit instructional programs
   a. Continuing education programs
   b. Adult education programs, including extension classes
   c. Management and supervision
   d. Requirements for personnel—kind, quantity, and quality, and standards for compensation
   e. Requirements for housing and equipment—kind, quantity, and quality
3. Organized research and field services
   a. Program projections
   b. Provision for management and supervision
   c. Requirements for personnel—kind, quantity, quality, and standards for compensation
   d. Requirements for housing and equipment—kind, quantity, and quality
4. Libraries
   a. Projections for character of services
   b. Requirements for personnel—kind, quantity, quality, and standards of compensation
   c. Requirements for housing and equipment—kind, quantity, and quality
5. Student personnel services
   a. Programs, including those for admissions, records, placement, organizations, financial aid, unions, chapel, health, communications, counseling, residential programs, and social, recreational, and cultural programs
   b. Management and supervision
   c. Requirements for personnel—kind, quantity, quality, and standards for compensation
   d. Requirements for housing and equipment—kind, quantity, and quality
6. Business and financial services
   a. Nature of program
      (1) Financial management and services—programs, including those

for cash receipts and disbursements, budget administration, auditing, investment services, personnel fringe benefits

(2) Purchases and stores—programs for purchasing, receiving, storing, distributing, reclaiming, and selling or discarding

(3) Plant management—programs for operations, maintenance, (including movable as well as fixed equipment), alterations, and improvements

(4) Auxiliary activities—programs for residence halls, dining halls, bookstores, and others

b. Management and supervision

c. Requirements for personnel—kind, quantity, quality, and standards for compensation

d. Requirements for housing and equipment—kind, quantity, and quality

7. Public information and fund procurement

a. Programs of public information

b. Programs of fund procurement

c. Requirements for personnel—kind, quantity, quality, and standards for compensation

d. Requirements for housing and equipment—kind, quantity, and quality

8. Institutional research and planning

a. Programs of institutional research

b. Programs of coordination of plans

c. Requirements for personnel—kind, quantity, quality, and standards for compensation

d. Requirements for housing and equipment—kind, quantity, and quality

9. President as leader, chief executive, and coordinator of policies and plans

a. Programs of leadership, planning, coordinating

b. Leadership of, communication with, and involvement of faculty, executives, and board

c. Leadership in board and its committees

d. Leadership in community, including information, interpretation, and efforts for fund procurement

e. Requirements for personnel—kind, quantity, quality, and standards for compensation

f. Requirements for housing and equipment—kind, quantity, and quality

10. Governing board

a. Programs for review and modification of objectives, policies, plans

b. Programs for review of quality and adequacy of resources—personnel and facilities

c. Programs for review of operations and achievements

d. Programs to guide board functioning—including (1) systematic review of board concept of its public responsibility or role, (2) its ways of working defined, conducted, and systematically evaluated, and (3) needed services or resources identified.

In this projection the answers to key questions concerning the future of the institution can be found. What kinds of educational services will it perform? What will be the nature of curriculum design? What services for adults? what research? what public services? What will be the principal characteristics of library services? of student personnel services? of business and financial services? What provision will be made for public information and fund procurement? How will the institution develop its plans? How will the president be freed for leadership? And how will the board provide for its activities and its working relationships to achieve consensus with faculty, president, and executives on important elements of governance?

The future program plans represent the best available judgments of how the institution will employ its resources to achieve its purposes. The long-range program plans guide the development of the annual plans. The outline could well be expanded to include the operation of auxiliary activities and others, but it will suffice to indicate how basic the plans are. Here are concrete expressions of institutional effort as it will be employed to achieve purpose. Such plans have the great advantage of permitting decision in advance of action, and thus a number of alternatives can be reviewed before choice is made.

Each item in the foregoing outline will claim serious attention. A few observations made by competent observers concerning the curriculum, as just one of these items, will illustrate the nature of the questions that must be answered. Fischer finds that

Despite substantial progress during the past half century, we still have more questions than answers about effective methodology and the relation of instruction to the nature of the learner, the nature of the subject, and the nature of the teaching devices most appropriate for particular purposes.[18]

Wise observes that there is little encouragement of independent effort, and where practical, it tends to benefit but a few students.[19]

Henderson believes that the more common practice of dividing the curriculum horizontally, so that general education is a prerequisite to the special, is less to be desired than a vertically integrated pattern.[20]

Katz and Sanford observe that curricula appear to be based on an earlier and now outmoded theory of personality. The type of curriculum that seeks

[18] John H. Fischer, *Administration and the Leadership of Education, op. cit.,* p. 15.

[19] W. Max Wise, *They Come for the Best of Reasons, op cit.,* p. 44.

[20] Algo D. Henderson, *Policies and Practices in Higher Education, op. cit.,* pp. 142–144.

to achieve breadth of education through distribution requirements, and depth of education through a chosen area of concentration, may reflect our lack of knowledge of the most common developmental needs of entering students.[21]

Weidner points out that increasingly a four-year liberal arts program postpones vocational or professional specialization until the bachelor's degree has been obtained.[22]

Woodburne points to the difficulty of exercising a rational control over the curriculum. He finds that new appointees can rarely be fitted into an already existing course structure, and suggests the use of a rule that for each new course added an old one be eliminated.[23]

It will be noted that for each program activity, the requirements for both personnel and facilities are indicated. These represent institutional resources. They also represent the third long-range planning element. In many institutions this element is not treated with the formality and care it deserves.

LONG-RANGE PLANNING ELEMENT NUMBER THREE: RESOURCES—PERSONNEL AND FACILITIES

A. Personnel
  1. Categories of institutional personnel
    a. Faculty
    b. Nonfaculty professional personnel
    c. Clerical personnel
    d. Building service employees
    e. Dining hall employees
    f. Residential housing employees
    g. Bookstore employees
    h. Other nonacademic employees
  2. Planning aspects for each category
    a. Long-range staffing plan showing inventory and future requirements defining kind, quantity, and quality
    b. Standards for compensation
    c. Standards for fringe benefits
    d. Policies for upgrading professional or job competency, and for personal development
    e. Status and privileges

[21] Joseph Katz and Nevitt Sanford, "Curriculum in the Perspective of the Theory of Personality Development," in *The American College,* Nevitt Sanford, ed. (New York: John Wiley and Sons, Inc., 1962), p. 419.

[22] Edward W. Weidner, *The World Role of Universities* (New York: McGraw-Hill Book Company, Inc., 1962), pp. 5–16.

[23] Lloyd S. Woodburne, *Principles of College and University Administration, op. cit.,* pp. 92–93.

B. The Physical Plant (Land, Buildings, and Built-in Equipment)
   1. Master campus plan (this plan must look forward twenty-five to fifty years)
      a. Land and area layout—projection for land additions and improvements
      b. Roads and walks
      c. Buildings, present and projected
      d. Adequacy of projected facilities
      e. Requirements for finance
   2. Buildings (including built-in equipment)
      a. Building space and utilization standards
      b. Building requirements justified by the estimated needs for housing program
      c. Long-range projection for buildings (this may look forward twenty-five or more years)
      d. For buildings to be built within five years:
         (1) Projected date of completion
         (2) Specifications of educational needs
         (3) General design
         (4) Location, relationships with other aspects of the educational programs, accessibility, and communications considered
         (5) Nature of structure and standards for lighting, heating, and cooling, sound conditioning, and provision for preventive maintenance
         (6) Specifications for built-in equipment
         (7) Implications for finance
      e. For rehabilitation of existing buildings:
         (1) Long-range plan for overcoming deterioration and obsolescence
         (2) Projects described
         (3) Implications for finance
      f. For equipment additions and replacement:
         (1) Inventories of existing equipment, showing status, age, and utility in program
         (2) Policy of replacement
         (3) Implications for finance
         (4) Projected provision for equipment additions—kind, quantity, and quality
         (5) Implications for finance

In the outline above the long-range needs for personnel are estimated. For each category provision is made for the present inventory of personnel, and for assessing the needs for the future. This projection permits, for each category, an examination of standards for compensation and fringe benefits. It permits review of accorded status and privileges. And—of great importance—it permits review of what the institution is doing to improve its personnel.

Indicated in the outline are the long-range plans for the physical plant, including the master campus plan, the timetable and justification for new construction and for systematic replacement of equipment and additions to it. Here, too, emphasis can well be placed on preventive maintenance and obsolescence. But it is not enough to have well-developed purposes and programs; it is equally important that suitable personnel and materials be assigned to the task of achievement.

The fourth long-range planning element is finance, and it is outlined below.

LONG-RANGE PLANNING ELEMENT NUMBER FOUR: FINANCE

1. Long-range operational budgets—ten years
   a. Units for finance (separately financed) with sub-divisions as desired: education and general, organized research, auxiliary activities, student aid
   b. Income by source
   c. Expenditures by function, organization unit, and object
2. Long-range capital budget—receipts and expenditures projected for ten to twenty-five years for:
   a. Land (details)
   b. Buildings and building rehabilitation (details)
   c. Equipment additions (details)
   d. Equipment replacements (details)
3. Fund procurement plans—ten years or more
   a. Program plans and expectation each year of receipts by source for current operations, student aid, capital outlay, and endowment

This outline requires three long-range budgets: one for operations, one for capital outlay, and one for fund raising. The latter is included here because of its close relationship to over-all financial plans.

These four outlines reveal the interrelationships of the elements of long-range plans. The elements may be separately outlined and detailed plans separately shown, but they are integral parts of decisions that must be made.

Long-range planning should begin with an assessment or evaluation of the institution in its current setting—in both general and specific terms—including its objectives in relation to social needs, the suitability of its programs and resources, and a review of trends. This assessment not only will point up the requirements for the future, but will demonstrate the importance of continuous evaluation of all aspects of institutional life. A further advantage is that it may emphasize the need for adequate assistance to the president in carrying on this function in cooperation with his committee on policy, program, and finance and in close relationship with the governing board.

Annual Operational Plans in Relation to Long-range Projections

Institutions conduct their day-by-day operations on the basis of annual plans prepared in advance. These plans, like long-range plans, are for programs, resources, and finance, but they are much more definitive. The annual plans require definition of the academic calendar, class schedules, established positions staffed at full strength, staff assignment, and program and personnel requirements for organized research and field services. They should be consistent with the long-range plans. Expediency may at times require that the annual program or finance plans be at variance with long-range plans. For example, a projected rise in tuition fees and general salary increases for faculty may be deferred because of an economic recession. Or the offering in a given subject is restricted in the particular year owing to a faculty vacancy for which a suitable candidate has not yet been identified. Or library accessions are fewer than planned because of a temporary difficulty in cataloguing which has now been resolved. If the actions taken are not of this nature, either the long-range plans require modification, or such deviation from the annual plan is not justifiable.

The annual program plans for instruction are rather fully defined in the institution's catalogue. Programs of organized research and of field services are generally not published, and plans often permit the president to authorize new projects as funds become available for purposes in harmony with the institutional purpose.

The annual budget expresses in money terms the provision made to finance the program. When approved, it represents authority to collect the income and incur the defined expenditures. The budget defines the year's relationship between income and expenditures. If the institution realizes the estimated income and is careful to limit expenditures to appropriations, any estimated operating surplus will surely be realized.

The third element in the annual plan has to do with resources. Personnel receive annual salaries and fringe benefits, and the level achieved is important. Established positions should be kept at full strength through recruitment and selection. Plans for facilities must be carried out. This may involve preliminary plans for additions, supervision of new construction, or the replacement of equipment. But the plans will carefully define what is to be done during the year.

Responsibility for and Participation in the Exercise of the Directive Function of Management

The relationships envisioned in the exercise of the planning aspect of the directive function of management are shown in Fig. 10. They are based on the delegation of responsibility and authority described in the preceding chapter. Participation of institutional personnel in the directive function of management is primarily a staff rather than a line responsibility. That is, the participants in this aspect of management are organized to provide their best advice and judgment. While these same relationships are depicted in Fig. 9, they are not as readily seen because in that chart the line relationships and responsibilities appropriate to operations are also shown.

As shown in Fig. 10, the president as the executive officer of the board is the chief planner. Because of the magnitude of the planning task he will need an assistant to aid him in coordinating plans and in carrying on or guiding studies of institutional operations related to the plans. Such an assistant may have the title of Planning Coordinator or Director of Institutional Studies.

The governing board has standing committees and *ad hoc* committees to which it assigns duties and responsibilities, the exercise of which contributes to the planning process. It is strongly urged that a standing committee take major responsibility for objectives, plans, and evaluation. The reason for grouping these responsibilities is that plans must relate both to goals sought and to a realistic assessment of present institutional resources and functioning.

To elicit the judgment of knowledgeable persons of the lay public, including alumni, concerning both social needs and the appropriateness of institutional programs (general or specialized), provision is made for lay councils to be appointed by the board. Through a program of visitation, evaluation, and advice, these councils, with overlapping term memberships, permit broad institutional identification with the public and greatly facilitate recognition of needed changes in institutional objectives and programs. The interaction of such councils with institutional personnel is arranged by the president.[24] In providing for widespread public participation, consideration must be given to the selection, term and rotation, status and service, and recognition of the participants.

The board, its committees, and its lay councils may be expected to exer-

---

[24] See discussion of organization of the board in *The Role of the College and University Trustee,* Annual Report 1961–62 (New York: The Carnegie Foundation for the Advancement of Teaching, 1962).

FIGURE 10.   Institutional relationships for planning

cise responsibilities with a sense of accountability to the public. Working relationships among institutional personnel and of representatives of such personnel with the president and (as arranged) with the board are provided to permit institutional personnel to contribute to the quality of policies and plans. Such working relationships will promote understanding of institutional affairs by the board, and will promote consensus of agreement on institutional polices and plans by board, president, executives, and faculty.

The key institutional agency is the committee on policy, program, and finance. This is a staff advisory committee chaired by the president. On it are faculty representatives and major executives. Objectives, policies, and plans initiated in any institutional area or by the president are considered by this committee. Because the search is for consensus, individual opinions are expressed, but no vote is taken.

The committee may meet with the faculty general committee or with any area planning groups or with other personnel as arranged by the president. The president, as guide to group interaction, may arrange joint meetings of trustees and institutional committees, of lay councils and faculty members or committees.

Each institutional area will have a central planning group under the direction of its chief executive, and the plans may be initiated either by the area executive or in the area's units of organization. Planning within each area may require interarea relationships.

Two primary responsibilities are to be found in the area of education. First, there is the exercise of policy responsibility delegated by the board and exercised by the faculty general committee. This institution-wide responsibility calls for the best talents of the faculty. The proposals of this committee, under the leadership of the president and the dean, are exposed to faculty debate, subjected to the search for implications by major executives in the committee on policy, program, and finance, evaluated by the board committee on plans, objectives, and evaluation, and acted upon by the board. Careful and mature consideration is thus assured. At any stage, if outside consultants, lay or professional, would be useful, such resources should be made available.

The second responsibility is the translation of the policy decisions into definitive plans, both annual and long range. Here the dean takes the leadership, aided by his administrative officers and committees. These plans are the bases on which the institution seeks to achieve its defined purposes. Defined are student programs, course offerings and schedules, faculty assignments, and the like. Correlative to the program plans are plans for personnel and facilities and a financial budget which makes careful provision for salaries of personnel, for materials, supplies, and contractual services. Such plans—for programs, resources, and finance—are submitted to the president for review and coordination with like plans from the areas of the supporting services. The president will be assisted by the committee on policy, program, and finance, and changes deemed necessary will be arranged by major executives in consultation with the unit head concerned.

The board committee on plans, objectives, and evaluation must be continuously involved, sometimes by briefing, sometimes by joint meetings. This is not a matter that can be acted on by trustees without the diligence to understand and assess. Some scholars deplore the placement of final authority for higher education in lay boards. They argue that lay boards cannot understand academic problems because they are not academic professionals. They overlook the fact that most lay trustees are highly skilled practitioners in making wise choices on behalf of the public—choices which have well served the academic community.

The area of public information and fund raising exercises leadership in seeking fuller public understanding of the institution and in strengthening financial support. The long-range academic plans define the need, and assessment of the outlook may in turn force modifications in the plans. The major executive in charge of this area serves as a member of the committee on policy, program, and finance, and exercises leadership under the general guidance of the president and the board committee on development. Program plans and financial plans of this area are subject to modification during the coordination process.

The area of student personnel services provides supporting services for the educational program. Its major executive is a member of the committee on policy, program, and finance. Proposals relating to area services are developed under the general supervision of the president; issues are evaluated by a trustee committee, which could well be the committee on education; and plans are subject to review by the board committee on plans, objectives, and evaluation. There are times when an activity is of concern to two areas. The management of residence halls affords an example. Here are responsibilities of concern to the student personnel area. The aspects of student residential life relate to student well-being and conduct, to counseling, and to provision for social, recreational, and cultural opportunities. Here, too, are responsibilities of concern to the area of business and finance. These include building maintenance, utilities, room care, security, room rentals, and budgets. In such circumstances, provision should be made for cooperation through either a regularized program of consultation or a standing committee exercising responsibility for the interests of both areas. Liaison between the two areas may permit early identification and action in relation to student needs or dissatisfactions. As in other areas, the projections are of three kinds: the activity programs, the correlative financial plans, and the plans for resources—personnel and facilities.

The area of business and finance, like student personnel services, exists to provide supporting services to the educational program. Aspects of financial management; contract negotiation; purchases and stores; physical plant management, improvements, and extension; and the management of dormitories, dining halls, and bookstores describe the more common services. For this area the executive in charge prepares plans under the general supervision of the president. These are reviewed with the advice of the committee on policy, program, and finance, of which the area executive is a member; evaluated by the board committee on business and finance; and coordinated by the board committee on plans, objectives, and evaluation. These relationships may be augmented by special committees as deemed necessary. Thus the development of a master campus plan, or major extensions within such a plan, may be assisted by a joint faculty–board committee. Effective utilization should be continuously measured against set standards so that knowledge of the unused plant potential is always available.

The relationships which have been described are desirable to achieve wide participation and understanding of the institutional community, and to provide the best available judgment on the course the institution should take. This is a continuous and difficult process, but one which holds the promise of consensus of the community.

Institutional Economics as a Conditioner of Institutional Policies and Plans

All institutions of higher education desire to improve or extend their services beyond the levels that their available incomes will finance. Despite the restrictions made in services, it is generally recognized that the salaries of teachers and other personnel are much too low, and large sums are needed for rehabilitation of the physical plant. Yet, ever present is the desire of a faculty to enrich the educational experiences of their students. Some want to offer new courses; some want smaller classes; some would prefer a less demanding teaching situation in favor of time for more adequate preparation. Administrators, too, seek to extend and improve the services of their areas. New and more costly processes of student selection may be proposed, or more extensive record keeping involving electronic data processing, or more assistance to relieve officers of some of the burdens of management. All these and many more claims that have substantial justification would, if authorized, greatly increase the cost of institutional operations.

EXPENDITURES ARE LIMITED TO AVAILABLE INCOME

The income available to institutional operations is limited. In public institutions the major source is public funds with student fees a secondary source. In private institutions the major source is student fees with philanthropy (endowment income and gifts) a secondary source. Other sources may include philanthropic support in public institutions and governmental support in private institutions, and income from sales and services of educational departments.

For public institutions, governments seek maximum institutional achievement with a minimum burden on taxpayers, and at the same time generally limit the amount of student fees. In private institutions, philanthropy bears a declining share of the cost, and the amount of fees chargeable to students is limited to some extent by the growing competition of public institutions and by low levels of family income which affect their ability and willingness to pay higher tuition fees.

Thus the management of each institution is faced with the necessity of reconciling the demand of society for quantity and quality of institutional services, the claims of institutional personnel to fair compensation for reasonable work assignments, the need to maximize the quantity and quality of institutional services, and the limited incomes available. The continuous exercise of judgment of value in relation to cost affords the basis for the difficult choices that must be made. In these choices, the interaction of policy, program, and finance is ever present.

THE HIERARCHY OF DECISIONS

The areas where important choices condition the performance of the institution can be illustrated by a flow chart, as in Fig. 11. This chart shows how the many choices that must be made have implications for money expenditures. An example will make this clearer. An independent four-year college chooses as its objective the operation of a residential coeducational liberal arts program leading to a bachelor's degree. It considers an enrollment of 1,800 to 2,000 students about right. In reaching this definition of objective, the college chooses not to add a graduate program, not to provide professional training in nursing and business management, not to proliferate courses with preprofessional programs such as premedical, pre-engineering, and the like. It chooses a size consistent with economy in operations.

The program of the college reflects its philosophy of education. In addition to a broad acquaintance with the liberal arts, study in depth in two subject areas is a requirement. Outstanding students may be granted privileges of independent study. In addition, knowledge of and interest in world affairs is encouraged for every student, as are experiences in other cultures and in social service, and work experience related to the student's major interest. Studies of the great books take their place with studies of modern science, social studies, and language.

Decisions are made concerning studies both in breadth and in depth, and concerning the policy of institutional participation in research and field services. In choice of program, the number of subject fields chosen falls between the extremes of many and few. The course offerings are consistent with the institutional purpose of providing a liberal education and avoiding professional and preprofessional courses.

When the program has been determined, choices must be made concerning processes or techniques which will be most suitable. For example, how can learning experiences be best arranged for those studying chemistry —how much lecture, how much laboratory, what size class or group? How secure balance in breadth and depth, and how relate this learning to that of other areas? How much independent study or group work? How can experiences be best scheduled—one period each day, or one or two longer

FIGURE I I.   Hierarchy of decisions relating to objectives that define
money expenditures

Complex One: Educational Objectives

For each component element $(1 \ldots n)$, choices $(1 \ldots n)$ are made. These choices form the frame of reference for choices of educational philosophies.

$\downarrow$

Complex Two: Educational Philosophies

For each component element $(1 \ldots n)$, choices $(1 \ldots n)$ are made. These choices join with the preceding to form the frame of reference for choices of services (programs) consistent with philosophies.

$\downarrow$

Complex Three: Services (Programs)

For each component defining the kind, quantity, and quality of program $(1 \ldots n)$, choices $(1 \ldots n)$ are made. These decisions now require choices of the processes or techniques to be employed.

$\downarrow$

Complex Four: Processes or Techniques

For each component of services $(1 \ldots n)$, choices $(1 \ldots n)$ of techniques are made. Such choices define the proportion of different productive services for each component and permit estimate of requirements for resources.

$\downarrow$

Complex Five: Means or Resources

For each component of services $(1 \ldots n)$, choices $(1 \ldots n)$ of kind, quantity, and quality of resources are made. The kind, quantity, and quality of management, of personnel, and of physical facilities are thus defined.

$\downarrow$

Complex Six: Money Expenditures

For each component $(1 \ldots n)$, choices $(1 \ldots n)$ are made. Such choices will relate to specifications for capital outlay, to levels of salaries and wages, to standards for purchases. The budgets for current expenditures and capital outlay are thus defined.

$\downarrow$

Complex Seven: Limiting Expenditures to Income

Preliminary choices made may require expenditures markedly above available income. In such case, the whole panorama of choices made is to be reviewed and compromises made in order to achieve maximum service within available income.

periods each week? The decisions made here have implications for use of space, equipment, teachers, library service, and student time. These resources of personnel and facilities, when used to achieve institutional purpose, may be termed productive services.

With the college program defined and techniques chosen, the requirements for kind and quantity of personnel services and physical facilities can be determined. Here, too, choices of standards must be made. With these requirements carefully determined, the requirement for personnel and facilities—both educational and residential—becomes evident. The requirement for expenditures for both current operations and capital outlay can be estimated.

This example illustrates the close interrelation of the decisions that must be made. If the requirement for expenditure resulting from the preliminary exercise of choice should exceed available income, or the requirement for capital outlay should be too great, then alternate choices must be considered until the most desirable combination is found that can be achieved within the means of the institution.

The example also indicates that in planning, a multitude of factors have important implications for costs, both current and capital, in an established institution. Five are selected for discussion here: the nature of the academic calendar, undesirable course proliferation, the quality of resources employed (human and material), their effective use, and a scale of operations consistent with economy. These will be taken up in order.

ACADEMIC CALENDAR

The academic calendar as discussed here means the schedule of institutional activity for each twelve-month period. It is common practice in American colleges and universities to operate on an annual academic calendar of two semesters of fifteen or sixteen weeks each. The normal time required for an undergraduate to qualify for his first academic degree is four years. Under this plan it is estimated that about half the experienced teachers have no summer assignments and for many more the assignment is a limited one. Ruml and Morrison see the need for change. They write:

Due to an intolerable level of compensation, the long vacations and the conventional sabbatical year, though respected as ideals, have in fact, unfortunately, largely lost their function. They no longer serve as ways of keeping the members of the faculty alert, in close contact with their subjects and their colleagues, with time to think, to discuss and to write without the pressure of assignments for which they receive specific compensation or grants.[25]

[25] Beardsley Ruml and Donald H. Morrison, *Memo to a College Trustee, op. cit.,* p. 5.

Rising enrollments, the high cost of facilities, and the increasing competition for able teachers have brought about an increasing amount of experimentation with calendars that permit more efficient use of resources.[26] In one study of the academic calendar Hungate and McGrath advocate an academic year of three fourteen-week trimesters, noting the advantages over the two-semester system to be opportunity for undergraduate students to qualify for the first degree in three instead of four years, fuller use of experienced teachers at higher salaries, more effective use of academic physical facilities including library, fuller use of residential and other auxiliary operations, and large savings in capital outlay.[27] Evidences of beginnings of change are at hand, and it is expected that the movement will accelerate in the future. Choice of academic calendar is in itself an important decision with respect to requirements for resources and for finance.

COURSE PROLIFERATION

There is a widespread tendency for proliferation of courses. Caplow and McGee describe this in the following words:

Perhaps the most important problem of this type is the indefinite expansion and proliferation of course offerings and service functions, without much regard for the instructional needs answered, or the quality of service rendered.[28]

Unnecessary and undesirable course proliferations are an indefensible waste of student time and institutional resources and money. The design of the curriculum must afford a rich and varied offering to students, but courses that are too narrowly specialized or that duplicate or overlap others should be avoided.

The need to achieve more effective use of resources has caused many institutions to examine their practices with respect to course offerings. Authorities on practices in higher education have written on this subject.[29] The problem has been studied by McGrath with special reference to the independent liberal arts college. In *Memo to a College Faculty Member*[30]

[26] There are now several excellent general references. For a comprehensive review, see Hugh Stickler and Milton C. Carothers, *The Year-Round Calendar in Operation* (Atlanta, Ga.: Southern Regional Education Board, 1963).

[27] Thad L. Hungate and Earl J. McGrath, *A New Trimester Three-Year Degree Program* (New York: Bureau of Publications, Teachers College, Columbia University, 1963).

[28] Theodore Caplow and Reece J. McGee, *The Academic Marketplace* (New York: Basic Books, Inc., 1958), p. 236.

[29] See, for example, Beardsley Ruml and Donald H. Morrison, *Memo to a College Trustee, op. cit.*

[30] Earl J. McGrath, *Memo to a College Faculty Member* (New York: Bureau of Publications, Teachers College, Columbia University, 1961), p. 11.

McGrath presents data for 14 institutions with enrollments ranging from 620 to 1,591 students. The range in credit hours offered in the major subjects is shown to be wide; for example, in biology, the range is from 38 to 98; in sociology, from 24 to 64; in English, from 54 to 146; and in mathematics, from 38 to 94. These ranges in subjects chosen as examples illustrate the diversity of practice. They may be compared with a proposed optimum offering in like subjects drawn from a liberal arts curriculum as proposed by McGrath:

Subject Examples	Range in Practice	McGrath's Proposal
Biology	38 to 98	41
Sociology	24 to 64	50
English	54 to 146	52
Mathematics	38 to 94	39

McGrath's proposal is based in part on what professors in leading graduate schools want for the undergraduate education of entering students who seek to major in their fields of specialization. Provision is made for general education offerings in each subject.[31] The comparative figures above serve to show that course proliferation needs serious consideration. It lowers class size; it increases the work involved. This waste of resources is reflected in cost.

QUALITY OF RESOURCES

A third major concern that has an important bearing on expenditure is the quality of the resources employed. Thus an able professor will (generally) receive a higher salary than an instructor, and a well-equipped building will cost more than one with the bare essentials. In the selection of resources, the criterion must be their suitability for the purposes they are to serve.

Effective use of resources is governed by the law of variable proportions, which may be stated as follows: If the quantity of one productive service is increased by equal increments and the quantity of other productive services remains fixed, the resulting increments of output will decrease after a certain point is reached. Consider, for example, room temperature at an uncomfortable 55°; as more fuel is added, the temperature rises to increase comfort, but above a certain point, say 72°, subsequent additions provide increasingly negative benefits. Or consider a class in which student discussion is desirable. A class size of, say, two students is too small to permit a

[31] Earl J. McGrath, "The College Curriculum—An Academic Wasteland?" Address delivered to Academic Deans of the Southern States, Dallas, November 27, 1962.

range of viewpoints. If a class enrollment of twenty students is assumed to be an optimum size, subsequent additions may be of negative value for this class. Again, consider the degree of specialization in a given curriculum. Up to a certain point, such specialization is advantageous. Beyond this point more specialization may be detrimental. For example, the professional schools prefer, for entering students, a well-rounded, liberal education to one that includes specialization in premedical or pre-engineering courses. Or, another example, extended study of costs in a paper box factory may provide the student of accounting with a highly specialized knowledge, for which he may have little later use, at the expense of a fuller knowledge of the general principles and procedures of cost accounting and cost analysis which are widely applicable in business affairs.

EFFECTIVE USE OF RESOURCES IN OPERATIONS

There is also a wide range in the decisions that must be made in institutional operations. Evidence of the play of the law of variable proportions is found in comparison of expenditures among similar institutions. In *The Sixty College Study* of 1957–1958 conducted by the National Federation of College and University Business Officers Associations, a percentage analysis of educational and general expenditures of 26 institutions with enrollments of 600 to 1,000 students revealed the following interesting distributions: [32]

	Percentage Distribution of Educational and General Expenditures		
Expenditure Category	LOW	MEDIAN	HIGH
General administration	5.5	8.9	15.9
Student services	3.8	8.4	16.4
Public services and information	1.1	5.9	10.4
General institutional expense	1.7	3.7	8.9
Instruction and departmental research	41.7	48.2	59.0
Organized research	0.1	2.0	9.2
Libraries	0.7	4.7	6.2
Plant expense	9.1	15.7	26.2

For each category of expenditures a wide range in the proportion of total expenditure assigned to it is shown, reflecting the diversity of decisions that have been made. In each institution the distribution is unique, and so correspondingly will be the character and quality of the environment for learning and the expenditure per student. Consider, for example, the rela-

[32] *The Sixty College Study . . . A Second Look,* National Federation of College and University Business Officers Associations, 1960, pp. 27 ff.

tion of expenditures for all other services to that of instruction. For the median distribution it is 1.074 times that for instruction; for the distribution with a low proportion assigned to instruction, it is 1.398; while for that with a high proportion assigned to instruction, it is .610. No qualitative judgments can be made; the data serve only to emphasize the variability that exists and to prompt search for the underlying causes—whether the requirements of excellence or the uselessness of waste.

From this consideration of variability in the distribution of expenditures, attention is turned to the existing variability in teaching practices. These selected data relating to nonlaboratory courses for freshman and sophomore students for 14 institutions are drawn from the *California and Western Conference Cost and Statistical Study* for the year 1954–1955: [33]

	LOW	MEDIAN	HIGH
Weekly student class hours taught per full-time teaching staff—Lower level:			
Mathematics	256	391	511
History	364	499	932
Art	118	550	756
Class size:			
Mathematics	17	26	39
History	18	48	89
Art	7	35	91
Weekly class hours taught per full-time teaching staff—Lower level median:			
Mathematics		15½	
History		12½	
Art		23½	
Total one semester teaching salary expenditure per weekly student class hour—Lower level:			
Mathematics	$4.22	$5.34	$12.07
History	2.69	4.23	8.95
Art	2.50	4.55	21.58

In the above data a wide range is shown in weekly student class hours taught, class size, teaching load, and cost per weekly student class hour. These variations doubtless include such uneconomical practices as classes that are small, teaching assignments that are low, and teaching costs that are high. They may also include classes that are very large, teachers with

[33] *California and Western Conference Cost and Statistical Study,* Financed by a Grant from the Fund for the Advancement of Education (Berkeley: University of California Printing Department, 1955).

heavy loads, and costs that are low. Some practices are guided by considered decisions; others result from lack of attention. What is needed is an awareness of the economic implications of decisions, and a practice guided by careful consideration.

Harris notes that

The trend [of student-teacher ratios] *in recent years* is upward through larger classes, more independent work, elimination of unnecessary classes, less formal requirements. But on many points teachers still oppose the rise of student-teacher ratios.[34]

Concerning class size, he writes,

Innumerable controlled experiments, inclusive of some that test beyond the usual objective tests, reveal either that results are equal in large and small classes or that the large class yields better results. Indeed some of the gains of small classes may escape measurement.[35]

The results of studies of class size at Minnesota and Purdue are reported by Woodburne. He says,

The general results of those studies is that for the transmission of pure information the large class or lecture is just as effective as the small quiz section . . . the concept of the effectiveness of large classes is limited to the transmission of information. It does not extend to group discussion, the formation of sound judgment, the development of analytical power, or the ways to accomplish a new synthesis.

Woodburne reports an actual study that showed that

. . . chemistry with an average student contact hour load per teacher of 13 hours each week had an average total work week of 50 hours; mathematics with a teaching load of 9 hours per week averaged a 47-hour total work week for the whole department . . . .[36]

Caplow and McGee observe that

. . . the average teaching load has been falling precipitously in all the major universities in recent years. They also note that "There is also considerable evidence to support the belief that, along with the general reduction of average teaching load in the universities studied, teaching itself is regarded more and more casually."[37]

The variations in practice are not restricted to instruction. They are common to all aspects of operations. For example, in the *California and*

[34] Seymour E. Harris, *Higher Education: Resources and Finance* (New York: Mc-Graw-Hill Book Company, Inc., 1962), p. xxxiv.

[35] *Ibid.*

[36] Lloyd S. Woodburne, *Principles of College and University Administraton, op. cit.,* pp. 94, 96, 97.

[37] Theodore Caplow and Reece J. McGee, *The Academic Marketplace, op. cit.,* pp. 145–146.

Western Conference Cost and Statistical Study mentioned earlier, utilization of physical facilities is shown. On 15 campuses, the use of student stations in nonlaboratory instructional rooms ranged from four hours a week to 14, with a median of 10. The data reflect either the housing of small classes in large classrooms, a low assignment rate per week, or both. In any case, there is need for more economical use of space, which represents a substantial proportion of current expenditures.

Harris finds that

Plant use is much less efficient than it might be. Resistance of students and faculty to afternoon and Saturday classes is one important cause of waste. But the responsibility lies in part with the administration also. They have shown little interest in studying the utilization of plant.[38]

Morris finds that in many cases space problems are in reality problems of scheduling. He says,

It is not uncommon to find an 80 to 90 per cent classroom utilization rate for morning hours and a 10 per cent rate for afternoon periods. To schedule afternoon periods to the same extent as morning periods will, in some cases, virtually double classroom capacity.[39]

These data are presented to show that the law of variable proportions is active; that day-by-day decisions utilize institutional resources in varying ways, and all are reflected in the quality and cost of the environment for learning that is provided.

An example will illustrate the importance of economics in institutional operations. In Tickton's *Needed: A Ten Year College Budget,* a ten-year financial projection is made for a hypothetical college designated as Ashford College. In this projection several basic fiscal policies were recognized. The salaries of teachers must be raised markedly. The primary source of support must be from fees, and such support could be anticipated despite a substantial increase. Some charge for plant replacement should be made to be financed by current income, and philanthropic support should be sought for student aid. Class size could be increased about 20 per cent. While an increase in enrollment was projected, no change was anticipated in objectives, educational philosophy, or program, or in teaching assignments.

The projection for Ashford College was, of course, a result of choices from among many variables. Obviously there are many alternate proposals that might be considered in making a choice. To illustrate, a second pro-

---

[38] Seymour E. Harris, *Higher Education: Resources and Finance, op. cit.,* p. 620.

[39] John B. Morris, "Space Utilization and Increased Efficiency." Proceedings of Second National Assembly of National Federation of College and University Business Officers Associations, 1960, pp. 37–38. Printed by News-Review Publishing Co., Inc., Moscow, Idaho.

jection is presented by the writer in which different choices have been made. This alternate projection (see Table 14) is not presented in any qualitative relationship to the first, but solely to show how different assumptions affect choice. For this new projection, it is assumed that there is doubt whether the kind of student body desired can be assured under the circumstance of high tuition, and whether philanthropy will provide the needed funds for adequate student aid. Hence the second projection seeks high standards at a lower tutition cost.

In the writer's alternate projection, the number of students is placed at 1,500 to assist in achieving a larger average class size, which is placed at 24. The calendar consists of three fourteen-week trimesters in order to make more effective use of faculty and facilities, and to permit students to qualify for the degree in three years, instead of four. The faculty will normally teach 10⅔ semester credit points each term, and will have leave of one trimester every third year. Annual salaries of professors will range from $14,000 to $24,000, with an average of $16,000, plus fringe benefits. In-

TABLE 14. Ten-year projections for Ashford College

Items	Actual[a] 1957–1958	Tickton's[a] Projection 1967–1968	Writer's Alternate Projection 1967–1968
1. Number of students—average annual	759	1,250	1,500
2. Student load—credit points	30[b]	30[b]	40
3. Academic calendar	2 semesters	2 semesters	3 14-week trimesters
4. Normal time for student to qualify for bachelor's degree	4 years	4 years	3 years
5. Average annual credit points taught per teacher	24[b]	24[b]	28 4/9
6. Number full-time teachers	63	84	87.9
7. Average annual teacher's salary	$5,637	$11,172	$12,185
8. Per cent salary is of total expenditure	36.33	37.42	42
9. Total student educational expenditure	$977,477	$2,633,274	$2,550,297
10. Fee income	$611,678	$2,301,274	$2,218,297
11. Aggregate annual tuition points	22,770	37,500	60,000
12. Student fees per point	$26.86[c]	$61.37[c]	$36.97

[a] Sidney G. Tickton, *op. cit.,* (Col. 1, pp. 21, 22; Col. 2, pp. 23, 24, 33).
[b] Assumed.
[c] Computed.

structors will receive an average of $9,000, and the average for the entire staff will be $12,185. Expenditures for salaries are expected to reach 42 per cent of the total. On the basis of the assumptions made, the average fee per point will be $37 rather than $61. In addition, year-round operations will permit a more effective operation of residence and dining halls, and may permit substantial saving of capital outlay.

The writer's example seeks to recognize assumed controlling factors that were not present in the choices made by Ashford College. In all institutions the choices that are made are many and each choice affects program, resources, and finance.

INSTRUCTIONAL VARIABLES THAT AFFECT COST

The example in Table 14 can now be summarized in terms generally applicable to all undergraduate instructional programs. The relationship of some of the instructional variables to total cost of instruction is seen in the following equation presented by Harris: [40]

$$\text{Cost of instruction} = \frac{NL}{CF} S(1 + O)$$

In this equation, N is the number of equivalent full-time students; C, average class size; L, average full-time student credit-hour load; F, average full-time faculty credit-hour load; S, average academic year salary of the teacher; and O, teaching overhead rate on teaching salary. This formula is useful in showing the economic relationship of the variables. Note that NL is equal to the total student credit hours for the academic year. If this is divided by CF, the average number of student credit hours taught by the average faculty member, the result is the number of full-time teachers. Total salary expenditures are arrived at by multiplying the number of teachers by the average salary. And total expenditures are found by adding to teaching salaries all other expenditures for supporting services which are here described as the overhead on teaching salaries. It can be ascertained, for example, that if average class size is increased 10 per cent, the number of required teachers will decline 9.1 per cent. The variability in the use of resources affects costs.

SIZE OF ENTERPRISE

Another important factor affecting institutional economy is the size of the enterprise. It needs to be big enough to permit full realization of specializations of personnel, physical facilities, and management. In a small college one is likely to find poor utilization of plant, small classes, and relatively high cost of administration. The following average percentages of educational

[40] Seymour E. Harris, *Higher Education: Resources and Finance, op. cit.,* p. 519.

and general expenditures for these categories of expenditures are drawn from *The Sixty College Study* of 1957–1958:[41]

Number of Institutions	Enrollment	Instruction (Per Cent)	Library (Per Cent)	Administration (Per Cent)
10	200–600	47.8	4.6	11.0
26	601–1,000	49.7	4.7	9.2
12	1,001–1,400	50.9	5.4	8.3
8	1,401–up	51.2	4.8	6.5

These data show that as size of institution increases the proportion of expenditures for instruction and library tends to increase, and the proportion for administration tends to decline. There is some evidence that the proportions tend to stabilize in institutions with enrollments above 2,500 students.

The large institution or component can provide economically for a specialization; the small one cannot. In the large institution maintaining a wide range of opportunities for specialized study, class sizes can permit economically feasible operations. In a small institution, such range would necessarily involve small classes with resulting high costs. Economy in operational procedures results in a lower unit cost per student. The implications of decisions for the unit cost per student are relevant because it is toward this cost that student fees are paid. For each institution and each program, a desirable size and scope of operations must be determined, and management's decisions must be guided by the assessment of net advantages —educational and financial.

From the examples given here, it becomes evident that considerations of policies and programs are intermingled with those of finance. It is thus vital that considerations of proposals seek understanding of the implications for both program and finance. Institutional economics is an ever-present factor in the exercise of the directive functions of management. What an institution achieves depends on wise choices with respect to objectives, educational philosophies, programs, and the quality and use of resources. Planning permits study of the desirability and feasibility of alternate choices of action before choice is made. The implications of choice—educational and financial—must be made known to all who participate in the directive function of management—faculty, executives, and board.

The Institutional Records Systems as the Foundation for Planning

The records necessary to management are of vital concern, and this concern increases as institutions become more complex. Records are expen-

[41] *The Sixty College Study . . . A Second Look, op. cit.*

sive to make and to maintain. Requirements for records-management procedures, and for retention schedules for each activity must be considered. A realistic and economical program of record keeping and processing will afford ready information for assessment and decision making.

An important criterion for a records system is the kind of information that is needed, and how frequently it is needed, for (1) operating decisions, (2) reporting to central management, (3) presidential planning and evaluation, and (4) use in relation to decisions by the governing board.

Institutional records—designed, for the most part, in the past—have been adapted through the years to meet changing requirements. Usually, the determination of record content, method, and procedure, including retention schedules, has been the responsibility of departmental administrators. It is understandable that in a single institution some departmental administrators far advanced in records management may be found while others give only relatively limited attention to improvement.

The new requirements of management of institutions of higher education stress long-range planning and evaluation and these in turn have put new importance on records and record keeping.

It is likely that concern for records will be institution-wide in scope, and that records will be systematically evaluated whether in relation to adequacy, availability, economy, or use. In this continuous review, duplication may be avoided and some multi-use obtained. Modern procedures, such as electronic data processing, must be employed to the extent warranted. The value of records essential to management will justify the cost of efficient record keeping by qualified personnel trained for the work.

Two types of records, drawn from widely different fields, are chosen to illustrate the value of records to management. The comprehensive institutional records system should comprise all records which, like the ones illustrated, have value to management.

CLASSROOM UTILIZATION

The first type of record is that incident to classroom utilization. These records are but a segment of those needed for effective plant utilization and management. The records will consist of (1) an inventory of classrooms showing the nature of each room, its size, lighting, equipment and furniture, and its relative attractiveness, and (2) the assignment of each room to use.

To the office that exercises responsibility for scheduling classes and that deals with class needs and the preferences of teachers, the records serve as aids in suitably housing the instructional program. But this is not enough. The faculty and major executives and board members are also concerned with the suitability of the rooms to their assigned purposes, and whether reasonably effective use is being attained. Such information is essential to planning for the future.

Because the quality of classroom space has an important bearing on learning and because such facilities are costly, a periodic review of the quality of classrooms and their utilization has implications for planning. Classrooms in need of modernization and improvement can be identified and such improvements planned. Low utilization may be due partly to a wasteful practice of designating a building or a plant area to exclusive use of one department, partly to the preference of professors to hold classes in mid-morning hours, and partly to the preference of all for modern, well-equipped rooms. Plans for new structures may appropriately relate to the manner of use of present buildings. Thus by providing means of ready assessment of quality and use, these classroom records are useful to management.

FACULTY RECORD

The second type of record is one useful in furthering the career of one professor. For the services of this professor the institution may through time spend as much as a third to a half million dollars or more. His services are sometimes performed with public recognition but most often are confined within the classroom. His compensation and the aids to his development provided by the institution (leave, travel, exchange, etc.) are based both on objective evidence of achievement and on subjective judgments of achievement and promise. The value of adequate, comprehensive, and continuous faculty records can readily be appreciated.

Following is an outline of the elements of a continuous faculty record. This record is designed to be added to annually.

Suggested Elements of a Continuous Faculty Record

1. Personal Data
   Name, date of birth, residence, citizenship, family data, education

2. Professional Status
   Rank, degrees, honors

3. Professional Achievement
   Prior to service in this institution
   Date of appointment and rank
   Promotions

   Annual Record of Activity
   Instruction—classes taught and class size, type of teaching
   Advisement responsibilities
   Research and field service

Institutional service assignments—committees, conferences, special leadership activities—national or regional associations
Public services
Publications, addresses, honors
Professional improvement activities—annual record of evaluation, annual notations of health

4. SALARY DATA

Annual record of amount, and accounts charged
Estimated distribution of time

5. FRINGE BENEFITS

Annual record—retirement allowance, major medical insurance (hospital and surgical insurance), life insurance, leaves of absence, sabbaticals

Record keeping finds justification in use. Once properly systematized, the recording of the information is a simple task. The test of the suitability of the record is its usefulness in promoting the effective service of the entire staff, in assigning suitable compensation, and in fostering personal development and identity with the institution.

These two examples are chosen from the many kinds of records that are required in institutional management. Among others are records of financial accounting and financial management, student selection, achievement, guidance, and evaluation; academic and nonacademic personnel—their selection, assignment, achievement, and evaluation; fund procurement—organization, information, solicitation of donors; plant management—plans, schedules, costs, performance; program records—courses, enrollments, course sequences. The opportunity exists to improve effectiveness of records in management, partly through new design, partly through new processes, and at the same time free, to some extent, the time of major executives.

The primary records are usually developed and maintained at the point of use. From the primary records are derived reports useful in control and planning. Records that are found to cost more than their estimated use value should be discarded. Where their use value in control and planning has been proved, records are justified; but both the record and the recording and evaluation process must be under constant revision lest the information provided be obsolete, inadequate, or inappropriate. Because of the interrelationships of all aspects of management, consideration should be given to procedures for the wide sharing of information provided by the records, in the form most useful.

Policies and Plans for Continuous and Systematic Evaluation of All Aspects of Institutional Life

A projection of institutional operations into the future, whether for an academic year or for a longer period, must be based on a wide range of value judgments with respect to activities, resources, and finance. Such judgments, carefully weighed and translated into coordinated policies and plans, will be reflected in the quality of institutional achievement.

Evaluation consists of a critical review of practice and its purpose is to improve the quality of institutional services. To be effective, institutional policies for evaluation should provide for continuous built-in systematic evaluation procedures and records. The test will be the degree to which value judgments are strengthened. An evaluation system—itself subject to rigorous review—that affords ready evidence for assessment of objectives, policies, plans, resources, and program, all in relation to financial implications, is basic to the exercise of the directive function of management. Although the personnel involved in institutional management is continually changing, the system of evaluation must afford a medium for continuity of operations and for institutional change based on value judgments.

Of all the functions of management, the evaluation function is perhaps the least systematized, partly because procedures are difficult to agree upon, partly because the evidence is often elusive, but primarily because its critical importance in institutional life often is not recognized.

Some of the evidence is objective, such as plant utilization, the incidence of program schedules, class size. Some is partly objective and partly subjective, such as student and teacher assignments, suitability of library resources, quality of a faculty. But for each important present or future decision, the evidence of experience will be valuable. This is the justification for a continuous built-in system of evaluation for all aspects of institutional life.

The Interdependence of the Plans for Program, Finance, and Resources

The responsibility for comprehensive long-range planning, involving as it must the clear definition of objectives and the difficult choices of the attainable optimum compromises imposed by financial and perhaps other limitations, is an imposing one. The range of the plans, the magnitude of the required efforts, the uncertainties attendant on the projection process itself, and the coordination of both the planning and the plans in a world of change give pause to an already burdened management as to acceptance of this responsibility.

Yet no other course is seen that will elicit systematic and over-all direction to the enterprise. A policy of making decisions when forced by necessity will surely place a premium on expediency, which is bound to be intensified by the changing membership of the management team. The institution unwittingly commits itself to programs that lag behind the social needs instead of anticipating and fulfilling them as they develop.

There are other and primary reasons for aggressively undertaking the responsibility of comprehensive long-range planning. The process itself is seen as the basis for cohesion of all aspects of institutional life. This does not mean that all members will agree, but it does mean that all will have had opportunity to assist in the search for values, and to understand and evaluate the nature and necessity of the compromises made. Moreover, it is likely that once established and systematized, these plans as the basis of management will not prove too great a burden. In the long run, it can be confidently predicted that the quality achieved in service and the economy achieved in cost will more than justify the efforts involved.

Planning must be carried on in each organization unit of the enterprise and in each major area, and must be molded by the president and governing board into comprehensive institutional plans. These plans must embrace the goals sought, the activity plans to achieve them, and the correlative financial plans. The interaction of the planning units must be such that proposals will secure careful attention and requests for alternates will be readily complied with. In well-conceived comprehensive plans the programs under existing limitations will be deemed the best it is possible to devise. Where, for example, a teaching program has been restricted or a desirable student personnel service denied in the interest of higher faculty salaries, then compromise will have been made in the over-all institutional interests and should be widely understood.

The interrelations of the plans must be recognized at the outset. The channels of communication and the participation of personnel are of great importance. The illustrations that follow indicate the nature of such interrelations.

Suppose an institution undertakes first to re-examine its *objectives.* It seeks to define what it wishes to achieve with how many of what kinds of students. Next it will be concerned with the *philosophy* for achieving its purposes. By what kind of organized experiences and environment can the objectives best be attained? Then it will wish to make *a projection of enrollments.* This will require specifications with respect to student qualifications for selection, sex, interest and aptitude, residential status, full time or part time, and academic-degree orientation. Account must also be taken of the desired student mix in terms of subject-matter specialization. In making this projection, account must be taken of enrollment trends in nation, state, and similar institutions; and in this institution, its constituency, economic conditions and outlook, and student cost. The size and nature of the student body will have implications for the character of the academic program. Now the *projections of the academic program* must be correlated with institutional objectives and philosophy and enrollment projections. Consideration of program values and financial economy may cause revision of any of these in the coordinating process. The academic program projections will indicate course sequences, required and elective, together with field experience, foreign study, work experience, internships, independent study, and the like.

The size of the enterprise and the program projection provide the basis for *projections for staffing*. Here standards for teaching assignments and class size are needed. In addition, there is need for guidelines concerning desirable over-all composition of the faculty in terms of qualifications, sex, age, rank, tenure status, and the like.

This definition of need for academic staff should now be supplemented by a *projection of faculty compensation*. The desirable standards for salaries and fringe benefits for each classification of personnel should be estimated, and thus permit estimates of annual expenditures for the various groups that compose the academic staff.

The size and nature of the student body and the institutional programs and the definition of personnel requirements permit an estimate of the requirements of space. *Projections for physical plant development* can now be made. A master campus layout, providing locations for plant extensions, and a campus development plan, providing for needed construction through time, together with a correlated financial plan, are essentials. Such a master plan permits optimum land use, with no violence to the over-all concepts of campus convenience and beauty, and it assures orderly development of new facilities as needed.

Important as it is to foresee the need for new facilities, it is equally important to plan adaptations of existing structures to meet the needs of program and to prevent obsolescence. This program must recognize the changing needs, whether in class size, in expanded research, in newer teaching techniques, or in accommodation of equipment. Standards for safety, lighting, heating and cooling, sound conditioning, visual aids, built-in equipment must be established, and *projections for rehabilitation* of existing structures established—both the requirements and the estimates of cost. Unless this is done, physical facilities may retard rather than promote the educational program. A third requirement is *projections for cyclical repairs and replacements*. If such requirements are to be financed from current income, it is desirable to foresee the needs and to make a constantly recurring annual charge so that through the use of resources the objectives will be met. Some parts of maintenance can be planned and budgeted on a recurring annual basis. Interior painting is one of these. But it is necessary to conceive of the total requirement, to set standards, and to schedule an annual program. Thus, the painting requirements for classrooms, offices, libraries, public rooms, and dormitory rooms need to be established and met through fairly constant charges to operations during the cycle. But the replacement of heating boilers and the heat distribution system, of plumbing lines, of exterior painting and repainting, of electrical wiring and fixtures, ordinarily require substantial outlays at one time. Unless the need is foreseen and provided for, current operations must deal with a widely fluctuating cost item in its annual operating program.

These examples are adequate to illustrate how interdependent all aspects of institutional operations must be. Assuredly the aspects of student personnel services, of business and finance, of public information and fund procurement, are similarly interwoven and require foresighted planning. In short, interdependence will require that planning approach in scope the outlines of the long-range planning elements one to four, presented on pages 127–136.

Correlated with all the plans must be the projections for finance. The *annual operating budget* of current income and expenditures is a financial plan in support of program for the ensuing year. The *annual budget for plant extensions,* showing estimated receipts and estimated expenditures for plant extensions, is a plan in support of the planned construction for the ensuing year. Both plans must be consistent with institutional objectives, philosophy, and long-range plans.

The *long-range operating budget is a projection of operational finance* for a series of years (ten or more) into the future. It includes estimates of receipts and expenditures, and represents the best available judgment with respect to institutional functioning in the years ahead. It must reflect fully the program projections outlined above.

The *long-range projections for financing plant extensions* will include by years (ten or more) the projections of estimated receipts and expenditure for plant extensions.

While in the planning process maximum understanding of institutional personnel must be sought, it is likely that proposals made by the various administrative units and by major executives will aggregate a cost much greater than estimated available income, even taking into account projected increases in income from all sources. It is also likely that for the most part these proposals are desirable and necessary. But the institution faces the limitations of finance; and the president, aided by his planning coordinator, his major executives, the committee on policy, program, and finance, and the faculty must, in consideration of the range of choices concerning policies outlined (see pages 120–123), revise the programs and estimates in a manner calculated to maximize institutional objectives.

The Coordination of Institutional Plans

Because of the interdependence of the plans, a major responsibility for coordination falls on the president. The task is seen as continuous. If the president is to perform it well, he must have as planning coordinator a staff officer with a supporting staff. Such an officer may also direct research studies that have implications for the plans. Coordination of plans will require their modification and reappraisal on the same broad bases of staff participation as did the original proposals. The post of planning coordinator will call for a dedicated officer with superior abilities both in the exercise of judgment and in the sustaining of desirable working relationships.

In addition to strengthening his own office to cope with the institutional planning function, the president must give attention to the adequacy of planning resources in the offices of major executives.

Summary

This review of the directive function of management has sought to emphasize the importance of forward-looking plans based on cooperative effort of faculty, administration, and board. It has noted how broad in scope the planning function is. It has sought to identify the key elements of a comprehensive long-range institutional plan. It has recognized the important relationship of the annual operating plans to the long-range objectives and plans. The economics of institutional operations are seen as a pervasive influence on objectives and their implementation. The institutional record system is termed basic to successful projection of institutional operations, and systematic evaluation of all aspects of institutional life is necessary to undergird the value judgments that guide the directive function of management.

The interdependence of the plans both in the near term and through extended periods of time impose on the president a major responsibility for leadership in the coordination process. The need to strengthen his office by adding a planning coordinator is present in all but very small institutions.

Looking to the future, the degree to which institutions of higher education appropriately and effectively fulfill their roles in the society they serve depends on how they individually perform the directive function of management.

CHAPTER 6

The Operative Function
of Management

The operative function of management is the exercise of responsibility for carrying out the program of activities envisioned in the institutional plans. In common with management of all enterprises, management of colleges and universities is concerned with (1) the kind, quantity, and quality of the work to be performed or the product to be produced, (2) the techniques, methods, and procedures for accomplishing the task, (3) the kind, quantity, and quality of resources, both personnel and material, necessary to achievement, and (4) the allocation of resources—personnel and material—best suited to the realization of stated objectives.

This chapter is concerned with principles and essentials that relate to these areas of responsibility: (1) operations consistent with an appropriate philosophy of management; (2) the kind, quantity, and quality of work to be performed; (3) the organization of the work to be performed; (4) the choice of techniques, methods, and procedures; (5) the definition, procurement, and care of resources; (6) the application of resources to the performance of the work; and (7) common essentials of the management of operations. Despite diverse delegated responsibilities every manager who seeks competent performance of work for which he is responsible must be concerned with each of these areas.

The discussion that follows emphasizes the common elements of the management of operations rather than the many tasks involved. If the observations are valid, they will be fully applicable to the diverse requirements for performance.

Responsibility of Management for Operations Consistent with an Appropriate Philosophy

The characteristics of management appropriate to the conduct of operations depend on the performance requirements of the enterprise, the setting in which it operates, and the influence of management practices and procedures on the institution as a whole.

The college or university operates in a public setting. Actions taken and methods employed are of immediate interest to the general public and to many special publics. Management must ever be prepared to interpret and justify its actions.

The students form a special segment of the public as well as an integral part of the immediate institutional community. The decisions and procedures of management affect them as community citizens and contribute to their educational experiences. The exercise of management that is consistent with democratic values, demonstrates respect for the individual, and adheres to ethical standards not only promotes the institutional purpose but provides for students examples that may influence their future actions and standards.

The faculty has recognized status, responsibilities, and relationships that condition the management process. The faculty member is not an employee in the ordinary sense of the term. He is a highly qualified specialist appointed to provide professional services and given wide latitude for self-direction. He exercises important delegated managerial responsibility. His assignment to service in any academic year may be guided by general standards, but it is defined on the basis of mutual agreement between him and the chief educational officer or his representative. He must be encouraged in the exercise of academic creativity and service through professional recognition, sympathetic attention to his service needs, opportunity for personal and professional development, and wise adjustments of his compensation. The greater the competence of the scholar, the greater his claim for special consideration.

THE DIVERSITY OF THE WORK

The work necessary to the operation of colleges and universities is highly diverse. This is true for educational program specialization and for supporting services. Basic to the educational program is the work of specialists in many areas and levels of instruction, research, and field services. Identification of some of the supporting services will illustrate their range: purchasing, storing, bookstore operations, physical plant operation and maintenance, residence and dining halls operations, health services, guidance and counseling, publishing, fund management, accounting, record keeping, data processing, telephone and mail services, and public relations. There are also many organized activities relating to instructional departments, such as creameries, museums, guidance clinics, teaching hospitals, and demonstration schools.

This range in kinds of work to be performed requires in turn a diversity of skills. Some examples on a single campus will illustrate—in the professional group a mathematician, a linguist, a surgeon; in the management group an accountant, an architect, a dietitian; in the nonprofessional group an elevator operator, a secretary, a cook. Standardized operating procedures cannot be applicable in a number of areas, even in the same institution, for several reasons: The requirements of teaching and learning vary in the several disciplines; courses within like subject fields are dissimilar; and faculty members are free to select their methods of teaching. The requirements of many minor operations often cause the choice of techniques to be exercised at the local level.

MANAGEMENT IS DECENTRALIZED

In response to conditions such as those outlined above, the management of colleges and universities operates on the basis of decentralization. The president as leader of the faculty and as executive officer of the governing board must delegate broad powers and responsibilities to chosen major executives. These areas represent groupings of related services. Customarily they are education, student personnel services, public relations and fund raising, and business and finance. The president places full reliance on each of the major executives to manage his area in a manner consistent with the plans, and to maximize achievement in furthering the realization of institutional objectives. This they are to be trained to do through full understanding of the objectives, the programs, and the plans. Each such major executive should serve as a member of the committee on policy, program, and finance, a service which will broaden understanding and promote cooperation.

The president must lead each major executive to greater achievement, both professionally and personally. He should encourage their attendance at professional meetings and provide time for visiting other institutions. He should promote interaction between them and the faculty, both to enhance their awareness of the central concern for program and to develop faculty understanding of the importance of the service areas to program. Personal counsel should also be available. This cultivation of a concern for service in an atmosphere of mutual respect is desirable. Management must ever be aware that arrogance, ill-temper, and disrespect have no place in higher education. Integrity, cooperation, respect, and humility are good companions of competence. In short, the president needs in his major executives a quality of leadership as effective for their areas as will be his for the institution as a whole.

Each major executive must be a generalist. He may have a background of specialization that aids him to understand and guide the affairs of his area, but the diversity of needed skills in each area is great, and he cannot be a specialist in all. Rather he serves as an interpreter to the personnel of his area of institutional objectives, philosophies, plans, and programs. He is a medium of communication both vertically and laterally. He fosters appropriate communication through contact channels. For his area he chooses those executives to serve with him who in turn possess the required specialized knowledge. He sees that they conduct operations in accordance with the plans of the institution. He is their leader, teacher, and guide. If the area is that of instruction, department or division heads are designated to facilitate the conduct of programs and to provide direct communication with faculty members. If the area is one of the supporting services, managers or second-line supervisors are assigned varying degrees of responsibility for direction of the work. In such areas the skilled worker and his first-line supervisor are primary resources of the manager to whom they are responsible and who guides and coordinates their effort.

Thus in higher education, because of the diversity of activity, management operates under a plan of decentralization in which responsibility is placed on executives chosen to head broad areas of specialization. They in turn build an organization based on specialized competence in performance, with supervision competent to guide, coordinate, and evaluate, and to ensure that the activity undertaken contributes to achievement of institutional purposes. Under such decentralization, when a policy is determined major executives are expected to interpret its implications for their respective areas, to see that subordinate executives and supervisors are well informed, and that plans for performance provide the kind, quantity, and quality of services needed. Associated with performance should be a systematic evaluation that will serve to improve performance. Such a system is described in a later chapter.

Principles Relating to Kind, Quantity, and Quality of Work to Be Performed

A major responsibility, shared by governing board, administrative officers, and faculty, is achievement at reasonable cost of the high institutional standards demanded. There are three requirements for the exercise of this responsibility. First, the work done must be of a kind that is needed to achieve the values sought. If the need of program is a course in the social sciences, an additional course in mathematics will not answer. If the need is for secretarial service, the provision of typing service will not adequately serve. Second, the work must be of a quality that promotes the values sought. Inferior quality of teaching, inefficient accounting procedures and services, or an inappropriate fund-raising program are examples of services that impede rather than promote the achievement of objectives. Third, the quantity of the service should be just equal to the need. An excess is useless; too little detracts from achievement. Needless proliferation of courses, a physical plant larger than the requirement, and duplication of records are examples of work loads that do not advance institutional achievement. Determination of the work that is essential reflects judgments based on experience. And this exercise of judgment is of first importance in meeting standards at reasonable cost.

Principles for Organizing the Work

Within each major area of operation the work must be organized in a systematic way. The basic aims to be considered are: (1) to relate in the best possible way the work to the achievement of the purposes sought; (2) to secure maximum use of specialized knowledge and skills; (3) to secure the advantages of the most effective techniques; and (4) to afford supervision of the highest competence. These aims are best realized when, consistent with the promotion of institutional objectives, the work is organized on the basis of like or related skills required for its performance. When thus organized, the volume of work to be done will permit use of advanced techniques, and individual performance units can be established according to the requirement of specialized knowledge and skills. This will provide optimum assignments of personnel and at the same time, by reason of grouping, greater flexibility in meeting work requirements of peak periods or needs caused by temporary absenteeism. It also allows for more effective supervision. For example, the volume of work in a centralized institutional admissions office justifies assignment of a supervisory officer of superior qualifications. It permits a layout of work in which specialists can be assigned to student records, correspondence, evaluation of transcripts, and decisions concerning admissions on the basis of consistent interpretation of the standards.

There are areas, however, where the controlling object requires organization on a different basis than that of like or related skills required for performance. Thus all instruction in a university may be divided into schools or colleges, each with a separate faculty. The reason for such grouping is that it provides a specialized environment for learning for a particular student group. The organization by faculties permits optimum interaction of student with student and student with faculty. Within the school or college the faculty is grouped in departments based on specialization in subject matter, or in divisions based on related subject matter. Under such organization, similar or related subject matter may be found in a number of separate schools or colleges. For example, the school of law will have a special interest in economics, as will education, business, engineering, and the graduate faculty. Other subjects, such as history, art, and statistics, may be taught in separate schools and colleges to serve their special needs. Such decentralization of teaching of similar or related subject matter in order to advance the achievement of purpose or objective of a particular school or college is brought about by decisions of management.

The work of the faculty and students of a school or college requires supporting services, most of which can, in cooperation with the school or college, be centrally directed to its net advantage, such as student personnel services, plant management and other business and financial services, and public information and fund-raising services.

While organization may successfully group work assignments that call for like or related knowledge and skills, there are instances where individual assignment of skilled personnel is required by the nature of the work. Thus an anthropologist may be assigned to work with professors in a school of education; a secretary may be assigned to work with an individual professor; or a porter may be assigned for a limited term to serve an activity under the direction of the officer in charge when need for such service cannot be specifically defined in advance. The keeping of records is an example of work calling for like or related skills that in the interest of performance can be centralized only to a limited degree. Student records are centralized, but the procedures in development, processing, and use differ markedly from those for financial records. Where records are directly related to performance they are wisely initiated and sometimes kept by the organization unit of which they are an integral part.

Where supporting services are centrally administered, the volume will justify a quality of supervision that cannot be provided in small decentralized units. The officer in charge can bring to bear a wealth of knowledge of service standards, procedures, and skills that an operation of lesser size would not justify. Concentration of library services in one organization to meet the complex needs of the institution is an example. The quality of accessions, cataloguing, lending, upkeep of reading materials and of audio-visual materials reflects the qualifications of the manager. The work is grouped on the basis of required skills. Even where specialized reading rooms are maintained for schools or departments, they operate best under centralized library management. This arrangement serves because a qualified library management is not divisible into small units, and centralized management will ensure the standards of service required at all locations. The library is brought to serve the purposes of the individual schools and departments through close cooperation with their staffs.

Another major service area that is organized on the basis of similar or related tasks to be performed is plant operation and maintenance. The utilities—heat, light, water, power, gas—are centrally controlled on the basis of fixed standards. But here, too, much of the service is decentralized. Some of this service, such as cleaning of rooms and public areas, can be performed on the basis of defined standards under supervision. But when individual offices are redecorated, the wishes of the occupants are desirably considered. In the services of plant operations and maintenance like skills are grouped, in so far as is practicable; for example, elevator operators, cleaners, porters, carpenters, painters, electricians. Such grouping permits the use of techniques designed for larger work loads, the fullest use of skills, and supervision by specialists. This centralization of supervision requires effective communication concerning assignments of the various rooms and the uses to which they are to be put. Where the services needed for a particular activity cannot be specified in advance, arrangements should be made for the assignment of personnel to meet the requirement. Sometimes geographic location, such as a campus on which the buildings are widely separated, so lengthens the lines of communication that services for certain buildings are administered under separate organization units. In such cases, both standards and assignments should be subject to centralized review.

A centralized financial office is organized on the basis of specialization. The officer in charge is a trained accountant. A central control of cash affords safety advantages and procedures not readily achieved through decentralization. Specialized skills in the collection of accounts, in recording, accounting, auditing, and reporting, require specialized supervision and direction, and improved techniques of record keeping are available for a volume of transactions that may not be justified at decentralized locations. Within this office, however, the skills are grouped—cashiers, accounts receivable clerks, bookkeepers, auditing clerks.

A centralized purchasing office and centralized stores serve the whole institution. This permits the application of standards to materials purchased and provides the skills necessary in securing advantageous prices and in storing and issuing materials. Within the organization, the skills are grouped—receiving clerks, stores clerks, order clerks, all under specialized supervision.

Food service is controlled by one manager, even though there may be a number of units of different types. The success of operation depends to a large degree on management—in food, labor, and cost control. In some institutions, food purchasing and processing are centralized, with food service decentralized to the several unit locations. In others, food purchasing may be centralized, with all other activities under the supervision of the local manager. But within the framework established, jobs are grouped and specialized supervision directs the work. Increasingly, institutions are contracting with firms to operate food services under general standards for services, costs, and prices fixed by the institution. Such an arrangement ensures continuity in management and over-all supervision by skilled, experienced personnel.

Residence halls, whether dormitories for men, women, or families, are centrally operated and controlled. A manager may be responsible to the chief student personnel officer or to the chief business and financial officer. In either case, these two officers must cooperate closely. The social, cultural, and educational objectives of operation must be defined, as well as the standards for furnishing and decorating and service. A local manager may be assigned to each unit. Utility services, structural repairs, and painting may be provided under the direction of the plant manager, or utilities may be supplied and all other needs for maintenance performed under contract. But within each unit, skills will be grouped. There will be specialists in room services, social directors, desk clerks, porters, and elevator operators, and each group will be under the direction of competent supervisors.

Supporting services need managers competent to direct and coordinate the work. The concern for standards of service must be constant. Failure to perform will ever be brought to attention by students and faculty. But to maintain services at standards above mediocrity requires dedicated management.

Principles Guiding the Choice of Techniques, Methods, and Procedures

It has been noted that the organization of work on the basis of like or related skills required for performance (so far as this is feasible) makes possible the optimum use of advanced techniques. Thus a centralized accounting system permits optimum use of machine methods. A centralized heating plant permits a high degree of automation in operation, and a centralized food service can economically use an automated dishwashing service. A centralized library assures economical use of teaching aids. New materials, equipment, and methods are constantly becoming available, and management must be alert to their use. Techniques are not necessarily related only to new products or new machines. There are better ways to design curricula, to arrange student programs, and to guide student life. There are better ways to improve the quality of teaching, to enlist faculty commitment to institutional purpose, and to promote faculty competence. There are better ways to relate research and field services to teaching and learning. There are better ways to answer the telephone, to improve the appearance of outgoing letters, to sweep, to dust, to clean.

The search for these better ways is a concern of personnel and of management. The choices have implications for man hours and for the physical facilities required, whether space or special equipment.

Vaizey observes that different trends in the prices of labor and capital have led to changes in educational techniques. He states:

Over the years the share of teachers' salaries in the total cost of education has declined; although the amount of teaching per child hour has increased substantially, the use of buildings, books, open space, ancillary labour, heat and light, specialist advisers and so on has increased proportionately faster. In general, therefore, the process of education has become *absolutely* more labour-intensive, but *relatively* less so.[1]

The choice of techniques to be used in teaching and research will ordinarily be made in agreement with the professional teacher or research worker who performs this service. In the supporting services, the responsibility will fall primarily on the second-line supervisor who may share it with his subordinates. Once made, the choice will be subject to the evaluation of the workers and the first-line supervisor, and to continuous review by senior executives in relation to new developments, to experiences in other institutions and in industry, and to evaluation as an essential service in institutional operations. The general management team—board, president, faculty, and major executives—is also interested in choices of techniques, methods, and procedures. Such choices have an important bearing on achievement and economy, as well as major implications for the plans. The management team will wish to receive informative reports for review and assessment.

CHOICE OF TECHNIQUES

There are certain considerations that guide the choice of techniques, methods, and procedures in operations:

1. The choice must take account of safety hazards and worker fatigue and morale.
2. It must take account of economy, including the use cost of capital assets involved (imputed annual value of interest, depreciation, and obsolescence), the drain on managerial attention, the wear and tear on existing resources, and the requirements for labor.

[1] John Vaizey, *The Economics of Education* (New York: The Free Press of Glencoe, Inc., 1962), p. 78.

3. It must meet the standards of performance, including (*a*) kind, quantity, and quality of service, (*b*) availability of the service at the right time, (*c*) least interference with other ongoing activities, (*d*) least detriment to physical facilities and employed personnel.
4. It must contribute to realization of institutional objectives at least equally as well as, and desirably to a greater extent than, any other available choice.

These considerations take on meaning when related to specific examples. Assume that the typewriters used are the manual type except for a few electrically operated machines assigned to offices of major executives. The electrically operated machines assure greater output, a better product, and less operator fatigue than the manual type. The proposal is made that where manual typewriters are employed on the average of four or more hours a day, electrically operated machines be used. Here the estimated annual additional equipment cost must be weighed against the advantages. It is possible that the complete use of electrically operated machines may afford a net cost advantage in addition to other recognized advantages.

The best time to paint the library reading room is not during the two weeks preceding examinations but between sessions, when interference with student and faculty use of the facility will be at a minimum.

An automatic telephone switchboard will save salaries of operators, but the annual use cost of the equipment and the effect on the quality of service must be weighed. This cost includes the imputed annual value of interest, depreciation, and obsolescence.

A proposal of a course that provides independent study for qualified students must be evaluated in terms of its educational merits, its cost to the institution in money and staff time and to the student in money and time.

As these examples indicate, new ways of doing necessary work should be constantly reviewed. In the decentralized management of the institution, the search for the best ways must be the responsibility of each major executive aided by his entire organization.

Principles Relating to the Definition, Procurement, and Care of Resources

When objectives are fixed, and the kind, quality, and quantity of work to be done are defined in the plans, the need for resources can be assessed. At the outset, however, the requirements for the work should be reviewed to assure that specified quantity and quality are fully adequate to the needs but not far beyond it. It is here that unnecessary expenditures can be avoided.

A curriculum that is characterized by a proliferation of courses represents an uneconomical use of teaching time. Class sizes that are very small may be both wasteful of teaching talent and educationally undesirable for students. Unused or little used physical facilities also represent waste because they must be operated and maintained regardless of use. Failure to provide the faculty with needed clerical service places an undue burden on them and wastes rare skills on tasks requiring lesser skills. Thus a review of projected institutional plans should seek to reduce the work load to be performed, and to secure economy of effort in performance.

STANDARDS OF PERFORMANCE

For most operations there are established standards of performance. These standards are based on practice, and represent norms on which first- and second-line supervisors can establish standards on local levels. These local standards will vary with the quality of work required, with the performance techniques adopted, and with the skills, health, and strength of the personnel. Executives should review constantly the appropriateness of the standards. Thus when standards for room service in a dormitory are set, the normal assignment per worker can be established. When painting standards and techniques are fixed, the normal performance expectation of output per painter can be determined. When courses and desirable limits for class sizes are established, a normal assignment per full-time teacher can be set, allowance being made for assignments to services other than teaching and for personal circumstances, such as health and strength. These performance standards should be used as guides only. At times the assignment norms for nonacademic personnel may exist only as background experience of the supervisor, but actual assignments should seek to secure for the institution the performance for which payment is made. Here is an area of management about which too little is known, and research is needed. There is an especially wide variation in the work loads assigned to teachers. Because the evidence of classroom hours assigned does not reveal the quality of teaching or class size, the reported practices of an institution cannot be accorded much weight in reaching judgment as to what constitutes a reasonable norm. Reliance must be placed on the judgment of the chief education officer and his staff and the faculty members involved. Yet every executive must be concerned with the rightness for the institution of the norms that are employed, and seek greater productivity, not by over-burdening personnel but by improving techniques.

PLANS FOR RESOURCES

On the basis of performance norms and techniques, it is possible to define in advance the requirements for personnel and facilities. These requirements must be defined in terms of jobs and the knowledge and skills needed for them. From such definition can be drawn the plans—both annual and long-range. These must cover the three aspects of institutional planning—programs, resources, and finance.

The plans for resources, including both personnel and material, have not received the recognition that is now required and will certainly be required in the future. Several factors call for more thoughtful attention to this phase of planning. First, there is keener competition for the services of qualified professional personnel at a time when turnover is rising. Second, the use of much more equipment in both teaching and nonteaching services is marked, and additions to plant are provided at more frequent intervals. There should be a long-range staffing plan for both professional and nonprofessional personnel, and a material resources plan—including plant extensions, new equipment, and replacement schedules for equipment in service. With such a staffing plan, the personnel resource is kept to strength through recruitment. Each worker recruited for an established position may serve the institution for years and hence through time will be paid many thousands of dollars. It is important, therefore, that great care be used in the selection process and that follow-up during the probation period justify retention.

In the plans for physical facilities are established the needs for supplies and equipment—their kind, quantity, and quality. Estimates are modified on the basis of performance experience. Most equipment, whether used for instruction and research or for supporting services, should provide several years' use. For each class of equipment there should be a policy of replacement, and inventories should be checked annually. The replacement policies afford a guide to annual requirements and cost. Obsolescence becomes more pronounced as new products vie with the old.

For example, the machines in use in the language laboratory must (generally) provide trouble-free operation. Systematic replacement of a certain number of machines a year may be found more justifiable than frequent machine repair, and the cost may not be appreciably greater. When new machines render the old obsolete, consideration should be given to accelerating the replacement program.

Both material and human resources employed by an institution must be maintained at the top level of usefulness.

CARE OF PHYSICAL FACILITIES

For physical resources there must be a program of preventive maintenance as well as systematic repair and replacement. Thus wooden floors will be sealed against deterioration. Typewriters will be kept clean and systematically replaced; library book collections, free of obsolete materials and in good repair; musical instruments, in tune and in good repair. Projection screens installed in classrooms will be regularly inspected and repaired or replaced as needed (where obsolescence is a major factor, as with types of audio-visual equipment, an annual rental may be found preferable to ownership). In particular, precautions against fire require systematic attention to hoses, motors, and fire doors. These examples serve to illustrate the need of the institution not only to acquire and maintain those physical resources useful to it but to keep them in fully operative condition.

CARE OF PERSONNEL

For the personnel resources, the policies that govern their services and relationships are of the highest importance. Ordinarily two groups are recognized: (1) the academic and professional group, which includes teaching staff, professional research workers, and administrative officers; and (2) the nonacademic group, consisting of building service workers, food service workers, residence halls workers, and clerical workers.

While the nonacademic personnel are similar to their counterparts in other kinds of endeavor, the academic personnel require wide latitude of independent action. Understanding of their attitudes, aspirations, motivations, and individualities is basic to constructive joint effort with management.

Mooney finds that there is often resentment and split between faculty and administration. He refers to this as a "psychological wedge."[2] Dodds describes faculty attitudes toward management in these words:

To many professors, the concept *administration* suggests regimentation; regimentation spells restriction on freedom; and the less there is of it the better . . . . The very terms "economy" and "efficiency" are apt to arouse faculty fear that its participation in decision-making will be diminished. This attitude should not be lightly dismissed. For it bears repeating that a certain incompatibility exists between organizational law and order and the play of individualism that produces an inspiring teacher or original scholar.[3]

Millett sees the scholars' professional endeavor

"inextricably bound up with the welfare of the community of which he is a part. . . . Yet often he senses little if any power in himself personally or in his immediate circle of colleagues to advance his professional status because the advancement of the material well-being of the college or university is beyond his range of activity.[4]

[2] Ross L. Mooney, "The Problem of Leadership in the University," *Harvard Educational Review,* Vol. 33, No. 1, p. 52, Winter 1963.

[3] Harold W. Dodds, *The Academic President—Educator or Caretaker?* (New York: McGraw-Hill Book Company, Inc., 1962), p. 69.

[4] John D. Millett, *The Academic Community: An Essay on Organization* (New York: McGraw-Hill Book Company, Inc., 1962), pp. 71–72.

The loyalty of the professor is often divided between his discipline and his institution. Dodds speaks of this in these words:

Since a university is a society of intellectuals and by definition intellectuals resist being organized, the loyalty of a professor is, to a greater degree than among businessmen, an ambivalent mingling of loyalty to the organization with an opposing loyalty—indeed an obligation—to himself and his profession to transcend, although he cannot ignore, the demands of team play.[5]

Corson observes this same characteristic. He says, "In effect, what has happened is that the average faculty member has become during the past 100 years oriented more to his discipline than to his institution."[6] Millett, too, observes this characteristic. He writes,

It is often said that faculty members have a major loyalty to their discipline or professional field of knowledge rather than to the College or University in which they practice their profession. To a considerable extent this observation is valid.[7]

The basic reason for such decided loyalty is identified by Caplow and McGee when they write:

In most large-scale organizations, the distribution of power conforms, more or less, to a ladder of rank and authority, and is supported by the formal assumption that rank and ability are closely correlated.

This kind of arrangement cannot be established in a university faculty because of the double system of ranking. Academic rank is conferred by the university, but disciplinary prestige is awarded by outsiders, and its attainment is not subject to the local institution's control.[8]

It is tenure which protects the individual freedom of the teacher, and the nature of this freedom must be understood and constructively supported. Ruml and Morrison describe this freedom. They state:

Once permanent tenure is granted, the teacher's relationship to the college community ordinarily is severed only when he reaches the established age of retirement. His behavior may be irresponsible, offensive, or even wrong as measured by the standards of a community of scholars; but unless he grossly offends the larger community, he is not likely to be disciplined by his faculty peers or by the President and Trustees. In short, individualism is not only condoned by the college community; it is encouraged and protected, because without it the institutional purpose cannot be fully accomplished. Short of gross offense, the re-

[5] Harold W. Dodds, *op. cit.,* p. 14.

[6] John J. Corson, *Governance of Colleges and Universities* (New York: McGraw-Hill Book Company, Inc., 1960), p. 27.

[7] John D. Millett, *op. cit.,* p. 70.

[8] Theodore Caplow and Reece J. McGee, *The Academic Marketplace* (New York: Basic Books, Inc., 1958), p. 206.

straints upon the individual teacher are chiefly those imposed by his own judgment, self-discipline and integrity.[9]

An institution of higher education can achieve a democratic climate only if it practices democracy. The dignity of the individual in his work must be recognized. The freedom of the teacher to teach and to search for the truth must be assured. The relationship of appointees and employees with officers of administration should be one of mutual respect. Each individual must understand what is expected of him and how he can progress in his work to the benefit of the institution.

Policies relating to recruitment, placement or assignment, probation, job evaluation, training, promotion, transfer, compensation, and individual growth and development are vital. Recruitment is a process of securing and evaluating candidates for a given position. The object is to select the person best qualified by education, experience, ability, and attitudes, keeping in mind the conditions under which the work is to be performed. Placement or assignment is the process of installing a person in a position; it involves not only an introduction to and full understanding of what work is to be performed, but also an introduction to conditions and personnel with which the new appointee or employee will be associated. Probation is an agreed-upon period in which the worker is tested and assessed, and if in this experience he fails to qualify, his service is discontinued without prejudice. Job evaluation is the process of judging the qualifications required to meet assigned responsibilities and work loads. Training seeks to promote job safety and job efficiency. These are all requirements of new workers. Every person also needs to know about policies for promotion and transfer from one job to another. All want compensation policies that recognize the value of their work and that are fairly administered. In addition, opportunities to broaden personal horizons, to learn and to achieve, are of interest to all. The manner in which executives and administrators exercise their responsibilities in this area is equally important.

In many institutions, a staff officer, generally made responsible to the president, exercises responsibilities for nonacademic personnel. He seeks the most effective policies and procedures to promote productivity and worker satisfaction. Personnel services for nonacademic employees may thus be centrally administered. A specialist in this area can open new channels for recruitment, can keep informed of workers' performance during probation, can set up training classes in job skills and other areas, and can see to it that there are lines of advancement. More than this, he can assist each employee in understanding the purposes of the institution and the employee's role, so that the significance of the work will be generally understood.

[9] Beardsley Ruml and Donald H. Morrison, *Memo to a College Trustee* (New York: McGraw-Hill Book Company, Inc., 1959), pp. 51–52.

For academic appointees, the dean exercises responsibility; for major executives, the president; and for administrative officers, the major executives in their areas. This placement of responsibility appears to be appropriate. Yet many deans have teaching as their primary background of experience and little or no training in personnel work. As a result they may spend too little of their time and effort on this phase of responsibility. It is likely that in the future more attention will be given to this requirement. When it is realized that an institution may pay out during his period of tenure a third to a half million dollars or more to a single professor, it is evident that the price an institution pays for lack of commitment or lack of well-directed effort on the part of just one professor can be too high. One may reason that faculty personnel can best chart their own course. But this requires a knowledge of the institution that they may not possess. If assistance is not offered them, they may fail to seek it. This attention to the search by the individual for personal growth and development, and assistance in forming his individual career design, is the responsibility of the dean. Despite the burdens the dean must assume, the exercise of responsibility for maintaining the faculty resource at a high level must come first. The dean's increasing responsibilities must not obscure his broad view of academic personnel nor nullify plans and services essential to individual faculty performance, satisfaction, and growth. Other burdens can be delegated to assistants. The president must see that the dean has adequate assistance in handling the pressing but more routine administrative matters in order that he may exercise leadership in matters concerning faculty personnel.

Principles Relating to the Application of Resources to the Performance of the Work

Within each area of operations major executives have the responsibility, through their organization team, of assigning personnel and facilities to achieve performance. In doing this, the timetable as well as the effects on other areas of operations must be considered so that needs will be met and maximum support, with the least temporary delay or upset to plans, will be given to achievement of over-all program goals.

PERSONNEL POLICIES

Clarence Frances, retired president of General Foods Corporation, once said,

You can buy a man's time, you can buy a man's physical presence at a given place, you can even buy a measured number of skilled muscular actions per hour or day. But you cannot buy enthusiasm, you cannot buy initiative, you cannot buy loyalty, you cannot buy the devotion of heart, mind and soul. You have to earn these things.[10]

"Our responsibility as managers," states Masterson, "is to motivate our employees to work at a pace clearly perceivable as more than adequate."[11]

The personnel policies of the institution may afford over-all standards for personnel, including qualifications, compensation, work load, and rating. In the assignment of each person to the work he is to perform, there is, however, the requirement that provision be made for his orientation to it, and sometimes for his training for it. For all personnel the following general policies in relation to their institutional service are suggested:

1. Each person (serving under institutional personnel policies) should be responsible to one and only one executive or supervisor. If a professor teaches in two separate departments or divisions, he should be assigned to the jurisdiction of one, and his assignment for service in the other may then be by mutual agreement.

2. Each person should have an assignment of work that promises to utilize his knowledge and skills. In making assignments, consideration should also be given to the habits and attitudes of the worker. A worker with interest in and enthusiasm for the work assigned will achieve more than one who is indifferent. Work requiring care and precision is best performed by a worker who practices care in his personal habits. Achievement in work that is a challenge to his capabilities will bring satisfaction to the worker. Assignments that require for performance a level of skills substantially below that possessed by the appointee or employee will tend to bring dissatisfaction.

3. Supervision should be based on leadership and respect. The supervisor should have close knowledge of worker qualifications and traits; knowledge of the performance, techniques, and skills required for the work; and awareness of the significance of the work to the institutional purpose.

   For nonacademic personnel such supervision makes clear to each worker what is expected of him. It will see to necessary orientation, job instruction, job safety, job relations, and worker rating. In this way there is motivation for better-than-average worker performance.

   Guidance of the work of faculty personnel and other academic officers is of a different order and is based on the appropriate relationship of academic appointees to their responsible officers. Yet here, despite the greater individual freedom of the faculty, the important need is to cultivate the

[10] Quoted from J. Roby Kidd, "Liberal Education for Business Leadership," in *Toward the Liberally Educated Executive,* Robert A. Goldwin, ed. (White Plains, N. Y.: The Fund for Adult Education, 1957), p. 76.

[11] Thomas Masterson, "Management Functions," *College and University Business,* 28:23, February 1960.

interest and capacity of the professional worker for his work, to arrange for appropriate assignments, to counsel as necessary on performance, and to recognize superior service through adjustments in compensation. Failure to recognize this need may result in less effective performance and in loss of satisfaction in position and service.

4. Each new appointee or employee should participate in a carefully planned program of orientation to his work. Experience has shown that time spent in such a program is a wise investment. Each person learns about the enterprise, his responsibilities in it, the privileges that are accorded, what management expects of him, what he may expect in return, and the conditions and working relationships of the work assigned.

5. Each person should receive fair pay for his work, inclusive of fringe benefits. In determining salaries and wages, management must consider the levels of salaries and wages for similar work outside the institution, the individual merits of the worker if merit scales are employed, and the pay levels of and among groups of workers.

6. Each person should receive the benefits of group security plans for which he may appropriately be asked to bear a share of the cost. Such plans safeguard the worker and his family against the financial burdens of ill health, disability, and death, and provide to the worker a reasonable retirement allowance.

7. Each person should have opportunities for self-development and growth, including job knowledge and skills in relation to present performance and possible promotion, as well as such general and cultural education as may enhance his self-realization, his work efficiency, his human relationships, and his exercise of citizenship. This does not mean that all things are to be taught to all people, but rather that an institutional policy of encouraging worker capacity and effectiveness will assist in performance and in promoting worker satisfaction.

8. Each person should have work assignments and conditions as free as possible of safety hazards, both through physical safeguards and through training in safe practices.

9. Each person should have the opportunity and encouragement for making constructive suggestions concerning the work—whether conditions, techniques, work load, or other related aspects. Such suggestions will normally be made through the first-line supervisor or administrative officer.

USE OF FACILITIES

There are two important guides applicable to the use of facilities:

1. Materials, supplies, and equipment should be available as needed. This means that requirements must be foreseen, and that where the timing of use is not readily predictable, a store may be essential.

2. Materials, supplies, and equipment should be of the kind, quantity, and quality that best serve the work to be performed. The kind and quantity

are generally understood. The quality requires the judgment of responsible officers, based on the knowledge and experience of the users. The quality should amply serve the need, but standards much in excess of need will waste funds. Examples of supplies that may at times meet specifications of quality beyond those required—and at a higher cost—are fuel oil, mimeograph paper, and canned food.

The Exercise of the Operative Function of Management

Serving in the complex matrix of institutional operations, under a management philosophy of decentralization responsible for performance of areas of specialized services, the common essentials of management may at the outset appear elusive. And it must be recognized that individual differences of those who manage, whether in knowledge, skills, habits, attitudes, or other personal characteristics, add to the challenge of identification of such essentials. Yet the president, each of his major executives, and each of the senior executives upon whom they rely, must each in his own way carry out assigned responsibilities that are similar. For their areas of responsibility they are each concerned with programs, finance, and the resources of personnel and material.

QUALIFICATIONS AND RESPONSIBILITIES OF MANAGERS

As noted before, under the institutional decentralized management plan each executive must be a generalist. The industrial world has found that the best generalist in management is one who has had previous experience as a specialist, preferably in one of the areas for which he becomes responsible. This characteristic as a requirement for management is an imperative for major executives, less imperative but highly desirable for senior executives, and a desirable qualification, in addition to specialized supervisory skills, for first-line supervisors.

Every manager should be dedicated to his work. He should understand the significance both of the institutional service and of his contribution to it. If managers lack this enthusiasm and understanding, it cannot be expected that desirable worker attitudes will be found within their areas.

Every manager should, according to his ability, contribute to the formulation of institutional objectives, philosophies, programs, and plans. Such participation will promote his identification with institutional purposes.

Every manager has the responsibility of building an organization consistent with his delegation of responsibility and authority. Such delegation will include responsibility for planning, operation, and evaluation.

Every manager has the responsibility of establishing channels of communication—both vertical and lateral—and of encouraging appropriate contact channels. Through channels he must continuously interpret throughout his organization institutional objectives, philosophies, plans, and programs as a basis for improving services performed. His superior should at all times be informed of progress under the plans—both operational and financial.

Every manager has responsibility for securing the performance of essential services through coordinated effective supervision of qualified workers. Such services are to be performed satisfactorily and on time, as envisioned in the plans.

Every manager has responsibility for personnel. Although guided by established policies, this is essentially a leadership responsibility. The procedures should assure that care and judgment are used in recruitment, selection, placement and assignment, training, rating, and compensation. But beyond this, interest in the personal development of workers, supervisors, and subordinate managers will make the difference between a possible average performance and an achieved superior one.

Every manager is responsible for records and reports. Care must be exercised to see that records are kept in useful form and that unnecessary records are dispensed with. The methods of record keeping and record processing, as well as retention schedules, should be carefully determined. Ready access at the point of use should be provided. Records at base afford historical information concerning persons, things, and activities. Analyses of records through appropriate processing afford views of resources or activities that can serve to guide managerial decisions. Such information is presented in reports. These reports generally present the historical evidence and may evaluate and/or assess implications of the findings for the future.

The institution has a heavy investment, and a high current cost, in the records that are kept. Among these are faculty records, student records, financial records, alumni records, nonacademic personnel records. It is undoubtedly true that in many institutions records and/or reports of academic personnel, plant and plant utilization, and the academic program are inadequate for decision making. They therefore are not serving their full purpose. Decisions require the information the records can provide, and failure to make full use of them is to substitute vague impressions and guesses for accessible facts. The use value of records and reports in relation to their cost is a continuing responsibility of every manager for all activities under his supervision.

Every manager must exercise responsibility for continuing evaluation of all aspects of plans, organization, resources, and performance. This responsibility is discussed in the following chapter. A manager who would learn by experience must be in a position to evaluate the experiences of his organization. This evaluation will identify the mistakes and confirm the elements of success. The manager must not only assess himself as a person and as a leader; he must also assess his methods of delegation and organization; the quality of his personnel in relation to the requirements; the decisions fixing the aggregate work load; the organization of the work; the methods, procedures, and performance; the treatment of personnel and facilities; the commitments to institutional purpose. In short, he must know his strengths and weaknesses and in the process permit assessment by his superiors.

Every manager, in addition to coordination of effort within his organization, must effectively coordinate such activities with other ongoing institutional operations to the end that performance will contribute most and will harm least.

Every manager should set aside some time each day to think, to plan, and to view his activity in the perspective of total institutional operations. Only then will he perceive ways of rendering more useful service that will equal or exceed its cost.

CHAPTER 7

The Evaluative Function
of Management

The decisions that guide American higher education are made in the present, are based on experiences of the past, and seek to meet the needs of society anticipated for the future. These decisions may be grouped according to five interrelated areas of concern: (1) the institutional objectives, (2) the educational philosophies chosen to achieve the objectives and basic to definitive educational programs, (3) defined services consistent with the philosophies—kind, quantity, and quality of instruction, research, and field services, (4) the processes employed in the services—the techniques used and proportion of productive services employed for each unit of achievement, and (5) the means used—the requirements and standards (kind, quantity, and quality) of management, personnel, and physical facilities.

Every institution operates under choices and decisions made in all these areas, and it is only through continuous evaluation with respect to each phase of operations that programs are adapted to changing social needs, and the economics of operations are brought to maximize service within the limits of available income.

The Nature of Evaluation

Evaluation is the process of securing value judgments essential to the improvement of the services of the institution. These judgments may be based on objective evidence, on experience, on subjective judgment, or on any combination of the three. Such judgments seek to assess the suitability or desirability of an activity or resource in relation both to institutional purpose and to cost. There can be no rational improvement in institutional services without the exercise of value judgments concerning all aspects of operations. Indeed, every act of management reflects such judgments. The concern is to provide more adequate bases for them and hence increase their reliability.

The criteria for value judgments, and the methods and procedures used in securing them, vary with the kind and purpose of the activity or resources. Thus the evaluation of student health services, or of faculty morale, or of a color scheme for an auditorium will require different criteria, procedures, and personnel. Probably the most widely practiced form of value judgment is the evaluation of student academic performance. Here the standards are fixed by the faculty, and achievement is often measured by periodic examinations. Yet here there are changing practices, such as raising standards of achievement, employing different measures of performance, or broadening the scope of evaluation to include other aspects of student development such as habits, attitudes, and social behavior.

Indeed, the rapidity of social and technological change may require ranking student ability in *how* to learn with achievement in learning. Thus criteria, methods, and procedures relating to evaluation may be expected to change as social conditions change, as techniques change, and as educational standards rise with the growth of knowledge and change in response to social needs.

Corson states:

The problem for decision making lies in the difficulty of evaluating the contribution to product of the various factors of production, of which the faculty is one, and of evaluating the particular individual in terms of the effectiveness of his contribution.[1]

More important, there is less acceptance of the need for regular reappraisal either of the educational product or of teaching. Faculty members, like counterparts in industry and government, manifest a resistance to change—in courses, curricula, programs, and teaching methods. Innovation, that fragile but vital force for progress in any human enterprise, finds tough going in the typical university.[2]

There is evidence, however, that scholars are seriously at work attempting to identify and improve appropriate methods of evaluation.[3]

[1] John J. Corson, *Governance of Colleges and Universities* (New York: McGraw-Hill Book Company, Inc., 1960), p. 23.

[2] *Ibid.,* p. 137.

[3] For example, see Paul L. Dressel and Associates, *Evaluation in Higher Education* (Boston: Houghton Mifflin Company, 1961); and John E. Stecklein, *How to Measure Faculty Work Load* (Washington, D.C.: The American Council on Education, 1962).

The Need for Evaluation Is Pervasive and Continuous

When an agency seeks to appraise the merits of an institution, the information it needs is often not readily available, and the academic program as a logical expression of stated objectives may be difficult to explain. Yet it seems reasonable that those entrusted with management should have at all times basic information easily accessible, and should have thought deeply about the affairs of the institution. Because planning and operations are continuous functions, it follows that the process of evaluation must also be a continuous function, indigenous to all aspects of institutional life. The quality and comprehensiveness of institutional evaluation that is carried forward continuously by management should far outweigh what could possibly be achieved by periodic appraisals within or outside the institution.

The eliciting or developing of value judgments on institutional objectives, philosophies, programs, and resources is a continuous responsibility of management. This does not mean that all aspects should come under review every day, but rather that such review should be provided at such times and in such ways as are deemed useful. For some activities, the procedure will be daily (food costs in the cafeteria); for some it may be monthly or quarterly (assessment of income and expenditures in relation to estimates); for some it will be at the close of each academic session (student examinations); for others it may be annual (the performance of indoor painting in relation to the long-range plan); for still others it may be periodic, say, every three years (assessment of program course sequences in areas of specialization). The requirement is that all aspects of institutional life be brought under appropriate review systematically. This is not a responsibility that can be left to the sole judgment of one individual. When a decision is made to appropriate funds to a particular activity or resource, the action is based on a judgment that this activity or resource will contribute most to the furtherance of institutional objectives. What can later be said of this use of funds? Had the activity or resource in fact so contributed? If it was essential at the time, does it continue to be? The answers to such questions can, through elimination of wasteful practices, conserve resources and funds to the advancement of the institutional purposes.

Evaluation in management in higher education is a widespread practice. Often, however, it is sporadic, fragmented, and limited to the use and purposes of managers on the local level. Local managers are not likely to have as full an understanding of institutional purposes as faculty, executives, and board. Hence their criteria and procedures for evaluation may be, to some degree, inappropriate. So long as evaluation is held in isolation at the local level, those primarily responsible for management lack the information essential to the effective discharge of their responsibilities.

There are certain requirements for an appropriate evaluation practice: (1) recognition by the governing board of its basic value to both plans and performance; (2) policies providing for a continuous comprehensive evaluating system with delegated responsibility for performance; (3) coordination of evaluation procedures by the president with the advice of the committee on policy, program, and finance; (4) systematic utilization of results in both plans and operations; and (5) wide understanding and participation of institutional personnel in the program.

Evaluation is measurement by criteria formed of identified knowledge and experience that permit wise choices in institutional affairs with respect to the six major concerns: objectives, philosophy, services, techniques, resources, and cost. Wisely nurtured, such measurement will favorably affect the plans and practices, the personnel, and the facilities of the institution. Lacking appreciation and official recognition of its usefulness by management it will receive uncoordinated, infrequent attention. The net result is almost certain to be drift, characterized by less effective and more costly operations.

In the evaluative process, experience has, by and large, centered on value judgments relating to the quality of activities and resources. Less attention has been given to cost, partly because in the past the disparity between the level of support and the demand for services has been less acute, partly because reliable techniques of cost analyses have been lacking, and partly because their values and uses have not been understood.

Harris, in a recent sampling of 115 private and 43 public institutions found that 38 per cent of the private and 56 per cent of the public institutions have made serious cost studies. Generally the larger institutions were more disposed to make such studies than were the smaller ones.[4]

It has been stressed throughout this work that policy, program, and finance are inseparable elements of management. Woodburne emphasizes these relationships.[5]

Coombs has characterized higher education as an increasing-cost industry; such increase he attributes to (1) the increases in services performed —the curriculum has been broadened and deepened, and many student services such as guidance, recreation, and health care have been added, (2) higher education is a high labor user, and salaries and wages have risen, and (3) "relatively few cost-reducing innovations and improved technologies have been introduced. . . . On the contrary, there has tended to be an

[4] Seymour E. Harris, *Higher Education: Resources and Finance* (New York: McGraw-Hill Book Company, Inc., 1962), pp. 501–502.

[5] Lloyd S. Woodburne, *Principles of College and University Administration* (Stanford, Calif.: Stanford University Press, 1958), pp. 40–43.

accumulation of 'built-in inefficiencies,' such as practices which result in low utilization of space, and low production of faculty."[6]

Vaizey sees the possibility of stopping the continuous relative rise in the cost of education through more effective utilization of teaching skills.[7]

Some decisive cost factors, identified by Harris, include

size of classes, teaching load, relative numbers in lower, higher, and graduate divisions, level of salaries and structure of pay and size of the unit. . . . Note lower division, upper division, and graduate costs per unit are roughly $1 = 2 = 6$."[8]

Serious attention to cost through the use of well-developed techniques of cost analyses, and through improved records descriptive of the use of resources is growing.[9] Dodds, speaking to this point, says, "Nevertheless, if present signs hold, the time may not be far distant when many legislatures will demand that comparative cost analyses be made available to buttress requests for appropriations."[10]

It is vital that knowledge of cost be available to guide decisions. This knowledge is not to be restricted to the financial office, but must be brought to the understanding of all who participate in the decision-making process, and, in more general terms, of those affected by the decisions.

The Scope of the Evaluative Program Should Be Broad

Any identification of areas of evaluation can be only suggestive. The list that follows will be useful as a basis for outlining in more detail the needs of an individual institution.

SUGGESTED INSTITUTIONAL AREAS FOR EVALUATION

1. Implications of social and technological changes for institutional objectives and programs.
2. Performance of graduates in relation to institutional program— educational, social, cultural.
3. Exercise of responsibility by the board of control—board personnel, pro-

[6] Philip H. Coombs, "An Economist's Overview of Higher Education," in *Financing Higher Education, 1960–70*, Dexter M. Keezer, ed. (New York: McGraw-Hill Book Company, Inc., 1959), p. 25.

[7] John Vaizey, *The Economics of Education* (New York: The Free Press of Glencoe, Inc., 1962), pp. 85–86.

[8] Seymour E. Harris, *op. cit.*, p. xxxiv.

[9] See, for example, references to cost and statistical studies listed in Chap. 1, p. 22.

[10] Harold W. Dodds, *The Academic President—Educator or Caretaker?* (New York: McGraw-Hill Book Company, Inc., 1962), p. 174.

cedures, policies, plans, legislation, public relations, institutional participation and cooperation.

4. Exercise of responsibility by president, faculty, and administration in planning, operation, and evaluation.

5. Instructional programs—philosophy, general and specialized courses, areas of specialization, course sequences; relation to research and field services.

6. Research and field service programs—philosophy, criteria for programs, quality and quantity; relation to instruction and to practical use.

7. Instruction—quality of teaching, teaching assignments, class size, student achievement, attitudes, and motivation.[11]

8. Library service—suitability, adequacy in relation to areas of specialization.

9. Student personnel services—admissions, student records, placement, student organizations, financial aids, student unions, recreational programs, residential programs, social programs, health services, chapel, nonacademic counseling, communications, student government.

10. Financial management—financial conditions, procedures, safeguards, policies, including those related to investments and student loans, accounting, reporting, auditing, cost analysis, economics of operations.

11. Purchases management—policies, practices, procedures for purchasing, storing, reclamation, and selling.

12. Dormitories operations, dining halls operations, bookstore operations—suitability and quality of service.

13. Plant management—utilities, operations, maintenance; and standards, procedures, supervision, cost.

14. Personnel—faculty, executive, nonacademic—qualifications, suitability in relation to standards.

15. Physical facilities—academic plant, kind and condition, suitability and utilization, account to be taken of spatial and structural provisions, student stations, office occupancy standards, lighting, heating, ventilating, cooling, floors, furniture and equipment, color.

16. Students as individuals in the environment, their attitudes, interests, experiences, growth, difficulties.

17. Academic staff as individuals in the environment.

18. Nonacademic staff as individuals in the environment.

[11] "The concept of motivation," writes Saupe, "relates to the *problem* aspect of the learning process. The recognition and acceptance of a problem or goal implies that the learner desires to solves the problem or attain the goal. The extent or depth of his desire determines his motivation . . . . The general principle is that *students learn only what they want or are motivated to learn.*" (Joe L. Saupe, "Learning and Evaluation Processes," in *Evaluation in Higher Education,* Paul L. Dressel and Associates, eds. (Boston: Houghton Mifflin Company, 1961), p. 59).

19. Personnel policies and practices—selection, placement, training, advancement, compensation, personal development, evaluation or rating, tenure.

20. Plans and planning procedures, performance and performance procedures, evaluation and evaluation procedures.

21. The institutional records system.

22. Public relations and fund procurement.

As this list shows, the evaluative program must be broadly based. Each area is capable of analysis, and such analyses should be carried to the point where anticipated value does not markedly exceed the time and trouble involved in making them.

The Responsibility for Evaluation Should Be Defined

As with other institutional activities, the basic responsibility for an institution-wide program of evaluation is that of the governing board, a responsibility it must delegate to the president. The board must retain direct responsibility for evaluating its own effectiveness and the effectiveness of its chief executive, the president. Beyond this, it will have a deep interest in the kind and quality of education the institution provides, in the kind and quality of institutional personnel, economics, physical facilities, and finance.

The president may delegate much responsibility for the administration of the evaluation process to his major executives. It will be desirable, however, to secure from each area executive an outline of the procedures to be used for review by the committee on policy, program, and finance, with a view to strengthening the procedure and improving the reliability of the conclusions. In this way needed coordination can be identified and interarea cooperation provided for.

The delegation of responsibility for evaluation may call for an organization that differs from the requirements for planning and operation. Usually institutional personnel, including students, will be involved in evaluative procedures but occasional consultants will be found useful.

The evaluation of endowment and other investment policies is a direct responsibility of the board, and ordinarily will not involve the faculty. But it will be desirable for the faculty and executives to be informed and to have an opportunity to express such opinions as they may care to give.

The evaluation of the quality of food service in a student dining room may call for something more than opinions of student patrons. Evidence on variety, nutrition, taste, and service may need to be judged by an experienced specialist.

In an undergraduate liberal arts college, the program of an area of specialization may serve a dual purpose—a survey of the subject field as a contribution to the education of students who major in other subjects, and as scholarly work preparatory for graduate work. To ascertain how well it has served its first purpose, the opinions of faculty members from other departments (or in some instances from other institutions) may be sought; to ascertain how well it has served its second purpose, opinions may be sought from professors of graduate schools in which graduates of the liberal arts college have enrolled and from professors in other graduate schools of high standards. But in such cases, the interest is not alone the graduates' later achievement in the graduate school, but also whether a change in the program would be desirable.

In evaluation use may be made of lay councils to advise board, faculty, and executives concerning social and technological changes, and their implications for institutional objectives, philosophies, and programs. Use may be made of outside consultants and of competent observers in one area to assist in the evaluation of activities or resources in another. While within the institution the basic area organization will be central, and each person in the organization will be responsible to one and only one administrator, the needs of evaluation will demand much attention to interarea services and to common effort in coordination. Moreover, the implications of evaluation of activities and resources in one area for those in another and for the institution as a whole must be shared.

The organization for evaluation is seen as starting with the organization for operations, and then being modified by interarea arrangements and by use of off-campus resources. The coordination of evaluation programs can be achieved by the president with the aid of the committee on policy, program, and finance. In the board it has been proposed that a standing committee give attention to objectives, plans, and evaluation. Evaluation is there related to objectives and plans in order to afford maximum justification for the value judgments required, and at the same time emphasize for the entire personnel of the institution the importance of evaluation as one of the basic functions of management.

Thus while the organization to achieve evaluation may involve many elements common to organization useful in performing the functions of planning and operations, each evaluation requirement must be served by appropriate resources of personnel, and supplementary organizational arrangements must be supplied as needed.

The Methods and Procedures of Evaluation
Should Be Determined

The methods and procedures used in each aspect of evaluation should have the general acceptance of those responsible for plans and operations—

the board, the faculty, the president, and his executives. The judgment of the executive in charge of an area concerning the methods and procedures for evaluation to be used in his area should be reviewed and modified as needed by the president and the committee on policy, program, and finance. Such review will assure more ready acceptance of the findings by those concerned, and will protect the executive from possible criticism of procedures employed. A schedule of systematic procedures is needed so that as often as is desirable appropriate attention can be given to the exercise of value judgments of any activity or resource.

The development of an effective system of evaluation within an institution is a major undertaking. Each item of evaluation calls for unique attention. If the concern is public relations, the relations of faculty to students and to the public, the manner in which telephones are answered, letters written, building service workers perform public services, and other pertinent procedures must be assessed. The most economical ways to make valid assessments and the frequency necessary must be determined. The great diversity of institutional activities calls for equally diverse methods and procedures of evaluation in each area.

Also, the necessary and desirable decentralization of the responsibilities of management adds to the difficulty of the coordination of evaluation.

Only when evaluation is seen as a major function of management, fully equal to its partners of delegation, direction, and performance, can the dimensions of its requirements be understood. An effective program will have taken years to develop, is at best incomplete, is ever under study to improve it, and is ever a primary concern of the board, the faculty, and the administration. It is not enough to seek the most desirable activity program. Equal attention must be given to cost and to the relative values of activity programs that compete for a share of income to finance them.

This quest for balance between value and cost in institutional achievement is the very essence of the management process. Also, the choice of activity based on value judgments rather than expediency or imitation is the mark of a good executive.

Some common characteristics of evaluation procedures deemed appropriate are summarized below:

1. Clear conception of the function to be served by the activity or use of resource.
2. Identification by competent persons of characteristics or qualities of the activity or resource essential to the performance of function.
3. Tests and measures—objective and/or subjective—devised by competent persons relative to such characteristics and qualities.
4. The fixing of time schedules for frequency and scope of evaluation.

5. Value judgments by competent persons with respect to the activity under review in its functional role in relation to possible alternates and cost, or with respect to the suitability and cost of resources employed both in relation to use and to alternate available choices of such resources.

6. Review and acceptance by responsible managers.

This summary applies both to activity programs and to management, personnel, and physical facilities. All resources—management, personnel, and physical facilities—are subject to variation in functional value. The functional value depends in part on the innate quality of the resource, and in part on how effectively it contributes to performance. What the maintenance programs are to physical facilities, the personnel programs and the exercise of leadership are to personnel.

The institutional plans that direct operations indicate the functions to be served by the activities and the use of resources. The persons competent to conduct or guide evaluation procedures and to exercise judgments will vary from activity to activity. It has been the practice for subject-matter teachers to evaluate student achievement. But questions have been raised concerning the nature and adequacy of examinations. Other instruments are called for. In addition to intellectual achievement, more attention is being directed to personal development—goals, motivations, habits and attitudes, social and cultural experiences. The search for evidence may extend beyond the campus. The qualities attained by graduates, say, five years after graduation, may have meaning for program. The views of lay council members on present and future requirements for competence in various occupations are relevant.

The entire student and staff personnel may evaluate the cafeteria and indicate the direction of needed change, but the evaluation of operations to effect change requires a competence based on specialized knowledge and experience. The entire community responds to and is affected by the color scheme used in the library, but devising a scheme that will contribute most to effective use also requires specialized knowledge and experience. Faculty and students can readily judge the quality and suitability of the library and the library services for their needs, but the choices that must be made can best be guided by those qualified to do so. Thus, in broad terms, the users of services should have an opportunity to express themselves, but the major reliance for change rests on the competency of specialists.

The frequency of evaluation may appropriately vary. Use in relation to cost is the criterion. An institution that chooses to seek review of its curricular offerings through the employment of authorities from other institutions may find the greatest value in periodic review, say at five-year intervals. But the financial audit is never less frequent than annual, and is more frequent in some institutions. For major repairs and alterations, evaluation of the work performed is made concurrently with its performance and never later than its conclusion.

Evaluations must be planned for and authorized, reviewed, and accepted by the management responsible. It is desirable for both the schedule and the methods to have approval of the president and concurrence of his committee on policy, program, and finance. Such approval in advance will secure more ready acceptance of the findings.

The Uses of Evaluation

Evaluation is useful both in planning and in performance. It justifies the plans for the program and for the resources. Appropriately used, it will ensure for the institution its most useful role in society; it will assure the use of an appropriate educational philosophy; it will maximize the usefulness of the program; it will achieve desirable economy; it will obtain for the program the essential resources and apply them by means of effective techniques.

Under a system of decentralized management, evaluation can be expected to be most widely used at the focal point of activities—the department or organization unit. It will be less widely used and understood by major executives, and perhaps least used and understood by the board. This situation exists because first- and second-line supervisors need and use evaluation in relation to the planning and performance of the work for which they are responsible. Major executives, however, have not generally stressed the importance of evaluation in management, and hence have not sought reports on either evaluation schedules, procedures, or results. The board in turn may receive from the president and major executives periodic evaluative reports, but these represent general impressions and spot evidence rather than a form of systematic appraisal. This lack does not permit the board to identify the strengths or weaknesses in specific aspects of programs or resources.

A focus of attention on a comprehensive plan of evaluation would strengthen local programs, provide evidence useful to major executives, and assist the board in meeting its responsibilities. While the records relating to evaluation may often be appropriately maintained by the local organization unit, what was done, how it was done, and what results were obtained should be made available to executives and, to the extent desired, to the board.

Evaluation is one of the major bases of decisions that are made in operating and in planning. It is knowledge of successful activities, and the ways of conducting them. Knowledge of better ways of performing is thus introduced into operations and projected in the plans. Evaluation will assist in limiting the total work load to that which is essential; it will assist in identifying effective and economical techniques; and it will focus attention on the quality and cost of performance. It is basic to assurance of wise expenditure of available income.

The very existence of the institution implies a wide exercise of value judgments. There is day-by-day evaluation in all phases of operations. It is seen in the choice of teachers, in the program offerings, in the catalogued books, and in the nature of building services. But often the value judgments are based on limited evidence, lack system, and are uncoordinated. In the institution in which evaluation is not recognized as a major function of management, the systematic use of what is known by decentralized management cannot adequately be reflected in the plans of top management.

In the institution that consciously recognizes the importance of a built-in system of evaluation, its personnel are made aware of what serves well and what is inappropriate. Agreed-upon foci, methods, and procedures for each subject, and systematic reporting will provide evidence that will serve to guide future activity. It will enable the president to keep the board informed of the quality of institutional effort. In this way institutional needs can be identified and given appropriate attention.

Attitudes of Institutional Personnel Toward Evaluation

Evaluation in the college or university meets with many difficulties. Important among these is finding acceptable procedures relating to professional services—teachers, research workers, and administrators. Yet these services are primary to achieving the very purposes of the institution. Together they aggregate between 40 and 50 per cent of current educational and general expenditures, and are in themselves the primary justification for the supporting services that account for the remainder of the educational services and expenditures. Both current operations and plans for the future are based on the premise—supported by such evidence as can be secured—that these professional services are altogether desirable. But reliable evidence on how the all-important group—the faculty—is achieving its assignments is difficult to secure. Whether as a group they wholeheartedly support the institutional purpose; whether morale is high; whether professional achievements are highly motivated; whether they are devoted to teaching and are faithful in conducting classes and office hours; whether they carry reasonable teaching loads, with desirable class size—all this is important to know, and not alone for a group, but for individuals, for it is here that remedial action can begin. Were this information available, it would be relevant both to the performance of operations and to the over-all plans.

There are many aspects of professional services of teaching that can be objectively observed, such as teaching assignments, institutional services, and class sizes. But the achievements of a teacher are difficult to measure. One teacher may have great skill in guiding many students into a field of knowledge; another may possess qualifications that cause him to be sought as a counselor; one may be a scholar in depth; another may be a generalist useful in relating fields of knowledge. Each as a person possesses certain traits that are deemed essential to the enterprise.

The scholar in his field, dedicated to the education of youth, free to teach, is rightly concerned lest his achievements be rated on some inappropriate scale of values by persons inadequate in conception of purpose, knowledge, or skill. Evaluation in this form would doubtless curtail the very freedom so hard won, for the talented and gifted teachers might not be selected for promotion or reward.

The administrator, unlike the teacher, does not have tenure. He may have impressive academic qualifications and be dedicated to his profession, but if he proves inept or fails to develop rapport with a new president, he may be asked to resign. In his day-by-day actions, aware of the values to be achieved and guarded, of the necessity of choice that will please some and displease others in his community, the administrator must rely on his judgment, his integrity, and his good will. Unlike the teacher, his actions are fully open to evaluation by all members of the community. If he does not have the confidence and full support of the president, there is danger that he may come to favor actions that please associates rather than actions that promote achievement of institutional purpose.

The evaluation of professional services is of key importance, hence inherent difficulties must be surmounted. The first requisite is achievement of a climate of mutual trust between faculty, administrators, and board. This can be done by cultivating understanding among those concerned and by establishing and maintaining channels of communication.

The first step is to develop principles and procedures of evaluation that will be understood and accepted by those concerned. The bases for evaluation are bound to be to some extent unique in each institution, but suggestions deemed appropriate are summarized below:

1. Evaluation of teachers in the selective process and during the period of probation will be rigorous.

2. Once a teacher has passed the probationary period and achieves tenure, he will be presumed to be a competent teacher. Visitation of classes by colleagues will be with the approval of the teacher and will not be related to evaluation.

3. Evaluation of teachers on tenure will be limited to the manner in which they fulfill their assignment responsibilities.

4. Assignments to service will be consistent with established policies. Teachers will be responsible for carrying out the requirements of such assignments in an appropriate manner.

It is considered that these bases for evaluation of teachers will in no way infringe on their freedom. A teacher may be expected to fulfill faithfully his assignment responsibilities. If he does not meet classes, if he does not keep office hours for students, or if he displays attitudes inappropriate to his role, these evidences should be noted and considered in relation to other evidences of achievement in scholarship and leadership that are available.

For the new teacher great care must be exercised in his selection, orientation training, and evaluation as a teacher. When it is realized that in each teacher placed on tenure an institution may invest as much as a third to a half million dollars, the importance of this precaution becomes clear. The procedures can best be devised with the aid of faculty representatives. The ability of the prospective teacher to teach should be known before selection. Class visitation during the period of probation should add to this knowledge and at the same time be helpful to the new teacher. By the close of the probationary period the new teacher should possess strong identity with institutional purposes, be well adjusted as a teacher, and his worth as a teacher be recognized by reason of the senior staff's direct acquaintance with his teaching.

The evaluation of major executives can best be the sole responsibility of the president. Each is his appointee; each has day-by-day contact with him; each has been guided by him. The president knows their strengths and weaknesses; he knows better than anyone the difficulties they face and their competence to surmount them. His wide association with faculty, trustees, and the public will inevitably bring to him many opinions—favorable and unfavorable.

For personnel as important to the institution as the teaching staff and administrators, adequate records should be kept, partly because memories are inadequate and partly because those responsible change positions from time to time.

Evaluation of all personnel and their services is best achieved in an atmosphere of mutual trust and confidence. And this atmosphere is developed on the basis of full knowledge of institutional purposes and procedures, in the formulation of which those being evaluated will have aided.

Cost of an Evaluation Program

The cost of conducting a coordinated, comprehensive, and continuous evaluation program is already being borne by most institutions. This is to say that evaluation procedures are in wide use, and the personnel to extend and improve them are already employed. What is often lacking, however, is institutional recognition of the value of the function, a systematic review of both procedures and findings, and the training of personnel. Under such a program major executives, the president, and the board can measure improvement, can readily identify problem areas, can focus adequate attention on them.

As stated above, the major cost of an evaluation program is already being borne by the institution; but its benefits in the exercise of management are largely lacking. The additional cost involved in improving and coordinating the program is seen as small, even when it includes the cost of reports and expenses of outside consultation if these are employed. Such a program of evaluation will afford management the greatest possible assurance concerning the quality of programs and the use of resources. The economies that will be achieved will far outweigh the additional cost incurred. The primary gain in continuous testing of all areas is that the results afford reliable guides to optimum institutional advancement.

Examples of Evaluation Programs

As noted earlier, evaluation consists of value judgments regarding institutional objectives, philosophy, plans, services, techniques, management, personnel, and facilities, in relation to an approved norm or standard. Because of the judgments required, the procedures are varied.

When an institution seeks to extend and improve its procedures and uses of evaluation, it faces a complex undertaking that requires continuous effort. A good evaluation system takes years to build and use effectively. But it is basic to good management.

A major program of evaluation found on every campus is the evaluation of student academic achievement. This program represents the exercise of delegated responsibility by the governing board. The minimal scope, frequency, and criteria are "fixed by the faculty, and conducted by the individual teacher as he deems best."[12] Such evaluation is indeed of central importance inasmuch as it concerns the product which the institution turns out. But, as indicated above, there is need for much more. There is need to evaluate the quality of the program itself, the whole range of student services from chapel to social life, to residential facilities. There is need to evaluate business affairs and other supporting services. There is need to evaluate public relations and the fund-raising effort. And there is need to evaluate both personnel and facilities. A manual based on research of

[12] See Paul Dressel and Associates, *Evaluation in Higher Education* (Boston: Houghton Mifflin Company, 1961), for an excellent treatment of this subject.

tested procedures relating to every one of these areas and their elements would assist an institution in devising its evaluation program.

Three examples of the process and use of evaluation in areas other than student achievement are described in the following pages. They indicate how institutional achievement can be maximized at least cost. The examples given are (1) the evaluation of visual factors in instructional areas, (2) the evaluation of course offerings in an undergraduate liberal arts college program, and (3) the evaluation of the undergraduate college calendar.

EXAMPLE I

The Evaluation of Visual Factors in Instructional Areas. This example is drawn from a fairly comprehensive program of evaluation of instructional areas carried out by the plant manager of Teachers College, Columbia University.[13] The evaluation took account of the following characteristics in measuring the suitability of lighting in 165 classrooms classified by function served and the number of student stations provided.

    a. Light sources: (1) fluorescent, (2) incandescent, (3) window

    b. Daylight controls: (1) roller shades, (2) venetian blinds, (3) vertical blinds, (4) curtains or draperies, (5) windows uncovered, (6) no windows

    c. General feeling of visual comfort: (1) good, (2) fair, (3) bad

    d. Reflected glare problems: (1) controllable, (2) not controllable

    e. Brightness: (1) range in lighting levels—footcandles, (2) balance in room brightness: (2a) good, (2b) fair, (2c) bad, (3) fixture brightness: (3a) too bright, (3b) acceptable

Lighting was but one of the classroom factors examined. Others were esthetic, special, sonic, and thermal factors, and teaching equipment. For the purposes of demonstrating the nature of the undertaking in evaluation, only the lighting factor is here considered. The visual factors in the 165 instructional spaces were evaluated by means of meters to measure light intensity and observations of sources of illumination, availability and control of exterior light, and presence and causes of glare. Relative to standards set, the general conclusion was reached that the visual comfort rating in 31 spaces was good, in 105 fair, and in 29 bad. Relative comments and recommendations from the report are given below.

Comments and recommendations. During the past several years there has been a growing concern for improving visual factors in the school environment. Major changes have taken place in both design and performance standards. Fluorescent lighting has replaced incandescent. Window light controls have been

    [13] Richard F. Tonigan, "Survey of Plant Management at Teachers College, Columbia University," unpublished Ed.D. project report, New York, 1962.

getting more light proof, glare resistant and decorative. Reflected and direct glare has been considered more troublesome and lighting levels have been increased. The securing of visual comfort has become a primary objective of plant design and operation. A joint task committee, consisting of representatives of the American Institute of Architects, the Illuminating Engineering Society and the National Council of Schoolhouse Construction, is expected to publish the results of a comprehensive school lighting study soon; it should be sought and studied for application to Teachers College's relighting program. (Preliminary discussions have indicated that the forthcoming reports will put more stress on performance standards.)

It should be noted that whereas classroom illumination levels of 25 to 35 footcandles provided acceptable working conditions a decade ago, 40 to 50 footcandle levels today comprise minimum standards with 200 to 400 footcandle levels being occasionally encountered. For the past four years remodeled areas at Teachers College have been designed to have an illumination level of 60 to 80 maintained footcandles.

One of the ways in which desired illumination levels can be secured is to continue the conversion from incandescent to fluorescent lighting systems. The importance of having adequate illumination levels has recently been stated: "The level of lighting—or number of footcandles—is one of the factors affecting visual acuity, and the type of lighting systems producing the light controls to a large degree the number of footcandles required for the efficient seeing of a given task."[14]

Just as glare can cause drivers to crash on the highways, glare can cause a student to miss seeing an important number, word, color tone, or demonstration detail. Most of the direct glare problems must ordinarily be resolved by improved design of fixtures, whereas reflected glare has more to do with general building conditions and the specific location of the task itself, and thus reflected glare can be affected by shifting the task or the student. A recent series of studies by John M. Chorlton in Canada has emphasized the direct relationship between readability and illuminating angles;[15] studies on glare should be watched for the development of better understanding of the causes of glare and its effects upon the learner.

It should be noted that footcandle readings are naturally affected by the conditions of cleanliness, or lack of it, on building surfaces as well as on the lighting fixtures. A review of the light fixture cleaning program showed that many fluorescent fixtures had not been cleaned, other than dusted, in the past three to five years, but that better than two-thirds of the building surfaces in the instructional areas have been washed or repainted in the last four years with a large proportion of the walls and ceilings having been properly painted with paints of high reflectivity so that more light would reach task areas. A fixture cleaning program should be established soon. Little was found in daylight controls materials that added to

[14]*Proceedings of the Thirty-Seventh Annual Meeting,* National Council on Schoolhouse Construction, Toronto, Ontario, Canada, October 4–7, 1960, p. 48.
[15]*Ibid.,* p. 60.

the attractiveness of the rooms, excepting perhaps in the thirty-four spaces having blinds, curtains, or draperies. Much could be done to make the rooms more pleasant appearing and sound absorbent if funds were available to install and maintain additional draperies, curtains, and blinds. The varying states of repair and cleanliness of the existing items indicated a more definite, scheduled cleaning of daylight controls is required, if suitable standards are to be maintained.[16]

It will be noted that this evaluation recognizes the importance of good glare-free lighting of instructional areas; that this is an important consideration in architectural design of new buildings; and that the trend is toward increasing standards for levels of illumination. The evaluation has implications for scheduling the installation of new lighting fixtures in those areas designated as bad, for action to reduce glare, for initiating a light-fixture cleaning program, and for a more effective cleaning and repair program for daylight controls. The evaluation serves to assure lighting standards for instructional areas that promote rather than retard the learning process.

EXAMPLE 2

The Evaluation of Course Offerings in an Undergraduate Liberal Arts College Program.   Differentiation in a program of an undergraduate college of liberal arts defines areas of specialization and course offerings in each area. The needless proliferation of courses may be an economic waste, and class sizes below a level conducive to desirable discussion may detract from the quality of educational experiences of students. Moreover, the extent of the offering should be consistent with the accepted philosophy of education. An examination of the offering in relation to an acceptable standard may be expected to identify questions the answers to which have important implications for the quality of the program and the economics of operations.

In the example given here, the credit hours offered in the selected subjects are shown for a selected college with a full-time enrollment of 1,000 students (designated as College A); the data were developed from the institution's catalogue for 1962–1963. These data are compared with a range of offerings found by McGrath in 14 colleges and with his proposals of an optimum offering based on opinions of graduate faculty members in the various subject areas.

It is evident from Table 15 that the program offering in College A, in relation to practice and standards, is high and is markedly higher than the optimum program proposed by McGrath. So extensive an offering for a relatively small student body indicates the presence of uneconomically small classes. The table does not answer the question whether the offering is too extensive; it is possible that the institutional philosophy of education sup-

[16] Richard F. Tonigan, *op. cit.,* pp. 112–114.

TABLE 15.   Program offering of College A in selected areas of specialization in relation to practice and standards

Selected Areas of Specialization	Credit Hours Offered College A[a]	Range in Credit Hours in 14 Colleges[b]		McGrath's Proposal[c]
		LOW	HIGH	
Biology	72	38	98	41
Chemistry	54	37.5	83.5	44
English	104	54	146	52
Philosophy	61	30	57	39
Mathematics	71	38	94	39
Religion	49	25	48	37
Political Science	78	27	81	36
Sociology	60	24	64	50
Spanish	64	24	63	31
Geology	59	37.5	58	31

SOURCES:
[a] Catalogue, College A
[b] Earl J. McGrath, *Memo to a College Faculty Member* (New York: Bureau of Publications, Teachers College, Columbia University, 1961), p. 11.
[c] Earl J. McGrath, "The College Curriculum—An Academic Wasteland?" Address before Academic Deans of the Southern States at Dallas, Texas, November 27, 1962.

ports the existing practice. But the comparative data clearly indicate the need for serious consideration of the wisdom of so many courses. It must be emphasized that the decisions made will have important implications for the quality of education, for operations, and for finance.

EXAMPLE 3

The Evaluation of the Undergraduate College Calendar.   This example involves the examination of the suitability for the future of the traditional two-semester academic year, with a four-year period as the normal span of time to qualify for the bachelor's degree. This study (referred to also in Chapter V) is one of a growing number that are being made.[17] In it the authors (Hungate and McGrath) make these observations on some of the shortcomings of this traditional calendar. They note: (1) In a period in which the demand for qualified teachers exceeds the supply, over one-half of employed teachers are not employed in the summer. (2) In a period when there is unprecedented growth of knowledge, students are idle about one-

[17] Thad L. Hungate and Earl J. McGrath, *A New Trimester Three-Year Degree Program* (New York: Bureau of Publications, Teachers College, Columbia University, 1963).

third of each year. (3) In a period when there is concern to construct adequate collegiate facilities, whole college plants lie idle all summer and are in far from full use in the academic year. (4) In a period when teachers' salary levels are low, increased productivity with its accompanying increase in salary is barred by the character of the traditional academic calendar.

The search for a calendar that could overcome the disadvantages of the traditional academic year was made in light of the basic condition that any change must sustain or raise the present standards of intellectual achievement. The proposal offered was a calendar of three 14-week trimesters that would fix the normal time for qualifying for the bachelor's degree at three years. In addition to saving time for students, it would permit more effective use of faculty, with substantial increase in salary (in the range of 18 to 27 per cent), and it would markedly improve utilization of plant, thus obviating the need for much new construction.

The economics of the proposal were examined. It could be expected to reduce per student institutional current student education cost by 6.3 per cent or more. The imponderables which only experimentation will resolve are: (1) How many weeks each year can the average teacher wisely teach? (The authors propose an average work period of $38\frac{1}{3}$ weeks per year compared with 30.7 to 33 weeks in the traditional academic year.) (2) Can students be brought to regard three years as a normal period for qualifying for the bachelor's degree?

In an examination such as this for the evaluation of present practice and the appraisal of possible future action, many implications must be assessed. For example, how would the athletic program be affected? What additional financial help will full-year students require and how can it be provided? What benefits will accrue from year-round bookstore, dining hall, and dormitory operation? Is the proposed trimester leave every third year an adequate faculty provision? Can the elementary and secondary school teachers who are taking further courses be accommodated in the trimester program? Can the new calendar be undertaken by individual institutions, or will its adoption require adoption first by state systems?

The evidence presented in the study revealed basic weaknesses in current academic calendar practice. The criteria for new practices were developed and a plan was proposed. The advantages of the proposed calendar appear impressive. Because of the anticipated resistance to change, however, it was concluded that only a state system or colleges with strong demands for their services could bear the risk of experimentally adopting the new calendar.

This example is typical of many problems in higher education, where evaluation reveals weakness and there is no ready-made course of action to follow. The best that can be done is to weigh the foreseeable implications of proposals.

These three examples are, of course, but random samples drawn from a large and heterogeneous population. But they serve to show that continuous concern for every element of operation and every class of resource, in relation to objectives and philosophies deemed appropriate for modern life, will produce far more effective plans and performance than are possible under a management content with laissez faire.

Suggestions for Initiating a Comprehensive, Continuous Evaluative Program

The bases of plans for the future are the value judgments concerning the effectiveness of performance. These value judgments are ever present in the appraisals by first- and second-line supervisors of performance of nonacademic personnel, and in the appraisals by academic department heads of departmental programs and personnel. Often those responsible for policies and plans fail to assure to themselves adequate knowledge of the conduct of evaluation in the institution; fail to provide for systematizing and improving it; and fail to use it effectively in the development of institutional plans. It is strongly believed, however, that (1) such value judgments can be improved; (2) they can be more effectively related to over-all institutional achievement through review and coordination; (3) faculty, major executives, the president, and board need to be kept informed and need to recognize their responsibility for review, coordination, and use in formulation of policies and plans.

For those institutions planning to initiate a comprehensive and continuous program of evaluation, these steps would appear appropriate: (1) the development of a broad understanding on the part of the board, the executives, and the faculty of the values and uses of evaluation as a major function of management; (2) an institution-wide examination of what evaluation is currently being carried out, the procedures used, and the results derived; (3) the securing from major executives of outlines of proposed continuous, comprehensive programs of evaluation for each area; (4) modifications as needed to take account of all areas of concern—objectives, philosophies, policies, plans, operations, management, facilities, personnel, and finance; (5) a review, evaluation, and modification as needed of the records system to maximize use and economy; (6) a review and rating of proposals in relation to priority in value, and in relation to frequency; (7) definition of frequency and content of reports expected by major executives, by the president, and by the board; (8) modification of requirements on the basis of experience.

The program does not require that the system be fully operative at any given time. Local conditions may suggest that areas be taken in sequence, or that focus first be on only those matters most in need of attention. The principal essential is the concept of the vital use of the evaluative function to institutional well-being. Once understood and undertaken it will gradually become an integral part of institutional life.

Summary

Evaluation is a value judgment obtained through comparison of characteristics of activities or resources with a norm or ideal of recognized merit. All aspects of management involve the use of such value judgments. It is therefore a management responsibility to improve both their quality and their usefulness. Although use of evaluation is likely to be pervasive in the conduct of operations, it is not generally fully recognized by faculty, major executives, and the board. It is here proposed that evaluation be recognized as one of the major functions of management; that each institution develop a coordinated, comprehensive, continuous program, subject to continuous review, that the procedures be improved as needed, and that results be fully utilized in the development of policies and plans. This institution-wide system is seen as available through time with much effort but with relatively small cost. The values to be gained are far-reaching, whether in clearer definition of the institutional role, in a more effective program, in increased quality of service, or in the improved economics of operation.

CHAPTER 8

Management and
State Responsibility

The management of institutions of higher education considered in the preceding chapters has assumed a lay governing board for each individual institution. The theory of management, already expressed, is based on the principle that the faculty has a vital stake in the development of plans and policies and that it has a special competence to contribute to such development. Unless its participation is sought and nurtured, the freedom to teach will be restricted or negated by conditions which the faculty member may deem inappropriate, by objectives which he may not approve, and by programs in which his work is less well oriented. In short, unless a governing board seeks the fullest understanding and cooperation toward a consensus on major matters, it may find that the faculty will have less identity with the institution. Some members will become routine employees and seek advance in status and pay through union activity; some will be content with the status quo, and develop a laissez-faire attitude; some will become active in developing opposition to the plans of executives and the board; and some of the most creative minds will undoubtedly seek a new environment for their talents. The students will be directly affected by whatever affects the environment created for them, and in this environment the faculty occupies a central place.

The new developments in higher education have imposed major responsibilities on state governments. In this chapter the way in which the states have responded to the challenge is reviewed, and recent trends are identified.

State Responsibility and Degree-credit Enrollments

One way to obtain perspective on the exercise of state responsibility for higher education is to consider it in terms of degree-credit enrollments, the procedure followed in Chapter 2. In using this base, we are aware that the major programs of research and field services, which are found in the universities, will not be made apparent.

In Table 16 a summary of 1959–1960 degree-credit enrollments is given for the fifty states, classified according to institutions directly responsible to state boards and those responsible to local public boards, whether municipal, district, or county. The states are divided into three groups according to size of enrollments in institutions directly responsible to state boards. This division is an entirely arbitrary one. It permits examination of certain practices in relation to the weight of state responsibility as measured by the size of degree-credit enrollments.

It is readily apparent from Table 16 that the responsibility for public higher education, as indicated by student enrollment, varies widely. The sixteen states that have enrollments of less than 17,500 students in institutions responsible to state boards account for but 7.5 per cent of the total enrollment in the public institutions of the nation, whereas the sixteen states with the highest enrollments (over 35,000 students) account for two-thirds of all students enrolled in public institutions.

A second significant fact is that as the responsibility grows, so does the tendency to place more of it on local boards, usually under the supervision of a designated state board. The percentage of enrollment found in institutions governed by local boards is 7.8 in states with the smaller enrollments, 12.8 in the middle group, and 26.3 in states with the larger enrollments.

In Table 17 the number of institutions and their average size are shown for the three groups of states classified according to size of enrollment under state boards. In this tabulation are included 75 units that are institutional branches or separate campuses.

It is evident from Table 17 that institutional size (as measured by student enrollment) tends to grow as state responsibility for higher education grows. In institutions under the governance of state boards, the average size in the group of states with smaller degree-credit enrollments is 1,888; in the middle group, 3,011; and in the group with largest enrollments, 4,048. The average size of institutional enrollments under local boards in the group of states with largest enrollments is 1,832 compared with 649 and 695 in the lowest and median groups.

TABLE 16. Degree-credit enrollments in institutions under public control in fifty states, classified by size and by type of governing board: 1959–1960

Size of Enrollment Under State Boards[a]	Total Enrollments		Enrollments in Institutions Governed by State Boards		Enrollments in Institutions Governed by Local Boards	
	NUMBER	PERCENTAGE OF TOTAL	NUMBER	PERCENTAGE OF GROUP	NUMBER	PERCENTAGE OF GROUP
Group I: Less than 17,500 students (16 states)	149,481	7.5	137,849	92.2	11,632	7.8
Group II: 17,500 to 35,000 students (18 states)	517,621	25.9	451,608	87.2	66,013	12.8
Group III: Over 35,000 students (16 states)	1,329,609	66.6	979,792	73.7	349,817	26.3
Total (50 states)	1,996,711[b]	100.0	1,569,249	78.6	427,462	21.4

[a] The classification of states is arbitrarily made to provide about the same number of states in each group. The criterion of classification is the size of degree-credit enrollments in public institutions governed by state boards, irrespective of the size of enrollments in institutions governed by local boards.

[b] Enrollments of federal institutions, District of Columbia, and Puerto Rico not included.

SOURCE: Appendix B-3.

TABLE 17. Degree-credit enrollments and number of institutions in fifty states: 1959–1960

Size of Enrollment Under State Boards	Number of Institutions	Student Enrollment	Average Institutional Size
Group I: 17,500 students (16 states)			
Under state boards	73	137,849	1,888
Under local boards	18	11,632	649
	91	*149,481*	*1,643*
Group II: 17,500 to 35,000 students (18 states)			
Under state boards	150	451,608	3,011
Under local boards	95	66,013	695
	245	*517,621*	*2,112*
Group III: Over 35,000 students (16 states)			
Under state boards	242	979,792	4,048
Under local boards	191	349,817	1,832
	433	*1,329,609*	*3,071*
Total, 50 states			
Under state boards	465	1,569,249	3,375
Under local boards	304	427,462	1,406
Total	769	1,996,711	2,596

SOURCE: Appendix B-3.

The state responsibility for public higher education is at base one that rests with the people, their legislature, and the governor. The legislature and governor have, traditionally, assigned responsibility to state boards. The general nature of these boards is shown in Table 18.

Within the fifty states are 214 state boards that exercise responsibility for higher education. In twelve states are found coordinating or planning-coordinating boards that plan, assign functions, and coordinate institutional programs and finance, but do not govern. More will be said of these later. There are 108 governing boards, each responsible for governing a single institution, and 66 boards responsible for governing and coordinating a group of institutions. The total number of boards charged with responsibilities of governance is thus 174. In addition there are 28 boards in 23 states[1] having

[1] For details, see Appendix B-3.

assigned responsibilities that vary but include such functions as supervision of institutions governed by local boards, accrediting programs, setting standards, and the like.

The student enrollments for which the 174 state governing boards (108 governing and 66 governing-coordinating boards) are responsible are summarized in Table 19. In this table institutions governed by local boards are not included.

It will be seen that 66 governing-coordinating boards, or 38 per cent of the total of 174 boards, exercise responsibility for 1,128,803 students, or 72 per cent of the total enrollment of 1,569,249 degree-credit students governed by all state boards. The table reveals that as state responsibility for higher education grows, the responsibilities exercised by state boards as evidenced by the size of degree-credit enrollments also grow. The average enrollment in institutions governed by governing-coordinating boards is 5,648 per board in the group of states with least enrollment, 15,112 in the median group, and 23,593 in the states having highest enrollment. Individual institutions governed by state boards also grow in average size, ranging from 2,928 in the low group to 4,946 in the high group. The average governing-coordinating board exercises responsibility for more than four times the enrollment in the average institution responsible to an individual governing board.

The distribution by size of degree-credit enrollments in institutions responsible to state boards is shown in Table 20. State boards responsible for

TABLE 18. Types of state boards responsible for public higher education in fifty states: 1959–1960

Size of Enrollment Under State Boards	Coordinating and Planning Boards	Governing-Coordinating Boards	Governing Boards	Supervising or Accrediting Boards	Total
Group I: Under 17,500 students (16 states)	2	13	22	5	42
Group II: 17,500 to 35,000 students (18 states)	3	23	31	13	70
Group III: Over 35,000 students (16 states)	7	30	55	10	102
Total, 50 states	12	66	108	28	214

SOURCE: Appendix B-3.

TABLE 19. Degree-credit enrollments in institutions in fifty states governed by state boards: 1959–1960

Size of Enrollment Under State Boards	Totals			Under Governing-Coordinating Boards			Under Governing Boards		
	NUMBER OF BOARDS	ENROLLMENT Total	Average	NUMBER OF BOARDS	ENROLLMENT Total	Average	NUMBER OF BOARDS	ENROLLMENT Total	Average
Group I: Under 17,500 students (16 states)	35	137,849	3,939	13	73,434	5,648	22	64,415	2,928
Group II: 17,500 to 35,000 students (18 states)	54	451,608	8,363	23	347,586	15,112	31	104,022	3,355
Group III: Over 35,000 students (16 states)	85	979,792	11,529	30	707,783	23,593	55	272,009	4,946
Total, 50 states	174a	1,569,249	9,019	66	1,128,803	17,103	108	440,446	4,078

a Only boards responsible for governance are included; 12 coordinating boards and 28 supervisory or accrediting boards are omitted.
SOURCE: Appendixes B-3 and B-4.

TABLE 20. Size of degree-credit enrollments in institutions responsible to state boards: 1959–1960

Size of Degree-credit Enrollment	Under Governing-Coordinating Boards		Under Governing Boards		Total	
	NUMBER OF BOARDS	ENROLLMENT	NUMBER OF BOARDS	ENROLLMENT	NUMBER OF BOARDS	ENROLLMENT
Under 2,500	4	5,302	64	76,904	68	82,206
2,500 to 4,999	5	17,325	19	62,572	24	79,897
5,000 to 9,999	12	80,547	13	98,933	25	179,480
10,000 to 19,999	28	411,552	7	85,606	35	497,158
20,000 to 29,999	10	261,514	5	116,431	15	377,945
30,000 to 39,999	4	139,577	—	—	4	139,577
40,000 and over	3	212,986	—	—	3	212,986
Total	66	1,128,803	108	440,446	174	1,569,249

SOURCE: Identification of state boards: S. V. Martorana and Ernest V. Hollis, *State Boards Responsible for Higher Education*, 1960. Enrollments: U.S. Office of Education, *Education Directory, 1960–1961*, Part 3.

211

institutions with degree-credit enrollments of less than 10,000 number 117, or 67 per cent of the total, and the aggregate enrollment in institutions responsible to them is 341,583, or less than 22 per cent of the total. Thus 57 boards exercise responsibility for institutions that enroll 1,227,666 students, or more than 78 per cent of the total. Included in this category are 22 boards responsible for an aggregate enrollment of 730,508, or over 46 per cent of all students enrolled in institutions responsible to state boards. This analysis reveals that there exist great concentrations of responsibilities for higher education in a relatively few state boards.

Organizational Patterns for State Responsibility for Higher Education

The states are not uniform in the provisions they have made for exercising state responsibilities for higher education. While each state has some unique provisions in its organization, the general organizational patterns are as shown in Table 21.

In the first category in Table 21 are six states in which the individual institutional governing boards are directly responsible to the governor or general assembly. In these states there is no state board to plan institutional design for the state system, to allocate functions, or to coordinate programs and finance. In the second category are thirteen states in which one board performs all functions—planning, coordination, and governance. The third category comprises eleven states and is similar to the second except that there are either two governing-coordinating boards or one such board and a single institution with its own governing board. In the latter case, the single institution is likely to be the state university. The fourth category, with eight states, can only be characterized as complex. There may be a number of institutions with separate governing boards and one or more governing-coordinating boards each responsible for a number of institutions; or there may be three or four governing-coordinating boards. In none of these states is there a state board charged with responsibility for statewide planning and coordination. The fifth category, with twelve states, like the fourth is complex, but here each state has a statewide coordinating board. These coordinating boards have no power to govern. Basically they are central planning agencies for higher education for the state and coordinate institutional programs and finance. All except one of these boards were established after 1950, and four were established in 1961. Included is the recently formed California Coordinating Board.[2]

---

[2] This board has only responsibility and power of recommendation to state authorities, but its composition and relationships are such that action based on its recommendations can be expected.

To illustrate the general characteristics to be found in the five organizational patterns, an example will be drawn from each category.[3]

ORGANIZATION PATTERN I

For this category (states with institutional governing boards directly responsible to governor or general assembly), the example chosen is the state of Washington. In this state are fifteen institutions that in 1960 enrolled 47,355 degree-credit students. Five institutions, with a 1960 aggregate degree-credit enrollment of 37,084 students, are directly responsible to five state governing boards, one for each institution. These boards in turn are responsible to the governor of the state. Ten institutions are two-year colleges governed by local boards under the supervision of the state board of education. They had a 1960 aggregate degree-credit enrollment of 10,271 students.

Each state governing board of a four-year (or more) college or university exercises responsibilities similar to those for the University of Washington. Martorana and Hollis describe its responsibilities as follows:

The board is responsible for the government of the institution; its authority for general policy determination encompasses budget approval, program endorsement, establishment of personnel policies, financing of current operations, and planning and financing of physical facilities.[4]

Of the five colleges and universities with four-year (or more) programs, each governed by a state governing board, one is a state university (1960 enrollment, 22,948), one is a state university and land-grant college combined (1960 enrollment, 6,943), and three are four-year (or more) colleges of education (1960 enrollments, between 2,000 and 3,000) that grant the bachelor's and master's degrees.

In addition to the state institutional academic programs, Washington also participates in the cooperative academic programs operated under arrangements made by the Western Interstate Commission for Higher Education.

Thus in the state of Washington, the legislature, the governor, and the leadership in the state boards of education are responsible for planning for public higher education. There is no single state board charged with responsibility for planning and coordination. In this category, with problems similar to those of Washington, are Ohio and South Carolina, each with five or six institutions under separate boards for which the machinery for state-

[3] Data in Appendix B-5 will permit fuller understanding of the wide variation in state organizational patterns for discharging the responsibilities for higher education.

[4] S. V. Martorana and Ernest V. Hollis, *State Boards Responsible for Higher Education* (Washington, D.C.: U.S. Department of Health, Education, and Welfare, Office of Education, 1960), p. 168.

TABLE 21.   Organization patterns in fifty states for exercise of state

Classification and States	Number of States	Number of Institutions	Degree-Credit Enrollment
Group I—States with institutional governing boards directly responsible to governor or general assembly: Delaware, Hawaii, Ohio, South Carolina, Washington, Wyoming	6	39^b	175,708
Group II—States with single governing-coordinating board: Alaska, Arizona, Florida, Georgia, Idaho, Iowa, Kansas, Mississippi, Montana, Nevada, North Dakota, Rhode Island, South Dakota	13	150^b	252,099
Group III—States with two governing-coordinating boards or one such and one governing board for a single institution: Connecticut, Louisiana, Nebraska, Minnesota, New Hampshire, New Jersey, New York, Oregon, Tennessee, Vermont, West Virginia	11	141^b	393,874
Group IV—States with complex organization without a statewide coordinating board: Alabama, Colorado, Indiana, Maine, Maryland, Massachusetts, Michigan, Pennsylvania	8	142^b	332,454
Group V—States with complex organization with a state-wide coordinating board; Arkansas, California, Illinois, Kentucky, Missouri, New Mexico, North Carolina, Oklahoma, Texas, Utah, Virginia, Wisconsin	12	297^b	842,576
Total, 50 states	50	769^b	1,996,711

^{a}State boards: C = Coordinating Board: G = Governing Board. For single than one institution: S&A = Supervisory, Accrediting Board.

^{b}Counted as institutions are branches and separate campuses as follows: in 5 states; Group IV, 33 units in 5 states; Group V, 23 units in 6 states—a total

SOURCE: Appendix B-5.

wide planning and coordinating is not presently available. In this category, too, are three states—Delaware, Hawaii, Wyoming—with but one or two institutions where the problems pertaining to large numbers are not acute.

ORGANIZATION PATTERN II

In this category (states with a single governing-coordinating board) are thirteen states, each with a single governing-coordinating board to govern and coordinate state institutions of higher education. The university system of Georgia is chosen to illustrate this pattern.

In Georgia the single board exercises responsibility for 19 institutions that in 1960 enrolled an aggregate of 31,153 degree-credit students. In addition, 468 students were enrolled in two local institutions with local responsibilities for higher education: 1960

State Boards [a]				Governed by State Boards		Governed by Local Boards	
C	G	G–C	S&A	NUMBER OF INSTITUTIONS	ENROLLMENT	NUMBER OF INSTITUTIONS	ENROLLMENT
0	21	0	3	21[b]	136,111	18	39,597
0	0	13	8	73[b]	208,832	77	43,267
0	4	18	4	109[b]	356,738	32	37,136
0	31	14	7	109[b]	306,309	33	26,145
12	52	21	6	153[b]	561,259	144	281,317
12	108	66	28	465[b]	1,569,249	304	427,462

institution: G–C = Governing-Coordinating Board. For more

Group I, none; Group II, 6 units in 3 states; Group III, 13 units of 75 units in 19 states.

boards not responsible to state boards. This single governing-coordinating board also is responsible for assisting in the conduct of state participation in the academic programs conducted under the sponsorship of the Southern Regional Education Board. Such academic programs are cooperatively undertaken by the group of regional members to achieve quality of instruction and economy in cost not readily obtainable by the individual states.

In the state system are a state university and land-grant college combined, a technological college, eight four-year (or more) colleges, a medical college, one land-grant college, and seven two-year colleges. The university in 1960 enrolled 8,978 students; Georgia Institute of Technology, 6,530 students. Only two of the other institutions exceeded 1,000 students in enrollment.

The fifteen members of the governing-coordinating board are appointed by the governor with the advice and consent of the senate. The term of office is seven years. The board, in the words of Martorana and Hollis, is responsible for the government, control, and management of the University System of Georgia, comprised of 19 institutions; its authority for general policy determination encompasses budget approval, fiscal management, establishment of personnel policies, and determination of educational programs.[5]

The central office staff of the board comprises a chancellor, who is the chief executive officer of the board, and five other professional staff members.

The board meets eleven times a year. It has responsibility for continually assessing the responsibilities of the state for higher education; for developing long-range plans to meet these responsibilities; for institutional design, growth, and development; for coordination of functions and programs among institutions; and for decisions relating to operations.

The task is a demanding one, and may be greater than can appropriately be carried by a single board. The faculties of the 19 institutions cannot share with the board in developing objectives and long-range institutional plans. The president of an institution may from time to time journey to Atlanta to confer with the chancellor, but this is bound to be an inadequate sharing in institutional plans. The president ordinarily will have access to the board only through the chancellor, and his own scope of operations may be circumscribed by the rules and regulations imposed by the board. The board itself may rely heavily on the chancellor, who has the immediate need to solve the current problems of management and may not lead the board to consider in depth the appropriate objectives for the system and for each institution. He may not have the resources needed to develop the necessary long-range institutional plans, or to search for the best allocation of academic program responsibilities for each institution. Martorana and Hollis write of governing-coordinating boards that "they often are weaker in providing interinstitutional coordination, programing, and long-range planning than in their governing responsibilities."[6]

ORGANIZATION PATTERN III

In this category (states with two governing-coordinating boards or one such and one governing board responsible for a single institution) are eleven states. In this category are two states each with aggregate degree-credit enrollments of less than 10,000; two with between 10,000 and 20,000 each; and seven with more than 20,000 each.

The example chosen to illustrate this category is the state of New Jersey.

[5] *Ibid.*, p. 80.
[6] *Ibid.*, p. 50.

There are 11 public institutions in the state and the aggregate degree-credit enrollment in 1960 was 38,429 students. Nine institutions that in 1960 enrolled 34,132 students are governed by state boards; two that enrolled 4,297 students are governed by local boards and are supervised by a state board.

Rutgers, the combined state university and land-grant college, comprises three institutional units, and in 1960 the total enrollment in them was 16,250 students. The other six state institutions are governed by a second governing-coordinating board and all are four-year (or more) colleges, with 1960 enrollments ranging from 1,901 to 3,917 students. The Rutgers board consists of thirteen members, six appointed by the governor with the advice and consent of the senate, and five chosen by the university advisory board from among its members. In addition, the president of the Rutgers Corporation and the commissioner of education of New Jersey are ex officio members without voting power. This board is responsible for the governance of the three institutional units, including budgeting, personnel policies, program, and physical facilities. The second governing-coordinating board is the state board of education. It has twelve members appointed by the governor with the advice and consent of the senate for six-year overlapping terms. The responsibilities of the board for governing the six institutions entrusted to it are similar to those of the Rutgers board. In addition, it has responsibility for making recommendations to the governor and legislature concerning academic programs, budgets, and physical facilities of the state university. This board also exercises responsibility for supervision of institutions governed by local boards and for supervision of state elementary and secondary education.

It will be seen that in this category the problems identified for a single governing-coordinating board, as in category II, are present. They become more pronounced, however, in the obvious difficulty of securing adequate cooperation and communication between the two boards to effect comprehensive state objectives and plans and institutional coordination of programs, facilities, and finance. The opportunities for cooperative planning efforts of boards and faculties are bound to be limited, and the demands on board time will restrict the attention it can give to planning for the future.

ORGANIZATION PATTERN IV

This category (states with complex organization without a statewide coordinating board) comprises eight states with institutional governmental relationships described as complex and with no over-all coordinating board. Of the eight states, the 1960 degree-credit enrollment in public institutions governed by state boards was under 10,000 in one state, from 10,000 to 20,000 in one state, and over 20,000 in six states. In these eight states are 109 institutions responsible to state boards.

The state chosen as an example to illustrate this category is Michigan. There are twenty-four public institutions of higher education in the state: five governed by five individual governing boards, four by a governing-coordinating board, and fifteen by local boards supervised by the state board of education. The total 1960 degree-credit enrollment in public institutions in the state was 118,679, of which 100,591 were in institutions responsible to six state boards and 18,088 in institutions responsible to local boards. The institutions responsible to individual governing boards and their 1960 enrollments were University of Michigan, 28,117; Michigan State University (and land-grant college), 21,874; Wayne State University, 20,326; and two four-year colleges, 3,055 and 2,483. The state board of education serves as a governing-coordinating board for four four-year (or more) colleges, three of which have programs leading to the master's degree. The aggregate 1960 enrollment in these four institutions was 24,736. In addition, this board supervises the junior colleges governed by local boards.

The governing boards of the three universities are elected by the people for overlapping terms, with the president of each and the state superintendent of public instruction serving ex officio with voice but without voting power. The boards of the two colleges are appointed by the governor with the advice and consent of the senate. Each of these five governing boards is responsible for governing its institution, for budget, program, personnel, finance, and facilities.

The state board of education comprises four members, three elected to overlapping terms, with the state superintendent of public instruction designated as the fourth member. Its responsibilities for governance of the four colleges under its jurisdiction are similar to those described for the board of an individual institution. In addition, it has supervisory responsibilities for the junior colleges under local boards.

It is evident that the state has no central body to envision how best the state can define its objectives for higher education and perform the function of planning and coordinating. The four institutions under the governing-coordinating board are denied suitable participation in policy formation and planning for their respective institutions.

What is true for Michigan appears to be applicable to all eight states in this category. Separate boards, each responsible for one or more institutions, number three in Maine and Indiana; four in Alabama, Colorado, and Maryland; six in Massachusetts and Michigan; and fifteen in Pennsylvania.

ORGANIZATION PATTERN V

This category (states with complex organization with a statewide coordinating board), like the preceding, is described as complex but there is an important difference. Each of the twelve states has a planning-coordinating board. The state of Texas is chosen as an illustration of this category. Texas has 52 public institutions, 21 governed by state boards, and 31 by local boards subject to supervision of a state board.

The 1960 degree-credit enrollment in public institutions was 129,449, with 98,954 in institutions governed by state boards, and 30,495 in institutions governed by local boards under supervision of a state board.

There are nine state governing and governing-coordinating boards, six governing boards each responsible for a single institution, and three governing-coordinating boards each responsible for four, five, and six institutions respectively. In addition, there is an over-all coordinating board, and a board which, among other responsibilities, supervises institutions governed by local boards.

The governing-coordinating boards are appointed by the governor with the advice and consent of the senate for six-year overlapping terms. The state board of education, which has certain supervisory responsibilities for institutions governed by local boards, is an elected board.

The governing-coordinating boards, with responsibilities for four, five, and six institutions respectively, have the disadvantage of not being able to cooperate adequately with the faculties of the several institutions. But the existence of the over-all state coordinating board should do much to assist state boards on the one hand, and governor and legislators on the other, in developing suitable statewide plans for higher education and in promoting their realization.

The Texas coordinating board for higher education is the Texas Commission on Higher Education. It was established in 1955 and consists of fifteen members appointed by the governor with the advice and consent of the senate for six-year overlapping terms. The responsibilities of this board are described by Martorana and Hollis as follows:

The Commission is responsible for the coordination of public higher education systems in the State of Texas, except for 2-year colleges with local institutional boards. One of its major functions is to conduct continuous studies of the needs of the State in the area of public higher education. The commission's responsibility includes the approval of proposed new degree programs and the preparation and submission of recommendations to the budget office and legislature concerning all phases of higher education appropriation requests. The Commissioner receives the initial appropriation requests from the several institutions.[7]

Thus in Texas, as in all twelve of the states in this category, there is a central board that seeks continually to define for the state the objectives, plans, programs, and financial requirements for higher education consistent

[7] Martorana and Hollis, *op. cit.*, pp. 154–155.

with the best development of its people. Why the two-year college program is not included as a part of its responsibilities is not clear.

The foregoing illustrations of the five categories of state organizational patterns indicate the diversity of practice. In the first category are the states that look to *ad hoc* surveys for direction, and to legislature and governor for coordination. The states in this group lack provision for continuous direction of the development of higher education in the state, and each institution seeks its independent development. In the second category one state board exercises state responsibility for over-all state plans, for coordination, and for governance of individual institutions. This provision places too great a responsibility on one board and does not permit institutional governance by consensus. The pressing problems of governance detract from the exercise of the responsibility for planning and coordinating. The third group is like the second except for a second board responsible for one or more institutions. Responsibility is thus divided. This arrangement has the weaknesses of the second category, plus the disadvantage of requiring that the problems incident to over-all plans and coordination be resolved by the legislature and governor. The fourth category is more complex than the preceding categories in that there are a number of state boards, some governing, some governing-coordinating. But like the third category, the state lacks provision for continuous over-all state planning and coordination; the institutions under separate boards cannot make long-range plans with assurance, because many questions relating to over-all state designs for higher education are unresolved; and faculties in institutions governed by governing-coordinating boards cannot adequately participate in management. The fifth category represents a new organizational pattern. Here there is a statewide planning-coordinating agent for the state, responsible for guiding the development of higher education. Within the states and subject to such boards are to be found both governing and governing-coordinating boards. The weakness in this pattern lies in the inability of the governing-coordinating boards to involve adequately institutional faculties in governance.

These organizational patterns of the states may be further considered in light of the requirements and provision for statewide planning and coordination.

Principles and Practices in the Exercise of State Responsibility for Planning and Coordinating State Higher Education

It is generally recognized that higher education is human capital and that its possession by a larger segment of the population is vital to our national well-being; that the content of higher education is subject to change with the growth of knowledge and technological and social change; and that the existing stock of higher education is subject to obsolescence. All these factors impose on each state broad responsibilities for setting objectives and devising plans to achieve them for youth and adults, for initial and continuing education.

STATEWIDE SURVEYS

In the period prior to World War II, and in the years immediately following it, the various states sought to develop goals and plans on the basis of *ad hoc* state surveys. The legislature, at the request of the governor, would appropriate a sum for the purpose, and a team of experts drawn from outside the state would review and assess the current situation and the outlook and make recommendations as to what the state should undertake and how it should do so.

Martorana and Hollis find that in the period 1957–1961 thirty-one states authorized statewide surveys of facilities, finances, and administration of higher education. In 1961 alone, thirteen statewide surveys, each dealing with the broad aspects of higher educational development, were authorized.[8] Included were Colorado, Florida, Idaho, Indiana, Kansas, Maryland, Michigan, New Hampshire, Texas, West Virginia, and Wisconsin. Each state had already taken some steps to achieve statewide institutional coordination.

The scope of these authorized surveys is of interest here. Two examples are chosen as illustrations—Texas and West Virginia. Texas requested "the Texas Commission on Higher Education to make a study of the overall needs of the state in the field of public higher education for the next 10 years, with emphasis on the need for new institutions or expansion in the role and scope of existing institutions."[9] West Virginia urged that "another study be made on the organization of the higher education system. The 9-member study group, appointed by the Governor, is to report to the Legislature its findings and recommendations in January 1962."[10]

Studies such as these, sometimes to assist the state in the design of the system, sometimes to aid in fixing objectives and the requirements for them, are useful to all types of state organization for higher education. A number of states have relied upon them in lieu of long-range plans developed and integrated into over-all state plans and responsibilities.

It is becoming increasingly clear, however, that the exercise of state

[8] S. V. Martorana and Ernest V. Hollis, *Survey of State Legislation Relating to Higher Education* (Washington, D.C.: U.S. Department of Health, Education, and Welfare, Office of Education, 1962), Circ. 684, January 1, 1961, to December 31, 1961, p. 10.
[9] *Ibid.*, p. 228.
[10] *Ibid.*, p. 249.

responsibilities for higher education requires long-range statewide plans, including the number and location of institutions, their assigned responsibilities, and provision for their resources and financial support. It is also clear that coordination of institutional plans, programs, facilities, and finance is a continuing responsibility. It is in light of state plans and assigned responsibility that plans for individual institutions can be drawn.

STATEWIDE PLANNING
AND COORDINATING

It is for this reason that a number of states have imposed this responsibility on separate planning-coordinating boards. Effective coordination cannot be achieved except in terms of long-range plans. Such plans must envision the nature and extent of need, the implications for numbers and kinds of institutions, their size and functions, and correlative with such plans must be those of finance. These long-range plans afford orientation for necessary actions both in the annual plans and in day-by-day decisions. The twelve states that have established such over-all state coordinating boards (category V) realize the importance of the planning-coordinating function.

For statewide planning, as with planning in individual institutions, four factors impose the requirement for long-range planning. First, there is the speed of technological and social change, which has important implications for the scope, nature, and extent of higher education. Second, there is the span of time involved from decision to realization, whether a program change, a new building, or a new institution. Third, there is the span of time needed for consideration and debate. Fourth, there is the requirement of imaginative planning that sees the present fixed elements of program, staff, plant, students, and the like as variables in planning for the future. The responsibility for institutional coordination is inseparable from planning responsibility. Coordination implies action directed to defined objectives, and these actions as proposed are found only in the plans. And the constant guidance, understanding, and assistance of institutions is in fact the continuous official interpretation for each of the statewide plans.

Provision for a degree of coordination of public higher education is general among the states. In some states, the provision is voluntary; in others coordination is exercised through a board with authority for coordination of all public institutions of the state. The trend is away from voluntary coordination,[11] partly because it may not take into consideration the over-all needs of the state, and partly because needed decisions may be unduly deferred. Glenny finds that "The primary motive of participants in voluntary

---

[11] For further discussion, see T. R. McConnell, *A General Pattern for American Public Higher Education* (New York: McGraw-Hill Book Company, Inc., 1962), pp. 136–137.

systems is the welfare of individual institutions, not the system as a whole."[12]
McConnell expresses the view that coordination of public higher education is inescapable and that

when the motivation is positive and forward looking, when the purpose is to plan and support a diversified educational system of high quality and to use financial resources efficiently, and when the greatest possible degree of freedom is left to individual institutions, the result should be constructive. [13]

The responsibility for the coordination of public higher education is exercised in varying degrees under three types of organization: (1) a board governing and coordinating a complex state university having a number of campuses or centers; (2) a governing-coordinating board responsible for a number of separate institutions within a state; and (3) a statewide coordinating board that has responsibility for allocating functions to institutions, and interinstitutional coordination of plans, programs, and support, with no direct responsibility for governance. At present, in a majority of the states coordination is a responsibility exercised by boards charged also with responsibility for the governance of numbers of institutions. Martorana and Hollis observe that for these boards "the coordinating function is implemented much less overtly than the governing responsibility."[14] They find that statewide coordinating boards are assigned major duties of interinstitutional programming, budget coordination, and long-range planning.

STATE PLANNING-COORDINATING BOARDS

The following examples illustrate some of the responsibilities assigned to state planning-coordinating boards:

The Texas Commission on Higher Education was created in 1955. It is classed as a coordinating board. "One of its major functions is to conduct continuous studies of the needs of the State in the area of public higher education."[15]

The Utah Coordinating Council of Higher Education was created in 1959. Martorana and Hollis describe its responsibilities as follows:

The council is charged with the responsibility of exercising leadership in the coordination of higher education institutions in the following areas but is admonished to do so "without imposing operational control": (1) Statewide plan-

---

[12]Lyman A. Glenny, *Autonomy of Public Colleges; The Challenge of Coordination* (New York: McGraw-Hill Book Company, Inc., 1959), p. 262.

[13]McConnell, *op.cit.*, pp. 143–144.

[14]Martorana and Hollis, *State Boards Responsible for Higher Education, op. cit.*, p. 48.

[15]*Ibid.*, p. 155.

ning of public higher education in Utah, including defining its objectives; (2) defining the role and program of each institution; (3) establishing criteria for determining operating budget and capital budget needs; (4) establishing criteria for determining needs for new programs and new institutions, or for eliminating existing programs; (5) studying new methods and techniques for increasing efficiency; (6) defining standards and regulations for student admissions; and (7) creating standards for plant utilization.[16]

In the conduct of its responsibilities this board presents to the legislature a recommended combined request for appropriations. It may call joint meetings with the governing boards of institutions. Reports are made to the governor and to the legislature.

The Council of Higher Education for Virginia was created in 1956. It is classified as a coordinating board. "The board is responsible for the coordination of public higher education in the Commonwealth of Virginia. . . . It prepares and submits to the Governor a coordinated budget request and reports to him and to the general assembly biennially regarding future needs of higher education."[17]

The Wisconsin Coordinating Committee for Higher Education was created in 1955. It is classified as a coordinating board. It is responsible "for coordination of activities of the University of Wisconsin and the State colleges, including coordination of program planning, planning of buildings, and preparation of budgets."[18]

In California the new master plan submitted to the California legislature in 1960 provides for voluntary coordination through a coordinating council of twelve members with equal representation of the university, the state colleges, the junior colleges, and the private colleges.[19] The legislature approved the recommendation, adding three public members to be appointed by the governor. McConnell reports that the legislature defined the duties of the council as follows:

To review the annual budgets and requests for capital outlay of the university and state college systems and to comment on the general level of support sought.

To interpret the functional differentiation among the publicly supported institutions, in the light of this differentiation to advise on programs appropriate to each system, and to submit to the governor and the Legislature within five days of the beginning of each general session recommendations for desirable changes, if any, in the functions and programs of the several segments of public higher education.

[16] *Ibid.,* p. 160.
[17] *Ibid.,* p. 165.
[18] *Ibid.,* p. 173.
[19] Martorana and Hollis, *Survey of State Legislation Relating to Higher Education, op. cit.,* p. 18.

To make plans for the orderly growth of higher education and to make recommendations concerning the need for, and the location of, new facilities and programs.[20]

Thus in California the transition has been from reliance on *ad hoc* surveys as the basis for development to continuous statewide coordinated planning.

These five examples indicate the broad scope of the responsibility assigned to a single central state board. Within each state system, as McConnell says, "the pressing problem is how to leave particular institutions room for initiative, experimentation, and striving for excellence while they play their appropriate roles in the general plan."[21] In discussing the merits of voluntary versus formal authoritative provisions for coordination, McConnell sees the choice as involving "a balancing of values." He states, "The values of independence, initiative, and responsibility weigh heavily in the quest for institutional excellence and integrity. The end to be gained is a *productive* compromise between the values of autonomy and coordination."[22]

Among the responsibilities recently assigned to the newly created coordinating board of Illinois were the following, as reported by McConnell:

to analyze the present and future aims, needs, and requirements of higher education in the state; to propose a master plan for the development, expansion, integration, coordination, and efficient utilization of the facilities for public higher education in teaching, research, and public service; to engage in continuing evaluation and revision of the plan; and to submit to the General Assembly the legislation necessary for the implementation of the plan.[23]

This board was given power to approve any new unit of instruction, research, or public service, whether department, institute, or branch. All institutional budgets are to be analyzed and recommendations concerning them made to the legislature. To carry out its assignments, the board was given authority to employ a professional staff.

The state planning-coordinating board is new. Oklahoma's coordinating board (1941) was the only one established before the close of World War II. Seven were established in the fifties—Kentucky, New Mexico, North Carolina, Texas, Utah, Virginia, and Wisconsin. And four—California, Illinois, Arkansas, and Missouri—in the early sixties. The purpose of these boards was to foresee and effectively provide for the state responsibilities for higher education—kind, quantity, and quality—and their creation was clear recognition of the necessity for continuous statewide planning and coordination.

[20] McConnell, *op. cit.*, p. 153.
[21] *Ibid.*, p. 82.
[22] *Ibid.*, pp. 161–162.
[23] *Ibid.*

Twelve states is an impressive number to have made provision for state-wide planning and coordination, but there remain thirty-eight states in which action is yet to be taken. While it may be said that over-all responsibilities for planning and coordination have already been assigned to some governing-coordinating boards, it has been pointed out that this provision is inadequate, partly because of the burden involved, and partly because there is often conflict of interests in the performance of this dual role.

INTERSTATE COOPERATION

The exercise of state responsibilities for higher education in addition to statewide institutional planning and coordination for public institutions within the states has in numerous instances extended to interstate cooperation. A number of states have entered into regional compacts to share resources and programs where mutually advantageous and to exchange information. There are at present three such groups: the Southern Regional Education Board (sixteen states); the Western Interstate Commission for Higher Education (thirteen states); and the New England Board of Higher Education (six states).

Principles and Practices in Exercising State Responsibilities for Governing Individual Institutions

The achievement of an institution in fulfilling its role as defined in the over-all state plan can be facilitated but not assured by actions taken by a coordinating board, or by a board removed from direct involvement in institutional affairs.

WEAKNESS OF GOVERNING-COORDINATING BOARD

Understanding and participation by the faculty is essential to such achievement. Such understanding and participation cannot be suitably fostered by and through boards responsible for governing and coordinating a number of institutions. This fact is recognized by some governing-coordinating boards that provide advisory boards for each institution. This roundabout process cannot be satisfactory. The advisory board does not have responsibility for decision, and it is the weight of responsibility that often conditions the quality of advice. It is here contended that each institution should have its own governing board, with the maximum of autonomy that can be provided to it. Only under these conditions can the more able board members be enlisted to serve. Only as the board has authority to act can there develop the community of consensus which for higher education is an essential of governance.

The governing-coordinating board has neither the time nor the energy required for effective governance and effective planning and coordination. Because of the weight of its responsibilities, it may not share adequately in decisions relating to each institution, or it may act on advice of central staff without adequate involvement of the institution's president and faculty. If it is occupied with the immediate requirements of governance, there is little time to develop long-range plans cooperatively.

This type of board cannot effectively reconcile the conflicts that attend plans and governance. The responsibilities are too great. It thus carries an assignment of responsibility that is inappropriate. The alternative is a state-wide planning-coordinating board with an individual board to govern each institution.

To the extent that the membership of a board assumes the added responsibilities for both governance and coordination of a number of institutions, it can be expected that their full knowledge of and sense of identity with any single institution will decline. In such circumstances, the board may place greater reliance on the president or on an employed central staff external to the individual institution. And to the extent that in the exercise of governance reliance is placed on such a staff, the faculty of the institution is denied adequate participation in management.

A review of the responsibilities assumed by state boards as measured by the degree-credit enrollments and number of institutions which they govern will provide evidence in support of the foregoing arguments against the assignment of responsibilities to individual boards for the governance as well as the coordination of more than one institution. The data are summarized in Table 22.

TABLE 22.   State governing boards for higher education in fifty states classified according to number of institutions and degree-credit enrollment for which responsible: 1960

Number of Institutions Governed by Each Board	Degree-credit Enrollment for Which Each Board Is Responsible			Total Number of Boards
	UNDER 10,000	10,000– 20,000	20,000 AND OVER	
1	96	7	5	108
2 or 3	15	6	5	26
4 or 5	6	8	4	18
6 or 7	—	6	2	8
8 or 9	—	6	1	7
Over 9	—	2	5	7
Total	117	35	22	174

SOURCE: Appendix B-4.

It will be noted from Table 22 that of thirty-five boards each responsible for a degree-credit enrollment of 10,000 to 20,000, fourteen boards are each responsible for six or more institutions. Of twenty-two boards each responsible for more than 20,000 degree-credit enrollments, seventeen exercise responsibility for two or more institutions. These thirty-one boards represent 17.8 per cent of all governing boards. Together they govern 245 institutions that in 1960 enrolled 818,547 degree-credit students, or 52.2 per cent of the total enrollment of 1,569,249 under direct governance of state boards. These boards have responsibilities that are beyond their powers.

The larger and more complex the undertaking and the greater the number of institutions involved, the more remote a governing board must become from the faculties of these institutions. The executive officers of the boards generally employ central professional staffs to assist them, but as Martorana and Hollis[24] testify, these staffs are frequently inadequate and often overburdened. A central board cannot seek consensus with the faculties of a number of institutions. The process is too involved and too time-consuming. When in lieu of faculty consensus reliance is placed on a central professional staff, this bypassing of faculties can adversely affect institutional achievement. Moreover, the board as proponent of a proposal of a particular institution must as a board sit in judgment on it from the point of view of system-wide plans. Such conflict of interests is bound to reduce the effectiveness of the board, whether in the exercise of responsibility for planning and coordinating or of its responsibility for governance.

LARGE, COMPLEX INSTITUTIONS ALSO PRESENT PROBLEMS OF GOVERNANCE

Another dimension of the problem of complexity concerns the single institution. When an institution enrolls more than, say, 20,000 students in a complex of undergraduate, graduate, and professional programs, and has further contracted to spend many millions annually for research, the responsibilities of management are much greater than those for a smaller institution. There are a number of such institutions within the states and some are adding branch campuses. In these institutions there is need for effective communication and for securing faculty involvement and identity with the institutional objectives. This is an area of management in which practices should be observed and evaluated in order to identify those that have proved most successful. Information concerning the effectiveness of managements in relation to institutional size would assist those responsible for higher education in the several states to answer such questions as this: Is it wiser to

[24]Martorana and Hollis, *State Boards Responsible for Higher Education, op cit.,* p. 50.

enlarge a single institution to accommodate, say, 35,000 or more students, or will achievement be enhanced by developing two or more institutions? Evaluation of practice in the management of large institutions is needed to assist in the determinations that in the future must be made.

Henderson takes a positive position which in the opinion of the writer has great merit. He says:

> . . . the personal factor in education is of the greatest significance. Our aim then should be to preserve this factor. This, in my judgment, requires a decentralization of programs and facilities. The most essential step in this direction is the creation of new institutions rather than making the big ones bigger. Our universities are going mad with the illusion that size is a measure of greatness.[25]

APPROPRIATE STATE ORGANIZATION

On the basis of the examination presented in preceding chapters of the requirements for the exercise of the functions of management, it must be concluded that only that state organization is appropriate which provides a separate governing board for each institution, subject to the supervision of a statewide planning-coordinating board. The question as to what constitutes optimum institutional size remains unresolved.

Principles and Practices in the Participation of State Agencies in the Governance of Higher Education

In a study made under the auspices of the Council of State Governments in 1952 entitled, *Higher Education in the Forty-Eight States,*[26] a chapter on organization explores the theory and practice of state agency participation in the governance of higher education.

Starting with the premise that "The most desirable organizational structure is one which assures that each individual decision will be made by the agency or official best qualified to make it,"[27] the study goes on to say:

> But meaningful distinctions can be made in terms of (1) whether the decision can and should reflect the broad public will, as in the determination of how much state money should go to higher education; (2) whether and what kind of expert knowledge or technical or professional competence the decision calls for, as in determination of the subject matter to be covered in a course in physics;

[25] Algo D. Henderson, *Policies and Practices in Higher Education* (New York: Harper & Row, 1960), p. 195.
[26] The Council of State Governments, *Higher Education in the Forty-Eight States* (Chicago: The Council, 1952).
[27] *Ibid.,* p. 120.

and (3) whether the judgment required involves a viewpoint and a breadth of public responsibility which only agencies with state-wide authority possess.[28]

The participating agencies are the legislature, the governor, the central state administrative agencies, and the responsible board for higher education. The central state administrative agencies are importantly concerned with functions including budget, pre-audit, post-audit, legal matters, personnel, and purchasing functions. The summary that follows is descriptive of how the governor and central state agencies participated in the conduct of higher education in 1950.

An inquiry made of the then 168 state governing and governing-coordinating boards yielded responses from 162 boards governing 361 institutions in forty-eight states concerning their responsibility for determining policy matters on admissions requirements, programs in extension and adult education, requirements for graduation, degrees to be offered, and programs or courses to be offered. The study reports that

Two-thirds of the boards, governing 74 per cent of the institutions, exercise full discretion in the determination of all five policy matters in question; and 15 per cent of the boards, governing 10 per cent of the institutions, exercise final authority over none of these matters. The remaining 18 per cent of the boards, governing 16 per cent of the institutions, exercise final discretion with regard to some but not all five.[29]

Where a central administrative agency was called on to exercise authority in this area, it was usually the state board of education.

Concerning budget formulation, 154 boards governing 353 institutions in forty-seven states submit budget requests in the form, scope, and degree of itemization prescribed by central state administrative authorities. A majority of the boards (140 boards governing 327 institutions in forty-three states) reported that their budget requests are subject to revision by a central budget authority before consolidation and submission to the legislature. Almost two-thirds of the boards reported that appropriations may be reduced by administrative action after the appropriation law is enacted.

Concerning audit, one-third of the boards reported that expenditures from all kinds of funds received are subject to central state pre-audit before payment is made. This practice, while widespread, is not universal. Five-sixths of the boards, governing 87 per cent of the institutions, reported that funds of all kinds are subject to central state post-audit.

As many as 127 boards indicated that funds are released to their institutions through periodic allotment. The most common allotment period is three months, but for some, allotments are made monthly.

[28] *Ibid.*, pp. 120–121.
[29] *Ibid.*, pp. 135–136.

Concerning purchasing, one-third of the boards reported no central state participation; fewer than one-tenth reported that all purchasing is performed by a central state agency. For the rest, central state agency participation to some extent is indicated.

The survey disclosed that a majority of the boards exercise full discretion over most aspects of personnel policy for both academic and nonacademic institutional personnel. Yet the minority is important. For example, 52 boards (governing 138 institutions in seventeen states) have no authority for the creation of positions, and 54 boards (governing 136 institutions in seventeen states) have no authority for salary determination.

In a recent survey conducted under the auspices of the Committee on Government and Higher Education, 284 institutions reporting,

164 reported that they were obliged to route purchasing through a central agency. Of the remaining schools, 34 did their own buying; 37 had the option of using the facilities of a central agency if they wished; and 56 reported that the school's purchasing was carried on independently although in accord with a uniform state purchasing law.[30]

Pre-auditing controls of higher education are not found in fifteen states. Such controls for part of the funds, including all appropriated funds, are found in fourteen states, for most funds in six states, and for all funds in thirteen states.[31]

The centralized state building agency, now found in most of the states, has developed rapidly since World War II. According to Moos and Rourke,

These agencies have ordinarily been established as a regular staff unit under the immediate direction of the governor or the commissioner of administration, standing alongside centralized purchasing, personnel, and accounting offices. Their authority is varied, but normally they supervise the planning, design, and often the construction of buildings for all state agencies. But not all building control is confined to specialized building agencies. The state budget office also oversees the development of the capital budget and often has authority over priorities in planning and construction.[32]

The Committee on Government and Higher Education inquired into the budgeting process. Of 345 inquiries made, 289 replies were received. It was found that

two-thirds of the schools (230) are compelled to submit their budgets for actual review by an executive agency. And in the case of 138 of these schools, only the revised budget is thereafter submitted to the legislature. (In the case of 48 insti-

[30] Malcolm Moos and Francis Rourke, *The Campus and the State* (Baltimore: The Johns Hopkins Press, 1959), p. 105.
[31] *Ibid.,* p. 123.
[32] *Ibid.,* p. 132.

tutions a permanent legislative agency also steps into the picture for the purpose of reviewing proposed expenditures.)[33]

Most of the institutions received appropriated funds under the allotment system. "Only 43 out of 284 schools . . . were entirely free from this control over the rate at which they expended funds. A large number (139) of institutions surveyed are subject to a system of quarterly allotments."[34]

Budget appropriations are usually made in broad categories, such as salaries, supplies and expenses, contractual services, and capital outlay. There are few lump-sum appropriations. "Out of 284 institutions covered by the Committee Survey, 166 reported that it was necessary for them to obtain the approval of a state fiscal agency before diverting any funds from the purpose for which they had originally been allocated."[35]

In the area of control of personnel, the report states:

Twenty-seven states still leave educational personnel in the hands of the colleges, but the remaining twenty-one states now apply personnel regulations to higher education. Customarily these controls are moderate and apply only to nonacademic personnel. But occasionally, as in Massachusetts, New York, and New Jersey, controls have been exceptionally rigid and have left deep marks on the educational program. Yet with rare exceptions, state and academic officials are in complete agreement that faculties themselves should never be exposed to state personnel controls.[36]

The foregoing summary of some of the findings of the survey made by the Committee on Government and Higher Education reveals the widespread practices of centralized state agencies under the delegated authority of state government to fix rules and procedures for higher education that limit the authority of, or interfere with the exercise of, institutional management. Such limitation or interference places handicaps on institutional management, and the burden of proof on the state that the exercise of such controls results in economy or advances the state purposes for higher education.

There can be no valid objection to the determination by the state of how much state money should go to higher education. This is a basic responsibility of state government. But objection can rightly be made to procedures that permit state agencies other than higher education to modify or alter the claims of higher education for support before being presented to the legislators. The practice whereby a budget director can impose his judgment on which of the requests the legislators should consider deprives the state of

---

[33] *Ibid.*, p. 76.
[34] *Ibid.*, p. 90.
[35] *Ibid.*, p. 91.
[36] *Ibid.*, p. 179.

the benefits both of its educational leadership and of its legislative decision made on the basis of full knowledge of the recommendations.

There can be no valid objection to a state-defined format for presenting budgets. The colleges and universities of the nation through their business and financial officers, after years of cooperative study and with the approval of the American Institute of Accountants, have established standard accounting classifications that are widely followed. These classifications are useful in the conduct of institutional affairs.[37] Some states have adopted them as a basis for the budget format they require. Others, however, continue to classify the affairs of higher education after the pattern of classification of other state departments. This affords little or no advantage to the state and imposes a heavy task on the institutions by requiring them to keep financial accounts in a form prescribed by a state agency and, in their own interest, to keep them in a form useful to management. Where there is failure to adapt state practice to the needs of higher education, objection would appear justified.

There can be no valid objection to state allotments so long as the practice is confined to its purpose of rationing state money as needed. But if the practice permits a state noneducational officer to withhold or reduce allotments by imposing his judgment or his interpretation over that of the responsible education officer, then objection is justified.

There can be no valid objection to the appropriation of state funds in broad categories so long as reasonable procedures are developed to effect transfers. It must be recognized, however, that the fewer arbitrary restrictions imposed, the greater the freedom of management to employ resources to the achievement of its purposes. The plans cannot take account of all contingencies, and appropriations should recognize the need for flexibility. Appropriations in too many categories, without ready provision for transfer, place handicaps on institutional management, and objections to this seem justified.

There can be no objection to state post-audit. Verification of institutional income, expenditures, and resources is a responsibility of government. Opportunity is provided here to see that finances have been administered as intended. It has been shown that the practice of pre-audit is widespread. In this pre-audit proposed expenditures are verified as consistent with appropriations before the transaction takes place. Experience has shown that the practice has not been satisfactory for many institutions. It invites constant question of educational decisions, through the questioning of proposed expenditures. Such questions seek to superimpose the views or interpretations of a lay representative of a state agency on those of the educational

[37] See American Council on Education, *College and University Business Administration*, Vol. I (Washington, D.C.: The Council, 1952).

leader, and result in delay, and sometimes unwilling acceptance of undesirable interpretations. The procedure in practice often constitutes interference in management and delays in desirable actions. Most institutions have competent financial officers, and their quality is improving. It is quite possible that this practice of pre-audit may be far more costly to the state than its discontinuance.

The requirements imposed by the state for centralized purchasing have produced widespread criticism. The objections are generally based on the delays encountered and the quality of material received. The best arrangement seems to be to permit appropriately staffed institutions to do their own purchasing, using as fully as possible the resources of a centralized purchasing agency.

Control of institutional personnel policies by a central state agency is not general with respect to faculty. Where exercised it enters into the central responsibility of institutional management. To the extent that the interests of the state appear to require it, personnel controls should be in terms of broad definition with maximal freedom to the appropriate board of higher education to define the specified terms. The direct control of nonacademic personnel by a state agency is objectionable because the implementation of its policies is difficult to articulate with the institutional program and financial operations. In higher education there are many special job classifications not found in other areas of state government. When a state agency attempts to use existing job classifications and pay scales suitable to other areas of state service, more problems are created than solved. Woodburne ably presents his views on this matter in the following:

While it is important in the state institution that the classification of persons or positions and the salary rates have some relationship to those in state government in general, it should be borne in mind that not exactly the same kind of work is involved because a university has a different goal than a department of public works or a department of highways and must reach it by different means. While there should be, therefore, comparable scales in relation to comparable responsibility, and in a sense, comparable classification programs, there should not be any real *identification* of the university nonacademic people with the civil service program of the state. This has occurred or has nearly occurred in several state institutions within recent years. In the instance where it has been tried or been proposed, there have been the most serious kinds of repercussions. It is quite impossible for a state director of civil service to determine in a really effective way the classifications and the pay rates of a teaching institution.[38]

The University of Illinois, faced with this problem, cooperated with the State Civil Service Authority for a separate code that it could administer.

[38] Lloyd S. Woodburne, *Principles of College and University Administration* (Stanford, Calif.: Stanford University Press, 1958), p. 135.

In this way, the needs of the university were recognized, and the standards employed were coordinated with general civil service regulations. There can be no objection to the exercise of state supervision of institutional capital outlay. But when this supervision permits final responsibility for building design and architecture to be lodged with other than the governing board of the institution, then noneducational judgment is given priority over educational judgment, and affords grounds for objection. In some states expenditures in small amounts for repairs or rehabilitation must have prior approval of an officer of the state building department. This appears to be unnecessary and undesirable interference with the management of the institution.

In brief, then, higher education as an agency of state government is to be held to account for its plans, its operations, its resources, and its expenditures. But its operations call for management skills and judgments that differ from those required for other state affairs. The practice of the states in seeking to centralize certain responsibilities for higher education in state agencies should be carefully re-examined to see whether the money economies that may have resulted are in truth real. It may be found that the exercise of responsibilities by state agencies for higher education have cost, in the form of lessened institutional achievements and restrictions on freedom, much more than the economies achieved. More autonomy in management of higher education is needed, with coordination and audit as necessary, but with freedom from interference of state agencies.

Former controller of the state of Michigan, John Lederle, has expressed this point of view: He notes:

Recent management literature has shifted the emphasis away from centralized managerial controls. Hierarchical values, while important, are being challenged by new concepts such as "Bottom-up Management." Present thinking is that we should decentralize, that the role of central control officials is to assist the departments and agencies and encourage them to develop their own control units. In purchasing, in budgeting, in personnel management, the new emphasis is to reverse the centralist trend of a few years ago. The federal Hoover Commission and most state Little Hoover Commissions have stressed decentralization.[39]

A summary by Martorana and Hollis clearly outlines the objectives that should guide the relationships between higher education and other state agencies in the future:

To argue that the leadership in public higher education should adopt a totally resistive attitude to cooperating or working with agencies of State government or with interstate programs would be illogical and unwise. To propose, on the other

[39] John W. Lederle, *The State and Higher Education: A Report from Michigan.* Quoted in Moos and Rourke, *op. cit.,* p. 335.

hand, that the historically proven advantages of autonomy and freedom of operation for academic institutions under lay citizen boards should be relinquished would be even more fallacious. The most fruitful course for the advancement of higher education and the strengthening of its traditional services to society would be to preserve as much as possible proven strengths and yet recognize new demands and conditions.[40]

Summary

In this chapter the extent of public higher education has been shown in terms of the size of state degree-credit enrollments in public institutions. Two-thirds of such enrollments are found in sixteen states. About one-fifth (21.4 per cent) are under the governance of local boards, most of which are supervised by state boards. The remainder (78.6 per cent), or 1,569,249 students, are responsible to the governance of 174 state boards.

The state patterns of organization are diverse and changing. They can be classified into five major categories descriptive of practice. The earlier pattern, in which institutional governing boards are directly responsible to the governor or general assembly, is now found in six states. Some states impose full responsibility for planning, coordinating, and governing higher education on a single governing-coordinating board. Others employ two or more such boards. Some have separate governing boards and governing-coordinating boards. But the trend is toward an over-all state planning-coordinating board with no direct responsibility for governance of institutions.

This trend is consistent with state needs for continuous long-range planning and coordination. Institutions must be required to fulfill the roles assigned them under the over-all state plans. Each institution has the responsibility to seek to maximize its services and may appropriately seek to change its role if such change is in the interest of the state. Many states have yet to assign over-all long-range state planning and coordination to a central state board. They continue to rely on *ad hoc* surveys and on appraisal of boards already overburdened with responsibilities of governance for a number of institutions. In such states, provisions for statewide planning and coordinating of higher education need to be strengthened. Each state needs a central agency for long-range planning and for coordination of functions, facilities, programs, and finance. But each institution also needs its own separate governing board with the maximum of autonomy for governance that can be accorded to it.

The evidence reveals that thirty-one boards have been assigned responsibilities for governing institutions that enroll over 800,000 students. It can

[40] Martorana and Hollis, *State Boards Responsible for Education, op. cit.*, p. 46.

be claimed that the task facing these boards is beyond their powers, partly because of sheer size, partly because the requirements of governance leave too little time for planning, partly because of remoteness from the faculties of the institutions they govern, but more importantly because of an inherent conflict in the roles assigned—conflict of the claims of the immediate with the claims of the future, of established practice with new requirements, of resistance to change with acceptance of innovation. Added to this, many such boards are in command of only a share of over-all state responsibility and hence can plan and coordinate with but limited effectiveness. The governing-coordinating board can be expected to plan inadequately and to govern unsatisfactorily. The real harm that may be cumulative is the bypassing of faculties in management, so that they are not brought to participate and understand and hence to be committed to the institutional purposes. Advisory boards can be no substitute for a board that exercises full institutional responsibility for a single institution. Such a board is essential to secure the consensus and understanding of faculty, executives, and the board concerning the primary purposes and policies of the institution.

The studies that have been made indicate that in their zeal for centralization states have given to centralized state agencies much authority over higher education that impedes its management and in some instances permits noneducational personnel to impose its judgment over that of designated educational personnel. This is harmful to the enterprise and, on balance, the economies that may be achieved are likely to be achieved at too great a cost. The trend in management today in business and industry is toward decentralization of authority. Such decentralization is being urged for governments. In recent legislation of some states, there is evidence of recognition of this trend for public higher education, but management in public higher education is at present operating with limited freedom.

In sum, the need is for a new emphasis on continuous centralized long-range statewide planning and coordination, in which responsibility is assumed by a designated state board. Such a board will study, consult, and propose in regard to objectives, system design, and institutional roles, and it will guide developments in light of the plans. A lay governing board is needed for each institution, and the freedoms of the institutions should be safeguarded through a strengthening of their autonomy. Management in higher education can be held to account by the state through defined policies and through post-audits of its programs, facilities, and finances.

CHAPTER 9

Meeting the Challenges to
Management—A Summary

This book has been written because the accelerating developments in higher education that have occurred and that are foreseeable demand for many institutions a new order of management. The present institutional and state resources for management are inadequate even now, and the gap between what will be needed and what present institutional adaptations portend is a growing one. Achievements in higher education in the next twenty to fifty years will depend in large extent on the quality and adequacy of institutional management.

The challenges to management result from society's insistent and growing demands on the higher educational establishment for an increase in the quantity, quality, and scope of its services. Two forces have activated this demand. The first is a new national concept of higher education as social capital as well as personal capital. This concept rests on the hypothesis that in a democracy the development of individual interests, aptitudes, and capacities under free choice will maximize the over-all social achievement and provide a qualified leadership. The second force is the requirement to guide wisely the adaptation of individuals and groups—in terms of readiness and capacity—to accelerating technological and social changes.

Society has called for extension of the opportunity of higher education to all youth who can qualify for and profit from it; for extended programs of basic research; for new and extended programs to serve adults; and for broader programs of field services. In response to this demand it is anticipated that degree-credit student enrollments may rise from the 3.5 million of 1960 to 7.1 million in 1976; that in this period the programs of research will multiply perhaps six times or more; and that public services and other organized activities may treble.

To provide such services it is estimated that annual current educational expenditures may rise from the $3.6 billion expended in 1957–1958 to a range of from $15.3 to $21.2 billion in 1975–1976, and that in the same period the capital outlay requirements may range from $23.2 to $33.3 billion.

The challenges to management are seen in the increased complexity of the enterprise, in the growth of knowledge, in the need to provide programs to match the increased range in student interest and capacity on the one hand, and the desired outcomes on the other. They are seen in the requirements for adequate and suitable resources and their effective use, and in the exercise of responsibilities of management with respect to changing institutional objectives, programs, resources, and operations.

In this analytical work, consideration was given to the four functions of management as a basis for assessing the needs for the future—the organizing and delegating function, the directive function, the operative function, and the evaluative function. The first is performed in determining how the responsibilities of management are to be borne—what the board will do, what the president and his executives will do, and what the faculty will do. This definition of the duties and responsibilities of the component elements of the institution fixes its organizations in the performance of the directive, operative, and evaluative functions. Not only do organizational elements relate differently for performance of the different functions, but the organization changes as a result of changes in program or through efforts to improve performance.

The directive function is the task of directing the institutional efforts to achievement of determined goals or objectives. Policies are the guides, and plans are the instruments. Every policy action has implications for finance, and financial plans must ever parallel program plans.

The operative function of management is the achievement of performance consistent with the plans. Such achievement requires knowledge of the work, the choice of techniques, the supply of necessary materials, and the assignment of qualified personnel to perform it. To this is added motivation both through appropriate personnel policies and through the leadership of management. Vital to performance are ready and well-used channels for communication, in order to assure common understanding.

Finally there is the evaluative function. Plans for the future require continuous assessment of all aspects of institutional affairs—whether objectives, philosophies, plans, programs, personnel, physical facilities, operations, or the evaluation process itself. Strengths and weaknesses are thus identified.

In the conduct of the institution these functions are carried on simultaneously.

The analyses of these functions, the assessments made, and their implications have been presented in some detail in the several chapters. In this chapter the more important needs of management that require attention to meet the challenges of the future will be identified. While some identified needs may relate more to one function than to another, others relate to several or all of them. In the summary that follows, therefore, the emphasis is on the needs of management, without identifying the nature of the functions involved. The order of presentation is not significant. All are important.

1. *Governance of institutions by consensus is essential.* This is a philosophy of management that seeks agreement on all major matters by the lay governing board, the president, the executives, and the faculty. This is a more difficult process than the simple exercise of authority, but it will not only secure faculty and executive identity with the institution and dedication to it; it will also enhance the quality of the policies, plans, and achievements.

To govern successfully by consensus, the board, in delegating responsibility and authority, must retain the authority to over-ride. To fail to do so is to transfer authority rather than to delegate it. The mere provision will do much to obviate the need for use of such reserved control.

It is in the development of objectives and plans and the process of evaluation that consensus of faculty, major executives, president, and board can evolve. Considerable attention must be given to how all may work together to develop and agree on objectives, major policies, and plans. Lay councils are enlisted by the institution to assist in relating aspects of program to the needs of the future. The faculty participates through proposals developed by divisional and general committees. Policies and plans relating to the areas of student personnel, education, and business and finance are prepared by the responsible officers. The committee on policy, program, and finance assists the president in considering and coordinating proposals. On this committee are the president, members of the faculty general committee, and major executives; a parallel committee is the board committee on objectives, plans, and evaluation. Joint meetings are held as arranged by the president.

Thus, in charting the institutional course, the faculty is accorded a leadership role, but its proposals are subject to review and coordination in which its representatives participate. The president has responsibility for seeking consensus on the plans. Because there is time for debate, and because change once determined will be fully understood in advance of action, this procedure seems most likely to achieve a unity of purpose of all the participants in management. In the focus on objectives and in the plans there must be machinery for working together, for communication and participation.

2. *Large delegation of board responsibility under its reserved control should be made to a unified organization with the president as the single chief executive. Such organization must be designed to facilitate the exercise of the directive, operative, and evaluative functions of management.* The interdependence of the three elements of management—policy, program, and finance—requires a unified organization with the president fully responsible for coordinating all three elements. Broad delegations of responsibility are made by the president, with the approval of the board, to major executives in the areas of educational services, student personnel services, business and financial services, public relations and development (fund-raising) services. A new major post is needed in the larger institutions to assist the president in coordinating research on institutional affairs and in coordinating the long-range plans. The president is the coordinator of policies, programs, and finance, the medium of communication between institutional personnel and board, and usually the spokesman for the institution to the public.

In management, the development of policies and plans may wisely enlist the aid of many, but in performance the responsibility is best exercised by the responsible executive. The organization must reflect the fact that institutional personnel are involved in different ways and in different degrees in the exercise of the functions of management. When the plans are made and the necessary personnel and facilities are available, performance is primarily a line responsibility, although the executive may seek advice on certain aspects of performance. In the line organization, which is primarily descriptive of organizations for operations or performance, each person is assigned to one and only one organization unit and is responsible to the head of that unit. It is in a line organization that the appointee or employee performs the special service for which he is prepared and to which he is assigned. For the faculty, it will be in an academic department or division; for the nonacademic employee it will be in an organization unit in which the employee will be under the supervision of and subject to the direction of the head of the unit. A proposed unit for the collegiate undergraduate instruction is the academic division rather than the traditional academic department because it permits more effective coordination of programs, better planning, and relieves professors from onorous administrative work as department heads.

In planning, and to some extent in the conduct of procedures for evaluation, the emphasis is on staff relationships. It is important that the extent and manner of involvement be defined. For the educational program a faculty general committee develops objectives and plans for the educational program. Divisional committees and subcommittees may be employed as needed. This faculty general committee is represented on the president's committee on policy, program, and finance, as are the supporting areas through their major executives. It is here that over-all plans are coordinated. The board has a parallel committee on objectives, long-range plans, and evaluation, and as arranged by the president these two committees may hold joint sessions. Other staff services are provided in each of the areas. When a person is performing as staff he is responsible only for the quality of the advice he gives.

Much responsibility for operations is decentralized. This decentralization is broadly achieved in delegating to major executives responsibility for broad areas of operations—education, student personnel, business and finance, public relations and fund raising. Each of these executives has responsibility for employing many specialists. Hence each executive must be a generalist capable of relating his area to the whole, but seeking performance consistent with institutional purposes. He must serve as an interpreter to the personnel of his area of institutional objectives, philosophies, plans, and programs. He will be the medium of two-way communication, both vertically and horizontally, but he will foster appropriate communication through contact channels. He will guide the senior executives—themselves specialists—in performing their roles. And within the area, as with the institution, the primary characteristic of management is decentralization.

Each officer is responsible for records and reports, and each should carry out continuous evaluation of all aspects of plans, organization, personnel, and performance. Each officer must seek to coordinate achievement with the achievement of others, in order that the value of service will be enhanced.

Thus delegation is reflected in organization. The test of delegation is its effectiveness in promoting wise planning, in achieving effective performance, and in fostering high morale of institutional personnel. It should be emphasized that in the performance of the management functions—directive, operative, and evaluative—the elements of organization, even though using established channels, may perform in different ways. Also, it must be emphasized that organization as outlined is to be flexible, and that countless *ad hoc* arrangements to achieve defined objectives are necessary and common.

3. *Procedures and channels for communication to, from, and among institutional personnel are essential to governance by consensus.* The participants in government at all levels must be informed, and opportunities

must be provided for expressing opinions and judgments. Information must be provided concerning objectives, policies, plans, finance, facilities, programs, and evaluation. Such information will relate to the institution as a whole, to the area, and to the particular organization unit.

The teachers of a given subject must relate their work to each other's, to other subjects, and to over-all student programs. The course sequences for those majoring in areas of specialization, the needed resources, the relationships with library services, the over-all educational objectives, the over-all curriculum design—all these and more call for understanding and discussion. Within the area of personnel, the plans for services include working relationships. The relation of standards for student selection to student achievement and the success of graduates; the relation of problem cases to health; the opportunities to improve the quality of student life through residential, cultural, and social programs—all these and more call for understanding and discussion. In the area of business and financial affairs, the quality of financial services to students and staff, the carrying out of programs of plant operations and maintenance, the suitability of services of purchasing materials and supplies, the quality of bookstore operations, and the recruitment and servicing of nonacademic personnel—all these and more call for understanding.

It will be recognized at once that care must be exercised to provide the right amount of information to elicit meaningful discussion. Information on trivial matters wastes time and risks loss of interest. The appropriate involvement of personnel in discussion is an art.

The most important and frequent form of communication is face-to-face discussion between individuals or in groups. Organization provides formal channels, but these may be supplemented by personal letters. For informing large groups, newsletters or newspapers can be used. To the fullest extent that is appropriate, contact channels should be encouraged.

The channels and practices of communication importantly condition achievement of governance by consensus. This is a matter worthy of serious study, for in addition to achieving the primary purposes, it can have important effects on personnel attitudes.

4. *Clear definition and continuous review of objectives, and the institutional guidelines for achieving them, are essential.* Each institution must carefully define its objectives or purposes, the nature of the undertakings it deems necessary to achieve them, and the general guidelines in accordance with which the undertakings are to develop. This is a joint responsibility of board, president, executives, and faculty. To define objectives clearly and to determine the nature and scope of institutional programs is in itself a major undertaking. These are matters which must be fully understood by all participants in management and by all institutional personnel. And this

understanding is to be renewed and deepened. It must be the constant focus of institutional effort.

These definitions and guidelines will have the interest of the public, and this interest should be cultivated. But they must not be regarded merely as expressions of ideals or hopes. Rather, they are the firm practical bases for developing the plans for achievement—plans for programs, for resources, and for finance. They are the decisions that set the institutional course.

Difficult as this requirement may be, it is not enough. In light of rapid technological and social change and the rapid changes in higher education itself, objectives and guidelines must be continuously reviewed and evaluated in order that desirable changes can be foreseen and acted upon.

In this review and evaluation the aid of lay councils, broadly representative of the public interest, may be enlisted. Such councils may bring to the institution broader views of present and future social needs in relation to institutional programs. They may also be helpful in evaluating programs.

5. *Long-range planning is fundamental to modern management.* The institution's plans are the instruments consistent with policies that translate the concepts expressed in policies into concrete proposals for action. Plans —both long-range and annual—always involve the parallels of programs, resources, and finance. Long-range plans are fundamental to effective management. They afford perspective; they permit consideration of institutional change that in the short term are not feasible; they afford time for necessary debate; and they permit an orderly array of priorities in effecting institutional change. While the span of time for long-range plans is seen as variable, a period of at least ten years is suggested. Short-range or annual plans should be consistent with the long-range plans. If a basic reason occurs that does not permit this, the propriety of that aspect of the long-range plans is brought into question.

The long-range projection must begin with programs designed to achieve institutional objectives. The faculty will evidence leadership here. It is necessary that the proposed plans for primary programs of instruction, research, and field services be coordinated with the supporting services of student personnel, plant operation and maintenance, other business and financial services, public relations and fund raising. And provisions for adequate assistance for the president and major executives must not be overlooked.

Plans for programs have implications for staffing and for physical facilities. There may thus be developed long-range plans for resources—plans for staffing, for campus development and improvement, for equipment replacements and additions, and for library facilities and books. The third long-range planning instrument is the financial plan. These three instruments are so interrelated that any change in one will doubtless cause change in the others. The long-range financial plan will demonstrate the financial feasibility of the plans for programs and resources, and to the extent that proposed expenditures exceed available income, the plans for programs and resources are altered until maximum achievement within the limits of available funds is possible for them.

The president is the coordinator of both the plans and the planning. In an institution of some size he will need a major executive to assist him in directing research on institutional affairs and in coordinating the plans. Proposals for educational objectives and long-range plans will be developed by a committee representative of the faculty. Each of the major executives will within his area devise long-range plans for supporting services. In coordinating these plans the president will have the aid of two very important committees—a committee on policy, program, and finance consisting of faculty representatives and major executives, and a parallel board committee on objectives, long-range plans, and evaluation. These committees may hold joint meetings as arranged by the president.

6. *In achieving the objects sought, the minimal requirement for work must be efficiently performed.* The kind, quantity, and quality of the work must be at a level to achieve the objective sought, but not much beyond it. The work must be organized to permit effective supervision and the choice of effective techniques.

At every level of activity, the kind, quantity, and quality of the work to be performed must be defined. This is implied in policy and further defined in plans, but it must be expressed in assignment of qualified personnel, appropriate materials, and standards of performance. Here the object must be to minimize the work requirement for the achievement of the requisite standard. It is the application of the principle of efficient allocation of resources in meeting standards that results in economical practice without lowering standards.

Every institution faces the need for decisions on how to organize the work. These decisions will importantly affect the achievement of the purposes sought, the effective use of specialized knowledges and skills, the feasibility of using effective techniques, and the quality of supervision. Should a professional school also provide for studies of the liberal arts, or should it rely on programs offered by the college of liberal arts? Should the library services be centralized or decentralized? Should plant operations be organized centrally or by building? Where possible, the grouping of skills permits competent supervision. But there are circumstances where other considerations are determinants.

Every supervisor and senior officer is directly concerned with the choice of techniques employed in work performance. Grouping similar skills under competent supervision promotes the use of techniques that are effective and economical. Improved techniques are often related only to new products and new methods, but there are better ways, for example, to answer the telephone, to improve the appearance of outgoing letters, to guide and teach students. This search for better ways is of concern to both workers and management. In choosing how the work is to be done account must be taken of safety hazards, worker fatigue and morale, economy, and standards of performance.

Norms or general guides for requirements of personnel and materials have in many instances been established. Thus work requirements can be translated into jobs and in turn into requirements for specialized personnel and materials. These afford the basis for plans and budgets for annual and long-range plans. This specification also permits recruitment of personnel as required as well as a review of their training needs.

7. *Personnel policies and practices that provide satisfaction in work, motivation to achievement, and personal growth are essential to the realization of institutional objectives.* The personnel policies that affect both the academic and nonacademic personnel are vital to institutional achievement. These policies must assure to the teacher the freedom to teach and to search for the truth. They must fix a democratic climate in which to work. Participation in management must be in an atmosphere of mutual respect and common purpose. Provision for tenure, compensation, health, security, and individual growth and development must be as full as institutional resources permit. For nonacademic personnel the policies should relate to recruitment, probation, placement, job evaluation, training, transfer, promotion, compensation, health, security, and individual growth and development.

The policies alone will not suffice. There is always need for leadership, for interpretation of the role of the individual in the undertaking, for interest in individual growth and development. This leadership must be exercised as fully as possible by all who exercise responsibility for personnel.

Most institutions have an officer who performs personnel functions for nonacademic personnel. For the academic personnel this function is assigned to the dean. In recent years, however, many deans have found their days filled with growing requirements related to schedules, staffing, contracts, and the like, and this function for the academic staff is often inadequately cared for. Yet here it offers the highest potential benefit. When a dean finds time lacking for guiding and encouraging faculty members, an assistant to perform routine administrative work is probably needed.

Each worker should be responsible to one and only one executive or supervisor, and should have an assignment of work that will utilize his knowledge and skills. He should be brought to understand the significance of the work in the enterprise. The exercise of supervision of his work should be based on respect and leadership and knowledge of the work. Each worker should have available opportunities for self-development and growth. His work should be free of hazard, and he should be free to express suggestions concerning all aspects of his work.

Each officer should be brought to participate in the development of policies and plans. Each must delegate responsibilities, establish channels of communications, and assure suitable performance of the work on time. Each must exercise leadership of the personnel under his jurisdiction, and through such leadership motivate them to superior performance.

8. *The institutional records system should more effectively serve management.* The records system of the institution must serve well the needs of management: the needs of the officer in charge of the activity, the needs of major executives, the faculty, the president, and the governing board. The records are those relating to operations or performance, to students, to personnel and physical facilities, and to finance. Such records are essential at the local level, but a careful review may identify important values to overall management, without increase in cost. The faculty personnel record can be an important aid in the recognition of merit or in developing a long-range staffing plan; a record of faculty assignments can be useful in devising assignments for the following year or for establishing a norm essential in long-range planning. A record of class size may permit assessment of experience with large classes, and it may point to very small classes that can scarcely be justified. A record of plant utilization may reveal maladjustments in office assignments and may forestall the erection of an unneeded building.

In the performance of operations, the records of the use of personnel and materials for a certain task permit consideration of possible alternate plans for the work in the future. Such records are basic to cost analyses and are thus useful in the assessment of the values achieved in relation to the costs and as estimates of values and costs of alternate procedures.

Records are useful not only in operations but also in the development of policies and plans, and in the evaluation of program activities, personnel, and facilities. They should be adequate to the need; and the information they supply should be readily available in planning, decision making, and evaluation.

To the extent justified, electronic data processing may assist in providing up-to-date information. The value of such information must be assessed in relation to the cost.

9. *More effective use of institutional resources can and should be achieved.* There exists an undersupply of suitable institutional resources— well-trained teachers and other personnel and adequate facilities. This shortage is expected to prevail for many years. At the same time, faculty salaries are low and many desirable improvements in programs are denied in order to limit expenditures to available income. There are also widespread evidences of uneconomic practices—proliferation of courses, small classes, low

utilization of plant, an academic year that in many institutions employs neither teachers nor facilities for the entire summer—to name a few. In many institutions, the introduction of more economical practices may improve the program and at the same time permit increases in the salaries of teachers without increasing the cost per student. Economical utilization of buildings may avoid heavy expenditures for capital outlay.

The primary purpose of the improvement in the economics of operations is to improve the quantity and quality of educational opportunities for students. This responsibility should be shared by the entire institutional personnel. The search for economy does not imply that faculty are to be overworked, buildings overcrowded, or curricula weakened. But it does mean that so long as resources are wasted, funds will be used needlessly rather than for increases in salaries or for other means of strengthening programs. Poor use of resources defeats the efforts to realize the purposes of the institution.

When proposals are made for programs, if the cost exceeds available income the plans must be reviewed until they represent the greatest value for the money to be spent.

It is now essential that all who participate in management understand fully the economics of the institution, the use of resources, and the costs. Finally, finance should be one of the considerations affecting choice with respect to all proposals.

10. *A comprehensive, systematic, and continuous evaluation of all aspects of the institution is an essential process.* Evaluation is the process of securing value judgments useful in improving the services of the institution. These value judgments may be based on objective evidence, on experience, on subjective judgment, or on any combination of these bases. Every act of management reflects such judgments. There can be no rational improvement of institutional services without them. It follows that any program that will improve the quality of such value judgments will improve the institution.

Evaluation may relate to any aspect of the institution—whether the plans, the physical facilities, the student, the program, the particular research project, or a method of teaching. The need for it in the institution is pervasive and continuous. In practice, while immediate supervisors actively employ it, it has not received the attention of executives, the president, and the board that it deserves. Properly employed, the evaluation program will secure to the institution its most useful role in society; it will assure use of an appropriate educational philosophy; it will maximize the usefulness of program; it will achieve effective economy; and it will secure to program the essential resources and apply them through the use of effective techniques.

The scope of the evaluation program should be broad. Executives should be brought to understand that evaluation is in fact a dimension of management, and their responsibilities for it should be defined.

The methods and procedures of evaluation should have general acceptance of those responsible for management—the faculty, the executives, the president, and the board. They should be developed by each executive for all aspects of his area and should be reviewed by the president's committee on policy, program, and finance. Such review will assure more ready acceptance of the results and will protect the executive from possible criticism of procedures employed.

Different procedures are required for evaluation of the different aspects of the institution. There should be clear conception of the functions to be served by the activity or by the use of the resource. Competent persons should identify characteristics or qualities of the activity or resource essential to the performance sought. Competent persons should devise tests and measures—objective and/or subjective—relative to such characteristics and qualities. Time schedules for employing the established procedures should be determined. The value judgments from competent persons should be secured and reviewed.

Not all evaluation can best be done by the institutional personnel. Sometimes the opinions of the employers of graduates will assist; sometimes the judgments of professional personnel from other institutions will be useful.

An effective evaluation program may take years to develop and is never complete. But a comprehensive, continuous program is seen as a basic need in each institution. It will require much thought and energy but probably very little additional money.

11. *The public should be informed concerning institutional affairs.* The growth of public interest in higher education is based on public expectation of benefit from its services, on commitment of public and philanthropic funds in its support, on personal observation of growth and development of sons and daughters who attend, and on the continued regard and loyalty of alumni. The public now recognizes that higher education for leadership is basic to the national well-being. Philanthropists, business enterprises, and governments are investing increasing amounts annually; the opportunities available to youth and adults are being enlarged; and programs of basic research and field services are growing. Millions of families entrust their sons and daughters to institutional guidance in their formative years.

The public is deeply interested in what the institutions are seeking to do and in how they are going about it. They are interested in the concepts that guide program development, in the objects of research, and in the nature of faculty services in the field. They are interested, too, in the quality of faculty personnel and in their competencies and achievements. And they are interested in cost.

This interest is entirely warranted and must be cultivated. It may be cultivated in part by a systematic provision of information and in part by the involvement of leaders in service on lay councils. The greater the interest and involvement, the greater the understanding and support of services in the public interest.

Information should be systematically provided and addressed both to the general public and to the special publics that have deeper interests. Various channels may be used—published newsletters, addresses, radio and television appearances, and discussion meetings. The special publics may include alumni, the membership of lay councils, the philanthropists, and members of the local community. At times the latter public is mistakenly ignored. It is both an educational resource for students and a potential friend of the institution. The needs of the community for adult education may well be provided for by the institution, and the needs for community leadership may well be partially met by members of the faculty.

The cultivation of broad understanding of programs designed to serve the social needs will gain public approval, and public approval will elicit financial support from philanthropists and governments.

12. *In the exercise of state responsibility for higher education, an over-all state planning-coordinating board, with each state institution governed by its own lay board, provides for over-all long-range state plans and affords a basis for institutional governance by consensus.* State patterns of organization for the exercise of responsibilities for higher education are diverse and changing. The earlier pattern in which institutional governing boards are directly responsible to the governor or general assembly is now found in only six states. Some states impose responsibility for planning, coordinating, and governing higher education in the state on a single governing-coordinating board. Others employ two or more such boards. Some states have one or more institutions, each responsible to its own board, together with one or more governing-coordinating boards, each responsible for two or more institutions. But a recent trend is to an over-all state planning-coordinating board that exercises no direct responsibility for institutional governance.

This trend is considered desirable to exercise the necessary state responsibility for continuous long-range planning, for guiding institutional design and development, and for appropriate allocation of institutional functions. Such a board is seen as necessary for each state.

Among the sixty-six governing-coordinating boards found within the fifty states, there are thirty-one that exercise responsibility for governing institutions that enroll over 800,000 students. The tasks facing these boards are considered generally to be beyond their powers to accomplish for several reasons: (1) The sheer size of the task makes it difficult. (2) The day-by-day requirements of governance leave too little time for long-range planning. (3) They are too remote from the institutions they govern to achieve consensus with institutional personnel. (4) The interests of individual institutions may conflict with the requirements envisioned in statewide plans. Many of these boards exercise only a share of state responsibility and hence can plan and coordinate with limited effectiveness. An over-all state planning-coordinating board, with each institution governed by a separate board, is desirable.

There is a strong trend toward delegation of authority over many aspects of higher education to centralized state agencies. But current management theory is in the direction of decentralization, and the states' provisions of centralization of authority in state agencies should be reassessed.

The exercise of state responsibility for higher education must recognize the importance of an appropriate philosophy for this responsibility. It must make wise provision for continuous statewide planning, system design, and coordination, for a maximum of autonomy for the enterprise, for a separate lay board to govern each institution, and for continuous evaluation of objects, plans, and institutional performance.

These twelve areas are seen as areas that in many institutions require strengthening. In many institutions the relationships that would permit governance by consensus are lacking. The president and the executives are often overworked and need assistance; the working relationships with faculty must be better established; the concept of the role of the board must be reviewed. Even when appropriate relationships are established, each institution tends to be isolated. It is true that each is unique and must solve its problems in ways suitable to it. But there is within the institutions research on institutional affairs and experiences in the solution of problems that would be useful to others. Moreover, even if common problems calling for research are identified, there exists no agency to undertake it. If regional centers could be established under private independent auspices and guided by the cooperative efforts of the institutions, they could provide services of value far in excess of the cost. These services could include dissemination of knowledge, of practices, of results of research, of sponsorship of research, and of staff advice and assistance to institutions that request such information. A single cooperative center sponsored by the states to assist in the development of state systems and of interstate cooperation could be of major service to the several states. Such centers would speed the identification and use of successful practices.

In these chapters new emphases have been placed on achieving consensus on major institutional matters of policy by faculty, executives, president, and board; on communication and participation; on appropriate delegation and organization; on continuous search of objectives; on long-range plans for programs, resources, and finance; on effective and economical achievement of performance; and on comprehensive, continuous evaluation. In all aspects of management the importance of personnel policies and procedures that will afford the necessary climate for personal and professional achievement in promotion of student growth and development has been stressed.

Society has assigned to higher education responsibility for educating the national leadership for the future, and for the conduct of important research and field services. Institutional achievement will depend in large measure on the quality and adequacy of management. The expenditures for management are but a small portion of the large sums that are now being spent and that will be spent for higher education. It is safe to say that in the search for ways in which to strengthen the enterprise there can be no more strategic focus of attention than on the management of the higher educational effort.

Observations and Opinions Concerning Some Major Aspects of Management

The Governing Board

Serious studies have been made of the governing boards of colleges and universities—of their compositions, responsibilities, organizations, and practices. A summary of some of the more significant findings of these studies is the purpose of this brief summary.

Lay Boards of Control

Brubacher and Rudy write

It is a credit to the builders of American higher education that the foundations which they laid down in colonial times for the organization and administration of higher education were still standing in the twentieth century. Although in the meantime the colonial college had become a modern university, although student bodies had grown from hundreds to thousands, and although budgets had skyrocketed from thousands to millions of dollars, the frame of academic government remained basically unchanged. [3:339]

Rauh identifies the basic characteristics in the following words:

The distinguishing characteristic of college trusteeship in the United States is that control is vested almost without exception in lay boards. . . .

Under this system of lay control we have produced a concept of universal educational opportunity which has characterized the phenomenal development of American higher education. The diversity of our colleges and universities seems to have been encouraged by this system of control. [26:13]

These lay boards, notes Rauh, are invested with "complete powers of management, most of which they elect to delegate to professional educators. They operate without the checks and balances typical of our democratic society." [26:15]

Size of Boards

Governing boards vary greatly in size. Heneman finds the range from seven to as large as one hundred, with the average between fifteen and eighteen members. [18:124] The study by the Carnegie Foundation for the Advancement of Teaching finds size varying "from 3 to 115, with a median of 15. Public universities tend to have smaller boards—a median of 10 as against 24 for private institutions. There are excellent reasons for avoiding the extremes of smallness and largeness." [7:6]

Trustee Qualifications

Some qualifications deemed desirable for trustees were identified by the Columbia University Special Trustee Committee. Among those listed are an unimpeachable reputation, demonstrated qualities of leadership, a strong interest in the aims and purposes of higher education, an open mind. "He [the trustee] must actively recognize that conventionality and conformity, no matter how greatly they ease social interactions, are not the prime qualities through which a university grows, prospers and advances." The interest of the trustee must be directed much more at the general than at the specific. The Committee rejects any idea of proportional representation, whether of professions, social classes, or any other; it prohibits membership of its own faculty, but not members of faculties of other institutions. It stresses the value of willingness to work hard, and considers representation of a particular school or college inappropriate. The Committee endorses the policy of filling six trustee places with alumni. Approving of eighteen life members, the Committee recognizes the need to balance the advantages of wide geographic distribution with the need for accessibility of trustees to work in committee. A retirement age of seventy is recommended. The presence of vice-presidents at all meetings (except executive sessions) is recommended, the Treasurer to be present when his report is considered. Because of the responsibility of fund raising and fund allocation, the presence on the board of businessmen, lawyers, and bankers is deemed necessary and desirable, but the search for talent should consider the "widest possible" diversities. [8:15–18]

"It is surprising," states Rauh, "that so few professional educators are members of boards considering that almost without exception trustees and presidents who have served on boards with educators testify that they make firstrate board members." [26:62]

The Columbia University Committee finds that alumni are increasingly represented on boards. "Nowhere, so far as this committee knows, is there an anti-alumnus rule or tradition, but dependence on the alumnus-trustee naturally varies from institution to institution." [8:14]

Board Responsibilities

The Columbia University Committee, observing that control is vested in a lay board which in turn governs the professionals (the faculty) finds the reason for success of this arrangement

lies not only in the wisdom but in the restraint with which the individual trustee conducts himself in the unique situation he occupies. The legal supremacy of the trustees and their final authority to act as they wish is unquestioned, but the most experienced trustees are themselves constantly warning their newer colleagues that overactivity in certain areas—particularly in the area of education itself—is as great a sin against the modern spirit of trusteeship as is neglect. [8:8, 9]

The responsibilities of the board, and how these should be exercised, has had much attention. It will be of interest to review opinions of those who have studied this matter.

The Columbia University Committee summarizes the legal responsibilities of the board of control in these words:

Yet any board of trustees which rested entirely upon its legal supremacy would obviously be an imperfect board, deficient in the sensitivity which must guide and inform a university's progress. The major legal responsibilities which devolve upon the trustees are, in the opinion of this Committee, three:

    a) To select and appoint the president of the university;

    b) To be finally responsible for the acquisition, conservation and management of the university's funds and properties;

    c) To oversee and approve the *kind* of education offered by the university and make certain that the *quality* meets the highest standards possible. [8:20]

Rauh puts it simply—the responsibilities are the duties which the board can perform better than any other agency. They include:

1. To fill vacancies and make changes in the office of president. In this function the board oversees the basic purpose of the institution.

2. To hold title to and conserve property. The board thus supervises the financial well-being of the institution.

3. To act as a court of last resort.

4. To hold the charter and seek revision of it when it is deemed necessary.

And he adds a basic function recognized by the Columbia University Committee.

5. To oversee and approve the *kind* of education offered by the university, and to make certain that its *quality* meets the highest standards possible. [26:19]

Ruml and Morrison take a sterner view, and place emphasis on trustee over-all responsibility. They reason:

Since the liberal college is a body corporate in the public interest, the powers, privileges and immunities of its Trustees are in fact duties and obligations. These rights are given by the charter to the Trustees in order that they may be exercised, and exercised by these particular persons or by their lawful successors. A single Trustee or the Trustees collectively may abdicate from their position of authority, but they cannot annul it; they may vacate their posts, but they cannot destroy them; they may delegate activities and decisions, but they cannot thereby avoid their own responsibilities. [28:3–4]

In the exercise of responsibilities, as Corson notes,

. . . board members find themselves (1) dependent on others for the formulation and effective making of many decisions for which they are ultimately responsible, (2) inadequately informed about the basic operations for which their institution exists, and (3) unable to influence decisions that determine the basic character of the institution as an educational enterprise for which they (influenced by tradition) have delegated authority to the faculty. [10:49]

Heneman holds this view of board responsibilities:

The president should see that his board deals with major matters and not with trivia. Governing boards should seek to establish objectives and policies and to insist upon the selection of good people. They should ask for assistance from the president and his chief administrative and educational officers in defining educational objectives; developing a plan of organization for administration; establishing requirements for plant, money, and people; and planning for the longer periods of time. Once objectives and policies have been systematically defined and approved by it, the governing board should permit the administration to conduct its affairs within the framework of these policies. [18:123]

Millett describes the board as "an insulating arrangement standing between the political process as spokesman of the public interest and the faculty, students, and alumni as spokesmen of their particular interests." He sees oversight of the administration as a primary function:

The board is deeply concerned with educational leadership, not because it is competent to provide such leadership but because it realizes the tendency of a profession to become dedicated to tradition, to engage in introspection, and to subscribe to ingrown practices. The board is deeply concerned with the expansion and utilization of economic resources. The board is deeply concerned with the efficient and effective performance of the services needed to maintain the college or university as an on-going community. In a sense it might be said that the board of trustees is the keeper of the social conscience, the protector of the public interest in higher education. [24:183–184]

The Trustees of the Carnegie Foundation for the Advancement of Teaching summarize the role of trustees in these words:

Most observers agree that a major task of trustees is to represent the college or university to the world. Since they are generally drawn from the leadership of the larger community, they accomplish this in part just by being the kind of people they are. In the normal course of their lives they have innumerable opportunities to educate the community concerning the college or university.

In many ways the trustees also provide a bridge between the institution and the community. As leaders in the larger community they bring to their deliberations as board members a breadth of view that effectively supplements the academic concerns of the faculty and administration.

The fact that the trustees are rooted in the larger community is important in connection with another of their duties: to protect the institution from improper pressures or attack, and particularly from outside interference with legitimate teaching functions. Because of their status, they are often able to accomplish this defense in ways that would be impossible for faculty or administration.

The most important responsibility of the board is to select a president, to back him when he is doing a good job, and to remove him when he is not. . . . A great many institutions have had experience with trustee-faculty collaboration in selection of a president, and the results have been favorable, on the whole. [7:9]

In Corson's view, the board can contribute to faculty interpretation of the evolving needs of society. He writes:

This is not to suggest that board members are always more accurately sensitive to or even aware of the evolving needs of society than are historians, economists, sociologists, or political scientists. It is to suggest that board members should be able to light up angles of the problem not apparent to the professors and to provide an additional, more comprehensive, and pragmatic interpretation of society's course. [10:58]

Board Committees

Rauh states:

The vast majority of boards make extensive use of standing committees of trustees to accomplish their business. Their function in the administration of the college may be any combination of the following:

1. To accomplish a larger order of business than would be possible in meetings of the full board.

2. To "educate" trustees in the problems of the institution by giving them more occasion for intimate contact.
3. To utilize special skills of trustees more efficiently.
4. To provide more occasions for direct contact between trustees and members of the staff.
5. To provide readily available local groups of trustees where the board as a whole is geographically scattered.
6. To screen and prepare matters for action by the full board.

While the names of the various committees are legion, the most commonly used designations are: executive, finance, curriculum, buildings and grounds.

Additional or alternate names are audit, budget, development, investment, honorary degree, nominations, library, and so on. The functions of the committees are not uniformly described by the title, so that a finance committee may work on investments or a curriculum committee on the library. . . .

Some trustees feel that when committees are properly used, they offer the president an effective opportunity to draw on the trustees for counsel on management decisions, while at the same time giving the trustees a better basis for considering board matters of policy. [26:72, 74]

Heneman's observations are somewhat similar to Rauh's. He writes:

Usually, boards operate through committees. The committee structure of some boards is a bewildering maze of outmoded and outdated bodies which provide little support to the board as a whole in dealing with the major problems of institutional management and may complicate internal administration. However, the basic committees which normally are found to be most useful include the following: educational policies, budget and finance, buildings and grounds, student affairs, development and planning, and executive. It is surprising how many boards fragment these committees and create bodies which either confuse basic areas of management or fall into disuse. [18:124]

The Trustees of the Carnegie Foundation for the Advancement of Teaching describe the working of the committee system as follows:

Most boards, particularly the large ones, depend rather heavily on an active executive committee. As a rule, boards have two or three other standing committees whose decisions are formally ratified by the full board after the fact. The committees on finance and the budget are in this category. So are the committees on investment and endowment. And so, as a rule, are committees on physical plant.

In some boards all the significant work is done by the standing committees. The full board meeting concerns itself chiefly with formalities and the ratifying of committee decisions. A powerful committee system enables board members to become thoroughly familiar with some one aspect of university policy. Trustees gain significant education in such assignments and may bring to the work special skills that would never be called on in a general board meeting. Some boards have developed a rotation system among the various committees. This is useful from the standpoint of the institution because it enables trustees to become familiar with all aspects of the university functioning, but the trustees are not always enthusiastic about it. [7:6, 7]

Corson finds three types of committees to be common.

These are the committees on finance or budget or, in some instances, audit; on investment, endowments, or gifts and grants; and on physical plant or buildings and grounds. This and other evidences suggest that these three areas comprise the bulk of the decision-making of many governing boards.

Board Responsibility for Educational Policy

Corson continues:

On the other hand, the extent of the participation by boards in the making of educational decisions, i.e., in matters of degree requirements, curricula, and courses, was early suggested by the conclusions of Elliot et al. They indicated that only 6 per cent of the governing boards of 91 institutions surveyed had committees concerned with academic policies. [10:52]

The Trustees of the Carnegie Foundation for the Advancement of Teaching bring into question this lack of involvement in educational decisons:

Curiously it is not common practice to have a standing committee on educational policy. One study of 91 institutions found only five that had committees concerned with educational policies. This reflects the strong tradition that the board should concern itself primarily with finances and physical plant. Yet one may doubt the wisdom of making no provision for continuing study of educational policy by the board. Every major decision the board makes ultimately affects the educational program. A college or university is an educational institution, not just in part, but through and through. Decisions to build a new chemistry building, or launch a medical school fund drive, or raise salaries in the liberal arts college are educational decisions.

In other words, trustees are involved in educational policy whether they like it or not. They had better know what they are talking about. [7:6]

Rauh notes that trustees may wish to exercise some responsibility for the curriculum. He says:

Although it is generally agreed that the curriculum is the prerogative of the faculty, there seems to be some recognized limitations upon the faculty's right to action . . . it is possible that by gradual or complete modification of the educational program the purpose and character of the institution may change significantly. In such situations, the trustees may want to be involved. . . .

However, more and more boards are finding that it is possible to participate in educational matters without intruding upon the basic rights of the faculty in this area. [26:21, 34–35]

Carman fosters this view of joint participation. He writes:

Throughout the nation this division of labor between trustees and faculty, advocated by Laird Bell and other distinguished spokesmen in the field of higher education, is rapidly gaining acceptance. Both parties are learning that each can be helpful to the other. From the faculty, board members can obtain insight and points of view which will not only help them to understand current programs, but proposals for new programs, including educational innovations and experiments. The faculty, in turn, can frequently benefit by pondering intelligent questions raised by board members. The president of the institution can be immensely helpful in keeping the lines of communication open between board and faculty. Indeed, this is one way in which the president can display his leadership. Cooperation between faculty and board can be achieved in more ways than one. [5:92]

Ruml and Morrison find the trustees basically responsible for the curriculum. They state:

The program leading to the degree is the curriculum, and for this, too, the trustees are responsible, since it is by the quality and test of the curriculum that the degree is awarded. In general practice, the design and the operation of the curriculum have been referred by the Trustees to the faculty and other academic officers, but although the activities relating to the curriculum pass for the time being into other hands, the responsibility remains with the Trustees, who have the degree-awarding power. [28:6]

Ruml and Morrison regard academic policy as a basic responsibility of trustees. They express this view as follows:

The faculty has been the instrument for organizing the curriculum. It has depended on departmental initiative for substantive proposals and on balance of power for its decisions. Under this system, the liberal college has deteriorated, its economic and financial position has become untenable. It cannot draw to its faculty the outstanding talent of its generation, although it still holds the prestige embodied in the ideal of "liberal education as preparation for the good life."

The Trustees must be informed as to what the faculty's administration of curriculum and methods of instruction has done to the liberal college. The Trustees must set some informed standards of performance on which their administrative officers can rely. The Trustees, to be successful, must accomplish these purposes with the cooperation of all, and above all must preserve for the individual faculty member the personal rights and privileges that are essential to the character of the liberal college. [28:89]

McGrath, like Ruml and Morrison, urges trustees to exercise responsibility for educational policy. Noting the lack of graduate programs for the training of college teachers, he says:

Unless trustees initiate appropriate steps toward the reform of the graduate program, the education of college youth will deteriorate with accelerated speed. If the academic community had to make a choice between the education of research scholars or college teachers, it would be a serious question of national policy whether research should have priority over undergraduate teaching. No such troublesome choice is at present before the American people. Both can be done effectively. But neither can be done satisfactorily within the framework of present policies and practices. [22:63]

Trustee-Faculty Relations

If the trustees seek to cooperate and share with faculty the responsibilities related to educational policies, the method of working together becomes important. Communication becomes a basic need.

The Trustees of the Carnegie Foundation for the Advancement of Teaching speak to this point.

By all odds the most effective mechanism for communication between faculty and trustees is the system of visiting committees developed at Harvard and other institutions. The size and complexity of many institutions today is such that effective communication between faculty and board can be accomplished only by specializing—as the visiting committees do. The effect of these committees is to create innumerable channels of communication between board and faculty. And contrary to the predictions of many apprehensive college administrators, the existence of such multiple channels of communication has not been a source of difficulty to the president. [7:12]

The Columbia University Special Trustee Committee expresses its views of appropriate trustee-faculty relations as follows:

Many of the attempts to reconcile the legitimate interests of the trustees in the "kind and quality of education" with the legitimate insistence of the faculty upon the freedom of teaching have sought to bring the two bodies, trustees and faculty, closer together in working arrangements. Your Committee here suggests the precisely opposite course: That the separation *in fact existing* between these two bodies should be declared legitimate, healthy, and desirable, in addition to being now merely unavoidable.

Of course it must be understood that mutual respect and confidence between the trustees and faculty is essential to the healthy operation of a university. Official contact between the faculty and the board as a whole is at present made by the President of the University, who is also a Trustee. Part 2 of this report has recommended that Vice-Presidents of the University should officially attend all board meetings except executive sessions. The academic officers are members, *ex-officiis*, of the University Council, the chief deliberative and advisory body of the faculty; your Committee believes that this system provides, when coupled with the recommendations to be made later, efficient and adequate means of keeping these two senior bodies in contact with one another. [8:24–25]

The Columbia University Committee gave attention to the methods of trustee supervision of educational policy. It stated:

In their supervision of the kind and quality of education provided by the university, the Trustees already have the advantage of two regular streams of information. These flow from:
(a) The reports and recommendations of the University Council.
(b) Oral reports made by Deans to the Trustees at regular intervals.

The Committee recognized the value of written reports regularly made by four of its divisions and recommended:

That in future all Deans submit to the Trustees, through the President, annual written reports on the programs of their divisions.

As a further means of informing the Trustees of the kind and quality of education, the Committee proposed:

That a council system be introduced for all academic divisions. . . .
That advisory councils be nominated by the President, and appointed by the Trustees, for the appropriate divisions of the University; that each member of an advisory council serve a term of three years, under a plan of rotation; that the total membership of each council should be a multiple of three, but not exceeding thirty in number.
It would be desirable to have Trustee representation on each advisory council. Additional members might or might not be Trustees; might or might not be alumni; but in all cases would be selected to bring to the Trustees the most informed periodic reports of each academic division.

Concerning responsibilities of the Councils, the Committee recommended:

That each advisory council should have periodic meetings with the heads of its academic division; that the Office of the Secretary of the University provide necessary staff help to each advisory council; and that each council submit at least once a year a written report to the Trustees, through the President, conveying the council's review of the general program of the division to which it is assigned, together with any suggestions for changes and improvements the council may feel desirable. [8:31–33]

Summary

These observations and opinions relate to board size, trustee qualifications, board responsibility, and board organization. Also treated is the exercise of board responsibility for educational policy—an area now receiving renewed attention.

Comprehensive Long-range Planning

Planning—What It Is

Masterson states:

Planning is usually defined as "systematic mental effort about the future" or, in a more precise managerial sense, as "the mental effort that precedes the physical effort." In any administrative situation, a factory, a college, a hospital, a government agency, a charity drive, planning is made up of three steps: (1) forecasting the future and ascertaining a *need;* (2) ascertaining what resources are required to fill that need, and (3) making a detailed plan and program to fill the need. [21:22]

Wilsey defines long-range planning thus:

Long-range planning is an attempt by an institution to establish rational control over its own destiny. An institution is engaged in long-range planning when it selects and defines its educational objectives, determines the means required for achieving them, and prepares for systematic achievement of those objectives within stated periods of time. Five years is usually regarded as the minimum period to qualify as "long-range" planning, but for educational institutions a 10- to 15-year period is more desirable. Excellent long-range plans have been projected as far as 25 years.

Long-range planning cannot be casual or informal. Long-range planning must go beyond occasional brainstorming sessions or periodic weekend retreats for the administrative staff. It must have a definite pattern—tailored to the individual institution and its objectives. It must be firm enough to provide guidance, but flexible enough to meet changing needs. Long-range planning is not an administrative straight jacket, but a flexible tool for helping an institution define and achieve its objectives. Above all, it must lead to effective action in a desired direction. [31:64–65]

Umbeck expresses these views:

Planning is one of the most important functions of good management. Planning involves the presence of clearly stated objectives, careful inventory of resources, thorough understanding of operations, and thoughtful development of realistic goals and schedules. The long-range plan must never be looked upon as a fixed unchangeable blueprint for the next decade—it is, rather, a thoughtfully developed set of *guidelines* to be used as a tool in charting the institution's course. . . . Rare, indeed, is the college which has a comprehensive plan for development of curriculum, faculty, staff, student body, plant and funds. Institutions which plan in this fashion are institutions which take their destinies into their own hands. Colleges which plan are colleges which know *where* they are going and *how* they propose to get there. [29:18, 19]

Coombs writes as follows:

Attention is usually focused on this year's budget and the next, but most colleges seldom pause to see where they have been over the past ten years and where they hope to be ten years hence. It often comes as a shocking surprise to discover that great shifts have occurred in such critical factors as student-teacher ratio, the faculty work load, the number of courses being taught, the distribution of classes by size, the utilization (or underutilization) of physical facilities, and the proportion of the budget going into faculty compensation or into general administration.

There is a strong need for better tools for fact-finding, planning, operations analysis, and reporting so that the president, trustees, and faculty will have a clearer frame of reference within which to make programs and management decisions and check progress against predetermined plans and goals, all in the interest of getting the best possible educational results from the resources available. [9:23]

Woodburne writes:

To most administrative officers and to most faculty policy committees, "the proposal outlined [for developing an over-all educational plan] will seem so time-consuming and so fraught with controversy as to be of very doubtful value. Perhaps the consequences of not formulating any plan would be more impressive than the advantages of going through the process. The lack of any plan of this kind has resulted, in several instances, in a complete distortion of the normal balance between fields of work. [32:146]

The Status of Planning

Wilsey describes the status of planning as he observed it in 1960. He says:

While many institutions are engaged in planning activities of some kind, the total planning effort is not adequate to meet the needs of the coming decade. Survey responses from 831 colleges and universities show that 59 per cent have future plans of some kind, 33 per cent are in process of developing plans, and 8 per cent have no plans at all.

Only one third of the institutions are making plans that can be classed as adequate or comprehensive, and less than half are making plans that extend beyond five years into the future. Quite a few institutions laying claim to long-range planning were only in the very early stages. The larger institutions, many state supported, have done the most thorough job of planning. [31:66]

The Scope of Planning

Authorities of management testify that appropriate planning must be both comprehensive and long-range.

Carmichael stresses the importance of the long view in planning programs. He states:

It is of the utmost importance that we take the long view in planning education for the youth of tomorrow. . . . What should we be giving them as preparation for life at that time? Surely it must be an understanding of the fundamentals of our culture—the concepts and ideals that underlie it; the meaning of science and technology and the changes they impose; the difference between the trivial and the significant, the temporary and the lasting, and a sense of values that will guide them along the high road. [6:198–199]

Woodburne, too, stresses the value of the over-all educational plan. He writes:

The advantages of such an over-all [educational] plan should be self evident but do not seem to be so. In the first place, it supplies basic information for a great many of the educational policy and budget decisions, and allows an intelligent examination of these questions consistent with the major purposes of the institution. Second, it develops a clear concept of the major purposes of the institution, around which it is possible to gather the loyalty and enthusiasm of most of the faculty and staff. This leads to a good deal better integration of program at the teaching level than would otherwise be possible. Such integration does not seem to occur on the campuses of most of the large universities, as is made evident by the extent of course duplication. Not the least advantage of such a plan is that it informs the entire campus as to the major line of effort. [32:145]

Long-range plans must include plans for finance. Dodds states as follows:

Five- or ten-year budget projections, strongly urged by management consultants, are still in embryonic states in most colleges and universities. One presidential assistant remarked of his chief that he preferred to "fly by the seat of his pants." Many presidents do, among them some conspicuous for the instructional and scholarly improvements which they have brought. We submit, however, that their success would have been greater had they operated more according to plans implemented by long-term budgets. It is the latter that give reality to planning and keep administration and faculty "sensitized" to changing factors in the life of the institution and the constituency it serves. [12:191–192]

Long-range plans should include plans for staffing. Woodburne states his views as follows:

In addition to the integration of the various aspects of staff problems, any long-time planning for an entire institution must take into account the competing claims of the different units. This is not at the level of the annual budgetary requests, but represents a realization that these annual requests for support are part of a larger pattern of intent with respect to the desired development of a department or a college. For if the yearly recommendations for additions to the staff or equipment are approved, the major decision of the direction of development has already been made. An officer should be able to see the place which any series of recommendations has in the larger framework, because that is the point at which integration of policy and practice occurs. [33:157, 158]

Of the need to include planning for buildings, Woodburne states:

At all stages of planning and in alterations of plans costly mistakes will occur unless educational plans and building plans are integrated one with the other. A lack of such coordination will certainly result in costly alterations as soon as the construction is completed in order to allow the building to function adequately. [32:26, 27]

Planning Procedures

Dodds states:

The first step toward a master plan is naturally a comprehensive self study. The impetus may come from within the faculty, but often it is in response to some external influence, such as pressure by the trustees, stimulation by an accrediting association, or a grant by a foundation. [12:168]

Wilsey identifies stages in the projection process, as follows:

There are at least five stages in the process of projection: (1) establishment of initial intent of the institution, including assignment of general priorities; (2) identification and analysis of key factors affecting initial intent, including prediction of future trends; (3) revision of initial intent in light of these predictions, including the setting of tentative goals, adjustment of priorities, and establishment of time schedules; (4) evaluation of tentative goals against funds obtainable, people involved; and (5) setting of final unit and institutional goals and schedules. [31:70]

Heneman outlines planning procedures he deems appropriate. He states:

To get planning under way, a president should obtain from each of his principal administrative and educational officers a definition of policies and objectives in his own area of responsibility, whether it be curriculum, admissions standards and student affairs, business and finance, management, plant, or alumni relations. These specific plans should be reviewed and coordinated into an over-all plan and submitted to the governing board for consideration and approval. Projections of requirements for resources based upon this over-all plan should be made for a five- or ten-year period. The annual budget and the supporting justifications for funds submitted with the budget should be in terms of the longer-range plan. Annual reprojections should be made in the light of experience so that the intermediate or longer-range plan may be adjusted to experience. The board should request regular reports on actual developments in order to evaluate the soundness of planning and determine the need for revision in projections. [18:126–127]

Need for Continuous Review of Plans

Dodds recognizes the need for continuous review of the master plans. He writes:

Nothing would keep a faculty in turmoil and uncertainty more than to be summoned constantly to consider major changes in a master plan. Nevertheless, no plan can be viewed as iron bound. To keep it viable, it requires repeated reexamination to identify parts which have been, or are being achieved and which are not, and to expose those which, because of changed conditions, need to be modified or even abandoned. [12:176]

Summary

The foregoing selected observations and opinions reveal findings and judgments concerning the status of planning, the values to be derived, the scope to be desired, the procedures to be followed, and the need for continuous review.

Faculty Role in
Policy Formation

Practices in the extent and methods of faculty participation in institutional policy formation vary from institution to institution. Institutional growth poses problems of methods and procedures. Here are presented observations and opinions concerning practice, rationale, faculty goals, faculty limitations, and procedures of faculty participation in policy formation.

Current Practices

Committee T of the American Association of University Professors identifies the groups that bear institutional responsibilities. It states:

Three groups play the most important roles in the government of American Colleges and Universities—faculties, administrations, and governing boards. Criteria for college and university government must define the respective responsibilities of each of these groups, since the interests of society in the conduct of higher education has been entrusted to all three jointly. The responsibilities of each group should depend on its own particular competence for the formations it undertakes. . . .

Actual practices of institutional operation are now based on the principles of joint responsibility of faculties, administrators and governing boards. [1:321]

Dodds describes his observations of practice in these words:

We may add that among the samples of colleges and universities which we studied those of accepted educational eminence were characterized by a large measure of faculty self-governmnt, although in varying degrees and forms, and that in each the trend in recent years has been to draw the faculty more and more into advance consultation on broad institutional policies formerly considered to lie within the exclusive domain of the trustees, advised by the administration. Our findings also support Wilson's opinion that if extreme authoritarianism exists, it is in less favored and secure institutions, although there are naturally striking exceptions among them. [12:15, 16]

Millett describes practice as follows:

Every member of a faculty of a college or university has a dual status. He has an individual role and a collegial role. As an individual a faculty member has various important duties to carry out in the performance of his profession. In addition, each member of a faculty has certain duties to perform as part of a company of scholars. Ordinarily these collective duties are performed at three levels of operation: the department, the college or school, and the university. While some individuals tend to have more influnce than others, every faculty member has some voice in the determination of matters of academic policy at all three levels of collective or group decision making. The individual contributes to the group process; he is not absorbed by it.

At the departmental and at the college or school level the system for decision making is one of direct democracy. Every person of stated academic rank has an equal voice and vote in the realization of collective action. At the university level the system for decision making may be either direct or representative. [24:74, 75]

Woodburne expresses observations and opinions concerning faculty policy role as follows:

In colleges or universities of prominence, the educational and personnel policy formation often involves some activity or participation of the college faculties or the faculty senate. The amount of faculty participation varies from senate committees which effectively run the school, to senates which are pale, anemic, consultative bodies. Neither of these extremes is healthy. A college where consultation is purely formal has a poor system for formulating wise policies, while the ultimate control by senate committees places faculty in roles for which they were never appointed. As noted before, it is important that faculty be used in policy determination, but from that point on their continued use becomes inefficient, since, once established, policies can be more ably implemented by trained administrative officers. [32:18]

Mooney observes a trend toward participation through representation. He states:

The university has lost access to a center of responsive power. What was formerly taken as a clear center of power, i.e., the assembled faculty, is no longer an effective instrument for making institutional decisions. It is too big, too diverse. . . .

In lieu of government by the total faculty, what has evolved by a series of accretions are several smaller faculty units set up to carry out specific responsibilities of the institution. Typically, a university has a sizable faculty council, made up of representatives of the academic staff, to take up the prerogatives formerly held by the total faculty assembly. Feeding into this council are a number of sub-councils, made up of appointive and ex-officio personnel, taking responsibility for monitoring different major functions of the university. [25:49]

Rationale of Faculty Participation in Policy Formation

Hickman expresses the following opinion:

Above all, however, there is one fundamental method of maximizing the gains and minimizing the losses of change. This method is to so involve all possible members of the academic community, that each person may feel that he has had at least some voice in the shaping of new goals, new values and criteria, and the basic policies of his academic society. This often time-consuming process of participation may sometimes seem an impediment to the rapid introduction of change, but it will make a world of difference in the way that the faculty, especially, feels about the change and the new ways of life that it will bring. It is even possible that such participation may prove to be the quickest way of bringing lasting, rather than abortive, institutional change. [19:130]

Woodburne recognizes the common cause of faculty and administration. He writes as follows:

Much of the misunderstanding and disagreement that arise between faculty and administration rests on a false conception of internal university or college relations. Because sometimes vociferous, unreasonable faculty have been joined to arbitrary presidents or deans, the fiction has been created that the interests of the faculty clash with those of the administration. Nothing could be further from the truth. The fact is that both groups are working merely on different facets of the same functional task. They should be partners in the same enterprise with a reasonable division of labor. The faculty cannot do their teaching and the job of the administrator as well; the reverse is likewise true of presidents, deans and business officers. Effective consultation can serve to keep the two parties together on the major policies. [32:21]

Woodburne describes the conditions essential to cooperative action in these words:

This discussion has led us to the position that the essential conditions of co-operative action—information by the administration and impartiality by the faculty and administration—are vital to develop a working partnership. Although this contention will be subscribed to by most faculty and administrators, it is violated as often as observed. The efforts of the administration and faculty complement one another. There is, in reality, no divergence of their proper interests. . . .

. . . the faculty must have confidence in the integrity of the administrative officers if an effective partnership is to develop. But this is no more necessary than administrative confidence in the impartiality of the faculty. A general practice of consultation often develops and confirms the good faith of the entire staff of the institution. The absence of effective two-way communication and the mutuality which it engenders are the basic cause of many if not most internal university conflicts and breakdowns. [32:19, 20]

Corson recognizes a breadth of interest as appropriate in faculty participation in policy formation. He says:

In long-range perspective, the practice of consulting the faculty or a faculty committee (even on the subject of faculty salaries) has proven a sound one. This practice tends to establish among the central staff of the educational enterprise a cohesiveness and sense of responsibility for decisions. To deny the faculty's capacity intelligently to participate or their interest in financial matters and capital improvements can prove detrimental. These areas of decision relate too closely to educational matters. [10:109]

Dodds cites basic advantages to be derived from faculty participation in policy formation. He says:

Faculty participation at levels of high policy makes the members more willing to entrust administrative matters to the administration—where they belong. If excluded from this level, they will concentrate attention on minor things as the only way to preserve their self-esteem. But the fundamental argument why presidents should respect faculty discretion is the cardinal truth that if an administration is to prosper, it must utilize the intellectual application and imaginative thinking of more than the president, vice-presidents and deans. [12:97]

The goals of the consultative process are identified by Dodds as follows:

The goals of the consultative process are a wiser decision than the president alone is equipped to make, a wider sense of ownership in the decision, and a more direct responsibility for carrying it out. To treat it as a manipulative tool for securing one's way is treason to the principle. It is also foolish because the fraud is soon found out. [12:73]

Woodburne finds that wide consultation is essential in curriculum development. He writes:

For an *effective* curriculum is in no sense a theoretical framework, but a pattern made up of the strength and limitations of staff, library, space, and competing departmental interest. A true composite of these forces provides reasonable stability of program, and a good program of training at the same time.

One of the most essential elements in the formation of such a change in program is the widest possible consultation with all the departments. This is in no sense pure courtesy, but an opportunity for wide consultation which looks in two directions at once. Explanations to departments allow them to understand the proposals in all their details, while discussions with departmental faculties help the committee to appreciate the difficulties and opposition the program may encounter in open faculty meetings. [32:88]

Faculty participation is also deemed by Woodburne to be essential. He says:

Long-time planning is difficult to achieve partly because of conflict of interest, and partly because of the short period of administrative service. The major continuity is in the faculty. For this reason a joint administrative faculty committee can achieve much more than administration alone. It will also have infinitely greater chances of widespread support and acceptance. When an institution decides upon the major educational direction without the cooperation and assistance of faculty it will not become fully effective at the teaching level. [32:63]

Faculty Goals of Participation in Policy Formation

Committee T of the American Association of University Professors has outlined its conception of appropriate faculty participation in institutional policy formation. They state, in part:

The faculty should have primary responsibility for determining the educational policies of the institution. If this responsibility is not conferred or defined by the charter of the institution, it should be expressed in legislation of the governing board.

Educational policies include such fundamental matters as the subject matter and methods of instruction, facilities and support of research of faculty members and students, standards for admission of students, for academic performance and for the granting of degrees. They also include those aspects of student life that relate directly to the educational process, for example, limitations, in aid of academic performance, on extra-curricular activities, and regulations affecting freedom of expression. On these matters, the power of review and final decision retained by the governing board should be exercised adversely to a faculty determination only in exceptional circumstances and for reasons that are communicated to the faculty.

The faculty is also properly concerned and should actively participate in decisions made on other matters that may directly affect the educational policies for which it is primarily responsible. The matters include major changes in the size of the student body, significant alteration in the academic calendar, the establishment of new schools or divisions, the provision of extension services to the community, and assumption by the institution of research or service obligations to private or public agencies. [1:322]

Corson outlines faculty claims to authority as follows:

By and large, however, the faculty usually claims authority to decide questions of curriculum, degrees, examinations, entrance requirements, academic standards, and related questions without formal approval or even consideration by the president or governing board. With respect to educational issues having substantial financial implications, the faculty will be authorized to (or will insist on the right to) express its judgment, even though the president and governing board reserve the authority for final decision. . . .

The relatively substantial authority that the faculty exercises over educational decisions in many institutions is founded more on tradition than on its formal establishment in university by-laws. [10:102, 103]

Corson further states:

Faculties, by and large, have sought a larger role in decision making relating to educational and faculty policy. Together these forces—the incapacity of governing boards and the ambitions of faculties—have accounted for the large and increasing control that the faculties have gained over educational policy. [10:46]

Some Faculty Limitations

Some observers express the view that substantial improvement in faculty participation is desirable. Dressel and Lorimer state their views as follows:

Although faculties would like to view administrative officers and even the board of control as deputies of the faculty in financing and carrying out faculty determined policies, this conception is unrealistic. Specialization and resulting lack of anything approaching unanimity in the faculty, coupled with the size, diversity of functions, and complicated financial problems of the modern college or university, make full faculty control inefficient if not actually impossible. The governing board is the legal representative of the supporting clientele of the college, and its ultimate authority is entirely in accord with democratic principles, although the exercise of that authority by the board and its appointed officers may be undemocratic. Usually, by common consent, authority on matters pertaining to curriculum and instruction is delegated to the faculty, but the financial implications of the curriculum decisions make faculty autonomy less than complete even here. Furthermore, the excesses of faculties in course proliferation have even led some persons (Beardsley Ruml, for example) to suggest that the board should exercise authority even on curriculum matters. [13:411, 412]

Dodds expresses his views concerning the manner in which faculties have exercised their responsibilities for policy formation as follows:

Nevertheless, the serious question has been put by some thoughtful trustees and by occasional faculty members themselves: Are faculties exercising their governing powers as well as they should? We discovered little evidence that they are giving any systematic thought to a general theory of the optimum scope and nature of their part in government and what in their own interest can better be left to the administration in this day of growth in size and diversity. The truth is that they have paid more attention to their rights than to their own internal problems of government. Faculties find the same difficulty in drawing the line between policy framing and administrative execution that trustees do. Too many individuals nourish the erroneous idea that the only way to keep control is to have a finger in every issue, to control the details and perhaps administer them as well. [12:99]

Corson, too, sees need for careful consideration of the manner and extent of faculty participation in policy formation. He states:

Against the advantages of involving faculty members in collaborative effort—and it is clear that the process of consultation strengthens their allegiance to the institution and their individual zeal and satisfaction—stand some reservations. Do faculties have time for participation in decision-making on issues of physical development and finance? Do faculty members have a sufficently broad understanding of the total operation to participate intelligently in making such decisions? How and to what degree can such views and time as they have be incorporated in the decision-making process? These and similar questions which relate to the increasing size and complexity of modern higher institutions need to be given careful consideration. [10:109]

Corson identifies factors which limit the capacity of the faculty to make decisions:

Four factors significantly limit the capacity of the faculty to make efficient and progressive educational decisions:

1. Only a few institutions accumulate and have readily available analytical data about the capacity of applicants for admission and about class size, course proliferation and faculty work load to facilitate decision-making.

2. A minority among the members of most faculties have thought deeply and analytically about educational programs (e.g., curricula make up) or teaching methods (e.g., size of class) or factors influencing instructional costs (e.g., course proliferation and size of class). Most faculty members are subject-matter specialists; few are educators in a comprehensive sense.

3. Much educational policy is formulated in bits and pieces by the approval of a new course, the modification of a requirement for completion of a curriculum, or the alteration of an admission requirement. These bits and pieces sel-

dom force comprehensive consideration of the educational program or prevailing practice.

4. Being subject-matter specialists, faculty members tend to resist proposals that, in their opinion, might encroach on the established preserves (e.g., number of courses offered, courses "required") of each subject-matter discipline.

The tendency of faculties to resist change usually means that the impetus for innovation . . . comes from a dean or president." [10:104]

Procedures for Faculty Participation in Policy Formation

Committee T of the American Association of University Professors outlines agencies of faculty participation that it deems appropriate. The Committee states:

The agencies employed may consist of meetings of all faculty members of the department, school, college, division or university system or may take the form of faculty-elected executive committees in departments and schools and a representative faculty-elected senate or council for the institution as a whole or one or more of its divisions. Where executive powers are conferred on a committee, one appropriate device is the election by the faculty concerned of a panel from which administrative officers select the committee's membership. The advisory committee, elected by the faculty from its own membership, can be a useful means for communicating faculty opinions to presidents and other high administrative officials, though it is no substitute for the agencies above described. [1:322–323]

Dodds sees advantage in faculty committees. He says:

Now that direct democracy no longer suffices, the efficiency of faculty self-government is closely related to its committee system. . . . Where faculty government is extensive, a proliferation of committees—some active, some dormant, and some which were never of any consequence—is common. [12:107, 109]

Horn, like Dodds, sees advantage in committees. He writes:

In practice, in a majority of America's two thousand colleges and universities, decisions on matters under faculty control are still made by the entire faculty of the institution, or of the separate schools and colleges that comprise the university. Generally such faculty decisions involve consideration by standing or *ad hoc* committees.

Once faculties get beyond two or three hundred in size, either in a single college such as that of arts and science, or in the entire institution, some sort of representative government is essential. The usual mechanism for faculty government of this kind is a faculty council or senate. Its organization varies considerably from institution to institution. In some, only faculty having tenure are eligible for membership, or even to vote for members of the senate; in others only full professors are eligible for membership. In general, however, all regular full-time members of the faculty should be eligible both to vote for and to serve as senate members. [20:75]

Corson describes the influence of administration on faculty action as follows:

The influence of the administration in the decisions that constitute educational advance is usually exerted subtly through (1) the service of major officers, i.e., presidents and deans, as chairmen of faculty governing bodies; (2) the membership on faculties of these same administrative officers; (3) the appointment to faculty committees or as committee chairmen of individuals the presidents and/ or deans know to be sympathetic with their ideas, or capable of generating educational forward movement, and (4) in a few instances, trustee-faculty consultation.

The central question is: Should the faculty's traditional right to decide educational issues be so comprehensive "that every matter involving educational policy is to be decided only by and with the consent of the faculty?"

Observations of the governance of colleges and universities suggest that the answer should be "no." ...

What is needed is not as Ruml has contended that "the Trustees [or the president one might add] ... must take back from the faculty as a body its present authority over the design and administration of the curriculum." What is needed is greater collaboration than obtains in most institutions among trustees and president, deans and faculty, in continually evaluating and reshaping the educational program. The interest and capacity of the ablest trustees and presidents are ineffectively utilized if they are limited to the exercise of judgment on administrative and financial matters." [10:105, 106]

Summary

This brief review of faculty participation in policy formation is drawn from the writings of competent observers. The points of view expressed vary, but in one respect they all agree—the best talents of trustees, administration, and faculty must be joined in furtherance of institutional effectiveness.

The Academic Department

The academic department is predominantly the basic unit of academic organization. Its strengths and weaknesses should be understood. The views of competent observers are summarized below.

The Nature of Departments

Woodburne states:

Departments of instruction within the college or university organization are, in one sense, primarily convenient budgetary units to provide for ease of operation and assignment of funds. These units also happen to be convenient groupings of instructional faculty into fairly unified blocks of subject matter. [32:107]

Henderson speaks of it thus:

In most colleges the department is the avenue for working out an intensive study for the student. The procedure of the department is to stipulate the courses that constitute this major. The student may, of course, be given some option. Thus the intensive study is identified with the departmental organization. There are advantages in this, in that it enables the staff to be mobilized and to work closely together and with coordination of effort. It also is a convenience in the counselling of a majority of the students. [17:132]

Millett expresses the view that research should be tied to the departments. He states:

Even where separate research institutes are established at the university level of operation, I believe strongly that all such research endeavors should be closely related to departments. In this way staff members have a home base in the specialized field of scholarship whose knowledge and techniques are being applied to general or specific research problems. Moreover, an interchange of student and faculty participation in research and instruction can be helpful to all concerned. [24:87]

The Department Chairman or Head

Millett writes:

The department chairman may be appointed by the president upon nomination by a dean, or he may be elected by members of the department. Each selection process has its faults and its virtues. Appointment after careful consultation with members of the department seems the preferable practice. The term of office may be indefinite or fixed. Some rotation seems desirable in most circumstances. A department chairman may stay too long. [24:89]

Woodburne presents views on the term of office of department chairmen as follows:

A considerable number of chairmen have indicated that a five-year term is the shortest period in which any constructive work could be accomplished. The same group has said also that a term longer than ten years may freeze the program of the department just when new ideas or course arrangements are needed. [32:47]

Woodburne describes the work of the department head in these words:

In general, then, the department head, if he is wise, concentrates his direct attention upon the budget, on the questions of staff appointments, promotion, tenure, and salary; and his indirect attention, through his stimulation of the rest of the staff in the department, on the course offerings, upon which their cooperation is essential, if any functional change is to take place. There are, of course, a great many details of room assignments, of handling of requisitions, of examining fellowship applications, and a whole series of questions of detail. [32:126]

Corson has given careful consideration to the potential of the department and its chairman. He writes:

In the departmental organization of most universities and colleges, the department chairman does hold substantial personal authority because of his influence over personnel policies and instructional assignments and his position in the formal communication between faculty members and administration.

The above suggests two considerations. First the departmental structure can serve, and often does, as a bastion of the *status quo* in opposition to any creative leadership. . . . On the other hand, the departmental structure can serve as the means by which presidents, provosts and deans can make effective their leadership. . . . Second, within the framework of these two possibilities, the chairmen are the key personnel for administrative relations with faculty members and with students. Therefore, the position and responsibilities, administratively, of chairmen offer a fruitful area of scrutiny. To the degree that chairmen primarily associate themselves with their colleagues, they will tend to reinforce the decentralized autonomous nature of academic organization. Thus they will tend, more often than not, to reinforce existing educational philosophies and commitments and resist educational change. To the degree that they recognize their administrative responsibilities, chairmen can better implement institutional policies and creatively participate in formulating polices. [10:92, 93]

Corson writes of the manner in which department heads serve as media of communications. He states:

The department heads (and sometimes deans)—scholars, not administrators by training and bent—usually accept little responsibility for communication. They recognize an obligation to voice the views of their departmental colleagues to the deans and president, but do not regularly take the initiative in assembling those views and then presenting them to the administration. On the other hand, department heads less often recognize an obligation to translate positively to their colleagues the views of the president. [10:132]

McGrath observes the positions taken by department heads in liberal arts colleges with respect to the improvement of economic efficiency. He states:

In the matter of eliminating small classes to improve economic efficiency the department head is typically the most conservative force in these liberal arts colleges. . . . The majority, however, appear to measure the status of their departments and their own personal fortunes in terms of the number of courses offered, the number of faculty members involved, and the compass of advanced specialized instruction provided, regardless of cost. [23:46)

Departmental Role and Performance

Corson writes of the departmental role in decision making in these words:

As institutions grow larger, the locus of decisions on courses, curricula, and faculty tends to slide down to the departmental faculty. Even the dean focuses his time and energy on matters of finance, buildings and public relations.

The environmental cause of this diffusion of responsibility lies in the range and depth of specialization among the university's staff. . . .

The result of this diffusion and decentralization of decision making is often costly. Decisions by faculties regarding educational program are often the result of compromise among specialists made without the leavening and stimulating influence of thoughtful leaders of the society who (sometimes) serve on boards of trustees.

The areas of decision making entrusted to faculties are in practice inseparable from those reserved for the president and his trustees: the determination of the educational program or the establishment of admissions policy necessitates financial support, may also preclude increased expenditures for faculty salaries, and may require substantial additional facilities and the raising of funds. The president, when given only a limited opportunity to participate with the faculty in programing courses and curricula, is ill equipped to make informed decisions on matters of budget, fund raising, and the need for new capital expenditures. [10:126]

Millett describes departmental decision making as follows:

Under the guidance of leadership of a chairman or executive officer, each department has a number of vital decisions to make. Ordinarily it is the department as a group which decides the general scope and specialization of subject matter to be undertaken in the course offerings. Ordinarily it is the department which determines the individual member who shall be invited to join the group, within the staffing limits established by the dean or the president of the college or university. Ordinarily it is the department collectively or through consultation of its senior members which decides whom to recommend for promotion in rank and for increases in salary. These recommendations may be reviewed by another group of academic personnel, but departmental recommendation is usually a vital step in the process.

A department ordinarily determines both what courses it shall provide its students and what sequence and number of courses shall be required for a "major." These decisions are subject to further review at the college and university level, but they are generally accepted without great questioning. The department is expected only to keep its demand upon the total time allowance of the college or school within the limits of a general scheme of distribution and concentration of courses. [24:83]

Departmental Problems and Shortcomings

Gross observes a failure of the department to deal with institutional problems. He writes:

The decentralization principle that sub-organizational units should make decisions about their basic problems because they are most knowledgeable about them has wide currency in many types of complex organizational settings.

The fact that work units are granted considerable autonomy in dealing with their basic problems does not insure that they in fact will resolve them—be seriously concerned about them, or even recognize them. It seems a reasonable assumption that departmental autonomy will result in the definition, examination, and solution of departmental problems only when the following conditions exist: (1) members of the group have a basic concern for the welfare and productivity of the department as a collectivity; (2) the departmental members can work together in an effective unit; and (3) group members have ample time to devote to departmental problems.

I submit that these conditions are the exception rather than the normal state of affairs in most departments. Although the university is organized on a departmental basis and one can speak of a departmental product the producing unit in universities is essentially individual academic man. The most highly rewarded activities, scholarship and research publications, are not departmental products, but the products of individual faculty members.... The frame of reference of academic man is *his* own specialized area of competence, *his* courses, *his* students, *his* research publications, *his* consulting activities; and the reward system of the university and the disciplines is based on individual, not group activity. [16:65]

Ruml and Morrison observe that the department has weakened the liberal arts curriculum. They write as follows:

The character and quality of the curriculum is directly, but of course not exclusively, affected by the balance of power within the faculty's specialized departmental structure. The departmentalized structure gives a prevailing and powerful vocational bias. It stimulates recruiting and the offering of highly specialized content courses attractive to a highly specialized student constituency. As a consequence, there is a pervasive deterioration of instruction that should be of a general and liberal character. Too often the importance of a course to the curriculum is determined by departmental voting strength in faculty meetings. Decisions are necessarily arrived at by *Roberts' Rules of Order* not by the Rule of Reason. Too often the dominant motivation is to advance and protect the professional status of the department and its subject matter, not the liberal education of the student.

The result is that the curriculum is of low quality judged by any standard by which one would evaluate an authentic liberal educational program, wisely founded on today's past and projected as best can be into today's uncertain future. It is of low quality judged by the high individual teaching competence of most members of the faculty. They do not look to teaching performance for professional advancement, for they are rarely so judged. [28:7, 8]

Henderson, too, sees possible shortcomings of the department. He states:

But a department may also become very rigid, isolated and self-contained. Rivalries for budgetary appropriations create animosities between departments that should not exist. It is easy for provincialized departments to become stereotyped. ... There is advantage, I think, in not identifying too closely with the department the field of concentration for the student. Even though the intensive study for most students would conform to the curriculum of a department, there should be opportunity for the non-conformist to work out a plan of his own. [17:132]

Horn finds departments contributing to narrow specialization. He writes as follows:

There is another problem stemming from department strength and organization —how to overcome narrow specialization, or at least how to bring about more cross fertilization of academic disciplines, in both teaching and research. The oldest organizational device for accomplishing this is the divisional pattern. Harvard has had divisions since before the turn of the century. The three divisions most frequently operative are the humanities, social sciences and natural sciences. . . .

Other attempts at crossing departmental lines occur through inter-disciplinary programs, as in the various area studies dealing with a particular geographical region of the world. In most cases, interdepartmental committees are the organizational medium for such arrangements, although increasingly such programs have a "director." [20:59, 60]

Woodburne finds that departments present problems of coordination, as follows:

Sometimes, unfortunately, the unity within a department may be reflected in a degree of separateness and autonomy from other teaching units so that there is very little coordination between the various disciplines. Many teaching institutions in the past ten years have wondered whether there was sufficient coordination between the various teaching disciplines as they are reflected in the course programs of students. It is possible to find, for instance, that a major program in zoology may be made up of 60 to 70 semester hours of nothing but zoology and similarly that a major program in chemistry contains little except more and more advanced courses in chemistry itself. This type of development, which fortunately is going out of fashion, is not healthy either for the departments of instruction or for the students. [32:107–108]

Corson, too, finds departments posing problems of coordination. He writes:

It is the basic academic unit, the *department,* that poses problems of coordination that are unique to the college or university. . . .

The department is, at the same time, an organizational subdivision of an association of individuals with professional ties. The allegiance of its members to the profession or discipline in which they are trained, rather than to the institution as a whole, does reduce the effectiveness of efforts to enlist the enterprise of these individuals in modifying curricula, budgets and programs as the needs of knowledge and society may dictate. David Riesman has dubbed the departments "the intellectual veto groups" within a university. He has charged that it is frequently the department which impedes the making of decisions that would alter existing curricular arrangements (and indirectly the professional societies associated with each) and dynamically develop the institution's educational program.

American institutions of higher education have devised a variety of devices and methods to overcome the narrow specialization by discipline that is reflected by the department structure. Fundamentally, departmentalization is a consequence of research specialization. At Wesleyan and, in an earlier period, at Stanford, divisions were established in an effort to provide a means of interrelating the instruction offered by departments. At Princeton a number of offices concerned with geographical areas and broad fields of scholarship, e.g., the humanities, are designed to attract the interest of individuals from several disciplines. In other institutions, seminars are used to bring together teachers from different fields. [10:33, 34]

Summary

This review of the findings and opinions of these eight observers affords considerable insight into the nature of the department, the responsibilities borne by its chairman, and its strengths and weaknesses in modern higher education.

Research and Graduate Education

The universities have developed strong programs of instruction and research in their graduate schools. In 1930, the enrollment in the graduate schools was 47 thousand, or 4.3 per cent of the total of 1,100 thousand. In the first term of 1960, graduate enrollment had risen to 342 thousand, or 10.6 per cent of the total of 3,216 thousand [11.45]. Expenditures for organized research, which amounted to some $18 millions in 1930, had risen to $734 millions in 1958 [30:5].

In this same period, while the enrollment in the graduate schools was growing, and the Federal Government, along with foundations and corporations, was sponsoring massive programs of research, the demand for trained teachers to serve in both graduate and undergraduate staffs has been mounting.

The debate centers on the place of research in scholarship and in the training of teachers; on its appropriate relation to instruction; on its organization, its control, and its program; and on the consequences of sponsored research on the freedom of the university to choose its course of inquiry. Beyond this, the questions relate to the mission of the graduate school and how it may be strengthened. The following observations and opinions reveal, to some extent, the nature of the debate.

Research and Scholarship

A panel of advisors, in a report to the Board of Regents of the State of Kansas, included in its report the following:

A few months ago Chancellor Wescoe's ad hoc committee on university research of which Dr. W. J. Argersinger, Jr. was chairman, said: "The university exists to accommodate and implement the whole human learning process, and this must include creative scholarship and research. Thus research is not an optional activity in the university, not merely a legitimate pursuit of those who may be interested and willing to dedicate their spare time, nor an assignment justified to either the university or the professor by the resultant income in dollars and publicity. Rather, research is an inescapable responsibility of the university and an inseparable part of its total educational function."

The committee then went on to say: "At the graduate level the central importance of research is most obvious, for here the instructor, one-half of the learning team, bears the double responsibility of imparting both knowledge—a word that implies depth of understanding as well as volume of information—and the techniques of discovery, evaluation and interpretation." [14:30]

Impact of Research on Finance

Herbert Rosenberg describes the impact of research on financing higher education as follows:

. . . 186 universities and technological schools—less than 10 per cent of the 2000 institutions—consistently account for 97 per cent of the research funds.

Research activities do not now affect in any major or direct sense the financing of other equally vital institutions—liberal arts colleges, teachers colleges, theological and other professional schools, junior colleges and technical schools. But research does play a powerful role, sometimes the dominant one, in financing the activities of the 186 universities and technological schools. These institutions award more than one-half of all the bachelor's degrees granted in this country and constitute the nation's main resources for graduate and professional training. In these institutions, research influences the intellectual climate of graduate and undergraduate education, the character of the physical facilities, the size, composition, and ambitions of the faculty, the nature of instruction, the aspirations of students; it affects significantly the financing of all their other educational activities. [27:305–306]

Relation of Teaching and Research

Caplow and McGee see a trend away from teaching and toward research. They say:

The basic trend away from teaching and toward research in the major universities is accompanied by minor shifts away from teaching and toward public service, away from undergraduate and towards graduate instruction, away from the general involvement of the faculty in the curriculum and toward specialization. The effects of these trends are mutually reinforcing. An increasing proportion of the faculty regard their teaching duties as obstacles to the performance of essential tasks, and instruction falls more and more into the hands of academics of inferior standing. . . . In the long run, the present trends will culminate either in the separation of undergraduate instruction from academic research—a development already visible in the increase of full-time research positions on many faculties—or the establishment of a new balance between the ever-increasing demands and rewards of research and the equally urgent demands of students to be taught. [4:232–233]

Corson expresses his views in part as follows:

Contractual research, in short, can shape the destiny of a university without regard to what its administrators and faculty believe its appropriate function to be. A broadly balanced research program stimulates faculty growth, attracts good graduate students, and helps to keep the institution attuned to the needs of contemporary society. But research can consume faculty time needed for undergraduate teaching; the effort to produce research scientists can dissipate resources also needed to educate men in other professions and as citizens; the prestige of investigation can overshadow the importance of good teaching (even in institutions concentrating on teaching, the research scholar may enjoy greater prestige than his colleague who concentrates on teaching). [10:152]

Gross, too, sees research drawing talent away from teaching. He writes:

. . . my own observations lead me to suspect that the modal pattern for senior professors is to give minimum effort and time to their teaching responsibilities and greater attention to their research obligations and outside activities such as consulting. It is not difficult to see why this should be the case. The reward and prestige systems of the university are geared not to effective teaching, but to outstanding scholarship and research. [16:68]

Woodburne sees research in most institutions as an adjunct of teaching. He states:

Normally, except in a few institutions, research is an adjunct of teaching. It is usually carried financially as a part of the teaching budget, the funds for library acquisitions or laboratory equipment being a part of the current expense account, and the time for it being one of the unspoken assumptions in setting the hours of a full teaching load. [33:75]

Mooney considers it possible that new values will come to be assigned to teaching. He writes:

Although research, by tradition, is highly valued, teaching is also highly valued; as enrollment pressures increase, as fields of knowledge become more complex, as curriculum problems become more severe, and as research men leave teaching to do separated research work, the good teacher becomes a freshly valued man; in this line of reaction, some administrators and some teachers now choose to put higher value on teaching than on research; the split between teaching and research becomes an open and contentious issue, with defenders on both sides. [25:47]

Furnas and Ewall do not find imbalance in the relation of research to teaching. They state:

There is often the criticism that faculty members become so involved in and imbued with research that they neglect their teaching duties. In individual cases this may be true, but the impact is serious only in a few instances in which conventional undergraduate instruction is involved. Certainly in graduate instruction, with its necessarily large component of research participation, involvement in research of both faculty and student is the *sine qua non* of success. By and large the research versus instruction pattern is not imbalanced, and there is not very much danger that it will become so. [15:100]

Implications of External Controls of Research

Concern is expressed by some that grants for specified applied research introduce external controls into university programs. Mooney observes:

All along the line the precedent has been set that those who have the money have the power to control the specific research which they purchase.

These recent precedents do not include arrangements for using outside money to back the universities, as such, for what their professors, out of their own wisdom and experience, shall name as good research to be doing. The universities have been bypassed by agencies adequate in their own right to determine what research to do. They are seen by outside agencies as pools of people available for use as these agencies see fit. [25:43]

Woodburne too expresses views on this matter. He writes:

The other aspect of research programs involves the question of large government contracts or any contract from an agency which imposes restrictions upon the work which a research person may do. A good many times these research projects are very important to the country at large and the people are willing to give up some of their own freedom of activity in order to carry them on. It should not be forgotten, however, that in doing so, one of the primary rules of basic research investigation has been violated: that a person should be free to carry on wherever the beacon of inquiry and curiosity may lead. Most of the research projects which are drafted by the government for its own purposes involve this violation. . . .

The other main danger of large government contracts is that it takes a good scientist or a good research worker and makes him a manager of research projects concerned primarily with the procurement of staff, the assignment of projects, the supervision of activities, the procurement of materials, and all of the multitudinous forms, reports, and other procedures which are imposed under government regulations. There are, without doubt, scores of good scientists in universities and colleges around the country who are being ruined as scientists by devotion to the management of a research project over a period of years. [32:159-160]

Gross sees consequences of outside support for specified research as follows:

One is that since most foundations, industrial supporters of research and a number of government agencies have clearly developed notions of areas they are interested in, and since the university looks with favor on a man with a research contract, many academics are involved in inquiries that frequently do not represent their basic research interests. A second consequence is that although the universities proclaim that one of their major objectives is to advance knowledge they have in large part allowed external agencies to determine the problems to be investigated. A third consequence flows from the fact that *most*, although not all, contractors of university research will support only short-term research. . . . Not only are most universities not set up to support this type of enterprise, but some of the research they encourage many of their faculty to undertake is frequently of dubious value to the advancement of knowledge." [16:68-69]

Problems of the Graduate School

Berelson summarizes some of the problems of the graduate school as identified by critics. He states:

What precisely is the problem? According to the critics, it is threefold.

First, it is a matter of *policy:* The graduate school has wrongly given higher priority to research and research training as against preparation for college teaching.

Second, it is a matter of *program:* the graduate school is not selecting the right students in the first place and then not training them correctly. As to the latter, the program lacks (a) sufficient breadth and (b) sufficient training in teaching.

Third, it is a matter of *numbers:* the graduate school is not training enough people to staff the colleges in the next years of the expected "bulge" in enrollment. [2:45]

Administrative and organizational problems are noted by Berelson as follows:

Administrative and organizational problems have characterized graduate work so long that most people have become used to them. The subordination of the graduate school to the undergraduate college, the intermingling of graduate and undergraduate students in the same courses, the uneven struggle between the dean's office and the departments, the weakness of a dean with no budgetary or appointive authority—these matters have been remarked by generations of commentators on the graduate scene. [2:119]

Woodburne further describes the problems of organization and administration in these words:

Except for five or six institutions in this country, the graduate school has no faculty at all. Only in a few instances does it have a budget and a faculty separate from those of the undergraduate units. In most institutions the entire budget and faculty for both the undergraduate and the graduate teaching is in the undergraduate college. The reason for this is that the faculty of a department such as English, chemistry, or sociology is a unitary group, whether it is teaching undergraduates or is responsible for the graduate program.

There develops, as a consequence, a kind of anomaly whereby the graduate school is given certain responsibilities connected with the level of graduate work and the requirement for degrees, and yet has no budgetary control or authority over faculty as do the other units of the university. [32:160, 161]

Carmichael sees a lack of defined responsibility for the graduate school. He says:

In reviewing the discussions and criticisms of graduate education over the past twenty-five years, one is impressed with two facts. First, that no significant changes have resulted from the criticisms and, secondly, that in no instance, so far as I have observed, has the critic raised the question whether the graduate schools could, if they wished to, bring about basic changes. It seems increasingly clear that the reason why graduate schools have remained virtually unchanged in methods and procedures for more than half a century is that no one has had a primary responsibility for graduate education or authority to effect reforms, however badly they may be needed. [6:43]

Carmichael advocates that each graduate school should have its own faculty. He says:

Each graduate school should have at least a small full-time faculty responsible to the dean of the school who would have a budget sufficient not only for his full-time staff but for part-time faculty who might be chosen from other divisions of the university. The full-time status of graduate faculty members should not be interpreted as precluding their teaching undergraduate courses. Indeed, each member should be expected to give at least one semester or year course each year in the college. This plan, coupled with that of having undergraduate faculty members give graduate courses regularly, should assure that there would be no "isolation or insulation" of the graduate faculty. [6:199]

Gross, too, observes the lack of authority commensurate with responsibilities assigned to the graduate school as follows:

That the organizational structure of the university is geared primarily to instructional activities is also seen by the anomalous position of the graduate school in most American universities, the organizational unit whose basic concern is with the advancement of knowledge and the production of new research investigators and scholars. Yet, with the exception of a handful of American universities, for example the University of Chicago and Columbia University, the graduate school has no separate faculty of its own, and its small budget normally only covers the administrative costs related to granting advanced degrees. In consequence, although the graduate schools were designed to serve as the unit that would develop the research and scholarship function of the university, deans of graduate schools have largely been unable to take leadership in this connection because they have no control over fiscal and human resources. [16:63]

Carmichael sees the graduate school as importantly responsible for the decline of the liberal arts. He states:

The decline of the *liberal* arts is, by all odds, the most disturbing fact of American higher education. Any basic reforms looking to their rejuvenation must begin in the graduate schools, for they provide the teachers. They have the responsibility of undertaking to restore the arts college to its former central position in higher education. [6:89]

McGrath, like Carmichael, charges the graduate school with the decline of liberal education, as follows:

Under the spreading influence of graduate education, the liberal arts colleges shifted their emphasis from teaching to research; from instruction concerned with the key ideas of Western culture to instruction composed of the latest findings in ever narrower areas of scholarly investigation; from a concern with the complete development of mind and character which Milton believed fitted "a man to perform justly, skilfully, and magnanimously all the offices, both private and public, of peace and war" to the cultivation of the professional skills and the restricted subject matter of the various fields of intellectual endeavor—in brief, from the dissemination to the creation of knowledge. To a considerable extent the weaknesses, the ineptitudes, and the inadequacies of higher education today have their origin in these changes which occurred largely unnoticed by laymen, and which, further, were little understood by the profession. [22:14–15]

Millett observes the relation of undergraduate to graduate instruction. He writes:

It is at the departmental level of academic organization where conflict especially occurs between undergraduate and graduate instruction . . . The prevailing pattern of academic organization prescribes that a department shall offer both undergraduate and graduate courses. . . . Because of a feeling that departments are not evidencing a proper degree of interest in their undergraduate programs, some universities have tried the device of separating faculties into undergraduate and graduate groups, and even of establishing new departments in the undergraduate college. In my judgment both arrangements have their faults. The persons recruited for undergraduate instruction are likely to feel cut off from their colleagues in their disciplines and to believe that their own academic careers have been somehow curtailed. The great ambition of the faculty member in the undergraduate college is likely to be to see how quickly he can gain promotion to the graduate faculty. And graduate faculties unconnected with undergraduate study grow out of touch with the previous preparation of their students. Each department in a university has to work out for itself how best to meet both undergraduate and graduate instructional demands. This is a decision of major academic importance. [24:87, 88, 89]

Summary

The views above expressed reveal the concerns of these competent scholars for the kind and quality of graduate education, including the appropriate role for research that will best serve the country's needs.

References

1. AMERICAN ASSOCIATION OF UNIVERSITY PROFESSORS, COMMITTEE T. "Faculty Participation in College and University Government," *A.A.U.P. Bulletin,* Vol. 48, No. 4, 321–323, December 1962.
2. BERELSON, BERNARD. *Graduate Education in the United States.* New York: McGraw-Hill Book Company, 1960.
3. BRUBACHER, JOHN S., AND WILLIS RUDY. *Higher Education in Transition.* New York: Harper & Row, 1958.
4. CAPLOW, THEODORE, AND REECE J. MCGEE. *The Academic Marketplace.* New York: Basic Books, Inc., 1958.
5. CARMAN, HARRY J. "Boards of Trustees and Regents," *Administrators in Higher Education, Their Functions and Coordination,* GERALD P. BURNS, ed. New York: Harper & Row, 1962.
6. CARMICHAEL, OLIVER C. *Graduate Education, A Critique and a Program.* New York: Harper & Row, 1961.
7. CARNEGIE FOUNDATION FOR THE ADVANCEMENT OF TEACHING, *Fifty-seventh Annual Report, 1962.* New York: The Foundation, 1962.
8. Columbia University Special Trustee Committee Report on *The Role of the Trustees of Columbia University.* New York: Columbia University, 1957.
9. COOMBS, PHILIP H. "An Economist's Overview of Higher Education," *Financing Higher Education, 1960–70,* DEXTER M. KEEZER, ed. New York: McGraw-Hill Book Company, 1959.

10. CORSON, JOHN J. *Governance of Colleges and Universities.* New York: McGraw-Hill Book Company, 1960.

11. DEPARTMENT OF HEALTH, EDUCATION AND WELFARE. *Health, Education and Welfare Trends.* Washington, D.C.: U.S. Government Printing Office, 1962.

12. DODDS, HAROLD W. *The Academic President—Educator or Caretaker?* New York: McGraw-Hill Book Company, 1962.

13. DRESSEL, PAUL L., AND MARGARET F. LORIMER. "Institutional Self-Evaluation in Higher Education," *Evaluation in Higher Education,* PAUL L. DRESSEL AND ASSOCIATES. Boston: Houghton Mifflin Company, 1961.

14. EURICH, ALVIN C., Chairman, Panel of Advisors. *Kansas, Plans for the Next Generation: A Report on Higher Education in Kansas to the Board of Regents.* Topeka, Kansas: The Board of Regents, 1962.

15. FURNAS, CLIFFORD C., AND RAYMOND EWELL. "The Role of Research in the Economics of Universities," *Financing Higher Education, 1960–70,* DEXTER M. KEEZER, ed. New York: McGraw-Hill Book Company, 1959.

16. GROSS, NEAL. "Organizational Lag in American Universities," *Harvard Educational Review,* Vol. 33, No. 1, Winter 1963

17. HENDERSON, ALGO D. *Policies and Practices in Higher Education.* New York: Harper & Row, 1960.

18. HENEMAN, HARLOW J. "Opportunities for Improved Management in Higher Education," *Financing Higher Education, 1960–70,* DEXTER M. KEEZER, ed. New York: McGraw-Hill Book Company, 1959.

19. HICKMAN, C. ADDISON. "What Happens to the Social Structure and Inner Dynamics of a College in Process of Change?" *Current Issues in Higher Education: Higher Education in an Age of Revolution,* G. KERRY SMITH, ed., Association for Higher Education. Washington, D.C.: National Education Association, 1962.

20. HORN, FRANCIS H. "The Organization of Colleges and Universities," *Administrators in Higher Education: Their Functions and Coordination,* GERALD P. BURNS, ed. New York: Harper & Row, 1962.

21. MASTERSON, THOMAS R. "Management Functions," *College and University Business,* Vol. 28, No. 2, February 1960.

22. MCGRATH, EARL J. *The Graduate School and the Decline of Liberal Education.* New York: Bureau of Publications, Teachers College, Columbia University, 1959.

23. MCGRATH, EARL J. *Memo to a College Faculty Member.* New York: Bureau of Publications, Teachers College, Columbia University, 1961.

24. MILLETT, JOHN D. *The Academic Community: An Essay on Organization.* New York: McGraw-Hill Book Company, 1962.

25. MOONEY, ROSS L. "The Problem of Leadership in the University," *Harvard Educational Review,* Vol. 33, No. 1, Winter 1963.

26. RAUH, MORTON A. *College and University Trusteeship.* Yellow Springs, Ohio: The Antioch Press, 1959.

27. ROSENBERG, HERBERT H. "Research and the Financing of Higher Education," *The Economics of Higher Education,* SELMA J. MUSHKIN, ed. U.S. Department of Health, Education and Welfare, Office of Education. Washington, D.C.: U.S. Government Printing Office, 1962.

28. RUML, BEARDSLEY, AND DONALD H. MORRISON. *Memo to A College Trustee.* New York: McGraw-Hill Book Company, 1959.

29. UMBECK, SHARVY G. "The Challenge of the Decade Ahead," *Proceedings of the Second National Assembly, Held July 6–8, 1960, French Lick, Indiana.* National Federation of College and University Business Officers Associations, 1960. Printed by News-Review Publishing Co., Inc., Moscow, Ind.

30. U.S. OFFICE OF EDUCATION. *Biennial Survey of Education in the United States, 1956–58.* "Statistics of Higher Education, 1957–58. Receipts, Expenditures and Property," Ch. 4, Sec. II. Washington, D.C.: U.S. Government Printing Office, 1961

31. WILSEY, H. LAWRENCE. "Long-range Planning for Colleges and Universities," *Proceedings of the Second National Assembly, Held July 6–8, 1960, French Lick, Indiana.* National Federation of College and University Business Officers Associations, 1960. Printed by News-Review Publishing Co., Inc., Moscow, Idaho.

32. WOODBURNE, LLOYD S. *Principles of College and University Administration.* Stanford, California: Stanford University Press, 1958.

33. WOODBURNE, LLOYD S. *Faculty Personnel Policies in Higher Education.* New York: Harper & Row, 1950.

APPENDIX *B*

Some Quantitative Aspects of American Higher Education

APPENDIX B–I. Institutions and degree-credit enrollments in each state, classified by type of control: 1959–1960

State	Public Control		Private Control		Total	
	NUMBER OF INSTITUTIONS	ENROLLMENT	NUMBER OF INSTITUTIONS	ENROLLMENT	NUMBER OF INSTITUTIONS	ENROLLMENT
Alabama	9	33,541	19	12,597	28	46,138
Alaska	1	2,767	—	—	1	2,767
Arizona	5	31,893	2	892	7	32,785
Arkansas	8	16,829	11	6,700	19	23,529
California	85	350,020[a]	78	74,516	163	424,536[a]
Colorado	14	35,953[a]	9	9,887	23	45,840[a]
Connecticut	7	18,760[a]	26	29,339	33	48,099[a]
Delaware	2	5,586	2	848	4	6,434
District of Columbia	3	5,014[a]	19	41,497	22	46,511[a]
Florida	19	38,901	16	26,283	35	65,184
Georgia	21	31,621	26	15,850	47	47,471
Hawaii	1	8,798	3	847	4	9,645
Idaho	5	8,505	4	2,676	9	11,181
Illinois	19	85,187	87	102,432	106	187,619
Indiana	6	52,139	36	37,593	42	89,732

[a]Includes the following federally controlled institutions:

State	Number of Institutions	Enrollment
California	2	2,564
Colorado	1	1,524
Connecticut	1	615
District of Columbia	2	3,740
Maryland	1	3,730
New York	2	3,492
Ohio	1	374
Total	10	16,039

APPENDIX B–1, Continued

State	Public Control		Private Control		Total	
	NUMBER OF INSTITUTIONS	ENROLLMENT	NUMBER OF INSTITUTIONS	ENROLLMENT	NUMBER OF INSTITUTIONS	ENROLLMENT
Iowa	19	27,017	32	27,156	51	54,173
Kansas	21	40,713	24	9,389	45	50,102
Kentucky	8	27,594	31	16,058	39	43,652
Louisiana	10	38,755	12	15,241	22	53,996
Maine	7	7,329	15	4,619	22	11,948
Maryland	17	32,710[a]	21	20,676	38	53,386[a]
Massachusetts	17	19,479	71	110,125	88	129,604
Michigan	24	118,679	36	33,719	60	152,398
Minnesota	15	50,831	28	20,946	43	71,777
Mississippi	25	26,635	18	6,427	43	33,062
Missouri	14	36,455	47	44,507	61	80,962
Montana	8	10,345	3	1,578	11	11,923
Nebraska	10	22,539	13	8,759	23	31,298
Nevada	1	3,708	—	—	1	3,708
New Hampshire	5	6,578	6	5,535	11	12,113
New Jersey	9	38,429	30	43,633	39	82,062
New Mexico	7	15,733	2	842	9	16,575
New York	45	136,198[a]	122	234,027	167	370,225[a]
North Carolina	16	36,805	43	30,176	59	66,981
North Dakota	11	12,618	2	644	13	13,262
Ohio	10	89,943[a]	59	78,077	69	168,020[a]
Oklahoma	24	43,505	10	12,693	34	56,198
Oregon	8	24,854	18	9,474	26	34,328
Pennsylvania	16	37,878	106	144,066	122	181,944
Puerto Rico	1	17,891	4	6,178	5	24,069

Rhode Island	2	9	7,077	10,491	11	17,568
South Carolina	6	25	17,753	14,084	31	31,837
South Dakota	7	9	10,299	3,690	16	13,989
Tennessee	7	39	35,435	24,451	46	59,886
Texas	50	48	129,449	49,436	98	178,885
Utah	4	4	19,703	11,087	8	30,790
Vermont	4	12	4,123	4,613	16	8,736
Virginia	8	33	35,871	18,164	41	54,035
Washington	15	12	47,355	14,995	27	62,350
West Virginia	11	9	21,479	6,776	20	28,255
Wisconsin	33	29	47,989	22,489	62	70,478
Wyoming	6	—	6,647	—	6	6,647
TOTAL	706	1,320	2,031,915	1,426,778	2,026	3,458,693

NOTE: The following public institutional branches or separate campuses have not been separately counted in listing the number of public institutions: Alaska, 4; Arkansas, 1; Colorado 1; Connecticut, 4; Illinois, 2; Indiana, 14; Louisiana, 3; Maine, 1; Maryland, 2; Minnesota, 1; Mississippi, 1; Nevada, 1; New Jersey, 2; Pennsylvania, 15; Tennessee, 3; Texas, 2; Utah, 3; Virginia 6; Wisconsin, 9— Total: 75 in nineteen states.

SOURCE: Data from U.S. Office of Education, *Education Directory, 1960–61*, Part 3.

APPENDIX B-2. Student degree-credit enrollment, classified according to type and control of institutions attended: 1959–1960

Classification[a] by States	Public Control			Private Control			Total		
	NUMBER OF INSTITUTIONS	ENROLLMENT	PERCENTAGE	NUMBER OF INSTITUTIONS	ENROLLMENT	PERCENTAGE	NUMBER OF INSTITUTIONS	ENROLLMENT	PERCENTAGE
ALABAMA									
Type I	—	—	—	6	1,342	2.9	6	1,342	2.9
Type II	1	1,156	2.5	11	7,916	17.2	12	9,072	19.7
Type III	6	10,148	22.0	2	3,339	7.2	8	13,487	29.2
Type IV	2	22,237	48.2	—	—	—	2	22,237	48.2
Type V	—	—	—	—	—	—	—	—	—
Total	*9*	*33,541*	*72.7*	*19*	*12,597*	*27.3*	*28*	*46,138*	*100.0*
ALASKA									
Type I	—	—	—	—	—	—	—	—	—
Type II	—	—	—	—	—	—	—	—	—
Type III	—	—	—	—	—	—	—	—	—
Type IV	1	2,767	100.0	—	—	—	1	2,767	100.0
Type V	—	—	—	—	—	—	—	—	—
Total	*1*	*2,767*	*100.0*	*—*	*—*	*—*	*1*	*2,767*	*100.0*
ARIZONA									
Type I	2	5,929	18.1	—	—	—	2	5,929	18.1
Type II	—	—	—	2	892	2.7	2	892	2.7
Type III	1	1,648	5.0	—	—	—	1	1,648	5.0
Type IV	2	24,316	74.2	—	—	—	2	24,316	74.2
Type V	—	—	—	—	—	—	—	—	—
Total	*5*	*31,893*	*97.3*	*2*	*892*	*2.7*	*7*	*32,785*	*100.0*
ARKANSAS									
Type I	—	—	—	2	790	3.4	2	790	3.4
Type II	4	4,844	20.6	6	3,541	15.0	10	8,385	35.6
Type III	3	6,040	25.7	2	2,197	9.3	5	8,237	35.0
Type IV	1	5,945	25.3	—	—	—	1	5,945	25.3
Type V	—	—	—	1	172	0.7	1	172	0.7
Total	*8*	*16,829*	*71.6*	*11*	*6,700*	*28.4*	*19*	*23,529*	*100.0*

	No.	Enrollment	%	No.	Enrollment	%	No.	Enrollment	%
California[b]									
Type I	61	206,299	48.9	4	683	0.2	65	206,982	49.1
Type II	—	—	—	30	11,516	2.7	30	11,516	2.7
Type III	17	102,656	24.3	35	29,263	6.9	52	131,919	31.2
Type IV	2	36,562	8.7	8	32,011	7.6	10	68,573	16.3
Type V	3	1,939	0.5	1	1,043	0.2	4	2,982	0.7
Total	*83*	*347,456*	*82.4*	*78*	*74,516*	*17.6*	*161*	*421,972*	*100.0*
Colorado[c]									
Type I	7	3,959	9.0	1	548	1.2	8	4,507	10.2
Type II	—	—	—	3	1,782	4.0	3	1,782	4.0
Type III	2	2,853	6.4	3	1,600	3.6	5	4,453	10.0
Type IV	4	27,617	62.3	2	5,957	13.5	6	33,574	75.8
Type V	—	—	—	—	—	—	—	—	—
Total	*13*	*34,429*	*77.7*	*9*	*9,887*	*22.3*	*22*	*44,316*	*100.0*
Connecticut[d]									
Type I	1	159	0.3	6	1,766	3.8	7	1,925	4.1
Type II	—	—	—	9	3,270	6.9	9	3,270	6.9
Type III	4	7,343	15.5	9	16,279	34.2	13	23,622	49.7
Type IV	1	10,643	22.4	2	8,024	16.9	3	18,667	39.3
Type V	—	—	—	—	—	—	—	—	—
Total	*6*	*18,145*	*38.2*	*26*	*29,339*	*61.8*	*32*	*47,484*	*100.0*
Delaware									
Type I	—	—	—	2	848	13.2	2	848	13.2
Type II	1	356	5.5	—	—	—	1	356	5.5
Type III	—	—	—	—	—	—	—	—	—
Type IV	1	5,230	81.3	—	—	—	1	5,230	81.3
Type V	—	—	—	—	—	—	—	—	—
Total	*2*	*5,586*	*86.8*	*2*	*848*	*13.2*	*4*	*6,434*	*100.0*

[a] Classification of institutions:
Type I: Two but less than four years beyond the 12th grade
Type II: Only the bachelors and/or first professional degree
Type III: Masters and/or second professional degree
Type IV: Doctor of philosophy and equivalent degrees
Type V: Other and unclassified

[b] Also 2,564 students in two federal institutions.
[c] Also 1,524 students in one federal institution.
[d] Also 615 students in one federal institution.

APPENDIX B-2, Continued

Classification by States	Public Control			Private Control			Total		
	NUMBER OF INSTITUTIONS	ENROLLMENT	PERCENTAGE	NUMBER OF INSTITUTIONS	ENROLLMENT	PERCENTAGE	NUMBER OF INSTITUTIONS	ENROLLMENT	PERCENTAGE
DISTRICT OF COLUMBIA									
Type I	—	—	—	6	2,365	5.5	6	2,365	5.5
Type II	1	1,274	3.0	3	1,210	2.8	4	2,484	5.8
Type III	—	—	—	3	1,357	3.2	3	1,357	3.2
Type IV	—	—	—	6	36,510	85.4	6	36,510	85.4
Type V	—	—	—	1	55	0.1	1	55	0.1
Total	*1*	*1,274*	*3.0*	*19*	*41,497*	*97.0*	*20*	*42,771*	*100.0*
FLORIDA									
Type I	16	10,877	16.7	6	2,238	3.4	22	13,115	20.1
Type II	—	—	—	7	9,301	14.3	7	9,301	14.3
Type III	1	3,141	4.8	2	2,553	3.9	3	5,694	8.7
Type IV	2	24,883	38.2	1	12,191	18.7	3	37,074	56.9
Type V	—	—	—	—	—	—	—	—	—
Total	*19*	*38,901*	*59.7*	*16*	*26,283*	*40.3*	*35*	*65,184*	*100.0*
GEORGIA									
Type I	9	5,177	10.9	7	1,846	3.9	16	7,023	14.8
Type II	5	3,972	8.4	15	7,374	15.5	20	11,346	23.9
Type III	5	6,964	14.7	3	2,366	5.0	8	9,330	19.7
Type IV	2	15,508	32.7	1	4,264	8.9	3	19,772	41.6
Type V	—	—	—	—	—	—	—	—	—
Total	*21*	*31,621*	*66.7*	*26*	*15,850*	*33.3*	*47*	*47,471*	*100.0*
HAWAII									
Type I	—	—	—	1	520	5.4	1	520	5.4
Type II	—	—	—	2	327	3.4	2	327	3.4
Type III	—	—	—	—	—	—	—	—	—
Type IV	1	8,798	91.2	—	—	—	1	8,798	91.2
Type V	—	—	—	—	—	—	—	—	—
Total	*1*	*8,798*	*91.2*	*3*	*847*	*8.8*	*4*	*9,645*	*100.0*

Type I	2	2,038	18.2	2	1,150	10.3	4	3,188	28.3
Type II	—	—	—	1	599	5.3	1	599	5.3
Type III	1	2,324	20.8	1	927	8.3	2	3,251	29.1
Type IV	1	4,143	37.1	—	—	—	1	4,143	37.1
Type V	—	—	—	—	—	—	—	—	—
Total	4	8,505	76.1	4	2,676	23.9	8	11,181	100.0
ILLINOIS									
Type I	12	22,608	12.0	13	5,972	3.2	25	28,580	15.2
Type II	—	—	—	34	19,939	10.6	34	19,939	10.6
Type III	5	21,584	11.5	28	34,015	18.1	33	55,599	29.6
Type IV	2	40,995	21.9	8	40,880	21.8	10	81,875	43.7
Type V	—	—	*	4	1,626	0.9	4	1,626	0.9
Total	19	85,187	45.4	87	102,432	54.6	106	187,619	100.0
INDIANA									
Type I	1	572	0.7	1	331	0.4	2	903	1.1
Type II	—	—	—	23	18,250	20.3	23	18,250	20.3
Type III	2	10,716	11.9	6	7,794	8.7	8	18,510	20.6
Type IV	2	40,825	45.5	3	7,827	8.7	5	48,652	54.2
Type V	1	26	*	3	3,391	3.8	4	3,417	3.8
Total	6	52,139	58.1	36	37,593	41.9	42	89,732	100.0
IOWA									
Type I	16	3,076	5.7	6	1,643	3.0	22	4,719	8.7
Type II	—	—	—	25	18,491	34.1	25	18,491	34.1
Type III	1	3,900	7.2	1	7,022	13.0	2	10,922	20.2
Type IV	2	20,041	37.0	—	—	—	2	20,041	37.0
Type V	—	—	—	—	—	—	—	—	—
Total	19	27,017	49.9	32	27,156	50.1	51	54,173	100.0
KANSAS									
Type I	14	4,735	9.5	5	976	1.9	19	5,711	11.4
Type II	—	—	—	17	7,834	15.6	17	7,834	15.6
Type III	4	12,171	24.3	2	579	1.2	6	12,750	25.5
Type IV	3	23,807	47.5	—	—	—	3	23,807	47.5
Type V	—	—	—	—	—	—	—	—	—
Total	21	40,713	81.3	24	9,389	18.7	45	50,102	100.0

e Also 3,740 students in two federal institutions.

* Less than one-tenth of one per cent.

APPENDIX B-2, Continued

Classification [a] by States	Public Control			Private Control			Total		
	NUMBER OF INSTITUTIONS	ENROLLMENT	PERCENTAGE	NUMBER OF INSTITUTIONS	ENROLLMENT	PERCENTAGE	NUMBER OF INSTITUTIONS	ENROLLMENT	PERCENTAGE
KENTUCKY									
Type I	1	587	1.3	10	2,668	6.2	11	3,255	7.5
Type II	1	638	1.5	14	9,401	21.5	15	10,039	23.0
Type III	4	10,702	24.5	6	3,057	7.0	10	13,759	31.5
Type IV	2	15,667	35.9	1	932	2.1	3	16,599	38.0
Type V	—	—	—	—	—	—	—	—	—
Total	*8*	*27,594*	*63.2*	*31*	*16,058*	*36.8*	*39*	*43,652*	*100.0*
LOUISIANA									
Type I	—	—	—	1	75	0.1	1	75	0.1
Type II	5	10,240	19.0	6	4,129	7.6	11	14,369	26.6
Type III	4	15,791	29.2	3	3,656	6.8	7	19,447	36.0
Type IV	1	12,724	23.6	2	7,381	13.7	3	20,105	37.3
Type V	—	—	—	—	—	—	—	—	—
Total	*10*	*38,755*	*71.8*	*12*	*15,241*	*28.2*	*22*	*53,996*	*100.0*
MAINE									
Type I	1	108	0.9	5	500	4.2	6	608	5.1
Type II	4	1,427	11.9	9	4,019	33.6	13	5,446	45.5
Type III	—	—	—	—	—	—	—	—	—
Type IV	1	5,509	46.1	—	—	—	1	5,509	46.1
Type V	1	285	2.4	1	100	0.9	2	385	3.3
Total	*7*	*7,329*	*61.3*	*15*	*4,619*	*38.7*	*22*	*11,948*	*100.0*
MARYLAND [f]									
Type I	10	3,866	7.8	2	146	0.3	12	4,012	8.1
Type II	4	3,536	7.1	7	4,037	8.1	11	7,573	15.2
Type III	2	2,281	4.6	7	7,108	14.3	9	9,389	18.9
Type IV	1	19,297	38.9	4	9,094	18.3	5	28,391	57.2
Type V	—	—	—	1	291	0.6	1	291	0.6
Total	*17*	*28,980*	*58.4*	*21*	*20,676*	*41.6*	*38*	*49,656*	*100.0*

MASSACHUSETTS									
Type I	2	685	0.5	17	7,687	5.9	19	8,372	6.4
Type II	5	2,907	2.2	18	8,539	6.6	23	11,446	8.8
Type III	8	9,171	7.1	21	34,818	26.9	29	43,989	34.0
Type IV	2	6,716	5.2	12	58,748	45.3	14	65,464	50.5
Type V	—	—	—	3	333	0.3	3	333	0.3
Total	*17*	*19,479*	*15.0*	*71*	*110,125*	*85.0*	*88*	*129,604*	*100.0*
MICHIGAN									
Type I	15	18,088	11.9	4	513	0.3	19	18,601	12.2
Type II	2	4,604	3.0	24	18,857	12.4	26	23,461	15.4
Type III	4	25,670	16.8	7	14,258	9.4	11	39,928	26.2
Type IV	3	70,317	46.1	—	—	—	3	70,317	46.1
Type V	—	—	—	1	91	0.1	1	91	0.1
Total	*24*	*118,679*	*77.8*	*36*	*33,719*	*22.2*	*60*	*152,398*	*100.0*
MINNESOTA									
Type I	9	2,381	3.3	2	431	0.6	11	2,812	3.9
Type II	—	—	—	18	13,731	19.1	18	13,731	19.1
Type III	5	12,568	17.5	7	6,684	9.3	12	19,252	26.8
Type IV	1	35,882	50.0	—	—	—	1	35,882	50.0
Type V	—	—	—	1	100	0.2	1	100	0.2
Total	*15*	*50,831*	*70.8*	*28*	*20,946*	*29.2*	*43*	*71,777*	*100.0*
MISSISSIPPI									
Type I	17	6,968	21.1	9	1,114	3.4	26	8,082	24.5
Type II	5	5,673	17.2	8	3,686	11.1	13	9,359	28.3
Type III	—	—	—	1	1,627	4.9	1	1,627	4.9
Type IV	3	13,994	42.3	—	—	—	3	13,994	42.3
Type V	—	—	—	—	—	—	—	—	—
Total	*25*	*26,635*	*80.6*	*18*	*6,427*	*19.4*	*43*	*33,062*	*100.0*
MISSOURI									
Type I	6	5,414	6.7	11	5,282	6.5	17	10,696	13.2
Type II	3	6,463	8.0	24	10,651	13.2	27	17,114	21.2
Type III	4	9,394	11.6	8	3,291	4.1	12	12,685	15.7
Type IV	1	15,184	18.7	4	25,283	31.2	5	40,467	49.9
Type V	—	—	—	—	—	—	—	—	—
Total	*14*	*36,455*	*45.0*	*47*	*44,507*	*55.0*	*61*	*80,962*	*100.0*

! Also 3,730 students enrolled in one federal institution.

307

APPENDIX B–2, Continued

Classification * by States	Public Control			Private Control			Total		
	NUMBER OF INSTITUTIONS	ENROLLMENT	PERCENTAGE	NUMBER OF INSTITUTIONS	ENROLLMENT	PERCENTAGE	NUMBER OF INSTITUTIONS	ENROLLMENT	PERCENTAGE
MONTANA									
Type I	2	459	3.9	—	—	—	2	459	3.9
Type II	1	486	4.1	3	1,578	13.2	4	2,064	17.3
Type III	3	1,934	16.2	—	—	—	3	1,934	16.2
Type IV	2	7,466	62.6	—	—	—	2	7,466	62.6
Type V	—	—	—	—	—	—	—	—	—
Total	*8*	*10,345*	*86.8*	*3*	*1,578*	*13.2*	*11*	*11,923*	*100.0*
NEBRASKA									
Type I	4	1,201	3.8	2	215	0.7	6	1,416	4.5
Type II	—	—	—	10	5,639	18.0	10	5,639	18.0
Type III	5	10,519	33.6	1	2,905	9.3	6	13,424	42.9
Type IV	1	10,819	34.6	—	—	—	1	10,819	34.6
Type V	—	—	—	—	—	—	—	—	—
Total	*10*	*22,539*	*72.0*	*13*	*8,759*	*28.0*	*23*	*31,298*	*100.0*
NEVADA									
Type I	—	—	—	—	—	—	—	—	—
Type II	—	—	—	—	—	—	—	—	—
Type III	1	3,708	100.0	—	—	—	1	3,708	100.0
Type IV	—	—	—	—	—	—	—	—	—
Type V	—	—	—	—	—	—	—	—	—
Total	*1*	*3,708*	*100.0*	—	—	—	*1*	*3,708*	*100.0*
NEW HAMPSHIRE									
Type I	2	557	4.6	—	—	—	2	557	4.6
Type II	—	—	—	3	1,754	14.5	3	1,754	14.5
Type III	2	1,678	13.8	2	3,512	29.0	4	5,190	42.8
Type IV	1	4,343	35.9	—	—	—	1	4,343	35.9
Type V	—	—	—	1	269	2.2	1	269	2.2
Total	*5*	*6,578*	*54.3*	*6*	*5,535*	*45.7*	*11*	*12,113*	*100.0*

	No.	Enrollment	%	No.	Enrollment	%	No.	Enrollment	%
Type I	1	711	0.9	9	1,790	2.2	10	2,501	3.1
Type II	1	1,901	2.3	12	8,471	10.3	13	10,372	12.6
Type III	6	19,567	23.8	4	25,994	31.7	10	45,561	55.5
Type IV	1	16,250	19.8	4	7,274	8.9	5	23,524	28.7
Type V	—	—	—	1	104	0.1	1	104	0.1
Total	*9*	*38,429*	*46.8*	*30*	*43,633*	*53.2*	*39*	*82,062*	*100.0*
NEW MEXICO									
Type I	1	278	1.7	—	—	—	1	278	1.7
Type II	—	—	—	2	842	5.1	2	842	5.1
Type III	2	2,811	16.9	—	—	—	2	2,811	16.9
Type IV	4	12,644	76.3	—	—	—	4	12,644	76.3
Type V	—	—	—	—	—	—	—	—	—
Total	*7*	*15,733*	*94.9*	*2*	*842*	*5.1*	*9*	*16,575*	*100.0*
NEW YORK[f]									
Type I	22	28,784	7.8	27	7,784	2.1	49	36,568	9.9
Type II	2	1,931	0.5	40	22,702	6.2	42	24,633	6.7
Type III	15	97,086	26.5	32	53,119	14.5	47	150,205	41.0
Type IV	4	4,905	1.3	22	149,830	40.9	26	154,735	42.2
Type V	—	—	—	1	592	0.2	1	592	0.2
Total	*43*	*132,706*	*36.1*	*122*	*234,027*	*63.9*	*165*	*366,733*	*100.0*
NORTH CAROLINA									
Type I	4	1,623	2.4	18	6,775	10.1	22	8,398	12.5
Type II	4	2,276	3.4	21	15,632	23.3	25	17,908	26.7
Type III	5	15,249	22.8	2	1,992	3.0	7	17,241	25.8
Type IV	3	17,657	26.4	1	5,747	8.6	4	23,404	35.0
Type V	—	—	—	1	30	0.0	1	30	0.0
Total	*16*	*36,805*	*55.0*	*43*	*30,176*	*45.0*	*59*	*66,981*	*100.0*
NORTH DAKOTA									
Type I	4	1,137	8.5	1	20	0.2	5	1,157	8.7
Type II	5	3,968	29.9	1	624	4.7	6	4,592	34.6
Type III	—	—	—	—	—	—	—	—	—
Type IV	2	7,513	56.7	—	—	—	2	7,513	56.7
Type V	—	—	—	—	—	—	—	—	—
Total	*11*	*12,618*	*95.1*	*2*	*644*	*4.9*	*13*	*13,262*	*100.0*

[f] Also 3,492 students enrolled in two federal institutions.

APPENDIX B-2, Continued

Classification[a] by States	Public Control			Private Control			Total		
	NUMBER OF INSTITUTIONS	ENROLLMENT	PERCENTAGE	NUMBER OF INSTITUTIONS	ENROLLMENT	PERCENTAGE	NUMBER OF INSTITUTIONS	ENROLLMENT	PERCENTAGE
Ohio[b]									
Type I	—	—	—	4	3,775	2.2	4	3,775	2.2
Type II	1	1,343	0.8	37	38,678	23.1	38	40,021	23.9
Type III	4	32,670	19.5	15	25,124	15.0	19	57,794	34.5
Type IV	4	55,556	33.1	3	10,500	6.3	7	66,056	39.4
Type V	—	—	—	—	—	—	—	—	—
Total	*9*	*89,569*	*53.4*	*59*	*78,077*	*46.6*	*68*	*167,646*	*100.0*
Oklahoma									
Type I	13	5,732	10.2	4	947	1.7	17	6,679	11.9
Type II	3	2,229	4.0	4	5,463	9.7	7	7,692	13.7
Type III	6	12,110	21.5	1	1,126	2.0	7	13,236	23.5
Type IV	2	23,434	41.7	1	5,157	9.2	3	28,591	50.9
Type V	—	—	—	—	—	—	—	—	—
Total	*24*	*43,505*	*77.4*	*10*	*12,693*	*22.6*	*34*	*56,198*	*100.0*
Oregon									
Type I	1	930	2.7	2	825	2.4	3	1,755	5.1
Type II	1	3,997	11.6	9	2,377	6.9	10	6,374	18.5
Type III	3	2,981	8.7	6	4,740	13.8	9	7,721	22.5
Type IV	3	16,946	49.4	1	1,532	4.5	4	18,478	53.9
Type V	—	—	—	—	—	—	—	—	—
Total	*8*	*24,854*	*72.4*	*18*	*9,474*	*27.6*	*26*	*34,328*	*100.0*
Pennsylvania									
Type I	1	206	0.1	15	5,128	2.8	16	5,334	2.9
Type II	8	9,735	5.4	53	42,217	23.2	61	51,952	28.6
Type III	6	10,947	6.0	23	30,080	16.6	29	41,027	22.6
Type IV	1	16,990	9.3	13	66,611	36.6	14	83,601	45.9
Type V	—	—	—	2	30	0.0	2	30	0.0
Total	*16*	*37,878*	*20.8*	*106*	*144,066*	*79.2*	*122*	*181,944*	*100.0*

310

Type I	—	—	—	1	825	3.4	1	825	3.4
Type II	—	—	—	3	5,353	22.3	3	5,353	22.3
Type III	1	17,891	74.3	—	—	—	1	17,891	74.3
Type IV	—	—	—	—	—	—	—	—	—
Type V	—	—	—	—	—	—	—	—	—
Total	*1*	*17,891*	*74.3*	*4*	*6,178*	*25.7*	*5*	*24,069*	*100.0*
RHODE ISLAND									
Type I	—	—	—	1	299	1.7	1	299	1.7
Type II	—	—	—	4	1,294	7.4	4	1,294	7.4
Type III	1	1,877	10.7	2	3,686	21.0	3	5,563	31.7
Type IV	1	5,200	29.6	1	3,791	21.6	2	8,991	51.2
Type V	—	—	—	1	1,421	8.0	1	1,421	8.0
Total	*2*	*7,077*	*40.3*	*9*	*10,491*	*59.7*	*11*	*17,568*	*100.0*
SOUTH CAROLINA									
Type I	—	—	—	6	2,165	6.8	6	2,165	6.8
Type II	1	2,041	6.4	15	7,396	23.2	16	9,437	29.6
Type III	2	3,285	10.3	3	2,275	7.1	5	5,560	17.4
Type IV	3	12,427	39.1	1	2,248	7.1	4	14,675	46.2
Type V	—	—	—	—	—	—	—	—	—
Total	*6*	*17,753*	*55.8*	*25*	*14,084*	*44.2*	*31*	*31,837*	*100.0*
SOUTH DAKOTA									
Type I	—	—	—	3	313	2.2	3	313	2.2
Type II	3	1,757	12.6	6	3,377	24.1	9	5,134	36.7
Type III	2	2,645	18.9	—	—	—	2	2,645	18.9
Type IV	2	5,897	42.2	—	—	—	2	5,897	42.2
Type V	—	—	—	—	—	—	—	—	—
Total	*7*	*10,299*	*73.7*	*9*	*3,690*	*26.3*	*16*	*13,989*	*100.0*
TENNESSEE									
Type I	—	—	—	6	1,644	2.7	6	1,644	2.7
Type II	—	—	—	25	12,832	21.4	25	12,832	21.4
Type III	6	19,491	32.6	5	4,191	7.0	11	23,682	39.6
Type IV	1	15,944	26.6	2	5,565	9.3	3	21,509	35.9
Type V	—	—	—	1	219	0.4	1	219	0.4
Total	*7*	*35,435*	*59.2*	*39*	*24,451*	*40.8*	*46*	*59,886*	*100.0*

ᵇ Also 374 students enrolled in one federal institution.

APPENDIX B-2, Continued

Classification [a] by States	Public Control			Private Control			Total		
	NUMBER OF INSTITUTIONS	ENROLLMENT	PERCENTAGE	NUMBER OF INSTITUTIONS	ENROLLMENT	PERCENTAGE	NUMBER OF INSTITUTIONS	ENROLLMENT	PERCENTAGE
TEXAS									
Type I	31	34,659	19.4	8	1,195	0.7	39	35,854	20.1
Type II	2	6,600	3.7	21	9,112	5.0	23	15,712	8.7
Type III	11	30,179	16.9	11	13,601	7.6	22	43,780	24.5
Type IV	6	58,011	32.4	7	24,088	13.5	13	82,099	45.9
Type V	—	—	—	1	1,440	0.8	1	1,440	0.8
Total	*50*	*129,449*	*72.4*	*48*	*49,436*	*27.6*	*98*	*178,885*	*100.0*
UTAH									
Type I	2	2,690	8.7	1	412	1.4	3	3,102	10.1
Type II	—	—	—	2	410	1.3	2	410	1.3
Type III	—	—	—	—	—	—	—	—	—
Type IV	2	17,013	55.3	1	10,265	33.3	3	27,278	88.6
Type V	—	—	—	—	—	—	—	—	—
Total	*4*	*19,703*	*64.0*	*4*	*11,087*	*36.0*	*8*	*30,790*	*100.0*
VERMONT									
Type I	—	—	—	3	653	7.5	3	653	7.5
Type II	3	800	9.2	5	1,798	20.6	8	2,598	29.8
Type III	—	—	—	3	876	10.0	3	876	10.0
Type IV	1	3,323	38.0	1	1,286	14.7	2	4,609	52.7
Type V	—	—	—	—	—	—	—	—	—
Total	*4*	*4,123*	*47.2*	*12*	*4,613*	*52.8*	*16*	*8,736*	*100.0*
VIRGINIA									
Type I	—	—	—	11	3,274	6.1	11	3,274	6.1
Type II	1	1,054	2.0	15	8,662	16.0	16	9,716	18.0
Type III	4	14,208	26.3	6	5,946	11.0	10	20,154	37.3
Type IV	3	20,609	38.1	1	282	0.5	4	20,891	38.6
Type V	—	—	—	—	—	—	—	—	—
Total	*8*	*35,871*	*66.4*	*33*	*18,164*	*33.6*	*41*	*54,035*	*100.0*

	No.		%	No.		%	No.		%
WASHINGTON									
Type I	10	10,271	16.5	—	—	—	10	10,271	16.5
Type II	—	—	—	4	1,646	2.6	4	1,646	2.6
Type III	3	7,193	11.6	8	13,349	21.4	11	20,542	33.0
Type IV	2	29,891	47.9	—	—	—	2	29,891	47.9
Type V	—	—	—	—	—	—	—	—	—
Total	*15*	*47,355*	*76.0*	*12*	*14,995*	*24.0*	*27*	*62,350*	*100.0*
WEST VIRGINIA									
Type I	1	597	2.1	2	837	3.0	3	1,434	5.1
Type II	8	9,470	33.5	7	5,939	21.0	15	15,409	54.5
Type III	1	4,361	15.4	—	—	—	1	4,361	15.4
Type IV	1	7,051	25.0	—	—	—	1	7,051	25.0
Type V	—	—	—	—	—	—	—	—	—
Total	*11*	*21,479*	*76.0*	*9*	*6,776*	*24.0*	*20*	*28,255*	*100.0*
WISCONSIN									
Type I	23	2,392	3.4	3	251	0.4	26	2,643	3.8
Type II	6	12,765	18.1	19	9,263	13.1	25	22,028	31.2
Type III	3	4,798	6.8	5	1,841	2.6	8	6,639	9.4
Type IV	1	28,034	39.8	2	11,134	15.8	3	39,168	55.6
Type V	—	—	—	—	—	—	—	—	—
Total	*33*	*47,989*	*68.1*	*29*	*22,489*	*31.9*	*62*	*70,478*	*100.0*
WYOMING									
Type I	5	2,003	30.1	—	—	—	5	2,003	30.1
Type II	—	—	—	—	—	—	—	—	—
Type III	—	—	—	—	—	—	—	—	—
Type IV	1	4,644	69.9	—	—	—	1	4,644	69.9
Type V	—	—	—	—	—	—	—	—	—
Total	*6*	*6,647*	*100.0*	—	—	—	*6*	*6,647*	*100.0*

APPENDIX B-2, Continued

Classification[a] by States	Public Control			Private Control			Total		
	NUMBER OF INSTITUTIONS	ENROLLMENT	PERCENTAGE	NUMBER OF INSTITUTIONS	ENROLLMENT	PERCENTAGE	NUMBER OF INSTITUTIONS	ENROLLMENT	PERCENTAGE
GRAND TOTAL									
Type I	329	397,756	11.6	256	80,561	2.3	585	478,317	13.9
Type II	91	109,443	3.1	637	402,351	11.7	728	511,794	14.9
Type III	175	594,253	17.3	286	378,147	11.0	461	972400	28.2
Type IV	96	912,174	26.5	115	554,412	16.1	211	1,466,586	42.6
Type V	5	2,250	0.1	26	11,307	0.3	31	13,557	0.4
	696	2,015,876	58.6	1,320	1,426,778	41.4	2,016	3,442,654	100.0
Federal	10	16,039	—	—	—	—	10	16,039	—
	706	2,031,915	—	1,320	1,426,778	—	2,026	3,458,693	—

NOTE: The following public institutional branches or separate campuses have not been separately counted in listing the number of public institutions: Alaska 4, Arkansas 1, Colorado 1, Connecticut 4, Illinois 2, Indiana 14, Louisiana 3, Maine 1, Maryland 2, Minnesota 1, Mississippi 1, Nevada 1, New Jersey 2, Pennsylvania 15, Tennessee 3, Texas 2, Utah 3, Virginia 6, Wisconsin 9, Total 75 in 19 states.

SOURCE: Data from U. S. Office of Education, *Education Directory, 1960–1961*, Part 3.

APPENDIX B-3. State responsibility for higher education exercised by state and local boards

GROUP I: States with 1960 degree-credit enrollment in state institutions of less than 17,500 students

State	Number of Institutions	Student Enrollment	State Boards				Institutions Governed by State Boards		Institutions Each Governed by Local Board	
			COORDINATING	GOVERNING	GOVERNING-COORDINATING	SUPERVISORY ACCREDITING	NUMBER	ENROLLMENT	NUMBER	ENROLLMENT
Alaska	5a	2,767	1	—	1	1	1	2,767	4	—b
Arkansas	9a	16,829	—	7	1	—	9a	16,829	—	—
Delaware	2	5,586	—	2	—	1	2	5,586	—	—
Hawaii	1	8,798	—	1	1	—	1	8,798	—	—
Idaho	4	8,505	—	—	1	—	2	6,467	2	2,038
Maine	8a	7,329	—	1	1	—	8a	7,329	—	—
Montana	8	10,345	—	—	1	—	8	10,345	—	—
Nebraska	10	22,539	—	1	1	2	5	15,585	5	6,954
Nevada	2a	3,708	—	—	1	—	2a	3,708	—	—
New Hampshire	5	6,578	—	1	1	—	5	6,578	—	—
New Mexico	7	15,733	1	7	—	—	7	15,733	—	—
North Dakota	11	12,618	—	—	1	—	9	11,981	2	637
Rhode Island	2	7,077	—	—	1	—	2	7,077	—	—
South Dakota	7	10,299	—	—	1	—	7	10,299	—	—
Vermont	4	4,123	—	1	1	—	4	4,123	—	—
Wyoming	6	6,647	—	1	—	1	1	4,644	5	2,003
Total, 16 states	91•	149,481	2	22	13	5	73a	137,849	18	11,632

State	Number of Institutions	Student Enrollment	State Boards				Institutions Governed by State Boards		Institutions Each Governed by Local Board	
			COORDINATING	GOVERNING	GOVERNING-COORDINATING	SUPERVISORY-ACCREDITING	NUMBER	ENROLLMENT	NUMBER	ENROLLMENT
Alabama	9	33,541	—	3	1	—	9	33,541	—	—
Arizona	5	31,893	—	—	1	1	3	25,964	2	5,929
Colorado	14c	34,429	—	1	3	1	8c	30,871	6	3,558
Connecticut	10c	18,145	—	—	2	1	10c	18,145	—	—
Florida	19	38,901	—	—	1	1	3	28,024	16	10,877
Georgia	21	31,621	—	—	1	1	19	31,153	2	468
Iowa	19	27,017	—	—	1	1	3	23,941	16	3,076
Kansas	21	40,713	1	—	2	—	5	27,439	16	13,274
Kentucky	8	27,594	—	6	—	1	6	20,618	2	6,976
Massachusetts	17	19,479	—	5	1	2	17	19,479	—	—
Maryland	19c	28,980	—	2	2	1	10c	25,285	9	3,695
Mississippi	26c	26,635	—	—	1	3	9c	19,667	17	6,968
Missouri	14	36,455	1	7	—	1	7	29,560	7	6,895
New Jersey	11c	38,429	—	—	2	—	9c	34,132	2	4,297
Oregon	8	24,854	—	1	1	—	8	24,854	—	—
South Carolina	6	17,753	—	6	—	—	6	17,753	—	—
Utah	7c	19,703	1	—	3	—	7c	19,703	—	—
West Virginia	11	21,479	—	—	2	—	11	21,479	—	—
Total, 18 states	245c	517,621	3	31	22	13	150c	451,608	95	66,013

aCounted as institutions are branches and separate campuses: Arkansas, 1; Maine, 1; Nevada, 1; also, four Alaska institutions under local boards. Total: 7.

bNot available.

cCounted as institutions are branches and separate campuses: Colorado, 1; Connecticut, 4; Maryland, 2; Mississippi, 1; New Jersey, 2; Utah, 3. Total: 13.

APPENDIX B–3, Continued

GROUP III: States with 1960 degree-credit enrollments in state institutions of 35,000 and over

State	Number of Institutions	Student Enrollment	State Boards — COORDINATING	State Boards — GOVERNING	State Boards — GOVERNING-COORDINATING	State Boards — SUPERVISORY	State Boards — ACCREDITING	Institutions Governed by State Boards — NUMBER	Institutions Governed by State Boards — ENROLLMENT	Institutions Each Governed by Local Board — NUMBER	Institutions Each Governed by Local Board — ENROLLMENT
California	83	347,456	1	1	2	2	—	21	140,956	62	206,500
Illinois	21[d]	85,187	1	1	2	2	—	8[d]	58,094	13	27,093
Indiana	20[d]	52,139	—	—	3	1	—	18[d]	51,541	2	598
Louisiana	13[d]	38,755	—	—	2	—	—	13[d]	38,755	—	—
Michigan	24	118,679	—	5	1	—	—	9	100,591	15	18,088
Minnesota	16[d]	50,831	—	—	2	1	—	7[d]	48,450	9	2,381
New York	43	132,706	—	11	2	1	—	27	109,202	16	23,504
North Carolina	16	36,805	1	6	—	—	—	16	36,805	—	—
Ohio	9	89,569	—	4	2	—	—	6	62,246	3	27,323
Oklahoma	24	43,505	1	14	1	2	—	18	42,539	6	966
Pennsylvania	31[d]	37,878	—	14	1	2	—	30[d]	37,672	1	206
Tennessee	10[d]	35,435	—	—	2	—	—	10[d]	35,435	—	—
Texas	52[d]	129,449	1	6	3	1	—	21[d]	98,954	31	30,495
Virginia	14[d]	35,871	1	2	4	—	—	14[d]	35,871	—	—
Washington	15	47,355	—	5	—	1	—	5	37,084	10	10,271
Wisconsin	42[d]	47,989	1	—	2	1	—	19[d]	45,597	23	2,392
Total, 16 states	433[d]	1,329,609	7	55	30	10	—	242[d]	979,792	191	349,817

State	Number of Institutions	Student Enrollment	State Boards COORDINATING	State Boards GOVERNING	State Boards GOVERNING-COORDINATING	State Boards SUPERVISORY ACCREDITING	Institutions Governed by State Boards NUMBER	Institutions Governed by State Boards ENROLLMENT	Institutions Each Governed by Local Board NUMBER	Institutions Each Governed by Local Board ENROLLMENT
SUMMARY										
Group I (16 states)	91e	149,481	2	22	13	5	73e	137,849	18	11,632
Group II (18 states)	245e	517,621	3	31	23	13	150e	451,608	95	66,013
Group III (16 states)	433e	1,329,609	7	55	30	10	242e	979,792	191	349,817
GRAND TOTAL, 50 states	769e	1,996,711	12	108	66	28	465e	1,569,249	304	427,462

d Counted as institutions are branches and separate campuses: Illinois, 2; Indiana, 14; Louisiana, 3; Minnesota, 1; Pennsylvania, 15; Tennessee, 3; Texas, 2; Virginia, 6; Wisconsin, 9. Total: 55.

e Counted as institutions are branches and separate campuses: Group I, 7; Group II, 13; Group III, 55. Total: 75.

SOURCE: Identification of boards: S. V. Martorana and Ernest V. Hollis, *State Boards Responsible for Higher Education. Enrollment and control:* U.S. Office of Education, *Education Directory, 1960–1961,* Part 3.

APPENDIX B-4. Responsibility of state governing boards and state governing-coordinating boards measured in terms of 1960 student degree-credit enrollment

I. Governing boards, each board responsible for a single institution

State	Number of Boards	Number of Institutions	Total Enrollment	Under 10,000			10,000 to 20,000			Over 20,000		
				Number of Boards	Number of Institutions	Enrollment	Number of Boards	Number of Institutions	Enrollment	Number of Boards	Number of Institutions	Enrollment
Arkansas	7	7	10,884	7	7	10,884	—	—	—	—	—	—
Alabama	3	3	23,450	2	2	9,759	1	1	13,691	—	—	—
California	1	1	235	1	1	235	—	—	—	—	—	—
Colorado	1	1	1,080	1	1	1,080	—	—	—	—	—	—
Delaware	2	2	5,586	2	2	5,586	—	—	—	—	—	—
Hawaii	1	1	8,798	1	1	8,798	—	—	—	—	—	—
Illinois	1	1	12,223	—	—	—	1	1	12,223	—	—	—
Kentucky	6	6	20,618	6	6	20,618	—	—	—	—	—	—
Maine	1	1	285	1	1	285	—	—	—	—	—	—
Maryland	2	2	2,594	2	2	2,594	—	—	—	—	—	—
Massachusetts	5	5	8,037	5	5	8,037	—	—	—	—	—	—
Michigan	5	5	75,855	2	2	5,538	—	—	—	3	3	70,317
Missouri	7	7	29,560	6	6	14,376	1	1	15,184	—	—	—
Nebraska	1	1	10,819	—	—	—	1	1	10,819	—	—	—
New Hampshire	1	1	4,343	1	1	4,343	—	—	—	—	—	—
New Mexico	7	7	15,733	7	7	15,733	—	—	—	—	—	—
North Carolina	11	11	17,564	11	11	17,564	—	—	—	—	—	—
Ohio	6	6	62,246	3	3	17,899	2	2	21,181	1	1	23,166
Oklahoma	4	4	13,791	3	3	1,283	1	1	12,508	—	—	—
Oregon	1	1	930	1	1	930	—	—	—	—	—	—

Pennsylvania	14	14	20,682	—	—	—	—	—	—	—	—	—
South Carolina	6	6	17,753	—	—	—	—	—	—	—	—	—
Texas	6	6	30,026	—	—	—	—	—	—	—	—	—
Vermont	1	1	3,325	—	—	—	—	—	—	—	—	—
Virginia	2	2	2,303	—	—	—	—	—	—	—	—	—
Washington	5	5	37,084	4	4	14,136	—	—	—	1	1	22,948
Wyoming	1	1	4,644	—	—	—	—	—	—	—	—	—
Total	108	108	440,446	96	96	238,409	7	7	85,606	5	5	116,431

II. Governing-coordinating boards, each board responsible for more than a single institution

Alabama	1	6	10,091	—	—	—	1	6	10,091	—	—	—
Alaska	1	1[a]	2,767	1	1	2,767	—	—	—	—	—	—
Arizona	1	3	25,964	—	—	—	—	—	—	1	3	25,964
Arkansas	1	2[a]	5,945	1	2[a]	5,945	—	—	—	—	—	—
California	2	20	140,721	—	—	—	—	—	—	2	20	140,721
Colorado	3	7[a]	29,791	2	5	13,629	1	2[a]	16,162	—	—	—
Connecticut	2	10[a]	18,145	1	5	7,502	1	5[a]	10,643	—	—	—
Florida	1	3	28,024	—	—	—	—	—	—	1	3	28,024
Georgia	1	19	31,153	—	—	—	—	—	—	1	19	31,153
Idaho	1	2	6,467	1	2	6,467	—	—	—	—	—	—
Illinois	2	7[a]	45,871	—	—	—	1	4	17,099	1	3[a]	28,772
Indiana	3	18[a]	51,541	—	—	—	2	7[a]	26,892	1	11[a]	24,649
Iowa	1	3	23,941	—	—	—	—	—	—	1	3	23,941
Kansas	1	5	27,439	—	—	—	—	—	—	1	5	27,439
Louisiana	2	13[a]	38,755	—	—	—	1	4[a]	12,724	1	9	26,031

[a] Counted as institutions are branches and separate campuses: Arkansas, 1; Colorado, 1; Connecticut, 4; Illinois, 2; Indiana, 14; Louisiana, 3; Maine, 1; Maryland, 2; Minnesota, 1; Mississippi, 1; Nevada, 1; New Jersey, 2; Pennsylvania, 15; Tennessee, 3; Texas, 2; Utah, 3; Virginia, 6; Wisconsin, 9. Total, 18 states: 71 units. Also four branches of University of Alaska under local boards.

APPENDIX B–4, Continued

II. Governing-coordinating boards, each board responsible for more than a single institution (continued)

State	Number of Boards	Number of Institutions	Total Enrollment	Enrollment as a Measure of Board Responsibility								
				Under 10,000			10,000 to 20,000			Over 20,000		
				Number of Boards	Number of Institutions	Enrollment	Number of Boards	Number of Institutions	Enrollment	Number of Boards	Number of Institutions	Enrollment
Maine	2	7a	7,044	2	7a	7,044	—	—	—	—	—	—
Maryland	2	8a	22,691	1	5	3,394	3a	—	19,297	—	—	—
Massachusetts	1	12	11,442	—	—	—	1	12	11,442	—	—	—
Michigan	1	4	24,736	—	—	—	—	—	—	1	4	24,736
Minnesota	2	7a	48,450	—	—	—	1	5	12,568	1	2a	35,882
Mississippi	1	9a	19,667	—	—	—	1	9a	19,667	—	—	—
Montana	1	8	10,345	—	—	—	1	8	10,345	—	—	—
Nebraska	1	4	4,766	1	4	4,766	—	—	—	—	—	—
Nevada	1	2a	3,708	1	2a	3,708	—	—	—	—	—	—
New Hampshire	1	4	2,235	1	4	2,235	—	—	—	—	—	—
New Jersey	2	9a	34,132	—	—	—	2	9a	34,132	—	—	—
New York	2	27	109,202	—	—	—	—	—	—	2	27	109,202
North Carolina	2	5	19,241	1	2	732	1	3	18,509	—	—	—
North Dakota	1	9	11,981	—	—	—	1	9	11,981	—	—	—
Oklahoma	2	14	28,748	—	—	—	2	14	28,748	—	—	—
Oregon	1	7	23,924	—	—	—	—	—	—	1	7	23,924
Pennsylvania	1	16a	16,990	—	—	—	1	16a	16,990	—	—	—
Rhode Island	1	2	7,077	1	2	7,077	—	—	—	—	—	—
South Dakota	1	7	10,299	—	—	—	1	7	10,299	—	—	—
Tennessee	2	10a	35,435	—	—	—	2	10a	35,435	—	—	—

Texas	3	15[a]	68,928	—	—	—	2	10	33,323	1	5[a]	35,605
Utah	3	7[a]	19,703	2	5[a]	8,813	1	2[a]	10,890	—	—	—
Vermont	1	3	800	1	3	800	—	—	—	—	—	—
Virginia	4	12[a]	33,568	3	8[a]	20,647	1	4[a]	12,921	—	—	—
West Virginia	2	11	21,479	1	2	7,648	1	9	13,831	—	—	—
Wisconsin	2	19[a]	45,597	—	—	—	1	9	17,563	1	10[a]	28,034
Total	66	357[a]	1,128,803	21	59[a]	103,174	28	167	411,552	17	131	614,077

SUMMARY

I. Governing Boards	108	108	440,446	96	96	238,409	7	7	85,606	5	5	116,431
II. Governing-Coordinating Boards	66	357	1,128,803	21	59	103,174	28	167	411,552	17	131	614,077
TOTAL	174	465	1,569,249	117	155	341,583	35	174	497,158	22	136	730,508

SOURCE: Identification of boards: S. V. Martorana and Ernest V. Hollis, *State Boards Responsible for Higher Education*. Institutional enrollment and control: U.S. Office of Education, *Education Directory, 1960–1961*, Part 3.

APPENDIX B-5. State board organization patterns for the exercise of state responsibilities for higher education: 1960

I. Governing boards directly responsible to governor or general assembly

State	Number of Institutions	Student Degree-credit Enrollment	State Boards			Institutions Governed by State Boards		Institutions Governed by Local Boards	
			GOVERNING	SUPERVISORY ACCREDITING		NUMBER	ENROLLMENT	NUMBER	ENROLLMENT
Delaware	2	5,586	2	1		2	5,586	—	—
Hawaii	1	8,798	1	—		1	8,798	—	—
Ohio	9	89,569	6	—		6	62,246	3	27,323
South Carolina	6	17,753	6	—		6	17,753	—	—
Washington	15	47,355	5	1		5	37,084	10	10,271
Wyoming	6	6,647	1	1		1	4,644	5	2,003
Total, 6 states	39	175,708	21	3		21	136,111	18	39,597

II. All state institutions governed by a single governing-coordinating board

| State | Number of Institutions | Student Degree-credit Enrollment | State Boards | | | | Institutions Governed by State Boards | | Institutions Governed by Local Boards | |
			COORDINATING	GOVERNING	GOVERNING-COORDINATING	SUPERVISORY ACCREDITING	NUMBER	ENROLLMENT	NUMBER	ENROLLMENT
Alaska	5[a]	2,767	—	—	1	1	1	2,767	4	—[b]
Arizona	5	31,893	—	—	1	1	3	25,964	2	5,929
Florida	19	38,901	—	—	1	1	3	28,024	16	10,877
Georgia	21	31,621	—	—	1	—	19	31,153	2	468
Idaho	4	8,505	—	—	1	—	2	6,467	2	2,038
Iowa	19	27,017	—	—	1	1	3	23,941	16	3,076
Kansas	21	40,713	—	—	1	1	5	27,439	16	13,274
Mississippi	26[a]	26,635	—	—	1	3	9[a]	19,667	17	6,968
Montana	8	10,345	—	—	1	—	8	10,345	—	—
Nevada	2[a]	3,708	—	—	1	—	2[a]	3,708	—	—
North Dakota	11	12,618	—	—	1	—	9	11,981	2	637
Rhode Island	2	7,077	—	—	1	—	2	7,077	—	—
South Dakota	7	10,299	—	—	1	—	7	10,299	—	—
Total, 13 states	150[a]	252,099	—	—	13	8	73[a]	208,832	77	43,267

[a] Counted as institutions are branches and separate campuses: Mississippi, 1; Nevada, 1; also four campuses with local boards in Alaska.
[b] Not available.

APPENDIX B-5, Continued

III. States with two governing-coordinating boards or one such board and one governing board

State	Number of Institutions	Student Degree-credit Enrollment	State Boards				Institutions Governed by State Boards		Institutions Governed by Local Boards	
			COORDINATING	GOVERNING	GOVERNING-COORDINATING	SUPERVISORY ACCREDITING	NUMBER	ENROLLMENT	NUMBER	ENROLLMENT
Connecticut	10c	18,145	—	—	2	—	10c	18,145	—	—
Louisiana	13c	38,755	—	—	2	—	13c	38,755	—	—
Minnesota	16c	50,831	—	—	2	1	7c	48,450	9	2,381
Nebraska	10	22,539	—	1	1	2	5	15,585	5	6,954
New Hampshire	5	6,578	—	1	1	—	5	6,578	—	—
New Jersey	11c	38,429	—	—	2	—	9c	34,132	2	4,297
New York	43	132,706	—	—	2	1	27	109,202	16	23,504
Oregon	8	24,854	—	1	1	—	8	24,854	—	—
Tennessee	10c	35,435	—	—	2	—	10c	35,435	—	—
Vermont	4	4,123	—	1	1	—	4	4,123	—	—
West Virginia	11	21,479	—	—	2	—	11	21,479	—	—
Total, 11 states	141c	393,874	—	4	18	4	109c	356,738	32	37,136

326

IV. States with complex organization without a statewide coordinating board

State											
Alabama	9	33,541	—	3	1	—	9	33,541	—	6	3,558
Colorado	14[c]	34,429	—	1	3	1	8[c]	30,871	—	2	598
Indiana	20[c]	52,139	—	—	3	1	18[c]	51,541	—	—	—
Maine	8[c]	7,329	—	1	2	—	8[c]	7,329	—	—	—
Maryland	19[c]	28,980	—	2	2	1	10[c]	25,285	—	9	3,695
Massachusetts	17	19,479	—	5	1	2	17	19,479	—	—	—
Michigan	24	118,679	—	5	1	—	9	100,591	—	15	18,088
Pennsylvania	31[c]	37,878	—	14	1	2	30[c]	37,672	—	1	206
Total, 8 states	142[c]	332,454	—	31	14	7	109[c]	306,309	—	33	26,145

V. States with complex organizations with a statewide planning-coordinating board

State											
Arkansas	9[d]	16,829	1	7	1	—	9[d]	16,829	—	—	—
California	83	347,456	1	1	2	—	21	140,956	—	62	206,500
Illinois	21[d]	85,187	1	1	2	2	8[d]	58,094	—	13	27,093
Kentucky	8	27,594	1	6	—	1	6	20,618	—	2	6,976
Missouri	14	36,455	1	7	—	1	7	29,560	—	7	6,895
New Mexico	7	15,733	1	7	—	—	7	15,733	—	—	—
North Carolina	16	36,805	1	11	2	—	16	36,805	—	—	—
Oklahoma	24	43,505	1	4	2	—	18	42,539	—	6	966
Texas	52[d]	129,449	1	6	3	1	21[d]	98,954	—	31	30,495
Utah	7[d]	19,703	1	—	3	—	7[d]	19,703	—	—	—
Virginia	14[d]	35,871	1	2	4	—	14[d]	35,871	—	—	—
Wisconsin	42[d]	47,989	1	—	2	1	19[d]	45,597	—	23	2,392
Total, 12 states	297[d]	842,576	12	52	21	6	153[d]	561,259	—	144	281,317

[c] Counted as institutions are branches and separate campuses: Connecticut, 4; Louisiana, 3; Minnesota, 1; New Jersey 2; Tennessee, 3; Colorado, 1; Indiana, 14; Maine, 1; Maryland, 2; Pennsylvania, 15.

[d] Counted as institutions are branches and separate campuses: Arkansas, 1; Illinois, 2; Texas, 2; Utah, 3; Virginia, 6; Wisconsin, 9.

APPENDIX B-5, Continued

State	Number of Institutions	Student Degree-credit Enrollment	State Boards COORDINATING	State Boards GOVERNING	State Boards GOVERNING-COORDINATING	State Boards SUPERVISORY ACCREDITING	Institutions Governed by State Boards NUMBER	Institutions Governed by State Boards ENROLLMENT	Institutions Governed by Local Boards NUMBER	Institutions Governed by Local Boards ENROLLMENT
SUMMARY										
Type I, 6 states	39	175,708	—	21	—	3	21	136,111	18	39,597
Type II, 13 states	150	252,099	—	—	13	8	73	208,832	77	43,267
Type III, 11 states	141	393,874	—	4	18	4	109	356,738	32	37,136
Type IV, 8 states	142	332,454	—	31	14	7	109	306,309	33	26,145
Type V, 12 states	297	842,576	12	52	21	6	153	561,259	144	281,317
TOTAL, 50 states	769[d]	1,996,711	12	108	66	28	465[d]	1,569,249	304	427,462

SUMMARY: Group I, none; Group II, 3 states, 6 units; Group III, 5 states, 13 units; Group IV, 5 states, 33 units; Group V, 6 states, 23 units. Total, 19 states: 75 units.

SOURCE: Identification of boards: S. V. Martorana and Ernest V. Hollis, *State Boards Responsible for Higher Education.* Institutional enrollments and control: U.S. Office of Education, *Education Directory, 1960–1961,* Part 3.

BIBLIOGRAPHY

BIBLIOGRAPHY

AMERICAN ASSOCIATION OF UNIVERSITY PROFESSORS, COMMITTEE T. "Faculty Participation in College and University Government." *A.A.U.P. Bulletin*, Vol. 48, No. 4, 321–323, December 1962.

AMERICAN COUNCIL ON EDUCATION. *Higher Education and National Affairs*, Vol. XII, No. 46. Washington, D.C., December 20, 1963.

AMERICAN COUNCIL ON EDUCATION, OFFICE OF STATISTICAL INFORMATION AND RESEARCH. *A Fact Book on Higher Education*. Washington, D.C.: The Council, 1958.

BERELSON, BERNARD. *Graduate Education in the United States*. New York: McGraw-Hill Book Company, 1960.

BEARD, CHARLES A. *The Unique Function of Education in American Democracy*. Washington, D.C.: Educational Policies Commission, 1937.

BENSON, CHARLES SCOTT. *The Economics of Public Education*. Boston: Houghton Mifflin Company, 1961.

BLAKELY, ROBERT J. *The Changing University. A Report on the Seventh Annual Leadership Conference.* GEORGE H. DAAGNEAULT, ed. Chicago: Center for the Study of Liberal Education for Adults, 1959.

BOKELMAN, W. ROBERT, AND LOUIS D'AMICO. *Trends in Higher Education, Planning and Management Data, 1957–58 to 1959–60,* U.S. Department of Health, Education and Welfare, Office of Education. Washington, D.C.: U.S. Government Printing Office, 1961.

BOWMAN, MARY JEAN. "Human Capital: Concepts and Measures," *The Economics of Higher Education,* SELMA J. MUSHKIN, ed. U.S. Department of Health, Education and Welfare, Office of Education. Washington, D.C.: U.S. Government Printing Office, 1962.

BRANDON, ARTHUR L. "The Vice-President or Director of Public Relations," *Administrators in Higher Education: Their Functions and Coordination,* GERALD P. BURNS, ed. New York: Harper & Row, 1962.

BRUBACHER, JOHN S., AND WILLIS RUDY. *Higher Education in Transition.* New York: Harper & Row, 1958.

BUNNELL, KEVIN, ed. *Conference on the Measurement of Faculty Work Load,* Washington, D.C.: American Council on Education, 1960.

BURNS, GERALD P., ed. *Administrators in Higher Education: Their Functions and Coordination.* New York: Harper & Row, 1962.

BURNS, GERALD P. "Summary and Evaluation," *Administrators in Higher Education: Their Functions and Coordination,* GERALD P. BURNS, ed. New York: Harper & Row, 1962.

BURSCH II, CHARLES W. "The Vice-President or Dean of Students," *Administrators in Higher Education: Their Functions and Coordination,* GERALD P. BURNS, ed. New York: Harper & Row, 1962.

CAPLOW, THEODORE, AND REECE J. MCGEE. *The Academic Marketplace.* New York: Basic Books, Inc., 1958.

CARMAN, HARRY J. "Boards of Trustees and Regents," *Administrators in Higher Education: Their Functions and Coordination,* GERALD P. BURNS, ed. New York: Harper & Row, 1962.

CARMICHAEL, OLIVER C. *Graduate Education, A Critique and a Program.* New York: Harper & Row, 1961.

CARNEGIE FOUNDATION FOR THE ADVANCEMENT OF TEACHING. *The Fifty-seventh Annual Report, 1962.* New York: The Foundation, 1962.

CARR, WILLIAM G. *The Purposes of Education in American Democracy.* Washington, D.C.: Educational Policies Commission, 1938.

Columbia University Special Trustee Committee Report on *The Role of the Trustees of Columbia University.* New York: Columbia University, 1957.

CONGER, LOUIS H., JR. "College and University Enrollment: Projections," *Economics of Higher Education,* SELMA J. MUSHKIN, ed., U.S. Department of Health, Education and Welfare, Office of Education. Washington, D.C.: U.S. Government Printing Office, 1962.

COOMBS, PHILIP H. "An Economist's Overview of Higher Education," *Financing Higher Education, 1960–70,* DEXTER M. KEEZER, ed. New York: McGraw-Hill Book Company, 1959.

CORSON, JOHN J. *Governance of Colleges and Universities.* New York: McGraw-Hill Book Company, 1960.

COUNCIL OF STATE GOVERNMENTS. *Higher Education in the Forty-eight States.* Chicago: The Council, 1952.

COWLEY, W. H. *What Does a College President Do?* An Address presented at Oregon College of Education, Monmouth, February 5, 1956.

DODDS, HAROLD W. *The Academic President—Educator or Caretaker?* New York: McGraw-Hill Book Company, 1962.

DRESSEL, PAUL L., AND ASSOCIATES. *Evaluation in Higher Education.* Boston: Houghton Mifflin Company, 1961.

DRESSEL, PAUL L., AND MARGARET F. LORIMER. "Institutional Self-Evaluation," *Evaluation in Higher Education,* PAUL L. DRESSEL AND ASSOCIATES. Boston: Houghton Mifflin Company, 1961.

DURYEA, E. D. "The Theory and Practice of Administration," *Administrators in Higher Education: Their Functions and Coordination,* GERALD P. BURNS, ed. New York: Harper & Row, 1962.

EDDING, FRIEDRICH. *Targets for Education in Europe in 1970.* Vol. II, with INGVAR SVENNILSON AND LIONEL ELVIN. Paris: Organization for Economic Cooperation and Development, 1962.

ENARSON, HAROLD. "The Academic Vice-President or Dean," *Administrators in Higher Education: Their Functions and Coordination,* GERALD P. BURNS, ed. New York: Harper & Row, 1962.

EURICH, ALVIN C., Chairman, Panel of Advisors. *Kansas, Plans for the Next Generation: A Report on Higher Education in Kansas to the Board of Regents.* Topeka, Kansas: The Board of Regents, 1962.

FALVEY, FRANCES E. *Student Participation in College Administration.* New York: Bureau of Publications, Teachers College, Columbia University, 1952.

FIRST NATIONAL CITY BANK. *Monthly Economic Letter,* November, 1962. New York: The Bank, 1962.

FISCHER, JOHN H. *Administration and the Leadership of Education.* Alfred D. Simpson Lecture on Administration, given at Harvard University, April 26, 1962. Published by the New England School Development Council, Cambridge, Massachusetts.

FURNAS, CLIFFORD C., AND RAYMOND EWELL. "The Role of Research in the Economics of Universities," *Financing Higher Education, 1960–70,* DEXTER M. KEEZER, ed. New York: McGraw-Hill Book Company, 1959.

GARDNER, JOHN. *Excellence: Can We Be Equal and Excellent Too?* New York: Harper & Row, 1961.

GLENNY, LYMAN A. *Autonomy of Public Colleges: The Challenge of Coordination.* New York: McGraw-Hill Book Company, 1959.

GROSS, NEAL. "Organizational Lag in American Universities," *Harvard Educational Review,* Vol. 33, No. 1, Winter 1963.

HARRIS, SEYMOUR E. "Financing Higher Education: Broad Issues," *Financing Higher Education, 1960–70,* DEXTER M. KEEZER, ed. New York: McGraw-Hill Book Company, 1959.

HARRIS, SEYMOUR E. *More Resources for Higher Education.* New York: Harper & Row, 1960.

HARRIS, SEYMOUR E. *Higher Education: Resources and Finance.* McGraw-Hill Book Company, 1962.

HENDERSON, ALGO D. *Policies and Practices in Higher Education.* New York: Harper & Row, 1960.

HENEMAN, HARLOW J. "Opportunities for Improved Management in Higher Education," *Financing Higher Education, 1960–70,* DEXTER M. KEEZER, ed. New York: McGraw-Hill Book Company, 1959.

HICKMAN, C. ADDISON, "What Happens to the Social Structure and Inner Dynamics of a College in Process of Change?" *Current Issues in Higher Education: Higher Education in an Age of Revolution,* G. KERRY SMITH, ed. Association for Higher Education. Washington, D.C.: National Education Association, 1962.

HILL, WALKER H., AND PAUL L. DRESSEL. "The Objectives of Instruction," *Evaluation in Higher Education,* PAUL L. DRESSEL AND ASSOCIATES. Boston: Houghton Mifflin Company, 1961.

HOFSTADTER, RICHARD, AND C. DEWITT HARDY. *The Development and Scope of Higher Education in the United States.* New York: Columbia University Press, 1952.

HORN, FRANCIS H. "A Lifetime of Learning," *Toward the Liberally Educated Executive,* ROBERT A. GOLDWIN, ed. White Plains, New York: The Fund for Adult Education, 1957.

HORN, FRANCIS H. "The Organization of Colleges and Universities," *Administrators in Higher Education: Their Functions and Coordination,* GERALD P. BURNS, ed. New York: Harper & Row, 1962.

HUNGATE, THAD L. *Finance in Educational Management of Colleges and Universities.* New York: Bureau of Publications, Teachers College, Columbia University, 1954.

HUNGATE, THAD L. *Financing the Future of Higher Education.* New York: Bureau of Publications, Teachers College, Columbia University, 1946.

HUNGATE, THAD L., AND EARL J. MCGRATH. *A New Trimester Three-year Degree Program.* New York: Bureau of Publications, Teachers College, Columbia University, 1963.

JOHNSTON, W. NOEL. "The Vice-President or Director of Development," *Administrators in Higher Education: Their Functions and Coordination,* GERALD P. BURNS, ed. New York: Harper & Row, 1962.

JOHNSTONE, JOHN W. C. *Volunteers for Learning: A Study of the Educational Pursuits of American Adults.* Chicago: National Opinion Research Center, University of Chicago, 1963.

KATZ, JOSEPH, AND NEVITT SANFORD. "The Curriculum in the Perspective of the Theory of Personality Development," *The American College,* NEVITT SANFORD, ed. New York: John Wiley and Sons, Inc., 1962.

KEEZER, DEXTER M., ed. *Financing Higher Education, 1960–70.* New York: McGraw-Hill Book Company, 1959.

KENDRICK, JOHN W. *Productivity Trends in the United States.* National Bureau of Economic Research, Annual Report, 1962.

KIDD, J. ROBY. "Liberal Education for Business Leadership," *Toward the Liberally Educated Executive,* ROBERT A. GOLDWIN, ed. White Plains, New York: The Fund for Adult Education, 1957.

KLOPF, GORDON. *College Student Government.* New York: Harper & Row, 1960.

KNOTT, LESLIE W., ELLWYNNE M. VREELAND, AND MARJORIE GOOCH. *Cost Analysis for Collegiate Programs in Nursing. Part 1: Analysis of Expenditures.* New York: National League for Nursing, Division of Nursing Education, 1956.

LEDERLE, JOHN W. "The State and Higher Education," Appendix A, *The Campus and the State,* MALCOLM MOOS AND FRANCIS ROURKE. *Baltimore:* The Johns Hopkins Press, 1959.

LIVERIGHT, A. A. "Adult Education in Colleges and Universities," *Handbook of Adult Education in the United States,* MALCOLM S. KNOWLES, ed. Chicago: Adult Education Association of the U.S.A., 1960.

McCONNELL, T. R. *A General Pattern for American Public Higher Education.* New York: McGraw-Hill Book Company, 1962.

McGRATH, EARL J. "The College Curriculum—An Academic Wasteland?" Address delivered to Academic Deans of the Southern States, Dallas, November 27, 1962.

McGRATH, EARL J. *The Graduate School and the Decline of Liberal Education.* New York: Bureau of Publications, Teachers College, Columbia University, 1959.

McGRATH, EARL J. *Memo to a College Faculty Member.* New York: Bureau of Publications, Teachers College, Columbia University, 1961.

MARSHALL, ALFRED. *Principles of Economics,* Eighth Edition. London: MacMillan and Company, Ltd., 1936.

MARTORANA, S. V., AND ERNEST V. HOLLIS. *State Boards Responsible for Higher Education.* U.S. Department of Health, Education and Welfare, Office of Education. Washington, D.C.: U.S. Govrnment Printing Office, 1960.

MARTORANA, S. V., AND ERNEST V. HOLLIS. *Survey of State Legislation Relating to Higher Education.* Washington D.C.: U.S. Department of Health, Education and Welfare, Office of Education, 1962.

MASTERSON, THOMAS R. "Management Functions," *College and University Business,* Vol. 28, No. 2, February 1960.

MIDDLEBROOK, WILLIAM T., Chairman of General Survey Committee. *California and Western Conference Cost and Statistical Study.* Berkeley: University of California, Printing Department, 1955.

MILLETT, JOHN D. *The Academic Community: An Essay on Organization.* New York: McGraw-Hill Book Company, 1962.

Mooney, Ross L. "The Problem of Leadership in the University," *Harvard Educational Review*, Vol. 33, No. 1, Winter 1963.

Moos, Malcolm, and Francis Rourke. *The Campus and the State*. Baltimore: The Johns Hopkins Press, 1959.

Morris, John B. "Space Utilization and Increased Efficiency," *Proceedings of the Second National Assembly, Held July 6–8, 1960, French Lick, Indiana*. National Federation of College and University Business Officers Associations, 1960. Printed by News-Review Publishing Co., Inc., Moscow, Idaho.

Mushkin, Selma J., ed. *The Economics of Higher Education*. U.S. Department of Health, Education and Welfare, Office of Education. Washington, D.C.: U.S. Government Printing Office, 1962.

Mushkin, Selma J., and Robert W. Bokelman. "Student Higher Education and Facilities of Colleges and Universities: Projections," *Economics of Higher Education*, Selma J. Mushkin, ed. U.S. Department of Health, Education and Welfare, Office of Education. Washington, D.C.: U.S. Government Printing Office, 1962.

National Committee on the Preparation of a Manual on College and University Business Administration. *College and University Business Administration*, Vol. I. Washington, D.C.: The American Council on Education, 1952.

National Federation of College and University Business Officers Associations. *The Sixty College Study—A Second Look*. The Federation, 1960.

Ohio Educational Association. *Ohio Schools*, Vol. XVI, No. 6. Columbus, Ohio: The Association, September 1963.

President's Commission on Higher Education. *Higher Education for American Democracy*. Washington, D.C.: U.S. Government Printing Office, 1947.

Rauh, Morton A. *College and University Trusteeship*. Yellow Springs, Ohio: The Antioch Press, 1959.

Rockefeller Brothers Fund, Inc. *The Pursuit of Excellence: Education and the Future of America*. New York: Doubleday and Company, 1958.

Rosenberg, Herbert H. "Research and the Financing of Higher Education," *The Economics of Higher Education*, Selma J. Mushkin, ed., U.S. Department of Health, Education and Welfare, Office of Education. Washington, D.C.: U.S. Government Printing Office, 1962.

Ruml, Beardsley, and Donald H. Morrison. *Memo to a College Trustee*. New York: McGraw-Hill Book Company, 1959.

Russell, John Dale, and James I. Doi, *Manual for Studies of Space Utilization in Colleges and Universities*. American Association of Collegiate Registrars and Admissions Officers. Athens, Ohio: Ohio University Press, 1957.

Saupe, Joe L. "Learning and Evaluation Processes," *Evaluation in Higher Education*, Paul L. Dressel and Associates. Boston: Houghton Mifflin Company, 1961.

Seldon, William K. *Accreditation*. New York: Harper & Row, 1960.

STECKLEIN, JOHN E. *How to Measure Faculty Work Load.* Washington, D.C.: American Council on Education, 1962.

SUMMERSKILL, JOHN. "Dropouts from College," *The American College,* NEVITT SANFORD, ed. New York: John Wiley and Sons, Inc., 1962.

TICKTON, SIDNEY G. *Needed—A Ten Year College Budget.* New York: The Fund for the Advancement of Education, 1961.

TONIGAN, RICHARD F. "Survey of Plant Management at Teachers College, Columbia University." Unpublished Ed.D. project report. New York: Teachers College, Columbia University, 1962.

TOWNSEND, AGATHA. *College Freshmen Speak Out.* New York: Harper & Row, 1956.

UMBECK, SHARVY G. "The Challenge of the Decade Ahead," *Proceedings of the Second National Assembly, Held July 6–8, 1960, French Lick, Indiana.* National Federation of College and University Business Officers Associations, 1960. Printed by News-Review Publishing Co., Inc., Moscow, Idaho.

U.S. DEPARTMENT OF COMMERCE, BUREAU OF THE CENSUS. *Current Population Reports,* Series P-25, Nos. 250 and 251, July 1962.

U.S. DEPARTMENT OF COMMERCE, BUREAU OF THE CENSUS. *Statistical Abstract of the United States.* Washington, D.C.: U.S. Government Printing Office, 1962.

U.S. DEPARTMENT OF HEALTH, EDUCATION AND WELFARE. *Health, Education and Welfare Trends.* Washington, D.C.: U.S. Government Printing Office, 1962.

U.S. DEPARTMENT OF HEALTH, EDUCATION AND WELFARE, OFFICE OF EDUCATION. *Educational Directory, 1960–61, Part 3, Colleges and Universities.* Washington, D.C.: U.S. Government Printing Office, 1960.

U.S. OFFICE OF EDUCATION. *Biennial Survey of Higher Education 1936–1938.* Bulletin 1940, No. 2. Chapter IV, "Statistics of Higher Education, 1937–38." Superintendent of Documents, Washington, D.C., 1942.

U.S. OFFICE OF EDUCATION. *Biennial Survey of Education in the United States, 1956–58,* Chapter IV, Section I, "Faculty, Students and Degrees." Washington, D.C.: U.S. Government Printing Office, 1961.

U.S. OFFICE OF EDUCATION. *Biennial Survey of Education in the United States, 1956–58.* "Statistics of Higher Education, 1957–58. Receipts, Expenditures and Property." Washington, D.C.: U.S. Government Printing Office, 1961.

U.S. OFFICE OF EDUCATION. *Educational Directory, Part 3: Colleges and Universities.* Bulletin 1939, No. 1. Superintendent of Documents, Washington, D.C., 1939.

VAIZEY, JOHN. *The Economics of Education.* New York: Free Press of Glencoe, Inc., 1962.

WEIDNER, EDWARD W. *The World Role of Universities.* New York: McGraw-Hill Book Company, 1962.

WILSEY, H. LAWRENCE. "Long-range Planning for Colleges and Universities,"

Proceedings of the Second National Assembly, Held July 6–8, 1960, French Lick, Indiana. National Federation of College and University Business Officers Associations, 1960. Printed by News-Review Publishing Co., Inc., Moscow, Idaho.

WISE, W. MAX. *They Come for the Best of Reasons—College Students Today.* Washington, D.C.: American Council on Education, 1958.

WOLOZIN, HAROLD. *The Outlook for Higher Education.* New York: The Fund for the Advancement of Education, 1963.

WOODBURNE, LLOYD S. *Faculty Personnel Policies in Higher Education.* New York: Harper & Row, 1950.

WOODBURNE, LLOYD S. *Principles of College and University Administration.* Stanford, California: Stanford University Press, 1958.

INDEX

INDEX